*Proslavery and Sectional Thought*
*in the Early South, 1740–1829*

# Proslavery and Sectional Thought in the Early South, 1740–1829

## AN ANTHOLOGY

*Edited by*

## Jeffrey Robert Young

University of South Carolina Press

Published in Columbia, South Carolina,
by the University of South Carolina Press

www.sc.edu/uscpress

Manufactured in the United States of America

15  14  13  12  11  10  09  08  07  06     10  9  8  7  6  5  4  3  2  1

Library of Congress Cataloging-in-Publication Data

Proslavery and sectional thought in the early South, 1740–1829 : an anthology / edited by
  Jeffrey Robert Young.
    p. cm.
  Includes bibliographical references and index.
  ISBN-13: 978-1-57003-616-3 (cloth : alk. paper)
  ISBN-10: 1-57003-616-0 (cloth : alk. paper)
  ISBN-13: 978-1-57003-617-0 (pbk : alk. paper)
  ISBN-10: 1-57003-617-9 (pbk : alk. paper)
  1. Slavery—Southern States—Justification—Sources. 2. Southern States—Intellectual
life—Sources. 3. Sectionalism (United States)—History—Sources. 4. Slavery and the
church—Southern States—History—Sources. 5. Racism—Southern States—History—
Sources. 6. Slavery—Southern States—History—18th century—Sources. 7. Slavery—
Southern States—History—19th century—Sources. 8. Southern States—Politics and
government—To 1775—Sources. 9. Southern States—Politics and government—
1775–1865—Sources. I. Young, Jeffrey Robert.
  E449.P9495 2006
  306.3'62097509033—dc22

                                                                    2005029316

This book was printed on Glatfelter Natures Natural, a recycled paper with 50 percent
post consumer waste content.

For Laurie and Paris, with love

# CONTENTS

# PREFACE

I chose the texts in this anthology to shed light on the deep relationship between proslavery thought, Christian activism, and European imperialism in the New World. Spanning the years 1740 to 1829, these writings illustrate the early influence that proslavery thought exerted on the American South. They also reveal a perhaps unexpectedly complicated relationship between racism and the defense of slavery. And they provide evidence for the slow process by which proslavery thought became entangled with southern sectionalism. Given the scholarly tendency to associate southern proslavery thought with the "fire-eating" late antebellum politicians who pushed the South out of the Union, and given the almost reflexive tendency to equate the defense of slavery with the racist dehumanization of African Americans, this anthology offers a corrective. As revealed in the writings of these conservative authors, proslavery thought had deeper, more tangled, and more substantial roots in Western political and religious thought than most modern readers have been willing or able to recognize.

As a general rule, I selected the following thirteen texts as examples of defenses of slavery that were published by southern authors or publicly presented in the American South prior to the 1830s—the decade that for many years was widely and inaccurately assumed by scholars to be the watershed era for proslavery southern thought. To be sure, the first author included in the anthology, the famous evangelical revivalist George Whitefield, cannot be characterized as a southerner, but his religious empire was centered around his orphanage in Bethesda, Georgia, and he came to own a slave plantation in South Carolina. Moreover, his pronouncements on the morality of southern slavery provided the context for the second selection in this anthology: Alexander Garden's defense of the southern slaveholders' treatment of their slaves. For these reasons, I decided to begin the volume with Whitefield's tract. I concede that it is also a stretch to characterize William Knox as a southerner, but he did own vast property in slaves and estates in coastal Georgia. He also lived in Georgia from 1757 to 1762 and, following his departure, continued to play an active role in the governing of the colony. Most important, his perspective as both a colonial administrator and a religious activist reveals the historical trends that were most responsible for the genesis and dissemination of proslavery thought in the colonial American South. I have therefore stretched my definition of a "southerner" to include his work in the anthology.

I have attempted to balance the needs of the modern reader with respect for the typographical and grammatical conventions of the original publications. In transcribing and annotating the texts, I have employed the following principles when altering typeface, spelling, punctuation, and forms of citation.

1. I have silently corrected typographical errors and inconsistencies.

2. I have capitalized the first word in every declarative sentence, and, in the case of William Graham's lecture, I have introduced paragraph breaks in those places where the author embarked on a fresh line of argument. In Graham's lecture, I have also inserted commas in those instances where subordinate clauses and elements in a series needed to be more clearly offset from the rest of the sentence.

3. I have retained (em) dashes that were used to indicate parenthetical material as well as dashes used to indicate a shift in subject matter. I have inserted appropriate punctuation to replace dashes that were employed in lieu of question marks and periods.

4. Antiquated spellings of the words "today," "tomorrow," and "tonight" have been updated.

5. The words "Jesus," "Christ," "Christianity," "God," and the names of particular churches have all been capitalized in cases when authors employed the lower case.

6. My annotation of the text appears as notes at the end of each selection; the authors' notes appear as footnotes.

7. I have used square brackets to indicate missing or illegible words and to indicate my insertion of conjectural words into the original texts.

8. In places where authors included quotation marks, I have altered their usage to conform to the modern practice of using one mark to open a quote and a second to close the quote.

9. In my annotation of the texts, I have provided biblical references in those cases where authors were quoting directly from or closely following that source. All of my own biblical references are to the Revised English Bible.

# ACKNOWLEDGMENTS

With tremendous gratitude, I acknowledge the assistance of friends, colleagues, and archivists who supported me in completing this volume. First and foremost, I must recognize at the University of South Carolina Press Alex Moore, for his unfailing patience and enthusiasm, and Karen Beidel, for all her help and good cheer.

Several libraries and archives provided critical resources: Woodruff Library and Pitts Library at Emory University, Perkins Library at Duke University, the New-York Historical Society, the Library of Virginia (which kindly granted permission to reprint the Virginia proslavery petitions), and Special Collections at the Leyburn Library at Washington and Lee University (which generously assented to the republication of the Graham manuscript). In each of these institutions, I received uniformly superb treatment.

A grant from the College of Liberal Arts and Sciences at Illinois State University in 1997 was invaluable. I thank my colleagues there and at Georgia Southern University and Emory University for their good cheer and more-than-occasional advice. In particular I remain deeply indebted to Jim Roark (who continues to offer much-appreciated friendship and advice whenever I knock on his door). I also benefited from counsel tendered by William Cooper and Drew Faust (who helped steer this project in a fruitful direction during its early planning phase). Michael O'Brien and an anonymous reader for the USC Press guided me through significant revisions of an initial draft.

Over the years I perhaps too frequently retreated from my office to bask in the love and support offered by family and friends. For the resulting delays, I blame my brothers, Jason Young and Jonathan Young; my friends Todd Mages and Tommy Mowatt; my parents, Jack and Joanne Young; my grandmother Frances Kass; and my Atlanta family, Kristian Blaich, Mary Cain, Louis Corrigan Jr., and Patricia Vanderspuy. And I cannot begin to express how much I am thankful for the love offered by my darling ex-wife, Laurie Watel, and our son, Paris Watel-Young.

# Introduction

## A Transatlantic Perspective on the
## Problem of Proslavery Thought

OVER THE COURSE OF FOUR CENTURIES, slavery in the New World generated immense profit and political power for European investors and American masters at an almost inconceivable expense in human suffering. Destabilizing and depopulating Africa, white and African entrepreneurs transported more than eleven million African slaves to plantations and mines in the western hemisphere.[1] From its inception to its demise, this grotesque system of coerced labor existed as a means toward financial gain. Yet slavery in the New World was affected by cultural as well as fiscal imperatives. Religion, nationalism, imperialism, and racism offered principles that helped to structure the institution of slavery, to manage it, and, by the eighteenth century, to defend it from mounting criticism. By the mid-nineteenth century, proslavery thought exerted considerable influence over the culture, the politics, and the very identity of elite slaveholders across the Americas. This was particularly the case in the American South, where slavery rested at the heart of the economy. But if the proslavery ideological orientation of the southern elite had come into clear focus by the antebellum era, the specific process—the precise chronology—by which proslavery thought had first worked its way into the white southern worldview has been difficult for scholars to pin down.

### Early Scholarship on Southern Proslavery Thought

Few topics have attracted more scholarly attention than slavery in the American South. Since the late 1950s historians have investigated every conceivable aspect of the southern slave system and have spun numerous theories to make sense of the region's plantation culture.[2] Much of this work has explored the contours and implications of the defenses of slavery published by southern ministers, writers, politicians, and agricultural reformers. In particular, the historian Eugene D. Genovese has deployed southern proslavery writings as evidence of the "worldview" of the slaveholding elite.[3] While Genovese's interpretations of southern proslavery thought were controversial when they appeared—and remain so to this day—numerous historians have shared his interest in proslavery sources and have spent the last four decades placing the southern proslavery thinkers in the context of the culture and political system in which they operated. In consequence of historical studies written by Genovese, Drew Gilpin Faust, Larry Tise, and a host of other scholars, the proslavery authors who toiled in the three decades preceding the Civil War have become increasingly familiar figures. And thanks to Faust's anthology of proslavery sources published between 1830 and 1860, students and scholars have become directly acquainted with the writings of significant southern thinkers such as Thomas Dew, James Henry Hammond, and George Fitzhugh.[4]

This scholarly fascination with proslavery thought, however, is a relatively recent historiographical phenomenon. In the first half of the twentieth century, a few pioneering works written by William Sumner Jenkins and William B. Hesseltine dwelled at length on southern proslavery thought, but these studies remained curiously peripheral to historians' inquiries into the political and cultural identity of the slave-owning South.[5] Ulrich Bonnell Phillips, the doyen of early-twentieth-century southern historians, spent relatively little time investigating proslavery tracts in his major books on slavery. His inattention to this material is, on one level, perplexing given his willingness to believe in the principal tenets articulated by a large number of prominent antebellum proslavery writers. Far from finding their defenses of bondage to be distasteful, Phillips accepted at face value the slaveholders' self-serving claims that their slaves were flourishing under benevolent white stewardship. In his preface to *American Negro Slavery* (1918), a work that would serve as the standard authority on southern slavery for the next four decades, Phillips insisted that interracial relations in the South had been harmonious. Since he believed that twentieth-century blacks showed "the same easy-going, amiable, serio-comic obedience and the same personal attachments to white men, as well as the same sturdy light-heartedness and the same love of laughter and of rhythm, which distinguished their forbears [*sic*]," Phillips had little difficulty accepting that "good will and affection" set the tone for the master-slave relationship.[6] Perhaps because these notions mirrored the ones articulated by late antebellum proslavery authors, Phillips felt that the proslavery tracts required no sustained commentary. Perhaps too Phillips believed that the proslavery authors merely gave voice to the obvious trajectory of a culture best explored through planters' correspondence and diaries. If writers such as Dew said "little that was new," as Phillips claimed in one of his few essays that explored proslavery tracts as evidence, then the essence of the slaveholding South could be extracted through scholarship that paid little heed to these sources.[7]

Prevailing paradigms for the causes of the Civil War also kept scholars away from the proslavery sources. The notion that the war itself had been a blunder caused by statesmen's miscalculations held sway among leading historians of the South prior to World War II. Attributing sectional conflict to poor political decisions, scholars had little reason to focus on the antebellum proslavery authors' discussions of the South's fundamental differences from the North. Furthermore, even white southern historians, such as Phillips, who were nostalgic about slavery still wanted their readers to understand that they did not mourn the institution's passing. They could insist that southern masters had been paternalistic to a degree that left them unable to compete with industrial capitalism; early white historians could also assert that the regions had not been so different as to make sectional conflict inevitable. But they could simultaneously hold to both of these positions only by turning their scholarship from the very antebellum southern texts that intertwined discussion of the South's unique slaveholding society with discussion of the South's impending conflict with the free North.[8]

Historians' relative indifference to proslavery texts gave way, in the 1950s, to scholars' self-conscious hostility to the use of these sources. Rejecting the racist assumptions undergirding Phillips's interpretation of slavery, Kenneth Stampp and Stanley Elkins brought to modern readers' attention the almost incomprehensible cruelties of southern slavery. In so doing, they created a scholarly environment that was even less conducive to research into formal tracts defending southern slavery. In *The Peculiar Institution* (1956), Stampp referred to proslavery authors only in order to illustrate the "profound error" in their thinking. Although Stampp deftly explored the intricate psychology of slave resistance against white authority, he largely ignored the complicated state of mind that enabled slave owners to frame their mastery in moral terms. It was enough for Stampp to note the inaccuracies of the proslavery authors' portrayals of bondage—inaccuracies that would be corrected by insights that Stampp had gleaned from a more even-handed survey of the historical record.[9]

In *Slavery: A Problem in American Institutional and Intellectual Life* (1959), Stanley Elkins sought to move the scholarship on slavery past the confines of moral debate. According to Elkins, previous historians (including Kenneth Stampp) had allowed their indignation over the evils of slavery to interfere with their analysis. Interestingly enough, however, Elkins's claim toward a more objective approach did not lead him toward more meaningful analysis of the proslavery evidence. As much as Elkins wrote in the voice of a dispassionate social scientist, his distaste for the defenders of slavery led him to reject their work as "polemical literature." A postscript to his work grappled with the role played by proslavery intellectuals in southern society; yet Elkins refused to concede that their texts might serve as a window through which the dynamics of the white southern mindset could be deciphered. Instead, he maintained that the proslavery writers did not really "think about slavery" because they were so eager to defend the institution from outside criticism. Their ideas, he insisted, did not constitute "true 'conservative' thought—or, indeed, 'thought' of any kind as is commonly carried on" because the larger society in which they operated allowed them no freedom for earnest examinations of the social issues of their day. As much as Elkins wanted to move away from simple moral arguments about American slavery, his own distaste for the institution precluded any serious intellectual engagement on his part with works seeking to defend bondage as an integral element in a just hierarchical society.[10]

For Elkins, Stampp, and other liberal white historians working during the turbulent era of the post–World War II movement for black civil rights, the task of documenting the destructive impact of slavery on American society almost required that the antebellum defenders of slavery be minimized as historical actors. The degree to which this historiographical climate was inhospitable to scholarship on proslavery thought can be seen, ironically, in the tone adopted by the few historians who were devoting significant attention to proslavery texts. When C. Vann Woodward put together a modern edition of George Fitzhugh's *Cannibals All! or, Slaves without Masters* in 1960, he denied that Fitzhugh was "typical of Southern thinkers of his period or representative of the pro-slavery thought or agrarian thought." The proslavery Virginia intellectual, according to Woodward, was "not typical of anything" but was, rather, "an individual—*sui generis.*" In similar fashion, when Eric McKitrick compiled an anthology of southern proslavery tracts in 1963, he insisted that the proslavery authors' conservative ideas were at odds with their own society, which was actually as "capitalist-minded as the North." Early scholars such as U. B. Phillips had not devoted their energies to the proslavery intellectuals because their conclusions were apparently so obvious and accurate as to require no in-depth analysis. Woodward and McKitrick focused their attention on the proslavery authors because they were historical curiosities whose seemingly wild proclamations were divorced from the fabric of southern slave society. Neither historiographical development proved conducive to the broad scholarly interest in proslavery thought that would sweep through the academy in the 1960s and 1970s.[11]

## The Historiographical Problem

When Eugene D. Genovese first presented his interpretations of the antebellum planters, he sparked debate by describing them as "not mere capitalists" but as "precapitalist, quasi-aristocratic landowners who had to adjust their economy and ways of thinking to a capitalist world market." Whereas the liberal scholarship of the 1950s had depicted the plantation system as the product of an unchecked capitalistic mentality, Genovese framed the planters' mindset in terms of "paternalism" that caused them to embrace "family and status, a strong code of honor, and aspirations to luxury, ease, and accomplishment" as opposed to an unabashed concern for maximizing profit.[12] His first book advanced this thesis through an investigation of political economy; in his second book, he focused his attentions on the proslavery writings of George Fitzhugh, thereby establishing a scholarly inquiry into proslavery sources that he has continued to mine over the past three decades. Unlike Woodward, Genovese saw Fitzhugh as emblematic of a worldview that placed the planter elite at odds—culturally, economically, and politically—with the capitalist system in which the slaveholders operated their plantations. Fitzhugh, asserted Genovese, developed a proslavery argument that "was not so much new as [it was] a more rigorous and mature presentation of a line of thought which had been steadily gaining favor for years."[13]

Drawing on a deep pool of evidence from manuscript sources, Genovese's *Roll, Jordan, Roll* (1974) fleshed out more fully a paternalistic paradigm for understanding southern slave-owning society. The slaveholders' paternalistic proslavery culture, he argued, led white and black southerners into a psychological dance of intimacy and hostility. Like William Sumner Jenkins before him, Genovese depicted the master-slave relationship as "organic"—a term that evoked the southerners' belief that slavery comprised a natural element in the hierarchical society ushered into existence by God's will. For as Genovese was already perceiving in *Roll, Jordan, Roll,* Christianity provided the ideological foundation for this vision of a stratified yet unified society.[14] Scriptural passages such as Romans 12:4–6 sketched out this logic in terms that generations of slave owners in the American South found reassuring: "For just as in a single human body there are many limbs and organs, all with different functions, so we who are united with Christ, though many, form one body and belong to one another as its limbs and organs. Let us use the different gifts allotted to each of us by God's grace."

In Genovese's analysis, the planters' paternalism did not mean that they were actually kind to the slaves, but rather that they conceptualized their mastery in familial terms that encompassed blacks as well as whites.[15] Slavery was defensible, from their perspective, because it promised kindness and intimacy that compared favorably to the rampant individualism and chaos engendered by the emerging wage labor economies in the Western world. Prominent planters, as Genovese demonstrated, acknowledged that they were "bound under many sacred obligations to treat [the slaves] with humanity at all times, and under all circumstances." This defense of bondage, in Genovese's opinion, cast the South on an ideological path that would pit the region against the emerging bourgeois tendencies of the capitalistic markets responsible for the birth of their plantation system. Slaveholder paternalism, as Genovese delineated it, bred specific racist assumptions about African Americans' innately childlike personalities and their incapacity to govern themselves without guidance from concerned whites. Yet Genovese's paradigm primarily sought to explain the growth of a master class whose racism was a means rather than an end unto itself. His interest in Fitzhugh reinforced this point, as Fitzhugh was one of the few proslavery thinkers to explicitly discuss the need to subordinate white laborers as well as black ones within encompassing systems of interdependent social strata. In the southern proslavery argument as expostulated by Genovese, class trumped race.[16]

The 1960s and 1970s were unpropitious times in which to suggest that racial prejudice did not provide the principal bedrock for southern proslavery thought. The civil rights movement had a salutary impact on the scholarship on slavery by pressing historians to recover African American perspectives on and experiences in bondage that had previously been of little interest to professional scholars.[17] Yet this increasing sensitivity to black voices also fostered explanatory models for southern slavery that insisted that racial prejudice preceded, mandated, and subsequently justified the planters' system of bondage.[18] In ambitious and well-received books exploring race and slavery, Winthrop Jordan and George Fredrickson developed historical narratives that used racial prejudice as defining themes in American history. In *White over Black* (1968), Jordan briefly mentioned the proslavery theology promoted by colonial Anglican reformers but devoted little energy to unpacking its implications because racial prejudice was not a structuring theme in these early proslavery works.[19]

On many levels, Fredrickson's *The Black Image in the White Mind* differed from Jordan's argument by emphasizing the relatively late emergence of white theories about the inherent and unalterable inferiority of blacks. But even if Fredrickson's racial model contradicted Jordan's in significant ways, his book still conceptualized race as a primary analytical category. Hence, Fredrickson's observation that "slavery in the South had survived the Revolutionary era and the rise of the natural-rights philosophy without an elaborated racial defense" carried him to the assumption that there had not been "much of an intellectual defense [of slavery] of any kind" prior to the nineteenth century. Because the colonial slave owners had not defended slavery primarily on racial grounds, their proslavery tracts had no easy path into Fredrickson's narrative. Not surprisingly, Fredrickson would become one of Genovese's sharpest critics, charging that "he simply ignores the complexities resulting from the fact that the Old South was a society of racial castes as well as of social classes." Genovese's preoccupation with the planters' development as a ruling class, charged Fredrickson, "prevents him from applying [himself] to the problem of what role racism actually played in the South's defense of slavery."[20]

For Fredrickson, Genovese's reading of the proslavery texts was not only flawed because of its insufficient attention to white racial prejudice, but it was also dead wrong in its contention that the proslavery southern mentality was inherently organic and hostile to the liberal democratic values of northern capitalist society, a position that Genovese and Elizabeth Fox-Genovese would develop with increasing sophistication in the coming years. By contrast, Fredrickson's scholarly interest in southern racial prejudice opened the door to an interpretive paradigm that reconciled the slaveholders' fierce commitment to black slavery with their enthusiastic embrace of concepts of liberty and republican institutions of government. Tapping into the sociological literature on *Herrenvolk* (or "Master Race") democracy, Fredrickson sketched out an interpretation of southern proslavery thought that rested upon principles of liberty and egalitarianism but limited them as the prerogatives of white men. Politicians such as William L. Yancey of Alabama, according to Fredrickson, evoked these ideals of *Herrenvolk* democracy by voicing their support of two cardinal ideals: "the first is that the white race is . . . the master race, and the white man is the equal of every other white man. The second idea is that the Negro is the inferior race." Conceding that there was "some truth" in Genovese's contention that there did exist proslavery thinkers who advocated a distinctly hierarchical social order at odds with democracy, Fredrickson nonetheless insisted that these conservative theorists ran counter to the racist logic to which most white southerners adhered. "In the last analysis, therefore," he concluded, "*Herrenvolk* egalitarianism was the dominant public ideology of the South."[21]

In the 1970s and 1980s, a historiographical debate raged between those who saw the South in terms of organic conservatism and those who saw it in terms of republicanism that hinged on racial prejudice. Landmark works published during this period offered powerful evidence in favor of the latter formulation. In one of the most influential monographs of the late twentieth century, Edmund S. Morgan postulated an ideological interdependence between the early American reliance on slave labor and American concepts of freedom and broadened political inclusion. Slavery, according to his analysis of the seventeenth-century Chesapeake region, enabled whites to live on sufficiently egalitarian terms with each other to make republicanism and freedom viable social principles for the white population. Morgan was working primarily with seventeenth-century evidence, but he applied his findings to the Revolutionary era.[22] And, in short order, impressive studies would reveal the interplay between slavery and inclusive republicanism for white men in the nineteenth-century South.

These works took note of the considerable social and cultural role played by small slaveholders and white yeomen farmers. These modestly situated men obviously had little stake in a conservative social agenda that bestowed a God-given authority to a tiny minority of the white male population. J. Mills Thornton III's exploration of sectional politics in Alabama, for example, depicted white southerners as defining their commitment to the proslavery cause in a manner that enabled them to campaign for broadly defined white liberty. Lacy K. Ford Jr. and J. William Harris respectively authored nuanced studies of South Carolina and Georgia that spoke to the white southern acceptance of slavery going hand in hand with a heartfelt embrace of republican liberties. Most dramatically, James Oakes published a history of the southern slaveholders that emphasized the numeric and political sway of the small slaveholders over the grand planters. His *Ruling Race* asserted that the "paternalist" proslavery ethic had actually waned during the antebellum era as generations of white southern men migrated west to pursue their dreams of upward social mobility. Using concepts that were similar to those developed by scholars ranging from Kenneth Stampp to George Fredrickson, Oakes asserted that these slaveholders on the make were racist businessmen operating "factories in the fields" and building a slaveholding republic in which their human property and their political liberties as white men would be secure.[23] In these studies the white male majority advanced the ideal of consensual government authority managed in deference to the will of the governed. The liberal embrace of the individual's active role in a just republic was accompanied by deeply ingrained racist and sexist beliefs that cast African Americans and women outside the bounds of participation in the southern political system.

## Contextualizing Proslavery Thinkers within the South and the World

As had been the case in Fredrickson's work, the best of this scholarship exploring proslavery thought and white republicanism did not ignore the proslavery authors who espoused an organic vision for plantation society. The scholars interested in proslavery republicanism, however, did argue that paternalism exerted little influence on the political culture in which white southerners interacted.[24] Conservative proslavery thinkers such as Fitzhugh, who occupied a central place in Genovese's proslavery paradigm, were relegated to a marginal role in this historiography. But scholars did not have to agree with Genovese's contentions about organic proslavery thinkers' centrality in southern culture in order to concentrate their analysis on them. In 1961 Ralph E. Morrow "revisited" the proslavery thinkers not to argue that they articulated the planters' worldview but rather to suggest that they revealed the slaveholders' fundamental uncertainty about the morality of their mastery. "The common incidence of the themes of guilt and doubt" in their writings, observed Morrow, suggested that the proslavery intellectuals were attempting to shore up a shaky southern commitment to slavery.[25] David Donald also dwelled on the proslavery writers at the same time that he argued for their marginal place in southern slaveholding society. Donald did not buy into the theories of guilt advanced by Morrow, but he did aver that the authors who struggled to defend southern slavery were primarily concerned with rehabilitating themselves in a society that had seemed to pass them by.[26]

Drew Gilpin Faust launched her scholarly inquiry into southern proslavery thought from a perspective that was similar to Donald's. In her first monograph, *A Sacred Circle* (1977), she stressed the degree to which some of the most prominent proslavery writers deemed themselves to be "similarly lonely and unappreciated."

But whereas Donald had suggested that alienated southerners became writers and intellectuals in order to ingratiate themselves with the ruling planter elite, Faust contended that the proslavery ideologues were alienated exactly because they were writers and intellectuals. Investigating the network of intimate relationships that enabled these thinkers to converse with each other about the contours of an idealized proslavery society, Faust lifted up their ideas for incisive critical commentary. By the time that she assembled her anthology of late antebellum proslavery texts in 1981, she was beginning to emphasize the deep roots of proslavery thought not just in the South but also in the colonial North and across the British colonial empire. Without discarding her earlier thesis of the proslavery authors' sense of intellectual alienation in the South, Faust subtly changed her emphasis in her biography of James Henry Hammond published in 1982. Hammond, in this work, became emblematic of the slave society that he defended, "a Representative Southern man" in terms of his "social values." Conversely, in Faust's first book, Hammond had been portrayed as part of an "intellectual class" that "was not the South and often felt it had no place in it." The more that Faust studied the proslavery thinkers, the more central to slaveholding culture did their ideas become in her historical analysis.[27]

Throughout all of her work, Faust has consistently placed southern intellectuals in a broader context of concerns that they shared with thinkers across the Western world. Faust was one of the first historians to approach the proslavery writers as a group of reformers who reflected trends of social improvement that were surfacing in the North as well as the South.[28] Her contentions on this point have received considerable support from scholars such as Bertram Wyatt-Brown and Joyce E. Chaplin. Writing in 1982, Wyatt-Brown characterized the slave owners' proslavery thought using concepts that would eventually recast the traditional historiographical divide between the paternalist and republican paradigms for proslavery thought. For years the historiography of slave studies had led scholars studying conservative organic proslavery thought to depict it in opposition to capitalist or bourgeois individualism, the constellation of principles that surfaced in modernizing economies making the transition to wage labor. Wyatt-Brown, however, suggested that proslavery reformers espousing organic ideals were self-consciously pursuing a modern progressive agenda. In order to put (in Fitzhugh's words) "the South at the lead of modern civilization," the slaveholders planned to institute a humane philosophy of mastery that, over time, would improve the region and serve as a moral counterexample to the vice and suffering of the ostensibly free society in the North.

Chaplin's study of the colonial Lower South provided compelling evidence that this proslavery sensibility was surfacing in the guise of "humanitarianism" in the mid-eighteenth-century South.[29] Scholars had already linked humanitarian ideals and progressive campaigns for social reform to the growth of capitalism itself.[30] Consequently, the recognition that proslavery thought was built on a progressive ideological foundation led historians of the South to reevaluate the relationship between proslavery thought and the modern world. Genovese himself would move his analysis in this direction during the 1990s. In 1965 he had called the slave owners' paternalism a "premodern" mentality; in 1983 he and Fox-Genovese deemed their proslavery ideology to be a "non-modern" value system; by 1990 Genovese had concluded that southern defenders of slavery "saw themselves as men who sought an alternative route to modernity." They "repudiated neither 'progress,' nor 'science,' nor 'modernity.'"[31]

This new wave of scholarship recognized an innovative cultural dynamic and agenda lurking within the proslavery ideologues' commitment to an organic master-slave relationship. Far from speaking to the slave owners' removal from cosmopolitan intellectual life, the southern proslavery culture was produced by the slaveholders' constant intercourse with the literature, philosophy, science, and history of the early modern world. This new scholarly paradigm contradicted images of southern identity that were fostered by some white southerners during the late eighteenth and early nineteenth centuries—most notably Thomas Jefferson's agrarian ideal of the sturdy, self-reliant farmer providing a moral foundation for the American political system. The slaveholders were not isolated farmers. Had they been, they would have lacked the intellectual means by which to defend slavery with concepts of humanity and Christian reciprocity in an era that was rapidly defining slavery as a monstrous holdover from a barbaric past. (For that matter, had they been isolated farmers, they also would have lacked the resources through which to arrange sufficient capital to underwrite the largest forced migration in human history and the construction of a sprawling plantation network producing staple crops for sale on the global market.) That the southern elite's value system was as much in dialogue with the world stage as was their elaborate plantation economy underscores the inaccuracies of liberal scholarly assumptions about the shallowness of their proslavery culture. The southerners' proslavery ideas might well be characterized as repulsive and dangerous, but these notions traveled across vast distances and winnowed their way deep into the white southern political sensibility.

The stereotype of the Old South as a region that walled off and therefore stifled its own intellectual life in order to protect slavery, a cliché wielded by authors such as Wilbur J. Cash, has thankfully withered under the weight of recent historical studies of the vibrant mind of the slavery South.[32] One might more readily conclude, on the heels of recent scholarship into this topic, that the Old South as a region immersed itself in global intellectual currents in order to chart a path toward an effective justification of its own social order.[33] More than any other scholar, Michael O'Brien has uncovered the "transatlantic dimension of Southern thought."[34] O'Brien's biography of the Charleston intellectual Hugh Swinton Legaré, for example, reveals how a Carolina planter's son could, in the ordinary course of events, receive an education in the classics, mathematics, natural and moral philosophy, and the texts produced by the Scottish Enlightenment. Legaré traveled abroad to complete his education, intending to study in Germany but ending up in Edinburgh. Upon his return to South Carolina, he entered politics as a representative in the state assembly before involving himself with the *Southern Review,* a periodical launched with the intention of vindicating the character of the southern states. His cosmopolitan education therefore provided him and his region with a principal resource in the defense of the slavery South. And Legaré, although cognizant that slavery did pose social problems, certainly did his part to protect the institution from moral critiques offered by the disapproving North. At the same time, however, O'Brien's scholarship reminds us that southerners' complicated intellectual interaction with the rest of the Western world could not be reduced by them (nor should it be reduced by modern scholars) to a monomaniacal campaign to defend slavery and nothing else. As many passionately proslavery Carolina statesmen geared up for battle with the federal government in 1832–33, Legaré's principled opposition to nullification landed him, appropriately enough given his intellectual background, in European exile. If Legaré's life story speaks to the richness of the southern mind, it also demonstrates that men of learning and privilege often found themselves drawn into elite circles that transcended a particular region or concern. Indeed, the work of scholars such as Daniel Kilbride has suggested the degree to which the planter elite was physically and psychologically intermixed with the wealthiest segments of northern urban society.[35]

In recent years scholars have become far less inclined to treat southern slavery as an isolated institution. In the scholarship of Sylvia Frey, Betty Wood, Gwendolyn Midlo Hall, and Jane Landers, one can discern the maturation of a global paradigm for understanding slaveholding society.[36] Their work builds on earlier comparative scholarship on slavery—most notably Peter Kolchin's magisterial study of southern slavery and Russian serfdom. These studies contrasted the mindset of the southern planters with that of the ruling elite in other sharply stratified societies in the hopes of lifting up the defining characteristics of power in each setting. By stretching their analysis to encompass widely distant historical settings, scholars such as Kolchin offered important insights into the southern planters' thorny ideological problem of living especially close to their slaves in a republic that placed a strong significance on the principles of republican liberty and human rights.[37]

Scholars of Atlantic World slavery have likewise offered fruitful comparisons between slavery in the American South, slavery across the Western Hemisphere, and the interplay between these plantation systems and the European and African continents. This work is holistic, searching for the actual interactions between masters and slaves residing in seemingly far-flung—but actually meaningfully connected—regions within the Atlantic system. David Brion Davis's monumental studies on the intellectual tensions that swirled around the institution of slavery from the ancient into the modern era demonstrated the potential payoff of an analytical approach that tracked a historical problem across conventional boundaries of nation and historical period.[38] Ambitious scholars interested in the material dimensions of this topic—dimensions of economy and social structure—have also delineated the role of the plantation system within an Atlantic system or even a world system.[39]

The trajectory of this historiography has obviously carried scholars of slavery far from old notions about a unique southern planter class whose society and ideals ran counter to the rest of the Western world. The more that scholars such as Larry Tise and Thomas Krise dig into the parameters of proslavery thought in the Atlantic world, the less it seems that organic conservative ideas were the special province of a planter elite that identified themselves in stridently sectional terms.[40] Resting at the heart of this scholarship is a paradox that is unpalatable to modern readers who justly equate slavery with a cruel waste of human labor and lives. During the early modern period and even into the nineteenth century, organic proslavery assumptions were the hallmark of a cosmopolitan standard for moral and genteel conduct. Far from representing the interests of reactionary conservatives or profit-obsessed entrepreneurs, the promulgators of organic proslavery doctrines constituted a vanguard of religious reformers who approached moral problems from the widest possible moral and geographic perspective. That these doctrines could be turned into a philosophical foundation for southern sectionalism would have struck early proslavery authors as an improbable notion.[41] That an antislavery movement could one day cast self-consciously Christian slaveholders into the roles of tyrannical villains would have struck the early modern proslavery authors as patently absurd.

## Ancient and Medieval Foundations for Proslavery Thought in the Western Hemisphere

As we have seen, early white scholars of the South gave less-than-full attention to proslavery texts. Moreover, because they equated proslavery thought with southern sectionalism, they also tended to ignore almost completely proslavery literature that appeared prior to 1830.[42] This lapse did not flow from a scholarly unfamiliarity with the relevant evidence, but rather from historiographical rhythms that kept such evidence on the margins of scholarly concern. Back in 1935 the historian William Sumner Jenkins had already illustrated that "long before the first [European] settlements were made in the western hemisphere the arguments in justification of the social institution of domestic slavery had become hackneyed."[43] Subsequent generations of scholars routinely cited Jenkins but somehow lost sight of the considerable evidence of the ubiquity of conservative proslavery thought in the ancient, medieval, and early modern world.[44] Indeed, even a good number of superb late-twentieth-century historians subscribed to the time-honored and flawed chronology wherein white southerners had supposedly referred to slavery as a "necessary evil" until the 1830s, at which point they suddenly declared the institution a "positive good."[45] Although the pace of proslavery publications most certainly increased in the 1830s, this formulation mistimed by millennia the growth of "mature" proslavery thought and mistimed by almost a century its manifestation in the American South. The simple truth of the matter was that more defenders of slavery emerged in the South in the 1830s because more antislavery reformers were beginning to denounce human bondage during this era. The proslavery ideas underlying the late antebellum debates over slavery, however, were long since familiar.

In the preceding millennia when slavery stretched across every corner of the globe and touched practically every society in human history, slavery seldom needed defenders because no one was challenging its existence.[46] When the occasional ancient philosopher or medieval theologian weighed in on the morality of unfree labor, practically none of them found reason to question its morality or practicality. Hence, Plato perceived slavery as an appropriate reflection of the social stratification that justly established order in the universe. Aristotle vindicated it as a domestic institution, stating that "a complete household consists of slaves and freemen" and that "the first and fewest possible parts of a family are master and slave, husband and wife, father and children."[47] For Aristotle, it was "clear" that "some men are by nature free, and others slaves, and that for these latter slavery is both expedient and right."[48] Those on whom nature had bestowed the condition of slavery lacked, in Aristotle's opinion, the capacity to attain "any excellence at all . . . beyond those of an instrument and of a servant." Qualities such as "temperance, courage, justice, and the like" were forever out of the slave's reach because the slave supposedly possessed "no deliberative faculty at all."[49] Denying the slave any role as an individual with agency, Aristotle had little difficulty portraying the slave as the master's appendage, as "a living instrument; . . . a living possession"—"a part of the master, a living but separated part of his bodily frame." Far from leading to tyranny, this utter eradication of the slave's individuality created a context for a master-slave relationship marked by "a common interest" springing from nature. In the end, maintained Aristotle, the "rule of a household" could be only "a monarchy."[50]

When Christianity emerged as a religion four centuries later, it too upheld the existence of slavery. Although Christianity would promote the value of freedom to an unprecedented degree in the ancient world, the religion nevertheless up-held the earthly institution of unfree labor during its first seventeen centuries of existence. This paradox of early Christianity simultaneously valuing freedom yet accepting the institution of slavery was, in some respects, a harbinger of the complex juxtaposition of slavery and freedom in early America. The sociologist Orlando Patterson has demonstrated that the recently freed status of many early Christians prepared them to relish freedom as a spiritual metaphor. In conse-quence, St. Paul's writings develop the theme of a Christian salvation that deliv-ered sinners from spiritual slavery.[51] Although Paul made clear that spiritual concerns about freedom did not mean that the Gospel liberated slaves from their earthly condition of service, he had still opened the door to a theology that would one day undermine the legitimacy of slavery in general. Sadly for the slaves, the Christian critique of slavery would not mature for another seventeen hundred years. Meanwhile, masters had little difficulty finding passages in the New Testa-ment that portrayed slavery as a feature of human life that should be regulated rather than eradicated. In this sense, the Gospels continued proslavery themes running through the Old Testament wherein the faithful were urged to treat their bondservants in accordance with God's teachings.[52]

In subsequent centuries, slavery continued to play a significant role in Europe. True, upon the decline of the Roman Empire in the fifth century, slavery's cen-trality in the European economy did begin to lessen, particularly in Germany. Yet the scholarship exploring this subject suggests that the decline in European slav-ery should be discussed in relative terms that still recognize the vigorous role played by slavery, even if medieval Europe cannot be classified as a "slave society" in the same way as Ancient Greece or Rome. Slavery, we should note, persisted in the ninth and tenth centuries, sometimes maintaining itself as a feature within the feudal labor arrangements that largely supplanted slavery in late medieval western Europe. As late as the turn of the eleventh century, some one-tenth of England's population consisted of slaves. More strikingly still, as many as one-fifth of the West Country's population was enslaved at this point in England's history. And as western Europe slowly purged itself of slavery between the eleventh and fifteenth centuries, the institution remained critically important to the economies and societies of southern and eastern Europe. The Italian city-states, as the scholar Charles Verlinden has established, relied heavily on slavery as they expanded their colonies in the thirteenth, fourteenth, and fifteenth centuries.[53] Slaves, moreover, occupied a noticeable place in the domestic life of these city-states.[54]

None of these complicated economic developments sprang primarily from moral concerns with unfree labor. Slavery had yet to become a moral problem inviting sustained commentary. The medieval Roman Catholic Church, however, did render judgment on the propriety of slavery when it grappled with Islamic expansion into the Iberian Peninsula. Well aware that Islamic law barred Muslims from holding fellow Muslims in slavery, eighth-century Christian authorities began to push for a similar doctrine.[55] Still, this rather limited call for reform—which fell far short of a general opposition to slavery on moral grounds—made little headway during subsequent centuries. The *Siete Partidas,* a thirteenth-century Spanish legal code celebrated for its humanity, merely sought to regulate rather than to ban the ownership of Christian slaves by fellow Christians. Celebrated Catholic theologians such as the thirteenth-century thinker Thomas Aquinas fleshed out proslavery positions that were in many respects similar to those elucidated in the Pauline texts of early Christianity. Like Aristotle, Aquinas characterized slavery as a natural institution. For Aquinas, however, slavery's legitimacy sprang less from the innate deficiencies of those whom Aristotle had described as slaves "by nature" and more from the human race's shared state of sinfulness, a state that required all people to submit to earthly hierarchies designed to channel sinful human nature in more constructive social directions. The bottom line for medieval Christianity was that God mandated human acquiescence to a system of marked social stratification.[56]

## The Reformation and the Emerging Global Plantation System

The onset of the Protestant Reformation in the early sixteenth century led to a thorough reevaluation of Christian perspectives on moral order. Amid the theological wrangling that resulted in the foundation of new Christian denominations, however, religious thought concerning freedom and social order remained surprisingly consistent. To be sure, oppressed segments of European society sometimes gravitated toward the emerging Protestant theology because its radical rejection of established church order seemingly paved the way for an upheaval against society at large. Yet when German peasants organized into a revolutionary army in 1525, they discovered—during the brief interlude before they were crushed by their feudal lords—that leading theologians never intended to foster such social upheaval. In fact, by the late 1520s, Luther was explicitly grounding his vision of social order on the traditional imperative of paternal obedience, on the holy mandate that household dependents owed to the patriarch their loyalty and obedience. "As husband, father and master," observed the historian Robert Bast, "Luther's ideal patriarch ruled through kindly condescension, holding his subordinates to reasonable standards." Yet the patriarch also required that servants "must honor their 'Housefather' in the same way that children and wives do, and 'not only the good and moderate fathers, but also the corrupt, harsh, and evil ones.'" Organic assumptions about patriarchal authority, then, provided a consistent moral baseline on which religious authorities would develop coherent perspectives on the unfolding spectacle of the modern plantation system.[57]

In the sixteenth and seventeenth centuries, as Spain and Portugal extended their empires from the western coasts of Africa to the distant reaches of the Western Hemisphere, the Christian rationale for slavery remained in force. Indeed, the theology linking the doctrine of salvation to the subordination of earthly populations manifested itself during Columbus's first voyage to America. Among Columbus's earliest impressions of the New World native population was his sense that "they ought to be good servants and of good skill, for I see that they repeat very quickly whatever was said to them." To this observation, Columbus immediately appended his prediction that "they would easily be made Christians."[58] If the Catholic theological tradition supported rather than opposed the genesis of a plantation complex based on slavery, so too did economic trends that were underway during the early eleventh century. Italian capital and European military power had extended into the Levant and across the Mediterranean during the late medieval era. In locales such as Crete and Cyprus, European entrepreneurs experimented with the use of slave labor in plantations that produced sugar as a staple commodity. In time, as the *Reconquista* left the Iberian Peninsula under the control of Catholic monarchs, this plantation complex shifted westward to the Canary Islands, the Azores, the Cape Verdes, and Madeira. Columbus's use of the Canary Islands as a final staging point on his journey to America reinforces the point that the New World plantation system merely extended economic practices that had been in play for half a millennium.[59]

The seventeenth century would prove to be a critical period for England's development as a colonial power in the New World. In their first half-century of existence, English settlements in Virginia and in the West Indies developed plantation economies that used unfree labor.[60] The resulting profits for the emerging white planter class were often as spectacular as the slave mortality rates were grim. Because no sustained critique of unfree labor had yet emerged during this century, hardly anyone involved in the English plantation complex felt compelled to struggle, on a personal level, with the morality of slavery. This is to say that seventeenth-century slaveholders wielding power over African slaves did so without having to contemplate the justice of their actions. At the same time, however, jurists and political theorists during this era entered debates over the just management of government authority. The rising tide of monarchical power in Europe, the civil and religious conflicts that led to constant bloodshed, and the European nations' squabbles over the spoils of the New World actually nourished intense contemplation about how best to govern subordinate members of society. Within the context of this broader discussion, slavery became a topic for contemplation.

Authors such as Hugo Grotius, Thomas Hobbes, Robert Filmer, and John Locke forcefully disagreed with each others' positions on a range of issues concerning moral government—whether, for example, it was grounded in nature or in human consent, whether it was immutable or subject to reformulation by the governed, and whether the relationship between rulers and subjects differed substantively from relationships between husbands and wives, masters and servants, or masters and slaves.[61] Notwithstanding the variegated positions staked out by these authors, they found ways in which to defend slavery. For admittedly different reasons, these authors depicted slavery not in terms of unrestrained tyranny but as a potentially just institution. On one end of the philosophical spectrum, Filmer insisted that slavery was rooted in the natural order of the world. "A son, a subject and a servant or a slave," he averred, "were one and the same thing at first." To illustrate the dangers attending efforts of the governed to modify the terms of their rulers' power, Filmer offered the repulsive specter of a general emancipation of slaves followed by endless civil disorder. When John Locke attempted to dismantle Filmer's position, he nonetheless took pains to rationalize the ongoing existence of chattel slavery as an institution that could be reconciled with his doctrine of consensual government.[62] These were not matters of idle speculation for Locke. As the Carolina Lords Proprietors launched their colony in the late 1660s, Locke himself transcribed proslavery passages in the new settlement's "Fundamental Constitutions," and he would later invest in the Royal African Company, which monopolized the slave trade. Hence, as the earliest generations of English entrepreneurs launched their colonial plantation empire, they did so with the blessing of the brightest thinkers of their era. If the author Thomas More found a place for slavery in his *Utopia,* then surely New World planters could feel secure in their roles as masters.[63]

None of these authors, then, offered much in the way of short-term hope to the tens of thousands of African slaves pouring into North America by the turn of the eighteenth century. And the slaveholders themselves hardly needed to bother with intricate rationales for unfree labor. Yet lurking within these philosophers' schema for moral applications of power were the kernels of competing organic and republican proslavery themes that, to the endless confusion of twentieth-century scholars, would surface in tension within the American South. Filmer, for his part, took pains to argue on behalf of an organic conservative order that, in his opinion, did not entail rejection of the concept of political liberty per se. He differentiated the meaningful liberty that derived from the just reign of a monarch from the mere "pretexts of liberty," which flowed from the indefensible doctrine that "Mankind is . . . at liberty to choose what form of government it please." Without denouncing the earthly institution of slavery, Filmer was prepared to employ slavery as a metaphor for suffering under unjust government. He therefore likened the anarchy created by "popular" government to a "liberty only to destroy liberty," which was, in essence, "but several degrees of slavery." Without ironclad hierarchy, reasoned Filmer, the world would sink into a debasing confusion, a state that offered terrible misfortune rather than true liberty. By linking the slaveholders' authority to the father's and the monarch's, Filmer gave voice to an organic conservatism that could justify the subordination of certain populations without casting them as morally or physiologically deficient. This framework for the justification of unequal social stations would blossom into an organic proslavery tradition that reached its apogee in the late antebellum works of George Fitzhugh.[64]

John Locke, by contrast, conceptualized the master-slave relationship as operating on principles that were utterly unlike and outside the standards of authority by which a just society should be governed. Adhering to the position that nature had bestowed equality on men, Locke insisted that rulers could govern only with the consent of the governed. Like Filmer, Locke distinguished between slavery as an earthly labor system and slavery as a politically debased condition into which free citizens might sink. In the latter sense, slavery, Locke famously observed, "is so vile and miserable an Estate of Man, and so directly opposite to the generous Temper and Courage of our Nation; that 'tis hardly to be conceived, that an Englishman . . . should plead for it." Yet plead for it as a labor system Locke did, justifying slavery as an alternative to the death awaiting those defeated in war: "This is the perfect condition of Slavery, which is nothing else, but the state of War continued, between a Lawful Conqueror, and a Captive." Here was slavery as a form of social death, with the slave cast in the role of permanent outsider to the system of social contracts that bounded other social relationships with standards of reciprocity and justice.

Interestingly, Locke's notions of natural equality were malleable enough to allow for the possibility that "the Lord and Master of them all" sometimes "set one above another." Notwithstanding his claim "that all men by Nature are equal," he clarified, "I cannot be supposed to understand all sorts of equality: age or virtue may give men a just precedency: excellency of parts and merit may place others above the common level." Significantly, Locke also reasoned that some people might fall into permanently subordinate positions due to their innate incapacities. "But if through defects that may happen out of the ordinary course of nature," he wrote, "any one comes not to such a degree of reason, wherein he might be supposed capable of knowing the law, and so living within the rules of it, he is never capable of being a free man."[65] Locke did not attach racial significance to this category, but other subscribers to his philosophy—most notably Thomas Jefferson—would make that leap. The complexities are admittedly maddening. Locke's liberal assumptions would offer a moral foundation to the burgeoning antislavery movement of the next century. At the same time, his philosophy potentially placed the rights of a broadly defined citizenship off-limits to enslaved segments of the population and to those deemed naturally incapable of exercising their political liberties—categories that would be conflated in the "*Herrenvolk* democracy" of the slavery South.

## Christian Proslavery Thought Bridges the Atlantic

Even as philosophers wrangled over slavery's role in society, entrepreneurs and monarchs were launching a plantation economy in the New World. It would be Christian ministers who spanned the literal and symbolic gap between these groups' concerns. In part, the theological wrangling over slavery sprang from a game of moral one-upmanship played between established and dissenting denominations. In the English empire, dissenters pointed to the American plantations to reveal the Anglican Church's inability to uphold a Christian standard for slavery, and Anglican authors responded to these charges with proslavery logic of their own.[66] Still, ministers' preoccupation with the state of religion among enslaved or subordinated populations in the Americas extended far beyond the rivalries between competing churches. For many theologians and ministers, the extension of the English colonial system carried with it grave responsibilities. The wealth and political power created by the plantation empire were potentially accompanied by sinful preoccupations with earthly gain and a perilous disregard for God's teachings. The master-slave relationship rested at the heart of these concerns. Christian thinkers prayed that this engine for fantastic riches might also be a vehicle for the salvation of new souls. If so, England's glory and the slaveholders' fiscal gains could be interpreted as signs of God's bounty. But if the slave populations were denied access to the Gospels, then the irreligious nature of the plantation complex threatened the empire with disastrous and ignominious consequences.

In the 1660s, as a planter elite was materializing in the British West Indies and as the Virginia landowners began to rely heavily on African slave labor, the Puritan minister Richard Baxter contemplated the morality of slavery. In *A Christian Directory,* a work written in 1664–65, Baxter looked to the New Testament for evidence calling for an organic master-slave relationship. Citing Romans 8:28, Baxter urged English slave owners to remember that "if you would have good servants, see that you be good masters, and do your own duty, and then either your servants will do theirs, or else all their failings, shall turn to your greater good." Baxter was clearly not an abolitionist. Rather, he recognized the righteousness of slavery insofar as the institution was managed in deference to holy teachings. "There is a slavery to which some men may be Lawfully put," he wrote, "and there is a slavery to which none may be put." Lawful slavery, he opined, required the slaveholders' recognition that their mastery did not entitle them to abuse their bondservants or to neglect their spiritual development. "Remember that God is their absolute Owner, and that you have none but a derived and limited Propriety in them," he counseled the American planters. Conceding that masters might still have just cause to discipline recalcitrant slaves, Baxter encouraged the slaveholders in these cases to "find fault in season, with prudence and sobriety, when your passions are down, and when it is most likely to do good." God's teachings on slavery, as Baxter understood them, called for an appropriate amount of discipline to be applied. "If it be too little," he warned, "it will embolden them in doing ill; If it be too much, or frequent or passionate, it will make them sleight it and despise it."[67]

As early as the 1660s, two centuries before the American Civil War, ministers such as Baxter fully articulated a "paternalistic" proslavery rationale that cast masters in the role of loving parents and slaves into the position of childlike dependents. "Remember that in Christ they are your brethren and fellow Servants; and therefore rule them not tyrannically but in tenderness and love," he wrote. The standards of a loving family encompassed the slaves, argued Baxter, exactly because they belonged to the planters. "The greater your power is over them," he warned the masters, "the greater your charge is of them, and your duty for them. As you owe more to a Child than to a Day Labourer or a hired Servant, because being more your own, he is more entrusted to your care: so also by the same reason, you owe more to a slave, because he is more your own; and power and obligation go together." This organic Christian logic about earthly hierarchy was not, in Baxter's opinion, sufficient to justify the international slave trade that was just beginning to flourish in North America during this decade. Here, Baxter's position illustrates the degree to which organic and liberal proslavery thought could surface within a single author's work. For Baxter, like his contemporary John Locke, believed that slavery could justly flow only from a captured prisoner's decision to trade lifetime service in slavery for the sparing of his or her life. Because this transaction required a consensual agreement, it conformed to the liberal insistence on the natural equality of all humans. Baxter could not countenance the African slave trade of the 1660s on such terms because vast numbers of African slaves were obviously being captured by entrepreneurs with the sole intent of gaining profit through the slaves' sale. This cash nexus did not provide a suitable foundation for a moral master-slave relationship. Baxter cautioned the American planters to "make it your chief end in buying and using slaves, to win them to Christ, and save their Souls." This was to be an imperative that masters placed before their own profits. "Let their Salvation," urged Baxter, "be far more valued by you than their Service."[68]

The proslavery sensibility given voice by Baxter also surfaced in the writings of the Anglican minister Morgan Godwyn. After spending time in Virginia and the West Indies, Godwyn simultaneously defended slavery as a biblically sanctioned institution and denounced the slaveholders for their failure to exercise their power in a moral fashion. As to the morality of the institution as an abstract proposition,

Godwyn had no doubts. Biblical passages such as Ephesians 6, he wrote, established "the Authority of masters, over their Servants and Slaves, in as high a measure, as even themselves could have prescribed. . . . Requiring service with singleness of heart, as unto the Lord, and not unto Men." Faithful Christians, he insisted, were not required to emancipate their slaves. Indeed, argued Godwyn, masters who Christianized their plantations stood to benefit in material as well as spiritual terms. "Can any Man believe other," he asked, "than that . . . it is not the Master's great Interest to have his Servants minds possessed, with the principles of true Piety?" In addition to the spiritual benefit of having played an "instrumental" role in the salvation of the slaves' souls, the master would "also reap the desired fruit of his Servant's Fidelity: which whosoever [master] hinders, must therein be an enemy to . . . his own great [self-]Interest."[69]

Unlike proslavery authors in the eighteenth and nineteenth centuries, Baxter and Godwyn did not direct their organic Christian logic at antislavery reformers. There were none, although there would be in the near future. Instead, as Godwyn's defensive tone indicates, the ministers espousing an organic vision of plantation slavery were hoping to convince the most proslavery audience imaginable: the slaveholders themselves. Although every political and religious authority weighing in on the question of Christianity and emancipation asserted that Christianizing slave populations did not require their release from bondage, slaveholders in the New World fretted over this possibility.[70] The conflict between planters and ministers over the proper character of New World slavery would remain unsettled until the early nineteenth century when growing numbers of southern slaveholders finally warmed to the organic proslavery vision. Until then, ministers attempting to Christianize plantation slavery consistently collided with slaveholder hostility and suspicion.[71] Morgan Godwyn reported the slaveholders' claim that Christianizing their slave populations amounted to a "ready way to have all their Throats cut."[72] A steady stream of such grim reports on the state of religious life in the colonies led the Anglican bishop William Fleetwood to ask in 1711 "whether there be any Exception" to this trend of colonial slaveholders keeping religion from their slaves.[73]

Ministers combating such religious intransigence were forced to press their arguments in directions that were, at once, forcefully proslavery and highly critical of the conduct of slaveholders in the New World. As we have seen, passages in Baxter's and Godwyn's texts unabashedly defended the lawfulness of slavery. Yet after evoking imagery of an organic brand of slavery, both men surveyed the American plantation system to see if it reflected these ideals. They found much to deplore. Godwyn recounted with dismay the planters' routine employment of ear cropping, castration, amputation of limbs, and capital punishment as tools for disciplining their bondservants.[74] His early-eighteenth-century Anglican successor,

Francis Le Jau, reported similarly appalling conduct in South Carolina, where slaveholders burned some slaves alive and tormented others by incarcerating them in "hellish" contraptions. After witnessing such scenes, Le Jau concluded that "many Masters can't be persuaded that Negroes and Indians are otherwise than Beasts, and use them like such."[75] The slaveholders' disavowal of their slaves' humanity coincided with—and no doubt was augmented by—the explosive growth of the institution in the late seventeenth century. This period was marked by dramatically increased importation of African slaves and an attendant hardening of the legal and cultural boundaries between blacks and whites.[76] To the dismay of ministers such as Godwyn, a good number of slaveholders explicitly denied that African slaves were human beings. "It was told me with no small Passion and Vehemency," he sadly recalled, "and that by a Religious Person (for so in all things else she appeared), that I might as well Baptize a Puppy, as a certain young Negro."[77]

Despite such resistance, the Anglican Church redoubled its efforts at the end of the seventeenth century. Seeking to increase its influence over colonial life, the church dispatched into the southern colonies commissaries to represent the bishop of London's authority.[78] Thomas Bray, the commissary for the colony of Maryland, proved to be a particularly zealous advocate of the plan to Christianize the plantation system. After a brief residence in the New World, Bray returned to England and established, in 1701, the Society for the Propagation of the Gospel in Foreign Parts (SPG). This Anglican organization subsequently funded numerous missions to the colonial slave populations. Bray also willed a portion of his estate to fund a second missionary group (that later called themselves the Associates of Dr. Thomas Bray) whose primary function was the salvation of African slaves' souls. Together with regularly dispatched Anglican ministers, the missionaries funded by these groups functioned as a network linking the Anglican authorities in England to the distant world of plantation slavery.[79]

Across this network, proslavery texts began to flow from England in the early eighteenth century. Bray himself saw to it that more than thirty-three thousand books and tracts were sent to the colonies, and these works provided the foundations for numerous American libraries.[80] Among these texts were sermons that Anglican authorities delivered to the SPG on the topic of slave religion. Repeatedly, the authors of these tracts complained about the colonial slaveholders' inhumane treatment of a slave population that was kept in spiritual darkness. In keeping with the pattern established by Godwyn and the dissenter Baxter, the Anglican writers emphasized that slave conversion should not be confused with slave emancipation. Bishop William Fleetwood argued in 1711 that "there is no fear of losing the Service and Profit of Slaves, by letting them become *Christians*," because planters were "neither prohibited by the Laws of God, nor those of the

*Lord,* from keeping *Christian Slaves.*" Citing Corinthians 7:20, he maintained that Christ called for "every Man [to] abide in the same Calling, wherein he was called." This biblical justification for slavery, however, carried with it a price that Christian masters had no spiritual choice but to pay. Namely, the "commands of Christ" compelled them "to pity all Mankind, to do to all Men, indistinctly, the good we can," and "to shew all Pity and good Nature" to the slaves' bodies and souls.[81]

These sentiments did not remain in England. The SPG, according to one of its secretaries, judged Fleetwood's address to be "so useful a Discourse, that they printed and dispersed abroad in the Plantations, great Numbers of that Sermon." Likewise, in 1727 the SPG published ten thousand copies of the bishop of London Edmund Gibson's pastoral message to the American slaveholders and distributed them in the American South.[82] In this work, Gibson urged colonial planters to keep their slaves out of the fields on the Sabbath. Like Fleetwood, Gibson bemoaned the slaveholders' tendency to assume that slave baptisms would "destroy both the Property which the Masters have in them as slaves" and that "the making them Christians, only makes them less diligent, and more ungovernable."[83] Gibson responded that Christianity "makes no manner of change" in its adherents' "*outward* Condition, whatever that was before, whether bond or free, their baptism." Citing Corinthians 7, he insisted that Christian teachings placed the slaves "under stronger Obligations to perform those Duties with the greatest Diligence and Fidelity." Gibson even conceded that planters possessed the right to discipline their slaves, although he urged the slave owners to wield this power with "Humanity" and to "have Recourse to severe and rigorous Methods [of punishment] unwillingly, and only out of Necessity." His squeamishness at the prospect of masters whipping their slaves could not compete with his overarching concern with their conversion to Christianity. In his estimation, "the greatest Hardships that the most severe Master can inflict upon [the slaves], is not to be compared to the Cruelty of keeping [the slaves] in the State of Heathenism, and depriving them of the Means of Salvation." According to such logic, the planters did not sin merely by owning Christian slaves; rather, they sinned by owning slaves whom they kept from Christianity.[84]

## Christian Doctrines about Slavery, Race, and Equality

By the time that the Anglican Church had launched its mission to the plantations, slavery had become inexorably associated with the racial subordination of African populations. A wealth of recent scholarship has demonstrated that there was nothing inevitable about this historical development in the New World plantation complex. In other parts of the world, slavery had not required the maintenance of racial lines between free and unfree populations. For a variety of complicated demographic, economic, and cultural reasons, American planters came to rely almost exclusively on African slaves as their source for unfree labor by the turn of the eighteenth century.[85] In the wake of their collective decision to find their slaves in Africa, the planters hardened stereotypes about subordinate laboring populations into racial assumptions that linked essential personality traits to skin color and lineage. By the end of the eighteenth century, according to scholars such as Winthrop Jordan, white colonists assumed with increasing frequency that African slaves were naturally fit for that role. These racial conceptions, moreover, dovetailed with a theological rationale for slavery that stretched back to antiquity. Espoused in the Old Testament, Noah's curse of enslavement on the lineage of Canaan, son of Ham, offered a religious justification for the ongoing enslavement and inferior treatment of populations of laborers who were perceived to be the inheritors of that biblical curse.[86] As the scholarship of William McKee Evans has revealed, the "sons of Ham" story defended slavery in genealogical terms that did not necessarily coincide with coherent racial categories. Witness the incongruity of simultaneously held medieval Jewish beliefs that Africans were Canaanites and that the Slavic tongues of eastern Europe were the "language of Canaan."[87] Yet even before the planters of the American South had completed their transition from an economy based on white indentured labor to one based on African slave labor, they had come to believe that Africans were descendents of Ham who were fated to bondage. In work that was published in 1680, Morgan Godwyn already deemed the question worthy of extended analysis.[88]

Given the mounting antipathy toward African slaves in the English colonies, it is not surprising that some proslavery authors integrated racial concepts into their religious justification for the enslavement of Africans.[89] For instance, when the Massachusetts jurist John Saffin upheld the morality of slavery in 1701, he interpreted the Bible in racially specific terms. When an antislavery author charged that the bondage of Africans was tantamount to the morally indefensible enslavement of Joseph by his jealous brothers in Genesis, Saffin responded with scornful racism. Denying any "congruiety" between Joseph's slavery and African bondage, he offered doggerel that claimed to unlock the inherited deficiencies of "the Negroes Character":

> Cowardly and cruel are those *Blacks* Innate,
> Prone to Revenge, Imp of inveterate hate.
> He that exasperates them, soon espies
> Mischief and Murder in their very eyes.
> Libidinous, Deceitful, False and Rude,
> The Spume Issue of Ingratitude.
> The Premises consider'd, all may tell,
> How near good *Joseph* they are Parallel.[90]

In Saffin's estimation, Africans' moral shortcomings cast them onto a lower rung of the hierarchy that God had created when he "set different Orders and Degrees of men in the World, both in Church and Common Weal." Tinged with racist assumptions about black character, his organic logic led Saffin to conclude that it would constitute a "breach of good manners" to accept the notion that "all men have equal right to Liberty, and all outward comforts of this life."[91]

While Saffin's racism colored his reading of the Bible, he still must have noticed that the scriptural passages enjoining humans to accept different earthly stations also inculcated a mandatory attention to the spiritual unity of the human race —both the free and the enslaved. Passages in 1 Corinthians 12 state that "Christ is like a single body with its many limbs and organs, which, many as they are, together make up one body; for in the one Spirit we were all brought into one body by baptism, whether Jews or Greeks, slave or free." God no doubt "set different Orders and Degrees of men," but he also made clear that "God has combined the various parts of the body, giving special honour to the humbler parts, so that there might be no division in the body, but that all its parts might feel the same concern for one another." This standard of reciprocity did not compel an early-eighteenth-century author such as Saffin to forgo his racist ideas. But the theological implications of such passages did constrain his racism within certain limits. Notably, Saffin's contempt toward African slaves did not carry with it an acceptance of the "sons of Ham" doctrine as a rationale for their enslavement. Indeed, he explicitly rejected the possibility that "Blackamores are of the Posterity of Cham, and therefore under the Curse of Slavery." Instead, he postulated that "any lawful Captives of other Heathen Nations may be made Bond men." In so doing, he sunk his proslavery argument onto a theological bedrock that was spiritual rather than racial at its core.[92]

Saffin poses an unusual example because he was more inclined to frame his proslavery assumptions in racial terms than were other authors defending slavery during this era. Again and again, proslavery ministers such as Baxter, Godwyn, Fleetwood, and Gibson urged their readers to recognize the Africans' humanity and equal claim to the spiritual liberation of conversion. "Sufficiently difference between Man and Bruits," counseled Baxter. "Remember that they are of as good kind as you; that is, They are reasonable Creatures as well as you, and born to as much natural liberty." In his mind, Africans' underexposure to the Gospel rather than their innate deficiencies had left them in a position to be enslaved. "If their sin[s] have enslaved them to you," he concluded, "yet Nature made them your equals."[93] Upholding the slaveholders' right to keep their baptized slaves in bondage, Baxter nonetheless presented an egalitarian spiritual vision that countenanced explicit imagery of liberation from sin. "Carry your selves to them," he encouraged the slaveholders, "as those that are sensible that they are Redeemed with them by Christ from the slavery of Satan, and may live with them in the Liberty of the Saints of Glory."[94]

Godwyn agreed that "naturally there is in every Man an equal Right to Religion," and he argued, moreover, "that Negro's are Men, and therefore are invested with the same Right." Not satisfied with this declaration, Godwyn expounded on this theme over the next forty pages of his book, asserting that the "humanity of slaves" was established by the "shape and figure of our Negro's Bodies." As further evidence, he pointed to the slaves' intellectual capacity to read and to write, and to be entrusted with managerial roles as plantation drivers. Godwyn cited Acts 17:26 for evidence that "God hath made [of one Blood] all Nations of men." He denied that the darker pigmentation of African skin should be equated with barbarity or ugliness, suggesting instead that standards for human beauty were relative. He also pointed to the absurdity of white slaveholders who rejected their slaves' humanity but also exploited them sexually.[95] In short, Godwyn harbored extremely enlightened views about the contingent nature of racial boundaries and the Africans' ability to excel spiritually and intellectually if given the opportunity. Racial prejudice played scarcely any discernible role in his rationale for slavery. Indeed, his embrace of the doctrine of human unity fit neatly with his organic vision of a Christian slaveholding society in which a web of mutual responsibilities and concerns encompassed the high and the low. This is not to say that organic proslavery thought was incompatible with racist assumptions about African inferiority. Saffin, for one, subscribed to racist ideas that enabled him to conclude that Africans could occupy only an enslaved role in colonial society. It is interesting to note, however, that prominent Anglican authorities diminished race as a criterion for determining the morality of holding another human being in bondage.

Of course, the articulation of these ideals by Anglican ministers should not be equated with the genesis of a slaveholding culture that operated on these principles. The frustrated testimony of numerous Anglican and dissenting ministers makes abundantly clear that the slaveholders themselves maintained a reactionary position on the question of slave conversions to Christianity. From the standpoint of these colonial entrepreneurs, the missionaries' organic doctrines were threatening on many levels. In addition to the planters' aforementioned fear that slave baptism would necessitate emancipation, they also resented the idea that they must accept their slaves as spiritual equals. Hence, the Carolina missionary Le Jau listened to a white parishioner ask, "Is it Possible that any of my slaves could go to Heaven, & must I see them there?" Clearly, the slaveholders did not accept Le Jau's affirmative answer to this question, leading him to complain that "by their Whispers & Conduct, they wou'd not have me urge of Contributing to the Salvation, Instruction, and human usage of Slaves and free Indians."[96] However much ministers such as Le Jau insisted that they were not attempting to undermine slavery, they were advocating the radical doctrine of spiritual equality between master and slave, an unsettling proposition for American masters who lacked the security of an elite that had been entrenched for centuries. These masters not only worried about surrendering power to their slaves but also fretted at the possibility that English authorities ranging from the missionaries to their superiors in England would regulate plantation life from afar. The religious network that the Anglican reformers wanted to create appeared to the planters as a potential cage. Better, believed the planters, to maintain a clear ascendancy over their colonial society than to place faith in organic standards for mastery that suggested that all power needed to be exercised with restraint.[97]

## The Debate over Slavery in Georgia

As it turned out, the planters were not being paranoid when they jealously guarded their plantation system from interference that might potentially spring from the religious power of the metropole. At the very moment when the bishop of London's tract was making its way to the New World, religious activists in England were making radical plans for a new southern colony. Melding doctrines of spiritual equality and organic hierarchy, the Georgia trustees dreamed of a colonial society that eschewed the materialism of settlements in South Carolina and Virginia. In keeping with their faith that lower elements of society could be redeemed to play constructive roles in a stable organic social system, the trustees envisioned a colony of white farmers who would work in collective harmony. Drawn from the ranks of England's unproductive poor, these settlers were to provide England with valuable commodities while securing the border between the English colonies and the Spanish settlements in Florida. Given the trustees' strong links to the Associates of Dr. Bray and the SPG, American slaveholders might well have found it disturbing that slavery was to have no place in the new colony. Having spent decades insisting that slavery potentially conformed to their Christian conceptions about moral society, Anglican authorities in England were now taking the unprecedented step, in 1735, of banning slavery from a New World settlement.[98]

On one level, the Georgia trustees' antislavery stance did not signify moral ambivalence about slavery.[99] Practical concerns about the military and economic security of the new colony led the governing authorities in Europe to ban the importation of African slaves. As defenders of the trustees' plan observed, the colony had been envisioned "to provide for poor People incapable of subsisting themselves at home" and certainly incapable of purchasing slaves for themselves. Had the trustees invested in slaves, they would have exhausted their limited resources, leaving them "disabled from sending white People . . . who would be of Security to the Province." The trustees "also apprehended, that the *Spaniards* at

*St. Augustine* would be continually inticing away the Negroes, or encouraging them to Insurrections." To better establish a colony with a sufficiently large population of English settlers and to better secure the colony from domestic violence, the authorities "thought proper to make the Prohibition of [slaves] a Fundamental of the Constitution."[100] That the trustees did not recoil from the general prospect of unfree labor can be seen from their willingness to allow white indentured servants into Georgia.

Lurking within these practical concerns about slavery, however, were potentially radical challenges to slavery's role in a moral, stable society. Although the trustees did not extend their antislavery reasoning into a call to remove slavery from other American colonies, their assumptions about human behavior undermined the economic rationale for slavery. Decades before the Scottish political economist Adam Smith famously discussed the inefficiency of unfree economies, the trustees had figured out that slavery degraded the status of labor. "The white Man, by having a Negro Slave, would be less disposed to labour himself," reasoned the opponents of slavery. "It was likewise apprehended" by them "that if the Persons who should go over to Georgia at their own Expence, should be permitted the Use of Negroes, it would dispirit and ruin the poor Planters who could not get them, and who by their Numbers were designed to be the Strength of the Province." Witnessing the labor that was extracted by force from African slaves, these nonslaveholding whites "would be unwilling, nay would certainly disdain to work like Negroes." The trustees also perceived that slaves coveted freedom and would exploit any opportunity to seize it. In nascent form, these ideas presented the grim political economy of slavery that boded ill for colonies such as South Carolina and Virginia as much as Georgia (if the trustees' antislavery policy were overturned). On an even more dramatic note, the minority of settlers who favored the trustees' antislavery stance wove moral concerns into these economic reservations. In a petition dated January 1739, eighteen Georgia residents declared that "it's shocking to human Nature, that any Race of Mankind, and their Posterity, should be sentenced to perpetual Slavery." The injustice of African bondage, predicted these settlers, would result in "our Scourge one Day or other for our Sins; and as Freedom to them must be as dear as to us, what a scene of Horror must it bring about! And the longer it is unexecuted, the bloody Scene must be the greater." Attacked from this perspective, slavery was not only economically indefensible but also constituted a dangerous sin against human beings who claimed the same natural rights of freedom.[101]

The proslavery response generated by the trustees' policies reveals the limited degree to which organic concepts had permeated the mentality of the colonial planters and would-be planters. Hoping to acquire the kinds of fortunes that enabled their neighbors in Carolina to live in splendor, most Georgia settlers wanted to minimize the trustees' control over every aspect of their lives. They faced a formidable challenge, given the ambitions of the reformers who were planning Georgia's future. As the historian Mart Stewart has perceptively suggested, the trustees' idealized vision of their colony hinged on republican ideals that contrasted civic virtue with speculative economic ventures such as the staple plantation economies geared toward rice and tobacco production. The trustees' ban on slavery was just part of their broader campaign to build a cooperative social venture in which sober Christians worked the land in collective intimacy.[102] To combat this conception of Georgia, the proslavery settlers understandably steered clear of organic reasoning that could easily be used to justify careful oversight of the colonial economy and society. For to invoke biblical passages that legitimized bondage was also to underscore the scriptural injunction on slaveholders to elevate spiritual concerns above temporal and financial ones. Instead, the Georgia planters insisted that slavery provided a necessary resource in the erection of a prosperous republican colony.

As early as 1735, individual Georgia colonists were writing to the trustees to convey the "impossibility" of doing "without the Use of Negroes." In justification of slavery, these petitioners turned the trustees' assumptions about slavery and labor upside down. Whereas the trustees had suggested that slavery should be banned because it discouraged and degraded white labor and thereby rendered the colony vulnerable to foreign enemies, the Georgia settlers claimed that white labor undermined the stability of their colony. Not only were white indentured servants more costly to maintain, asserted the settlers, they also posed a serious threat to Georgia's security by "continually Stealing and Imbezzling our Goods; and which is of a worse Consequence, forming Plots and treasonable Designs against the Colony." Worse, when these white servants fled from their masters, which they did frequently according to the petitioners, they were able to elude capture by blending in to the free white population. "There is no Law as yet made to take up white People who are travelling, nor could it easily be distinguished whether they were Servants or not," complained the proslavery settlers. By contrast, masters could more easily control an African slave population of laborers because "Negroes would always be known and taken into Custody unless they could produce a Certificate from their Master." Here, slavery was equated with the stability of a republican society. By providing a readily identifiable and controllable workforce, slaves would minimize the specter of white civil discontent.[103] The slaves, moreover, would not "make the white Men grow idle and lazy," because nature had seemingly made blacks "fitter and abler" for plantation labor. This racist assumption led the proslavery agitators to ask, "May not white Men be still industrious, and to better Purpose, each Man furnishing that Part for which he is best qualified?"[104] A preference for white settlers, argued some petitioners, could be served by a loosening of the trustrees' strictures because the prospect of slave ownership would "occasion great Numbers of white People to come here."[105] Without rejecting the trustees' logic that Georgia's population should consist largely of whites, the proslavery agitators suggested that the importation of at least some African slaves was a necessary precondition to the growth of the desirable white population.

Strikingly, the trustees' antislavery policy rankled the colonists because they viewed it as just one of many heavy-handed strategies for denying them their "Civil Liberties." The settlers had migrated to Georgia expecting "a free Government" but found that they had been "singled out for a *State of Misery* and *Servitude*." Their lobbying effort for slavery assumed that "the Genius of the *British Nation*, so remarkably zealous for *Liberty* and the *Rights of Mankind*, will never suffer *British Subjects* . . . to be depriv'd of . . . the *natural* Liberties" that were their due. "Should it be said," asked another proslavery author, "that *Englishmen*, whose free Spirit rises at the least obscure, oblique Attempt on their Liberties and Properties at home, shall impose such Yokes, the very Badges of Infamy and Slavery, on their own, tho' unfortunate, Countrymen abroad, who have common and unalienable Rights to the same Privileges as them?" Within this proslavery perspective, white republican liberty required black slavery, and the proscription on black slavery was tantamount to the white settlers' enslavement to the trustees. The settlers' republican convictions led them to conceptualize the trustees as "but a Channel to convey . . . the King's Rights," as opposed to the stewards of an organic Christian scheme to better colonial and English society. The trustees' republicanism had led them to restrain the materialism of the plantation market economy. The Georgia colonists' republicanism prompted them to decry such interference with the plantation system.[106]

## Evangelical Awakenings

As the debate over slavery in Georgia reached its climax, a series of evangelical Christian revivals swept through England and its colonies. Known by scholars as the Great Awakening, this religious movement of the 1730s and 1740s offered a shift in both the style and the substance of church services. Affecting not only the Anglican Church but also the Congregationalists, the Baptists, and the Presbyterians, the Awakening led ministers to emphasize individual conversion. As worshippers listened to sermons about the need for religious rebirth, they responded with unprecedented emotional fervor. To conservative religious commentators, evangelical Christian revivals seemed to be chaotic and godless affairs in which impoverished segments of society escaped from necessary social restraints. Because many of these religious participants were African Americans and slaves, and because the evangelical preachers attached special importance to the spiritual welfare of the poorest segments of colonial society, the Awakening marked a turning point in colonial proslavery thought. As white and black worshippers gathered together within an intimate religious atmosphere, preachers spoke about the master-slave relationship with newfound emphasis. Evangelicals such as the charismatic itinerant George Whitefield (whose writings are reproduced in chapter 1 of this anthology) offered impassioned criticism of the slaveholders who refused to Christianize slavery. In this respect, Whitefield merely followed the example of religious authorities ranging from Baxter to Gibson. Whitefield's commentary on slavery, however, created a far greater stir among the colonists because he tackled inflammatory issues in a combustible religious environment of intensely felt spirituality.[107]

Many capable scholars have documented Whitefield's complicated role in this story.[108] After preaching to huge appreciative audiences in England, the nominally Anglican Whitefield arrived in Georgia in 1738. His initial visit to the colony lasted only three months, but during this time he established the foundations of a spiritual project that would consume his attention for the rest of his life. Conferring with the trustees of the new colony, Whitefield established plans for an orphanage that was constructed in 1740 in Bethesda, Georgia. The humanitarian venture echoed the philosophy of reform espoused by the trustees and the closely related Anglican missionary organizations. With compassion for the poorest, most vulnerable members of society—the unemployed English, the unconverted African slave and Native American, the unparented orphan—these groups constructed transatlantic networks through which they pursued their organic conceptions of social justice. The Bethesda orphanage served as the symbolic center of Whitefield's growing religious empire, seldom visited in person by Whitefield or his followers, but often discussed and cherished as an earthly manifestation of Christian enthusiasm for social improvement. On a practical level, Whitefield used the orphanage as a vehicle for fund-raising that even hardened skeptics found difficult to resist. Despite raising legitimate objections about Whitefield's venture in Georgia, Benjamin Franklin could not help but empty his pockets "wholly" after hearing in person Whitefield's call for contributions.[109] As Whitefield's supporters developed transatlantic lines of communication with which to publicize his sermons, they united worshippers across the eastern seaboard of America into one extended religious community devoted to servicing the needs of the most subordinate, most needy figures imaginable.

Given the scope and ideological orientation for this religious framework and given the ongoing debate over slavery's future in Georgia, Whitefield could not help but comment on the relationship between evangelical Christianity and African slavery. When he did, he provoked a furor in the American South. Like his missionary predecessors, Whitefield recoiled from the horrors of plantation slavery. Associating the influx of African slaves with a general state of irreligion, Whitefield did not hesitate to preach to blacks as well as to whites in southern towns and on those plantations owned by planters who were swayed by White-field's ministry.[110] Having embraced the slaves spiritually, he felt compelled to discuss their treatment at the hands of their masters. In 1740, to the utter dismay of the white planter class, he published his views on this subject. His *Letter to the Inhabitants of Maryland, Virginia, North and South-Carolina, Concerning Their Negroes* accused the slaveholders of "Abuse of and Cruelty to the poor Negroes."[111] Leaving aside the question of "whether it be lawful for Christians to buy Slaves," Whitefield expressly condemned as "sinful" the planters' proclivity to treat the slaves "as though they were Brutes." Contending that Africans labored under worse conditions than the slaveholders' horses and dogs, the minister lamented their suffering at the hands of "cruel Task Masters, who by their unrelenting Scourges have ploughed upon their Backs, and made long Furrows, and at length brought them even to Death itself."

Following the reasoning set forth by Edmund Gibson thirteen years earlier, Whitefield claimed that such physical mistreatment represented less of an injustice to the slaves than did their masters' refusal to admit them into the ranks of Christianity. "Most of you," he complained to the planters, "keep your Negroes ignorant of Christianity" out of the mistaken assumption that "teaching them Christianity would make them proud, and consequently unwilling to submit to Slavery"—a notion that he countermanded with biblical citation. In pushing the slaveholders to recognize their slaves' humanity and spiritual capacity, Whitefield rejected race as a meaningful social boundary. "Blacks are just as much, and no more, conceived and born in Sin, as White Men are," he concluded. "Both, if born and bred up here, I am persuaded, are naturally capable of the same Improvement." To this plea Whitefield added a threat. If the slaveholders did not change their ways, God would punish them. "Unless you all repent," he warned, "you all must in like Manner expect to perish." Most radical of all was Whitefield's suggestion that slave rebellion against sinful white authority "would be just" if it were to "be permitted by Providence."

Although Whitefield claimed to "heartily pray God" that the slaves "may never be permitted to get the upper Hand" in this fashion, such language spoken amid the uneasy racial climate of the early 1740s left the slaveholders in doubt about his intentions. For openers, South Carolina had experienced a bloody slave insurrection in 1739, the year before Whitefield published his tract. Armed African slaves, chanting "liberty," had come close to escaping from the colony after killing some twenty white settlers. Only by chance did South Carolina authorities manage to summon sufficient firepower to quell the uprising. In this context, the slaveholders must have bristled at Whitefield's queries as to why "they have not more frequently rose up in Arms against their Owners." Even worse, from the planters' perspective, Whitefield's own white converts posed a troubling threat to the security of their human property. Following his religious awakening in 1741, Hugh Bryan published a letter in the *South-Carolina Gazette* in which he echoed Whitefield's apocalyptic imagery of slaveholders being "humbled by scourgings" that included the "Insurrections of our Slaves."[112] Charleston authorities wasted no time before arresting not only Bryan but also Whitefield, who was briefly detained under the suspicion that he had some responsibility for Bryan's letter. The following year, as Whitefield continued his transatlantic travels, Bryan illegally gathered with lowcountry slaves for religious services that he conducted without their masters' permission. Unhinged, he prophesied the divine destruction of Charleston "by fire and sword" at the hands of the slaves. With white authorities hot on his trail, he retreated to the countryside, where he communicated with "an invisible spirit" that convinced him to part the waters of a nearby river with a stick—a religious experiment that went horribly awry and would have resulted in his drowning had not his brother plucked him from the water. The slaveholders were relieved when Bryan seemed to come to his senses and apologized for his erratic behavior. Needless to say, his conduct did nothing to endear Whitefield's teachings to the slaveholding elite.

The strangest aspect of this story is not that evangelical awakenings prompted some whites to challenge, at least temporarily, the institution of slavery. The recognition of spiritual and racial equality running through Whitefield's theology and call for spiritual rebirth lent themselves to radical shifts in earthly behavior. Should not have antislavery reform accompanied the evangelical campaigns against drinking and dancing? According to Whitefield, the answer to this question was "no," although the slaveholders remained suspicious of the reformer. In Whitefield's mind, the doctrine of black spiritual equality implied only their potential liberation from sin, not from earthly service to their masters. The New Birth elicited by evangelical conversion would foster slave obedience instead of rebellion. "I challenge the whole World to produce a single Instance of a Negroe's being made a thorough Christian," proclaimed Whitefield, "and thereby made a worse Servant." He concluded that "it cannot be." And when Whitefield likened the African slaves to the slaveholders' own children, he was not suggesting that the slaves be placed beyond the purview of rigorous discipline. Whitefield had no qualms about employing force against children to keep them in an appropriate state of spiritual discipline. A boy who behaved badly during one of Whitefield's sermons found this out the hard way. Whitefield "ordered him to be tied until he could say the 51st Psalm, which he repeated to-night very solemnly in the midst of the congregation." Liberation from sin required earthly discipline rather than emancipation.[113]

Whitefield's charismatic presence and unorthodox religious style prompted attacks from more conservative southern religious authorities. Alexander Garden, the bishop of London's commissary in Charleston, developed a particularly strong dislike for Whitefield.[114] Garden—whose response to Whitefield is reproduced as chapter 2 of this anthology—complained to Anglican authorities in England that Whitefield was making himself "to be some great One indeed, set forth from God . . . to give Light to the World and restore the true Doctrines of the Gospel." After Whitefield criticized the Anglican clergy for spouting "false Doctrine," Garden denied him permission to preach from Anglican pulpits. When Whitefield conducted services in the dissenting churches in Charleston, Garden watched in horror as the "Lower Sort" were captivated by his preaching.[115] To strike a blow for social order and to ingratiate himself with the slaveholders who recoiled from Whitefield's revivalism, Garden produced a tract that condemned Whitefield for criticizing colonial slavery. Published in 1740, the same year as Whitefield's work, Garden's *Remarks on [Whitefield's] Letter Concerning the Negroes* appears to be the first formal, extended defense of human bondage authored by a resident southerner.[116] In it Garden countered Whitefield's accusations of slaveholder misconduct with the same logic that Anglican authorities had espoused in preceding decades. In particular, Garden lectured Whitefield that had he "caused another Edition to be printed at Philadelphia of the Bishop of London [Edmund Gibson]'s Letter to the Masters and Mistresses of Slaves . . . and dispersed the Copies," Whitefield would have "done more effectual Service" than he accomplished "by the Publication" of his incendiary tract.

Garden vehemently denied that southern slaveholders mistreated their slaves, asserting that the "Generality of Owners use their Slaves with all due Humanity, whether in respect of *Work, of Food,* or *Raiment.*" Notwithstanding overwhelming evidence of miseries experienced by the slaves—the hardships reported by generations of visiting missionaries—Garden claimed that the slaves' "Lives in general are more happy and comfortable in all temporal Respects (the Point of Liberty only excepted) than the Lives of three fourths of the hired *farming* Servants, and Day Labourers, either in *Scotland, Ireland,* or even many Parts of *England,* who not only labour *harder,* and fare *worse,* but have moreover the Care and Concern on their Minds how to provide for their Families; which *Slaves* are entirely exempted from, their Children being all provided for at the *Owner's* charge."[117] Garden went so far as to compare the vicious corporal punishment directed toward slaves with the "due *Discipline,* or Rod of Correction exercis'd among Children" by their own parents. By denouncing Whitefield's attack against slavery, Garden simultaneously discredited in general Whitefield's heterodoxy and demonstrated to the local planter elite the Anglican Church's trustworthiness on the question of slavery.

Genuine ill will existed between these ministers. Yet Whitefield and Garden largely subscribed to the same Christian concepts concerning the morality of slavery. As Whitefield's supporters hastened to point out, his thoughts on slavery hardly differed from those given voice by leading Anglican figures. Siding with Whitefield in 1742, the dissenting ministers Josiah Smith and James Parker reminded the public that Whitefield's criticism of the planters was in keeping with commentary offered by the bishop of London himself.[118] Whitefield lent credence to these ministers' insistence that he did not harbor antislavery viewpoints. Although he had conceded the possibility that slave insurrections could be just, Whitefield obviously wanted no part of such transactions. When he passed through the South Carolina countryside in 1740 in the wake of the Stono slave revolt, he felt considerable anxiety at the prospect of rubbing shoulders with African firebrands. Encountering a suspicious "hut full of negroes," Whitefield and his companions "inferred . . . that these negroes might be some of those who lately had made an insurrection in the province, and had run away from their masters." This realization led the travelers to depart with all possible speed. For the rest of the evening, they moved through the woods in fear, "expecting to find negroes in every place," until they finally found refuge at "a great plantation, the master of which gave us lodging and our beasts provender." Safely tucked away under the roof of a slaveholder, Whitefield and his party learned with "much comfort" and rejoicing to God that their suspicions had been unfounded—that the "negroes" in question remained in a state of slavery.[119]

Perhaps in response to the controversy surrounding Hugh Bryan's antislavery actions, Whitefield broadcast with increasing clarity his proslavery sentiments. In 1743 he was likely the author of *A Letter to the Negroes Lately Converted to Christ in America,* a tract that emphasized that conversion to Christianity did not emancipate slaves. Although God "hath now called you into his own Family, to be his own Children and Servants," the author lectured the slaves, "he doth not call you hereby from the Service of your Masters according to the Flesh; but to serve him in serving them, in obeying all their lawful Commands, and submitting to the Yoke his Providence has placed you under."[120] On a more dramatic note, Whitefield personally involved himself in the colonial plantation system. As his Bethesda orphanage experienced financial difficulties in 1747, he acquired a South Carolina plantation to generate enough capital to keep the orphanage afloat. When the Carolina property made possible the survival of his humanitarian enterprises, the itinerant preacher exulted. "Blessed be God," he proclaimed, for enabling him to obtain "a plantation and slaves." By this point, Whitefield also entered the debate over slavery in Georgia, urging the trustees to recognize that "it is impossible for the inhabitants [of Georgia] to subsist without the use of slaves."[121] His proslavery lobbying contributed to the trustees' decision to surrender their opposition to slavery in Georgia in 1750.

Whitefield's proslavery views came into sharper focus during the 1740s, but these developments did not signify a fundamental change in his attitude toward slavery—only a change in emphasis. The controversial tract that he published in 1740 had melded criticism of the slaveholders' conduct with a defense of slavery as an institution reconcilable with Christianity. In this respect, he was no different from Richard Baxter or, for that matter, from Alexander Garden. Nestled within Garden's defense of the slaveholders' characters as humane masters was his criticism of their conduct with respect to slave conversion. "As to the little or no *proper Care taken by* Owners *of the Souls* of their *Slaves,* it is too sad a Truth," conceded Garden, "and I tremble to think, what Account they will give of it at the great Day!" When Garden proposed methods by which this flaw in the plantation system could be remedied, he implicitly conceded that his defense of slavery was not unconditional. Only a system of bondage characterized by reciprocity between masters and slaves could qualify for holy approval.

These tensions in Christian proslavery thought played themselves out in other areas of the American South. In Maryland in the 1740s, the Anglican minister Thomas Bacon (whose sermon is reproduced in chapter 3 of this anthology) expounded at considerable length on the organic themes given voice by Garden and Whitefield. In Virginia in the 1750s, the Presbyterian revivalist Samuel Davies (whose tract is reprinted in chapter 4 of this anthology) developed a reputation as a minister who was genuinely concerned with Christianizing the plantations in his parish. He sermonized on the reciprocal religious responsibilities that constrained the conduct of masters but that also turned slavery into a blessing for the African slaves. Despite their varying denominational affiliations, these ministers engaged in a common transatlantic project to extend the Christian faith to individuals in every rank of society. Hence, the Presbyterian Davies could exchange friendly letters with the radical Methodist John Wesley on their mutual concerns about slave conversions.[122]

Yet in pursuit of that spiritual goal, the colonial ministers walked a razor's edge. One aspect of their religious thought, their genuine empathy for the humanity of the slaves, motivated their criticism of slavery and enabled them to bring noticeable numbers of African worshippers into their churches. A few evangelical ministers, most notably John and Charles Wesley, cast their emphasis on slave suffering and were carried into the ranks of the antislavery movement.[123] Most Christian authorities and converts, however, attempted to balance their sympathy for the slaves with their commitment to maintaining order in human society. They stepped firmly into the conservative proslavery camp. Whitefield's radical follower Hugh

Bryan and his brother Jonathan, for example, eventually reconciled their spiritual fervor for slave conversions with their ongoing ownership of slaves. When the Salzburger pastor Johann Martin Bolzius visited Jonathan Bryan's property in 1742, he came away impressed by the "most beautiful order in the housekeeping and among the Negroes." Here, believed Bolzius, was living proof that Christianity could work in the mutual interest of master and slave. "Although the people in this land say that his Negroes do nothing but pray and sing and thereby neglect their work," he wrote, "this calumny was clearly contradicted by the very great blessing" of productive Christian slaves working efficiently in their master's fields.[124]

## Slaveholder Ideology and the American Revolution

Evangelical leaders obviously sought to impress on American slaveholders an understanding of the idealized Christian conception of the master-slave relationship.[125] As we have seen, an impressive number of missionaries and religious authorities during this period espoused an organic defense of the master-slave relationship as part of their broader project to Christianize the American plantation system. Yet the mere articulation of ideals by reformers did not mean that those ideals had been embraced by the local slaveholding elite. Alan Gallay, for one, has contended that the colonial ministers' religious prescriptions did in fact influence slaveholder ideology. For evidence, he cites the example of the prominent Georgia colonist James Habersham, who was an enthusiastic follower of Whitefield and one of the most vocal eighteenth-century supporters of the campaign to bring Christianity to the slave quarters.[126] Yet Habersham's experiences also offer signs that evangelical Christianity made only limited inroads into the slaveholders' collective culture of mastery. One of Whitefield's most devoted followers and one of Georgia's largest slaveholders, Habersham most certainly did find it "unaccountable, that any people calling themselves Christians, should have any objections against having their Servants instructed" in religion. In letters directed back to England, he took pains to portray colonial slavery in organic terms, "to evince . . . that we do not treat our Negroes as some people imagine." Yet Habersham himself repeatedly complained about his fellow slaveholders' adamant rejection of his organic proslavery perspective. "This work of instructing Negroes," he concluded after many failed efforts to Christianize the lowcountry plantation system, "will meet with all the opposition and reproach that men and Devils can invent."[127] Other colonial slaveholders who shared Habersham's vision of slavery offered similarly grim assessments of the popularity of their organic viewpoint on the master-slave relationship. In South Carolina, the planter Henry Laurens deplored that the "few who would wish to deal with [their] slaves as with brethren in a state of subordination" met with "difficulties" that "are almost insurmountable." That these men were struggling to enact organic proslavery doctrines in the 1760s, on the eve of colonial rebellion against English authority, is itself significant. The very institutions and forces responsible for conveying the Christian proslavery creed to the colonies also set the stage for increasing American resentment against imperial policy. For as church officials and imperial administrators pressed for organic harmony throughout the British Empire, white slaveholders saw in those efforts a sinister campaign to eradicate their liberties as independent citizens—liberties that were intertwined with their right to own slaves.[128] In the late 1730s the Georgia settlers' rhetorical response to the trustees' ban on slavery provided an early hint of how efforts to regulate slavery could trigger impassioned "republican" proslavery language. By the 1770s these issues would explode into a revolutionary movement that would forever change the context in which debates over slavery took place.

Starkly divided by denominational affiliation, colonial proponents of Christian proslavery thought nonetheless shared cosmopolitan perspectives on the institution of plantation slavery. By definition, those thinkers who sought to integrate distant plantations into a unifying Christian sensibility framed the master-slave relationship within a system of universal morality. That a particular planter resided thousands of miles from church authorities in Europe and tens of miles from the nearest American port did not alter the logic that both masters and slaves were bound to conform to holy teachings about slavery. Ministers such as Godwyn and Whitefield traveled from England into the colonies carrying assumptions about the application of moral principles in the New World. They were welcomed only by a small number of resident planters whose unusually cosmopolitan religious and economic viewpoints on colonial life pushed them into the ranks of the religious reform movement. James Habersham, for example, first traveled to Georgia in the company of Whitefield and later helped to manage the Bethesda orphanage. As a merchant, his economic dealings kept him in close contact with the culture of the English metropolis. As a wealthy planter, he developed partnerships with the colony's ruling elite. In consequence, when Georgia's royal governor James Wright was forced to return to England in 1771, Habersham served in his stead as the colony's highest-ranking administrator. In all of his endeavors in Georgia, Habersham was attempting to institute regular standards for colonial conduct. "Every thing with me in the planting Way," he noted, "is reduced into a kind of regular System."[129] Habersham's desire to Christianize his plantations represented merely one dimension of an outlook that treated the colonies not as isolated units but as integrated members of a holistic social system.

Amid increasing tensions between England and the colonies in the 1760s, it was exactly the cosmopolitan colonial cohort personified by Habersham that found itself at odds with radical American protestors against mercantilism. During the Stamp Act crisis of 1765, for example, both Habersham and Laurens decried the anarchy engendered by settlers seeking to overturn the obnoxious legislation. Habersham referred to the radical resistance against Parliament as an "Infection"; Laurens viewed it as a sign that "Riot is in fashion."[130] Moral power, in their view, hinged on reciprocity between rulers and their subjects. This organic vision of power cast its adherents into initially conservative roles in the unfolding break between England and the colonies. As Georgia's acting royal governor in the early 1770s, Habersham personified British imperial authority in America, and he remained a devout Tory until his death in 1775. Conversely, Laurens became a leader of American resistance and, ultimately, revolution after several of his ships were confiscated by aggressive customs officials—an act partially upheld by an English judge. Still, when Laurens threw himself into the cause of American independence, he did not abandon the principles that had defined his understanding of a justly ordered society.[131]

In this conservative group's advocacy of organic social ideals, one also can detect the manifestation of republican notions of government. Insisting on reciprocity between rulers and subjects, neither Habersham nor Laurens believed that England had the right to govern the colonies despotically. Habersham forcefully insisted that the colonists deserved direct representation in England's "mixed" system of government. Clearly, this cosmopolitan elite expected colonial society to be organized as a hierarchy. But within the hierarchy subordinating slaves to masters and the colonies to England, both slaves and white settlers had natural rights to certain minimal standards of treatment. Slaves could legitimately expect religious education and decent material circumstances in which to labor and to live. In return, reasoned these paternalistically inclined white men, slaves consented to work faithfully for their masters. The organic logic structuring their notions of slavery also facilitated their ideas about the proper relationship between American settlers and English government. If enslaved Africans could expect a degree of reciprocity in the master-slave relationship, then surely free white men could expect to be governed with benevolence. If not, suggested Laurens, then surely the colonists had a right to protest against the violation of their political liberties.[132]

To maintain these tangled convictions, however, required both firmness of spirit (which Laurens and Habersham certainly evinced) and some measure of support from peers on both sides of the Atlantic (which evaporated by the onset of the Revolution). By the 1770s it had become a decidedly lonely proposition to hold together organic notions of slavery and organic conceptions of the imperial system. As African slaves perceived the possibility for liberty lurking in their masters' protests, their masters struggled to reduce them to the status of unthinking property. After the American Revolution had stretched on for eight long years, after American masters experienced firsthand a massive disruption in their ability to control their slaves, Laurens grew increasingly convinced that his countrymen would not accept the humanity of their African slaves, even if "one should rise from the dead" to promote this doctrine. Habersham, for his part, remained a loy-alist in his final years of life, working to avoid war by reining in the imperial administrators' tendencies to govern with a heavy hand. Habersham, for example, rejected the mercantilist doctrines espoused by William Knox, a sometime resi-dent of Georgia who had become an officeholder in the Hillsborough ministry in England. The two saw eye to eye on slavery, as can be seen in Knox's proslavery writings reproduced in chapter 5 of this anthology. Knox's unrestrained mercan-tilism, however, made him an awkward figure for Habersham to defend in Geor-gia, where the vast majority of planters already rejected organic conceptions of power.[133]

If nothing else, however, the Revolution provided a powerful impetus for the republican proslavery ethos that had surfaced in colonies such as Georgia as early as the 1730s. Although British loyalists mockingly pointed to the fundamental incongruity of the patriotic rhetoric of freedom being articulated by slaveholders, slavery actually reinforced the American commitment to republican freedoms on several levels.[134] First, as historians such as Bernard Bailyn and Jack Greene have argued, the American political vocabulary was drawn from an English Whig tradi-tion that, for a century, had defined the liberties of citizens in contrast to the degraded state of slaves.[135] As firsthand witnesses to the subordinate position of African American slaves, colonial slaveholders attached vivid meanings to the political metaphor of slavery and therefore felt strong incentive to avoid falling into such an unenviable state of dependence. When American political resistance increased and was channeled by colonial statesmen and propagandists into a coherent movement for independence, the metaphor of slavery played a critical and almost ubiquitous role. To be sure, the application of the slavery metaphor to the American struggle against British mercantilism paved the way for antislavery agitation against the colonial plantation system. It was no accident that the north-ern states embarked on plans for gradual emancipation during the Revolution-ary era.[136] Even in the American South, where the plantation economy reigned supreme, a noticeable contingent of prominent statesmen such as Thomas Jeffer-son and Patrick Henry conceded that the institution contradicted the ideal values of the newly formed nation. Jefferson, most obviously, instilled Lockean language of natural equality into the Declaration of Independence and sought to portray African slavery as a crime for which George III had been responsible.[137] Still, the antislavery implications of this political language of protest did not pose to the slaveholders "an unanswerable argument" against plantation slavery (as the histo-rian Bernard Bailyn suggested).[138] Only a tiny minority of white southerners will-ingly acknowledged some measure of hypocrisy in their campaign for American liberty.[139] Instead of buckling under the weight of their own philosophical inconsistencies, southern planters embraced republican ideals that cemented their notions of liberty to their commitment to slavery.[140]

Americans mobilized against England because they believed their property could be taxed or interfered with only by a government that afforded them representation. As the wealthiest colonists in British North America, the slaveholders had the most to lose and were therefore the most receptive audience to political rhetoric that equated unjust taxation with a violation of political liberties. No matter how grandiose were the claims for those liberties, slaveholders never forgot that their enslaved workforce was the property that they most needed to protect. The scholarship of Robert Olwell, Sylvia Frey, and Woody Holton has revealed the proslavery dynamic behind the planters' decision to rebel against England.[141] By the early 1770s the colonial rhetorical campaign against their imperial superiors centered around the damning charge that an English campaign was afoot to liberate African American slaves in order to use them as weapons against their former masters. No such policy existed (although events would make the slaveholders' prophecies self-fulfilling). Nevertheless, with concern about taxation melding into fears about slave emancipation, otherwise conservative slaveholders took up arms against England precisely to protect the liberty to own slaves.

## Proslavery Responses to the American Revolution

To date, scholars have unearthed no formal defenses of slavery published by American authors during the American Revolution.[142] In part, the absence of proslavery writings during this period was the inevitable product of the havoc wreaked by the war. Moreover, once the fighting had resulted in a wholesale disruption of plantation slavery, slaveholders had little use for rhetorical defenses of the institution of human bondage. Instead, they defended slavery on the battlefield, attempting to kill the troops whom they associated with a campaign for emancipation. Given that some of their former slaves fought against them festooned in sashes bearing the word liberty, slaveholders hardly needed to stretch their imaginations to make that association. Revolutionary slaveholders' proslavery voices were also likely stymied by the colonial association between organic proslavery rhetoric and metropolitan reform movements that had long rankled the planter elite. Having attacked the presumptions of authors such as William Knox, colonial planters no doubt felt some reluctance to parrot organic proslavery language. As an organization visibly associated with the imperial campaign against American liberty, the Anglican Church—which had played such a crucial role in expressing Christian defenses of slavery—had been dealt an especially severe blow by the Revolution. Amid the campaign for disestablishment of the

Anglican Church, few American patriots were primed to take advantage of theological resources for proslavery arguments.[143]

By contrast, Tory authors occupied ideological territory that served as fertile ground for organic proslavery thought. Prior to the Revolution, the Anglican minister Jonathan Boucher staked out a position on slavery that mirrored the ones adopted by his counterparts, Alexander Garden and Thomas Bacon. From his pulpits in Virginia and Maryland, Boucher took pains to proselytize African American slaves. He claimed, on one Easter Monday in 1766, to have baptized more than three hundred slaves, and he corresponded regularly with the Anglican missionary organizations such as the SPG. As was the case with other ministers before him, Boucher's mission to the slaves provoked resistance from conservative planters, who did not approve of the minister's plan to "unfetter" the slaves from "the chains of ignorance" and "emancipate them from the bondage of sin, the worst slavery to which they can be subjected."[144] Notwithstanding the planters' suspicions, Boucher himself purchased slaves and used them to cultivate tobacco. Far from pushing him toward the antislavery camp, his Christian faith led him to value earthly slavery as an institution conducive to the establishment of a warm, mutually beneficial master-slave relationship. Later in life, he would reflect fondly on one of his slaves who thanked God that he belonged to Boucher.[145]

Boucher's Anglican affiliation and his adherence to organic conceptions about earthly power propelled him into the ranks of the Tories. In September 1775 "amid the tears and cries of our slaves," he later recalled, Boucher fled America for sanctuary in England. His former countrymen missed him only as a target for patriotic abuse. Upon his departure, the *Virginia Gazette* rejoiced "that America is in so fair a way of being disgorged of all those filthy, groveling vermin." In Annapolis more than a thousand patriots dragged an effigy of Boucher through town before staging his mock execution.[146] American revolutionaries despised him for his failure to stand up to British tyranny, "villainy and corruption." Boucher, not surprisingly, saw the situation in very different terms. He too rejected the specter of unlimited earthly power. However, in his mind, the imperial system of government offered a suitable restraint to the base instincts of the individual colonists. Without that proper restraint, the patriotic crowds sank into dangerous behavior. Significantly, Boucher drew a link between patriotic disorder and the misconduct of American slaveholders whose mastery reflected no deference to higher earthly or heavenly powers. Republican theorists and jurists such as John Locke had erred, according to Boucher, for awarding "every freeman of Carolina absolute power and property over his slaves." In general, he concluded, republican nations treated their slave populations far more harshly than did nations under strong centralized government. In work published after his return to England, Boucher expressly tied the immorality of the American Revolution to the immorality of American slaveholders, noting that the "most clamorous advocates for liberty were uniformly the harshest and worst masters of slaves." Boucher portrayed his own mastery in terms that differentiated it from the unrestrained selfishness of the revolutionaries. If slavery was "sometimes cruel," he wrote, "it is so only from being abused." He asserted that slavery was "not one of the most intolerable evils incident to humanity, even to slaves," because he had interacted with "thousands of slaves as well-informed, as well-clad, as well-fed, and in every respect as well-off as nine out of ten of the poor in every kingdom of Europe."[147]

So long as the Revolutionary War continued, American masters could never swallow the thinking of despised Tories such as Boucher. Once the war ended, the ideological wrangling over slavery began in earnest. The decades following the American Revolution would prove to be a formative period in a southern proslavery ideology. During this era, organic ideas about the master-slave relationship that had long been expressed by religious reformers crept their way into the minds of the slaveholders themselves. The historian Willie Lee Rose was perhaps the first scholar to explore the historical chronology for the "Domestication of Domestic Slavery"—the process whereby slaveholders increasingly conceptualized their mastery in benevolent familial terms. In her brief yet suggestive essay on this topic, Rose questioned whether this ideological shift "came into style during the Revolutionary epoch as a means of avoiding the blatant contradiction that property in human beings implied for the natural rights philosophy" promoted by American revolutionaries.[148]

On the level of the individual slaveholder, recognition of this contradiction sometimes did result in ideological contortions of a proslavery bent. In the 1780s, for example, Thomas Jefferson conceded that plantation slavery amounted to "a perpetual exercise of the most boisterous passions, the most unremitting despotism on the one, and degrading submissions on the other." Like the Georgia trustees a half-century earlier, Jefferson bemoaned the pernicious influence of slavery on free members of society, particularly impressionable white children. As a result of slavery, "the morals of the people" and "their industry also is destroyed," he reasoned, "for in a warm climate, no man will labour for himself who can make another labour for him."[149] Unable to endure the financial and social hardships confronting the few planters who emancipated their slaves during this era, Jefferson instead rationalized his ongoing complicity in an institution that, he once contended, provoked God's wrath with its iniquity. First, Jefferson employed scientific reasoning to establish innate African inferiority that rendered impossible the granting of black social and political equality in America. Claiming that racial "difference is fixed in nature," he associated blacks with "a very strong and disagreeable odour," a "want of forethought, which prevents their seeing a danger till it be present," an inability to "reason" or to understand "the investigations of

Euclid," and defective imaginations that were "dull" and "tasteless."[150] Because of these racial disparities, Jefferson forwarded a plan in the 1780s to colonize emancipated slaves to some distant place. By 1816 prominent Americans had adopted this plan as a political cause, but their organization, the American Colonization Society, did not inspire the confidence of the aging Jefferson.[151]

In 1814 he responded to an antislavery plea made by Edward Coles, a young Virginia planter who had transported his own slaves into Illinois, granted them land, and liberated them. Although Jefferson still claimed to sympathize with antislavery reform efforts, he spoke also of the slaveholders' obligations to care for the slaves "until more can be done for them." Jefferson suggested that the idealistic emancipator had not been "right in abandoning this property." Instead, Jefferson expressed the organic view that "we should endeavor, with those whom fortune has thrown on our hands, to feed and clothe them well, protect them from ill usage, require such reasonable labor only as is performed voluntarily by freemen, and be led by no repugnancies to abdicate them, and our duties to them." Jefferson's conflict over slavery permitted him neither to embrace emancipation nor to defend slavery in universally positive terms. Instead, between the 1780s and the 1820s, he slowly worked toward a nebulous middle position in which he maintained his abstract abhorrence of the institution but accepted the central proslavery argument that slaves needed white guidance. He doubted that "to turn them loose" would be "for their good," especially given his belief that American slaves enjoyed more comfortable lives than the working poor of England.[152] In a letter written a few weeks after his correspondence with Coles, Jefferson asserted that the slaves were "better fed in these states, warmer clothed, and labor less than the journeymen or day laborers of England. They have the comfort too of numerous families, in the midst of whom they live, without want, or the fear of it; a solace which few of the laborers of England possess."[153]

## Post-Revolutionary Evangelical Proslavery Thought

Jefferson poses the scholar with a highly unusual case of individual agitation over the morality of slavery. The vast majority of post-Revolutionary slaveholders felt little direct discomfort over the moral intricacies of slavery. Instead, they worried that misguided reformers would rob them of their slaves or of their future opportunity to become slaveholders. If Jefferson personified this age, he did so by embodying the debates over slavery that were taking place within religious and governmental institutions during the early national era. In particular, late-eighteenth- and early-nineteenth-century religious authorities struggled to fix their denominational positions on the morality of slavery.

The Methodist Episcopal Church provides a case in point, as it offered a brief yet powerful challenge against slavery in the post-Revolutionary South. Organized in 1784 under the leadership of Thomas Coke, the church initially set a clear anti-slavery standard for its adherents. In a Christmas Conference that assembled in the slaveholding city of Baltimore, the Methodists decreed that slaveholders who refused to liberate their slaves would be denied communion and expelled from the church. This bold pronouncement provoked a noticeable number of slavehold-ing Methodists to withdraw from the church. Amid the resulting furor, antislav-ery Methodist ministers conceded that they were pressing too far too fast and rescinded the stricture against slaveholding. However, they maintained that they "do hold in the deepest abhorrence, the practice of slavery; and shall not cease to seek its destruction by all wise and prudent means." As their church memberships grew from fifteen thousand in 1784 to fifty-eight thousand in 1790, the church leaders distributed antislavery literature and instituted regulations that required emancipation when local laws and "the circumstances of the case" made such action possible. They also joined with Quakers in Maryland and Virginia in pre-senting antislavery petitions to the state legislatures. All told, these actions sig-naled the ripening of an antislavery movement that would have been unthinkable prior to the arrival of the Revolutionary Era. In strongly Methodist and Quaker locales, thousands of slaves in the Upper South received their freedom as a result of these religious developments.[154]

Yet this religious attack against slavery never seriously challenged slavery in the American South and, within decades, had foundered against the white commit-ment to maintain the institution. By 1798 the Methodist bishop Francis Asbury was already conceding "that slavery will exist in Virginia perhaps for ages" because "Methodists, Baptists, and Presbyterians, in the highest flights of rapturous piety, still maintain and defend it." Scholars once tended to focus on the antislavery lamentations of Revolutionary figures such as George Mason and to depict post-Revolutionary Virginia in particular as a region struggling over the morality of slavery. By contrast, recent work by the historian Douglas Ambrose reveals that proslavery Christian forces structured white southern culture in the decades fol-lowing independence.[155] As can be seen in chapter 6 of this anthology, white men were quick to condemn antislavery activism when it surfaced in the post-Revolu-tionary era.

By the late 1780s a host of ministers in the Upper and Lower South were pub-licly presenting organic defenses of slavery. Some, such as the Anglican Devereux Jarratt, followed the precedent established by George Whitefield and mixed together their criticism of the institution with their conviction that the Bible ulti-mately upheld the morality of the master-slave relationship. Jarratt, on the one hand, hoped in 1790 that "it may be consistent with the deep and wise schemes of his Providence to open a way for the freedom of the whole human race; and espe-cially that the Africans in the United States of America may see an end to their bondage." Jarratt's hostility toward slavery stemmed from his sense that black slaves were treated with abuse. "Slavery," he averred, "as thousands of the slaves are treated, is indeed *shocking to humanity.*" On the other hand, like Whitefield, Jarratt refused to condemn slavery in the abstract. He "dare not say that it is inconsistent" with Christianity, unless he "reproach" God, who "blessed his friend Abraham with abundance of that property." Moreover, Jarratt believed that the New Testament upheld the morality of slavery, and he pointed to "the writings of the apostles, whose directions and exhortations to bond and free incline them to believe that such stations and relations were to exist under the Gospel."[156]

Jarratt was perhaps unusual for the extent to which slavery troubled him. Other ministers such as the Presbyterians Henry Pattillo and William Graham did not hesitate in the early national era to draw on the already well-developed proslavery Christian tradition. Pattillo, whose tract is reproduced in chapter 7 of this anthology, had received his religious training from Samuel Davies, a noted proslavery authority in the 1750s, and had subsequently settled in North Carolina. In 1787 he published *The Plain Planter's Family Assistant,* a didactic tract that bemoaned the general disorder of American society and called for greater attention to scriptural duties, including, of course, the reciprocal duties of masters and slaves. Graham—the author of the lecture transcribed in chapter 8 of this anthology—offered similar wisdom as an instructor at Liberty Hall Academy in Lexington, Virginia, in the late 1780s and early 1790s.[157] Their message was far from new, but the reception that they received from white southerners was, in fact, novel. These ministers took part in a broad and successful evangelical campaign to root Christianity firmly within the culture of the American South. By the turn of the nineteenth century, the evangelical denominations had largely abandoned their antislavery efforts in the American South, and many of the ministers were themselves entering the ranks of the slaveholding elite. Demonstrating the rapid evolution in the evangelical church's stance on slavery, the Methodist bishop Francis Asbury applauded the fact that slaveholders and slaves were flocking to his church in 1805, just seven years after he had complained about the persistence of slave ownership among Methodist church members.

As these Christian authorities increased the presence of their churches in the plantation South, their pronouncements on slavery tended to complicate and to refine the racial boundaries that had long separated southern masters and slaves. Early national authors such as Pattillo and the Baptist minister Edmund Botsford developed the theme of full-fledged African humanity to a greater extent than had their predecessors in the colonial era. Furthermore, they insisted that the Christian plantation household provided an environment perfectly conducive to the nurturing of black humanity. In 1787 Pattillo celebrated the fact that slaveholders increasingly acknowledged that mastery should be tempered by regard for the slaves' human needs—that "my country," as he put it, "increases in humanity." Because "the slaves you own," lectured Pattillo to his readers, "generally grew up with yourselves, or have been raised with your children," slaveholders "feel, then, a kind of brotherly or parental affection for them." As such, the proslavery luminary maintained that "the slaves of my *Plain Planter,* are among the happiest of human beings. Well clothed, and well fed; a warm cabbin, and comfortable bedding; with their hearty thriving children, growing up under their eye. Their daily labour they scarcely feel, being void of all the distressing cares of life; such as educating, and settling out children; procuring food and raiment for a family; paying taxes, and a thousand other cares, that never disturb their solid sleep, nor rack their waking thoughts." Pattillo emphasized that antislavery activists "who put freedom" into the slaves' "heads" were "by no means their friends." The prospect of emancipation should be left, he opined, to "divine providence."[158]

When the South Carolina minister Edmund Botsford penned his enormously popular tract *Sambo and Toney* in 1808—reproduced as chapter 9 in this anthology —he integrated into his work's narrative structure the theme of African American humanity. His work presented a dialogue between enslaved African Americans, who discussed at length the challenges and rewards of Christian faith. Botsford clearly designed his characters to reinforce the proslavery contention that bondage offered blacks as well as whites the benefits of a reciprocal relationship. This organic vision of slavery had long been a staple feature of Christian texts, but, in Botsford's work, the point is hammered home in the words of his black protagonists. For example, the principal slave character Sambo likened the plantation household to "heaven" as his companion Davy expressed sympathy for his master's desire to have the "work done." Over the course of Botsford's text, his readers grow acquainted with the black characters' very human struggle to lead a spiritual life. Whereas colonial authors such as Whitefield and Garden articulated claims about black humanity, Botsford and other early national proslavery authorities such as William Meade (who published the proslavery dialogue reprinted in chapter 10) presented black characters who gave a personal voice to these claims. Ultimately, some Christian authorities even hoped that pious black characters could serve as a model for white acceptance of the Gospels.[159]

Still, this mounting emphasis on black humanity was accompanied by the elaboration of stock characteristics associated exclusively with the black race. Pattillo, for example, contended that the plantation "family is a little community within itself, of which smaller bodies, states and kingdoms are composed." Segregating slaves into a distinct segment of this idealized community, Pattillo "readily acknowledge[d]" that "whoever has had the management of half a dozen Negroes, for as many years, has had his patience put to severe trials; . . . their obstinacy and laziness; their endeavours to evade, or flight their work, under his very eye; the universal practice of lying, to conceal or lessen their offences; their provoking or petulant answers . . . are doubtless made the occasions of very great guilt by many." Measured against the language of the colonial proslavery authors, this argument represented the advance of racialized thought among early national southern intellectuals. Yet even as Pattillo employed and elaborated on stereotypes of black personality traits, he also took pains to underscore their essential humanity. In his "Negroes Catechism," Pattillo insisted that "white folks and Negroes all come from one father," that notwithstanding their "black skin, and the curled head, their bodies . . . are just alike, within and without." Most important, the souls of whites and blacks were "related" because "we all seem to think alike. We all love and hate the same things; and what gives pain or pleasure to the one, does to the other." Race, concluded Pattillo, did not overshadow the human connections between masters and slaves.

## Emerging Sectional Tensions and the Political Uses of Proslavery Thought

Even as American politicians were designing a new federal union, sectional tensions over slavery surfaced. At the Philadelphia constitutional convention in 1787, delegates such as Charles Cotesworth Pinckney responded indignantly to the accusation that slavery was immoral, insisting instead that "if slavery be wrong, it is justified by the example of all the world."[160] Arriving at compromises over the issues of representation in Congress, the international slave trade, and the question of fugitive slaves, the delegates secured a place for slavery in the new American nation. But as the new Congress assembled in 1789, slavery almost immediately created sectional tensions. Antislavery congressmen criticized the institution, and activist constituents such as the Quakers presented petitions that publicly called into question the morality of the slaveholders. Amid these political pressures, white southerners appealed to proslavery logic in order to justify their mastery. In private correspondence during this decade, slaveholders increasingly took pride in the "order" and "humanity" that supposedly characterized the finest southern plantations. Early national slaveholding statesmen, moreover, also proved willing to hinge their regional identity on organic logic that had once been the hallmark of cosmopolitan religious reformers. In 1789, for example, the Georgia congressman James Jackson defended slavery on the grounds that it benefited both whites and blacks.[161] One year later, William L. Smith of South Carolina defended slavery in Congress, building his case with scriptural and racial reasoning.[162]

By no means should these early sectional debates over the morality of slavery be interpreted as signs that southern "fire-eaters" were already poised to withdraw their states from the Union in order to protect slavery. To the contrary, leading southern statesmen had just led the campaign to forge a new federal government, and slaveholding politicians from the South would dominate the executive branch of that government until the 1850s. Still, the burgeoning antislavery movement in the North did change the political context for contemplation and discussion of slavery. In the decades preceding the sectionally charged political confrontations over the admission of Missouri to the Union and nullification in South Carolina, southern slaveholders privately and publicly internalized organic assumptions about the nature of the master-slave relationship. As we have seen, these assumptions had flowed from transatlantic religious reform movements that colonial and Revolutionary slaveholders had resisted as ideologically unnecessary and dangerous in the sense that the reformers' proslavery logic seemed to invite outside interference with slavery. In the shifting political climate at the turn of the nineteenth century, however, slaveholders began to shroud their regional identity and their collective identity as masters in organic and religious terms.

These developments surfaced in 1806 during the congressional debate over the international slave trade. On the immediate issue of ending American participation in the international slave market, the slaveholding delegates had little quarrel. Because the American slave population was already growing through natural increase and because the Chesapeake region was already emerging as a major supplier of slaves for the expanding cotton economy, slaveholders did not believe that strictures against the international slave trade threatened their livelihood. The question of what to do with smuggled slaves intercepted by American authorities posed a thornier dilemma. Slaveholders' ideological commitment to African American bondage led them to resist provisions that would have freed the smuggled slaves. As an economic issue, the slaveholders could accept the closure of the African markets for slaves, but the prospect of the federal government freeing Africans from the shackles of bondage gave the slaveholders pause. Congressmen such as Peter Early of Georgia were already trumpeting the fact that "the large majority of people in the Southern States do not consider slavery as even an evil."[163] Even when northern and southern congressmen largely agreed about a measure concerning slavery, the mere broaching of the issue opened a political window onto the diverging sectional ideologies concerning the institution.

Barely perceptible sectional tremors became a full-fledged political earthquake when Congress deliberated over the question of slavery in the new state of Missouri. Perceiving that restrictions placed on slavery in the western territories would reduce the slaveholding states to a minority in Congress, southern statesmen squared off against their antislavery opponents in 1819. The South Carolina senator William Smith made a lengthy proslavery speech in 1820 that was notable not for its introduction of novel defenses of bondage but rather for its adaptation of proslavery rhetoric to the southern sectional cause. The year before the Missouri controversy erupted, Smith had advanced similar proslavery logic (as can be seen in chapter 11 of this anthology). Like Alexander Garden (who had written his tract eighty years earlier), Smith insisted that "there is no class of laboring people in any country upon the globe, except the United States, that are better clothed, better fed, or are more cheerful, or labor less, or who are more happy, or, indeed, who have more liberty and indulgence, than the slaves of the Southern and Western States." Reflecting the trends that had shaped proslavery thought during the early national era, Smith perhaps placed greater emphasis on the fact that slaves were "supremely happy," but, in general, he advanced traditional concepts in his defense of southern bondage. Predictably, he turned to the Bible for rhetorical ammunition, and he asserted that "the whole commerce between master and slave is patriarchal."[164]

Events over the next decade continued to exacerbate sectional tensions, and, as a result, proslavery rhetoric became increasingly intertwined with the planters' insistence that their regional society was built on the moral bedrock of slavery. In 1822 white authorities in Charleston, South Carolina, became convinced that slaves were plotting a massive rebellion.[165] During this period of perceived crisis in the slaveholding system, southern politicians and ideologues mobilized proslavery tenets in defense of their region. Like their colonial and early national predecessors, ministers such as the Baptist Richard Furman (whose proslavery tract is reproduced in chapter 12 of this anthology) and the Episcopalian Frederick Dalcho led the proslavery charge of the 1820s. And during sectional debates such as the one that took place over the fate of black seamen visiting southern ports and the one that raged over the increased tariff of 1828, southern authors began to make their case for slavery using sectional language.[166] Interestingly, fiercely negative stereotypes of Yankee abolitionists fueled racial imagery that portrayed black slaves in far more menacing terms than had been the case in the early national era. Blaming the Vesey plot on meddling antislavery activists, Edwin Holland, for example, suggested in 1822 that "our Negroes are truly *Jacobins* of the country . . . the *anarchists* and the *domestic enemy* . . . the barbarians who would, IF THEY COULD, become the DESTROYERS of our race." Three years later Whitemarsh Seabrook equated blackness with stupidity as he portrayed antislavery efforts to undermine the livelihoods and even the lives of the slaveholders. "As if we were buried in the labyrinth of Ethiopian stupidity," complained Seabrook, the antislavery forces were pretending that "our good is the impelling power of their hearts."[167]

The growing importance of race in southern proslavery thought, however, did not lead to the rejection of the organic premises that had traditionally been used to justify slavery. In fact, the rhetorical emphasis on the comfort and happiness of the slaves could be seen in the same tracts that made use of sharpened racial language. Holland, for one, presented page after page of slaveholder testimony that insisted the slaves were "perfectly happy and contented with their situation" and that they "enjoy a greater share of the blessings of life than falls to the lot of the laboring poor of most countries." Indeed, by the end of the decade, a new pattern in proslavery thought had emerged—one that increasingly recognized that racial differences cast slaves into an inferior social position, but also insisted, as did the Florida slaveholder Zephaniah Kingsley, that "there is no natural antipathy between the castes on account of color." That Kingsley advocated biracial sexual and marital relationships underscores the fact that on a variety of issues, proslavery authors could still diverge. Nonetheless, the principal ingredients for a self-consciously sectional proslavery argument were now in place and would be repeated hundreds of times in tracts published over the next three decades. With every passing year, southern ideologues would embroider their self-congratulatory depictions of their regional superiority with repeated references to the humanizing impact of slavery on the southern black population. Charles Cotesworth Pinckney's proslavery lecture of 1829—presented in the final chapter of this anthology—signified the degree to which traditional proslavery arguments had worked their way into the worldview of the planter elite. Meanwhile, the development of "scientific" theories about racial difference reflected the slaveholders' urgent need to affix an air of permanency and certainty to the social roles assigned to whites and blacks by the plantation system. These trends were parallel yet unfolded uneasily, and most southern defenders of slavery continued to emphasize the common ground between master and slave as much as the natural forces that cast them into different stations in life.[168]

From the earliest days of colonization, abstract defenses of slavery had rooted the institution within all-encompassing religious and political frameworks that supposedly lent moral structure to the world at large. Exactly for this reason, historians who have reflexively equated proslavery thought with sectionalism have been largely blind to the deep and longstanding intellectual traditions underpinning the southern defense of slavery. The intellectual and cultural dynamics supporting the defense of slavery were never entirely free of racial prejudice, but the colonial proslavery authors tended to minimize racial boundaries as part of their larger project of integrating American plantations more firmly into a Christian moral framework. As proslavery assumptions finally winnowed their way into slaveholder culture in the early national era, racial boundaries became both less and more important in the defense of slavery. The embrace of black humanity and the emphasis on black happiness became more prevalent features of proslavery thought even as early national authors cast African Americans into the seemingly permanent and racially dictated role of bumbling, loving, childish, and grateful recipients of their masters' love. Only with the unfolding of sectional political tensions in the antebellum era did proslavery thought come to be wielded as part of a campaign to insulate the South from the moral standards of the outside world.

And as the specter of the antislavery menace grew in the planters' minds, they responded with ever-deepening stereotypes of black identity coupled with ever-more-insistent claims about the humanity and happiness of southern slaves. During this final phase of American slavery's existence, the planters used their proslavery assumptions as the very measure of their moral distance from the rest of the Western world. Of course, when viewed from the context of a transatlantic proslavery tradition that stretched back thousands of years, this ideological development represented nothing more than a brief and paradoxical coda to a conservative religious tradition that matured in parallel with New World slavery.

## Notes

1. For a starting point into the massive scholarship exploring the scope and economics of the slave trade, see David Eltis, *The Rise of African Slavery in the Americas* (Cambridge: Cambridge University Press, 2000); Patrick Manning, *Slavery and African Life: Occidental, Oriental, and African Slave Trades* (Cambridge: Cambridge University Press, 1990), chap. 4; and Paul E. Lovejoy, "The Volume of the Atlantic Slave Trade: A Synthesis," *Journal of African History* 23, no. 4 (1982): 473–501.

2. For a wonderful overview of the literature, see Peter Kolchin, *American Slavery: 1619–1877* (New York: Hill and Wang, 1993).

3. The contested historiography surrounding the ideological orientation of the southern master class is explored in numerous essays. See Drew Gilpin Faust, "The Peculiar South Revisited: White Society, Culture, and Politics in the Antebellum Period, 1800–1860," in *Interpreting Southern History: Historiographical Essays in Honor of Sanford W. Higginbotham,* ed. John B. Boles and Evelyn Thomas Nolen, 78–119 (Baton Rouge: Louisiana State University Press, 1987); Peter J. Parish, *Slavery: History and Historians* (New York: Harper and Row, 1989), chap. 7; Allan Kulikoff, "The Transition to Capitalism in Rural America," in *The Agrarian Origins of American Capitalism* (Charlottesville: University Press of Virginia, 1992), 13–33; Douglas R. Egerton, "Markets without a Market Revolution: Southern Planters and Capitalism," *Journal of the Early Republic* 16 (Summer 1996): 207–21; and Mark M. Smith's very insightful work, *Debating Slavery: Economy and Society in the Antebellum American South* (Cambridge: Cambridge University Press, 1998), chaps. 1–2.

4. Eugene D. Genovese, *The World the Slaveholders Made: Two Essays in Interpretation* (New York: Pantheon Books, 1969); Drew Gilpin Faust, *A Sacred Circle: The Dilemma of the Intellectual in the Old South, 1840–1860* (Baltimore: Johns Hopkins University Press, 1977); and Larry Tise, *Proslavery: A History of the Defense of Slavery in America, 1701–1840* (Athens: University of Georgia Press, 1987). Tise's book merits special attention as the most exhaustively researched modern study of the deep historical roots and resonance of proslavery thought in eighteenth- and nineteenth-century America. Also see Douglas Ambrose, *Henry Hughes and Proslavery Thought in the Old South* (Baton Rouge: Louisiana State University Press, 1996). For the anthology of proslavery texts edited by Faust, see *The Ideology of Slavery: Proslavery Thought in the Antebellum South, 1830–1860* (Baton Rouge: Louisiana State University Press, 1981).

5. William Sumner Jenkins, *Pro-Slavery Thought in the Old South* (1935; repr., Glouces-
ter, Mass.: P. Smith, 1960); William B. Hesseltine, "Some New Aspects of the Pro-Slavery
Argument," *Journal of Negro History* 21 (January 1936): 1–14. For another example, see
Harvey Wish, *George Fitzhugh: Propagandist of the Old South* (Baton Rouge: Louisiana State
University Press, 1943).

6. Ulrich Bonnell Phillips, *American Negro Slavery: A Survey of the Supply, Employment and
Control of the Negro Labor as Determined by the Plantation Regime* (New York: D. Appleton,
1918), viii (first quotation); Phillips, *Life and Labor in the Old South* (Boston: Little, Brown,
1941), 211 (second quotation). Phillips characterized the plantation as "a school" in which
African savages were exposed to "civilizing" influences. Slavery, in Phillips's work,
emerged as an institution that evoked "good will and affection" between paternalistic masters and "submissive" and "affectionate" slaves. *Life and Labor,* 198–99, 211. For background and commentary on Phillips' writings, consult Merton L. Dillon, *Ulrich Bonnell
Phillips: Historian of the Old South* (Baton Rouge: Louisiana State University Press, 1985);
John Herbert Roper, *U. B. Phillips: A Southern Mind* (Macon: Mercer University Press,
1984); and John David Smith and John C. Inscoe, eds., *Ulrich Bonnell Phillips: A Southern
Historian and His Critics* (New York: Greenwood Press, 1990). I should make clear that long
before the white academy perceived the racist distortions in Phillips's work, African
American scholars were chronicling the hideous cruelties of the southern slave system.
See W. E. B. DuBois, *The Suppression of the African Slave-Trade to the United States, 1638–1870*
(1896; repr., New York: Dover, 1954).

7. Ulrich Bonnell Phillips, *The Course of the South to Secession,* ed. E. Merton Coulter
(New York: Hill and Wang, 1939), chap. 5 (quotation 108).

8. For discussion of the "blundering generation" historiography, see Charles E. Cau-
then and Lewis P. Jones, "The Coming of the Civil War," in *Writing Southern History: Essays
in Historiography in Honor of Fletcher M. Green,* ed. Arthur S. Link and Rembert W. Patrick,
224–48 (Baton Rouge: Louisiana State University Press, 1965). For the postbellum southern insistence that a proslavery agenda had not caused the Civil War, see James M.
McPherson, "Southern Comfort," *New York Review of Books,* April 12, 2001, 28–31. For a
particularly illuminating discussion of Phillips's tangled attitudes toward slavery, southern
identity, and sectionalism, see Eugene D. Genovese, "Ulrich Bonnell Phillips: Two Studies," in *In Red and Black: Marxian Explorations in Southern and Afro-American History* (New
York: Vintage Books, 1971), 259–98.

9. Kenneth Stampp, *The Peculiar Institution: Slavery in the Ante-Bellum South* (New York:
Knopf, 1956), 77.

10. Stanley Elkins, *Slavery: A Problem in American Institutional and Intellectual Life,* (1959;
3rd ed., Chicago: University of Chicago Press, 1976), 20–23, 2, 206–22 (quotation 216).
Of course, scholars such as Elkins and Stampp had good historiographical reason to avoid
treating proslavery tracts as serious evidence. They were, after all, seeking to overturn a
half-century of bogus conclusions promoted by influential racist scholars such as Phillips
and William Dunning. In his history of Reconstruction, Dunning ignored evidence of the
suffering and betrayal of African Americans during the period following the Civil War, and
he claimed that Republicans fabricated stories of black mistreatment at the hands of
whites. He also defended the notorious "Black Codes" passed by the former Confederate

States, claiming that the legislation was a prudent response to freemen who "were not, and in the nature of the case could not for generations be, on the same social, moral, and intelléctual plane with the whites." See, for example, his *Reconstruction, Political and Economic, 1865–1877* (New York: Harper, 1907), 250, 58.

11. George Fitzhugh, *Cannibals All! or, Slaves without Masters,* ed. C. Vann Woodward (Cambridge, Mass.: Belknap Press, 1960), x. Eric L. McKitrick, ed., *Slavery Defended: The Views of the Old South* (Englewood Cliffs, N.J.: Prentice-Hall, 1963), 5. McKitrick believed that the proslavery authors were worthy of study because their attacks on northern industrial capitalism forced the abolitionists "to think about their first principles" of liberal society. Although McKitrick recognized the "intellectual agility" of the proslavery thinkers, he averred that their "social thinking" was "barren" because "critical analysis" was "out of the question" in the South (2–3). Demonstrating the peripheral nature of this proslavery scholarship within the historiography of the American South, neither of these works was mentioned in the historiographical essay by Herbert J. Doherty Jr., "The Mind of the Antebellum South," in *Writing Southern History: Essays in Honor of Fletcher M. Green,* ed. Arthur S. Link and Rembert W. Patrick (Baton Rouge: Louisiana State University Press, 1965), 212. Louis Hartz's treatment of proslavery thought provides us with one more example of this era's low regard for proslavery tracts as meaningful historical evidence. Hartz referred to the proslavery tracts as evidence that "fraud, alas, was the inevitable fate of Southern social thought." *The Liberal Tradition in America* (New York: Harcourt, Brace, 1955), 147. For a notable historiographical exception, see Richard Hofstadter, "John C. Calhoun: The Marx of the Master Class," chap. 4 in Hofstadter, *The American Political Tradition and the Men Who Made It* (1948; repr., New York: Vintage Books, 1974), 86–117. Here Hofstadter acknowledges the rigor of Calhoun's "social analysis" and credits him with being "a brilliant if narrow dialectician, probably the last American statesman to do any primary political thinking" (87).

12. Eugene D. Genovese, *The Political Economy of Slavery: Studies in the Economy and Society of the Slave South* (New York: Pantheon Books, 1965), 28.

13. Genovese, *World the Slaveholders Made,* 130.

14. Eugene D. Genovese, *Roll, Jordan, Roll: The World the Slaves Made* (New York: Pantheon Books, 1974), 3, 245.

15. Genovese, however, has taken seriously the possibility that the paternalistic ideology of the southern planters did result in more favorable material circumstances for their slaves than would have otherwise been the case. See, for example, *World the Slaveholders Made,* 15; and his linkage of slaveholder paternalism to the closing of the African slave trade in 1808: *Roll, Jordan, Roll,* 5. Here Genovese seemed to pin the slaveholders' proslavery ideology firmly to material circumstances. Their need for a self-sustaining slave population pushed them toward a recognition of slave humanity, he suggests, and their ideological concession of their slaves' humanity led the planters to treat them in a fashion that permitted their population to grow. The growing anthropological, demographic, and archaeological literature on American slavery, however, suggests a grimmer portrait of the material circumstances on even the southern plantations owned by the most stridently paternalistic masters. See my "Ideology and Death on a Savannah River Rice Plantation, 1833–1867: Paternalism amidst 'A Good Supply of Disease and Pain,'" *Journal of Southern History* 59 (November 1993): 673–706.

16. Genovese, *Roll, Jordan, Roll,* 602 (quotation). For his analysis placing the planters' racial prejudices in the context of their broader concerns as a ruling elite, see 57–58. More recently, Genovese has complained that the antebellum "southern-conservative critique of modern Gnosticism has been wrongly equated with racism and white supremacy." Genovese, *The Southern Tradition: The Achievement and Limitations of an American Conservatism* (Cambridge, Mass.: Harvard University Press, 1994), xi.

17. For an overview of this wave of often-brilliant scholarship, see Charles B. Dew, "The Slavery Experience," in Boles and Nolen, *Interpreting Southern History,* 120–61.

18. For a summary of the "chicken-or-egg" debate over whether slavery or racism came first, see Alden T. Vaughan, "The Origins Debate: Slavery and Racism in Seventeenth-Century Virginia, *Virginia Magazine of History and Biography* 97 (July 1989): 311–54.

19. Winthrop Jordan, *White over Black: American Attitudes Toward the Negro, 1550–1812* (Chapel Hill: University of North Carolina Press, 1968), 190–215. Of course, Jordan was perfectly well within his rights to devote his project to studying racial prejudice rather than proslavery thought per se. Far from criticizing him, I am merely using his work to illustrate that the swirling concerns of this era in American history tended to push more scholars to approach race as a key organizing force in the American past.

20. George Fredrickson, *The Black Image in the White Mind: The Debate on Afro-American Character and Destiny, 1817–1914* (New York: Harper and Row, 1971), 3. Fredrickson maintained that slavery "had never actually been seriously threatened" prior to the post-Revolutionary period. He also suggested that many eighteenth-century slaveholders gave "theoretical assent" to "the abstract proposition that slavery was an undesirable institution" while they simultaneously clung to the institution because of "the power of white 'prejudices'" against free blacks. For Fredrickson's critique of Genovese, see *The Arrogance of Race: Historical Perspectives on Slavery, Racism, and Social Inequality* (Middletown, Conn.: Wesleyan University Press, 1988), 133. For a similar example, see William Stanton, *The Leopard's Spots: Scientific Attitudes toward Race in America, 1815–59* (Chicago: University of Chicago Press, 1960), 54–58.

21. Eugene D. Genovese and Elizabeth Fox-Genovese, *The Fruits of Merchant Capital: Slavery and Bourgeois Property in the Rise and Expansion of Capitalism* (New York: Oxford University Press, 1983); Fox-Genovese, *Within the Plantation Household: Black and White Women in the Old South* (Chapel Hill: University of North Carolina Press, 1988); Fredrickson, *Black Image,* 61, 65, 68. Summing up the differences between Genovese's paradigm and his own, Fredrickson observed that "emphasis on slavery per se as an organizing principle of society led to a genuinely reactionary and paternalistic theory of society; but if racial differentiation was seen as the heart of the matter, then the result, in the larger American ideological context, was 'Herrenvolk democracy' or 'egalitarian' racism" (64).

22. Edmund S. Morgan, *American Slavery, American Freedom: The Ordeal of Colonial Virginia* (New York: Norton, 1975). Morgan actually began the book with scenes of Virginians devotions to slavery and liberty in the Revolutionary era, and he called his study "an attempt to see how slavery and freedom made their way to England's first American colony and grew there together, the one supporting the other" (6).

23. J. Mills Thornton III, *Politics and Power in a Slave Society: Alabama, 1800–1860* (Baton Rouge: Louisiana State University Press, 1978); Lacy K. Ford Jr., *Origins of Southern Radicalism: The South Carolina Upcountry, 1800–1860* (New York: Oxford University Press,

1988); J. William Harris, *Plain Folk and Gentry in a Slave Society: White Liberty and Black Slavery in Augusta's Hinterlands* (Middletown, Conn.: Wesleyan University Press, 1985); and James Oakes, *The Ruling Race: A History of American Slaveholders* (New York: Knopf, 1982). For another example, see Laurence Shore, *Southern Capitalism: The Ideological Leadership of an Elite, 1832–1885* (Chapel Hill: University of North Carolina Press, 1986). A scholarly fascination with republicanism flowered at the very moment that this scholarship on the slavery South was being written. For elaboration on this term's many uses by historians, see Daniel T. Rodgers, "Republicanism: The Career of a Concept," *Journal of American History* 79 ( June 1992): 12–38. More recently, talented scholars have continued to refine our understanding of proslavery thought and white class and gender dynamics. See Stephanie McCurry, *Masters of Small Worlds: Yeoman Households, Gender Relations, and the Political Culture of the Antebellum South Carolina Low Country* (New York: Oxford University Press, 1995); Kathleen M. Brown, *Good Wives, Nasty Wenches and Anxious Patriarchs: Gender, Race, and Power in Colonial Virginia* (Chapel Hill: University of North Carolina Press, 1996); Michele Gillespie, *Free Labor in an Unfree World: White Artisans in Slaveholding Georgia, 1789–1860* (Athens: University of Georgia Press, 1999); Susanna Delfino and Michele Gillespie, eds., *Neither Lady nor Slave: Working Women in the Old South* (Chapel Hill: University of North Carolina Press, 2002); and Jennifer L. Morgan, *Laboring Women: Reproduction and Gender in New World Slavery* (Philadelphia: University of Pennsylvania Press, 2004).

24. See, for example, Ford, *Origins of Southern Radicalism,* 358–59.

25. Ralph E. Morrow, "The Proslavery Argument Revisited," *Mississippi Valley Historical Review* 48 ( June 1961): 79–94 (quotation 94). For the debate over whether the slaveholders experienced feelings of guilt, see Gaines M. Foster, "Guilt over Slavery: A Historiographical Analysis," *Journal of Southern History* 56 (November 1990): 665–94.

26. David Donald, "The Proslavery Argument Reconsidered," *Journal of Southern History* 37 (February 1971): 3–18.

27. Faust, *Sacred Circle,* 2, 6; *Proslavery Thought in the Old South;* and *James Henry Hammond and the Old South: A Design for Mastery* (Baton Rouge: Louisiana State University Press, 1982), 3. James L. Roark's groundbreaking study of the planter experience during the Civil War also emphasized the deep roots that proslavery notions had sunk into white southern culture. See *Masters without Slaves: Southern Planters in the Civil War and Reconstruction* (New York: Norton, 1977).

28. Drew Gilpin Faust, "Evangelicalism and the Meaning of the Proslavery Argument: The Reverend Thornton Stringfellow of Virginia," *Virginia Magazine of History and Biography* 85 ( January 1977): 3–5.

29. Joyce E. Chaplin, *An Anxious Pursuit: Agricultural Innovation and Modernity in the Lower South, 1730–1815* (Chapel Hill: University of North Carolina Press, 1993).

30. Thomas L. Haskell, "Capitalism and the Origins of the Humanitarian Sensibility," *American Historical Review* 90 (April–June 1985): 339–61, 547–66.

31. Genovese, *Political Economy of Slavery,* 3; Genovese and Fox-Genovese, *Fruits of Merchant Capital;* Genovese, *The Slaveholders' Dilemma: Freedom and Progress in Southern Conservative Thought, 1820–1860* (Columbia: University of South Carolina Press, 1992), 13. *The Slaveholders' Dilemma* was initially delivered by Genovese as a series of lectures in 1990. Also see Fox-Genovese, *Within the Plantation Household,* 54–58. Lacy Ford took note of the

evolution in Genovese's perspective on the planters' relationship with modernity: Ford, "The Conservative Mind of the Old South," *Reviews in American History* 21 (December 1993): 591–99. For fuller consideration of the slaveholders' alternative path toward modernity, see Mark M. Smith, *Mastered by the Clock: Time, Slavery, and Freedom in the American South* (Chapel Hill: University of North Carolina Press, 1997).

32. W. J. Cash, *The Mind of the South* (New York: Knopf, 1941), 94–96. Clement Eaton's scholarship likewise rendered a bleak portrait of southern intellectual life. See his *Freedom of Thought in the Old South* (Durham, N.C.: Duke University Press, 1940).

33. For my own efforts to develop this theme, see *Domesticating Slavery: The Master Class in Georgia and South Carolina, 1670–1837* (Chapel Hill: University of North Carolina Press, 1999).

34. Michael O'Brien, *Conjectures of Order: Intellectual Life and the American South, 1810–1820*, 2 vols. (Chapel Hill: University of North Carolina Press, 2004); O'Brien, ed., *All Clever Men, Who Make Their Way: Critical Discourse in the Old South* (Athens: University of Georgia Press, 1992); *A Character of Hugh Legaré* (Knoxville: University of Tennessee Press, 1985); *Rethinking the South: Essays in Intellectual History* (Athens: University of Georgia Press, 1988); and O'Brien and David Moltke-Hansen, eds., *Intellectual Life in Antebellum Charleston* (Knoxville: University of Tennessee Press, 1986).

35. For southern slaveholders' interactions with Europe, see Maurie D. McInnis, *In Pursuit of Refinement: Charlestonians Abroad, 1740–1860* (Columbia: University of South Carolina Press, 1999). On classical education in South Carolina, see Wayne K. Durrill, "The Power of Ancient Words: Classical Teaching and Social Change at South Carolina College, 1804–1860," *Journal of Southern History* 65 (August 1999): 469–98. For the intimate interactions between the northern and southern elite, see Daniel Kilbride, "Southern Medical Students in Philadelphia, 1800–1861: Science and Sociability in the 'Republic of Medicine,'" *Journal of Southern History* 64 (November 1999): 697–732; "Cultivation, Conservatism, and the Early National Gentry: The Manigault Family and their Circle," *Journal of the Early Republic* 19 (Summer 1999): 221–56; and "Philadelphia and the Southern Elite: Class, Kinship, and Culture in Antebellum America" (Ph.D. diss., University of Florida, 1997). On this point, also see Charles Hoffman and Tess Hoffman, *North by South: The Two Lives of Richard James Arnold* (Athens: University of Georgia Press, 1988). Historians have also been exploring the extent to which the colonial North was deeply reliant on slave labor. See, for example, Leslie M. Harris, *In the Shadow of Slavery: African Americans in New York City, 1626–1863* (Chicago: University of Chicago Press, 2003); and Shane White, *Somewhat More Independent: The End of Slavery in New York City, 1770–1810* (Athens: University of Georgia Press, 1991).

36. Sylvia R. Frey and Betty Wood, *Come Shouting to Zion: African American Protestantism in the American South and British Caribbean to 1830* (Chapel Hill: University of North Carolina Press, 1998); Gwendolyn Midlo Hall, *Africans in Colonial Louisiana: The Development of Afro-Creole Culture in the Eighteenth Century* (Baton Rouge: Louisiana State University Press, 1992); Jane Landers, *Black Society in Spanish Florida* (Urbana: University of Illinois Press, 1999).

37. George M. Fredrickson, *White Supremacy: A Comparative Study in American and South African History* (New York: Oxford University Press, 1981); Peter Kolchin, *Unfree Labor:*

*American Slavery and Russian Serfdom* (Cambridge, Mass.: Belknap Press, 1987); and Shearer Davis Bowman, *Masters and Lords: Mid-Nineteenth Century U.S. Planters and Prussian Junkers* (New York: Oxford University Press, 1993). Of course, comparative scholars had been publishing significant studies long before the 1980s. See note 39 below.

38. David Brion Davis, *The Problem of Slavery in Western Culture* (Ithaca, N.Y.: Cornell University Press, 1966); *The Problem of Slavery in the Age of Revolution, 1770–1823* (Ithaca, N.Y.: Cornell University Press, 1975); and *Slavery and Human Progress* (New York: Oxford University Press, 1984).

39. Frank Tannenbaum, *Slave and Citizen* (New York, 1947); Eric Williams, *Capitalism and Slavery* (1944; repr., Boston: Little, Brown, 1980); Herbert S. Klein, *Slavery in the Americas: A Comparative Study of Virginia and Cuba* (Chicago: University of Chicago Press, 1967); Eugene D. Genovese, *From Rebellion to Revolution: Afro-American Slave Revolts in the Making of the New World* (Baton Rouge: Louisiana State University Press, 1979); Immanuel Wallerstein, *The Modern World-System,* 3 vols. (New York: Academic Press, 1974–89); Peter A. Coclanis, *The Shadow of a Dream: Economic Life and Death in the South Carolina Low Country, 1670–1920* (New York: Oxford University Press, 1989); Robin Blackburn, *The Making of New World Slavery: From the Baroque to the Modern, 1492–1800* (London: Verso, 1997); and Ira Berlin, *Many Thousands Gone: The First Two Centuries of Slavery in North America* (Cambridge, Mass.: Belknap Press, 1998).

40. Tise, *Proslavery;* and Thomas W. Krise, ed., *Caribbeana: An Anthology of English Literature of the West Indies, 1657–1777* (Chicago: University of Chicago Press, 1999).

41. I make this statement forcefully yet I must confess that this point was sometimes lost on me as I struggled through early drafts of this anthology. I thank Michael O'Brien for urging me to disentangle southern sectionalism and southern proslavery thought.

42. See, for example, Thomas Jefferson Wertenbaker, *The Old South: The Founding of American Civilization* (New York: Scribner's Sons, 1942). In this massive study of southern history during the colonial and early national periods, Wertenbaker offers no discussion of proslavery thought and, instead, contends that slaveholders during this period conceded the moral flaws of their economic system (28).

43. Jenkins, *Pro-Slavery Thought,* 1.

44. For example, see Fredrickson, *Black Image,* 43–45. Here the author cites Jenkins (in n. 1 on p. 44) but nonetheless begins his discussion of southern proslavery declarations with evidence from the 1820s and 1830s. For very similar evidence, see John McCardell, *The Idea of a Southern Nation: Southern Nationalists and Southern Nationalism, 1830–1860* (New York: Norton, 1979), 49–50.

45. See William W. Freehling's study of proslavery thought and the nullification crisis in South Carolina: *Prelude to Civil War: the Nullification Controversy in South Carolina, 1816–1836* (New York: Harper and Row, 1966), chap. 9. It is unclear whether Freehling has changed his views of the chronology for the emergence of southern proslavery writings. However, we get some hint in his two-volume study of southern secession that he has not altered his perspective on this issue, for he has chosen to leave his discussion of proslavery thought for his yet-to-appear second volume dealing with the final years of the antebellum era. Freehling, *The Road to Disunion,* vol. 1, *Secessionists at Bay, 1776–1854* (New York: Oxford University Press, 1990), ix. Other recent scholars continue to work from the assumption that the proslavery argument became significant in the South in the 1830s. See,

for example, Manisha Sinha, *The Counter-Revolution of Slavery: Politics and Ideology in Antebellum South Carolina* (Chapel Hill: University of North Carolina Press, 2000), chap. 3.

46. Orlando Patterson, *Slavery and Social Death: A Comparative Study* (Cambridge, Mass.: Harvard University Press, 1982); David Brion Davis, *Problem of Slavery in Western Culture.* Here I must also thank the anonymous scholar who reviewed this anthology for the University of South Carolina Press for urging me to make this point with greater force.

47. David Brion Davis, *Problem of Slavery in Western Culture,* 66–68; Aristotle, *Politics,* ed. Stephen Everson (Cambridge: Cambridge University Press, 1988), 4 [1253b].

48. Aristotle, *Politics,* 7 [1254b].

49. Ibid., 19 [1259b].

50. Ibid., 5 [1253b], 9 [1255b].

51. Orlando Patterson, *Freedom in the Making of Western Culture* (New York: Basic Books, 1991), especially part 4.

52. Of course, we should also note that certain biblical passages could be interpreted in ways that thoroughly challenged slavery's ongoing existence. As such, antislavery reformers and proslavery intellectuals skirmished endlessly over their contrasting readings of the Bible. Their debates were fueled by the contradictory evidence found in their principal source. Compare, for example, seemingly proslavery verses such as Exodus 21:2–10, Leviticus 19:20, 1 Corinthians 7:20–24, and Colossians 3:22–24 with potentially antislavery verses such as Exodus 14:10–14, Galatians 4:7–8, 31, and Galatians 5:1.

53. Patterson, *Freedom in the Making;* David Brion Davis, *Problem of Slavery in Western Culture;* Blackburn, *Making of New World Slavery;* M. I. Finley, *Ancient Slavery and Modern Ideology* (New York: Viking Press, 1980); Pierre Dockès, *Medieval Slavery and Liberation,* trans. Arthur Goldhammer (Chicago: University of Chicago Press, 1982); Pierre Bonnassie, *From Slavery to Feudalism in South-West Europe* (Cambridge: Cambridge University Press, 1991); Iris Origo, "The Domestic Enemy: The Eastern Slaves in Tuscany in the Fourteenth and Fifteenth Centuries," *Speculum* 30 ( July 1955): 321–66; and Charles Verlinden, *The Beginnings of Modern Colonization,* trans. Yvonne Freccero (Ithaca, N.Y.: Cornell University Press, 1970).

54. Origo, "Domestic Enemy"; David Brion Davis, *Slavery and Human Progress,* 31.

55. For Islamic doctrine on this point, see William McKee Evans, "From the Land of Canaan to the Land of Guinea: The Strange Odyssey of the 'Sons of Ham,'" *American Historical Review* 85 (February 1980): 28.

56. Blackburn, *Making of New World Slavery,* 50; David Brion Davis, *Problem of Slavery in Western Culture,* 94–105; Thomas Gilby, *The Political Thought of Thomas Aquinas* (Chicago: University of Chicago Press, 1958), 294–300.

57. Peter Blickle, *The Revolution of 1525: The German Peasants' War from a New Perspective,* trans. Thomas A. Brady Jr. and H. C. Erik Midelfort (Baltimore: Johns Hopkins University Press, 1981); and Robert James Bast, *Honor Your Fathers: Catechisms and the Emergence of Patriarchal Ideology in Germany, 1400–1600* (Leiden: Brill, 1997). My thanks to Professor Bast for his generous assistance and advice on this point.

58. Samuel Eliot Morison, ed., *Journals and Other Documents on the Life and Voyages of Christopher Columbus* (New York: Limited Editions Club, 1963), 65.

59. Verlinden, *Beginnings of Modern Colonization.* Also see T. Bentley Duncan, *Atlantic Islands: Madeira, the Azores and the Cape Verdes in Seventeenth-Century Commerce and Navigation*

(Chicago: University of Chicago Press, 1972); and Philip D. Curtin, *The Rise and Fall of the Plantation Complex: Essays in Atlantic History* (Cambridge: Cambridge University Press, 1990).

60. Edmund S. Morgan, *American Slavery;* Richard S. Dunn, *Sugar and Slaves: The Rise of the Planter Class in the British West Indies, 1624–1713* (Chapel Hill: University of North Carolina Press, 1972).

61. On the proslavery consensus in the works of seventeenth-century jurists including Grotius, see Alan Watson, "Seventeenth-Century Jurists, Roman Law, and Slavery," in *Slavery and the Law,* ed. Paul Finkelman, 419–35 (Madison, Wis.: Madison House, 1997). Also see Thomas Hobbes, *Leviathan,* ed. Richard Tuck (Cambridge: Cambridge University Press, 1991); Richard Tuck, *Hobbes* (Oxford: Oxford University Press, 1989); Robert Filmer, *Patriarcha and Other Writings,* ed. Johann P. Sommerville (Cambridge: Cambridge University Press, 1991); James Daly, *Sir Robert Filmer and English Political Thought* (Toronto: University of Toronto Press, 1979); and John Locke, *Two Treatises of Government,* ed. Peter Laslett (Cambridge: Cambridge University Press, 1960).

62. Filmer, *Patriarcha,* 237, 30, 276; and Locke, *Two Treatises,* 284–85, 323.

63. David Brion Davis, *Problem of Slavery in Western Culture,* 107. In More's work, on the one hand, the condition of slavery was not passed on to the children of slaves as a matter of course, and slaves acquired from foreign countries were permitted to leave their state of bondage if they so desired. On the other hand, slaves were whipped for laziness, routinely suffered ear cropping, and were vigilantly policed for signs of planned insurrection or flight. More, *Utopia,* trans. Clarence H. Miller (New Haven, Conn.: Yale University Press, 2001), 29–31, 95–96.

64. Filmer, *Patriarcha,* 4, 2, and 30. On Fitzhugh's discussion of Filmer, see Genovese, *World the Slaveholders Made,* 211.

65. Locke, *Two Treatises,* 141, 284–85, 269, 304, 214. Thomas Jefferson, *Notes on the State of Virginia,* ed. David Waldstreicher (New York: Palgrave, 2002), 175–81.

66. Morgan Godwyn, *The Negro's and Indians Advocate, Suing for their Admission into the Church* (London, 1680), 4–7.

67. Richard Baxter, *A Christian Directory: Or, a Summ of Practical Theologie and Cases of Conscience,* 2nd ed. (London, 1678), pt. 2, pp. 70, 72, 71, 70. Baxter wrote this text in 1664–65. For background on his life and prolific writings, see N. H. Keeble, *Richard Baxter: Puritan Man of Letters* (Oxford: Oxford University Press, 1982); Hugh Martin, *Puritanism and Richard Baxter* (London: SCM Press, 1954); and William M. Lamont, *Richard Baxter and the Millenium: Protestant Imperialism and the English Revolution* (Totowa, N.J.: Rowman and Littlefield, 1979).

68. Baxter, *Christian Directory,* pt. 2, pp. 70, 71, 74.

69. Godwyn, *Negro's and Indians Advocate,* 112, 142, 75. For David Brion Davis's analysis of Baxter's and Godwyn's texts, see *Problem of Slavery in Western Culture,* 204–6.

70. For the clear disassociation between Christian conversion and compulsory emancipation, see the "Fundamental Constitutions" of South Carolina in 1669: "Since charity obliges us to wish well to the souls of all men, and religion ought to alter nothing in any man's civil estate or right, it shall be lawful for slaves as well as others, to enter themselves and be of what church or profession any of them shall think best, and thereof be as fully members as any freeman. But yet no slave shall hereby be exempted from that civil

dominion his master hath over him, but be in all things in the same state and condition he was in before. . . . Every freeman of Carolina, shall have absolute power and authority over his negro slaves, of what opinion or religion soever." Thomas Cooper and David J. McCord, eds., *The Statutes at Large of South Carolina* (repr., Columbia, S.C.: Republican Printing Company, 1872), 1:55.

71. See Frey and Wood, *Come Shouting to Zion,* chap. 3; John B. Boles, "Evangelical Protestantism in the Old South: From Religious Dissent to Cultural Dominance," in *Religion in the South,* ed. Charles Reagan Wilson, 13–34 (Jackson: University Press of Mississippi, 1985); Albert J. Raboteau, *Slave Religion: The "Invisible Institution" in the Antebellum South* (New York: Oxford University Press, 1978), 96–150; Philip D. Morgan, *Slave Counterpoint: Black Culture in the Eighteenth-Century Chesapeake and Lowcountry* (Chapel Hill: University of North Carolina Press, 1998), 420–37; and John C. Van Horne, ed., *Religious Philanthropy and Colonial Slavery: The American Correspondence of the Associates of Dr. Bray, 1717–1777* (Urbana: University of Illinois Press, 1985), 1–38.

72. Godwyn, *Negro's and Indians Advocate,* 107.

73. William Fleetwood, *A Sermon Preached before the Society for the Propagation of the Gospel in Foreign Parts* (London, 1711), repr. in Frank J. Klingberg, *Anglican Humanitarianism in Colonial New York* (Freeport, N.Y.: Books for Libraries Press, 1971), 203.

74. Godwyn, *Negro's and Indians Advocate,* 41.

75. Le Jau to the Society for the Propagation of the Gospel in Foreign Parts, March 22, 1709; and February 20, 1712, in Frank J. Klingberg, ed., *The Carolina Chronicle of Dr. Francis Le Jau, 1706–1717* (Berkeley: University of California Press, 1956), 55, 108.

76. Kolchin, *American Slavery,* 17–18.

77. Godwyn, *Negro's and Indians Advocate,* 38.

78. Jon Butler, "Enlarging the Bonds of Christ: Slavery, Evangelism, and the Christianization of the White South, 1680–1760," in *The Evangelical Tradition in America,* ed. Leonard I. Sweet, 87–112 (Macon, Ga.: Mercer University Press), 93.

79. Van Horne, *Religious Philanthropy,* 1–9.

80. John Wolfe Lydekker, *Thomas Bray, 1685–1730: Founder of Missionary Enterprise* (Philadelphia: Church Historical Society, 1943), 11.

81. Fleetwood, *Sermon Preached,* 205–8.

82. Edmund Gibson, *A Letter of the Lord Bishop of London to the Masters and Mistresses of Families in the English Plantations Abroad; Exhorting Them to Encourage and Promote the Instruction of Their Negroes in the Christian Faith* (London, 1727), repr. in David Humphreys, *An Historical Account of the Incorporated Society for the Propagation of the Gospel in Foreign Parts* (1730; New York: Arno Press, 1969), 250–77. For evidence of the number of these texts sent to America, see 248–49.

83. Ibid., 265–66.

84. Ibid., 267–68.

85. Morgan, *American Slavery;* Russell Menard, "From Servants to Slaves: The Transformation of the Chesapeake Labor System," *Southern Studies* 16 (Winter 1977): 355–90.

86. Genesis 9:21–27.

87. Evans, "From the Land of Canaan," 27.

88. Godwyn, *Negro's and Indians Advocate,* 43–54. Like most ministers, Godwyn rejected the "sons of Ham" rationale for slavery. See my discussion below.

89. Milton Cantor, "The Image of the Negro in Colonial Literature," *New England Quarterly* 36 (December 1963): 452–77.

90. Saffin, *A Brief and Candid Answer to a Late Printed Sheet, Entituled, The Selling of Joseph* (Boston, 1701), quoted in Lawrence W. Towner, "The Sewall-Saffin Dialogue on Slavery," *William and Mary Quarterly,* 3rd ser., 21 (January 1965): 48. Saffin's tract appears to be the earliest proslavery publication by a resident American colonist. The fact that he resided in Massachusetts underscores the degree to which slavery was a feature of the Atlantic colonial system rather than a "peculiar" element of southern society.

91. Ibid., 48.

92. Saffin quoted in Tise, *Proslavery,* 17.

93. Baxter, *Christian Directory,* pt. 2, p. 71.

94. Ibid., 74.

95. Godwyn, *Negro's and Indians Advocate,* 9, 12–13, 18, 20–21, 30. Edmund Gibson also urged the slaveholders to remember that "Humanity forbids all cruel and barbarous Treatment of our Fellow-Creatures, and will not suffer us to consider a Being that is endow'd with Reason, upon a Level with Brutes." *Letter of the Lord Bishop of London,* 267.

96. Klingberg, *Carolina Chronicle,* 102, 50.

97. On the tensions between slaveholders and missionaries arriving from the metropole, see Robert Olwell, *Masters, Slaves, and Subjects: The Culture of Power in the South Carolina Low Country, 1740–1790* (Ithaca, N.Y.: Cornell University Press, 1998), chap. 3.

98. On the Georgia trustees' overlapping relationship with the Anglican missionary organizations, see Van Horne, *Religious Philanthropy,* 9–20.

99. The best historical account of this issue is Betty Wood, *Slavery in Colonial Georgia, 1730–1775* (Athens: University of Georgia Press, 1984).

100. *An Account Shewing the Progress of the Colony of Georgia in America from Its First Establishment* (London, 1741), repr. in Trevor R. Reese, ed., *The Clamorous Malcontents: Criticisms and Defenses of the Colony of Georgia, 1741–1743,* 179–255 (Savannah: Beehive Press, 1973), quotations on 190–92.

101. *Account Shewing the Progress,* 190–92; New Inverness Petition, January 3, 1738–9, in Reese, *Clamarous Malcontents,* 249–50. Critics of the trustees' policies claimed that the signers of this petition had been bribed with promises of cattle extended from the principal authorities of the colony. See David Brion Davis, *Problem of Slavery in Western Culture,* 148. For the purposes of the discussion at hand, the legitimacy of this claim hardly matters. The significant point is that, on at least some level, the trustees' ban of slavery in Georgia opened the door to a fundamental challenge against slavery's existence across the New World. For evidence that the trustees themselves were complicit in slavery outside of Georgia, see Mart A. Stewart, *"What Nature Suffers to Groe": Life, Labor, and Landscape on the Georgia Coast, 1680–1920* (Athens: University of Georgia Press, 1996), 272–73n59.

102. Stewart, *"What Nature Suffers to Groe."*

103. Patrick Talfair and others to the trustees, ca. May 1735, in *The Colonial Records of the State of Georgia,* ed. Kenneth Coleman and Milton Ready, vol. 20, *Original Papers, Correspondence to the Trustees, James Oglethorpe, and Others, 1732–1735* (Athens: University of Georgia Press, 1982), 365–66. According to Edmund Morgan, exactly this fear of white civil unrest motivated Virginia planters to embrace slavery as their principal labor system following Bacon's Rebellion in 1676. See *American Slavery.*

104. Thomas Stephens, *The Hard Case of the Distressed People of Georgia* (London, 1742), in Reese, *Clamarous Malcontents,* 264.

105. Proslavery petition to the Georgia trustees, December 9, 1738, repr. in Patrick Tailfer, *A True and Historical Narrative of the Colony of Georgia in America* (London, 1741), and in Reese, *Clamorous Malcontents,* 78.

106. Tailfer, *True and Historical Narrative,* 58; Stephens, *Hard Case,* 266.

107. Sydney E. Ahlstrom, *A Religious History of the American People* (New Haven, Conn.: Yale University Press, 1972), 280–329; Jon Butler, *Awash in a Sea of Faith: Christianizing the American People* (Cambridge, Mass.: Harvard University Press, 1990), chap. 6; Raboteau, *Slave Religion,* 110–50.

108. Alan Gallay, *The Formation of a Planter Elite: Jonathan Bryan and the Southern Colonial Frontier* (Athens: University of Georgia Press, 1989); Harry S. Stout, *The Divine Dramatist: George Whitefield and the Rise of Modern Evangelicalism* (Grand Rapids, Mich.: W. B. Eerdmans, 1991); Stephen J. Stein, "George Whitefield on Slavery: Some New Evidence," *Church History* 42 (June 1973); Frank J. Lambert, "'Pedlar in Divinity': George Whitefield and the Great Awakening, 1737–1745," *Journal of American History* 77 (December 1990): 821–37; Harvey H. Jackson, "Hugh Bryan and the Evangelical Movement in Colonial South Carolina," *William and Mary Quarterly,* 3rd ser., 43 (October 1986): 594–614; William Howland Kenney III, "Alexander Garden and George Whitefield: The Significance of Revivalism in South Carolina, 1738–1741," *South Carolina Historical Magazine* 71 (January 1970): 1–16; S. Charles Bolton, *Southern Anglicanism: The Church of England in Colonial South Carolina* (Westport, Conn.: Greenwood Press, 1982); and Robert M. Calhoon, *Evangelicals and Conservatives in the Early South, 1740–1861* (Columbia: University of South Carolina Press, 1988).

109. For Whitefield's resolution to create an orphanage, see William V. Davis, ed., *George Whitefield's Journals, 1737–1741* (1905; Gainesville: Scholar's Facsimiles and Reprints, 1969), 150. On the Franklin episode, see Carl Van Doren, *Benjamin Franklin* (New York: Viking Press, 1938), 138. Whitefield himself marveled at his ability to procure donations for the orphanage from even the poorest congregations. See William V. Davis, *George Whitefield's Journals,* 195. Also see Neil J. O'Connell, "George Whitefield and Bethesda Orphan-House," *Georgia Historical Quarterly* 54 (Spring 1970): 41–62.

110. See William V. Davis, *George Whitefield's Journals,* 386; Young, *Domesticating Slavery,* 29.

111. The tract is reproduced in chapter 1 of this anthology.

112. My account of the Bryan episode (including the quotations) is drawn from Jackson, "Hugh Bryan."

113. William V. Davis, *George Whitefield's Journals,* 142.

114. For scholarship exploring their conflict, see Bolton, *Southern Anglicanism.*

115. Alexander Garden to unknown correspondent, ca. 1740, SPG General Correspondence, Fulham Papers, Lambeth Palace Library, London.

116. The tract is included as the second selection in this volume.

117. Anglican missionaries such as Le Jau also provided evidence that contradicted Garden's for the benevolent character of southern slavery. Across the lowcountry, slaves were expected to devote their Sundays to cultivating gardens that produced a significant portion of their diets. See Klingberg, *Carolina Chronicle,* 54.

118. Jackson, "Hugh Bryan," 611.

119. William V. Davis, *George Whitefield's Journals*, 380–81.

120. The tract was published anonymously, but Steven J. Stein makes a convincing case for Whitefield's authorship of it. See "George Whitefield on Slavery," 254–55.

121. Ibid., 245.

122. On Davies, see George William Pilcher, *Samuel Davies: Apostle of Dissent in Colonial Virginia* (Knoxville: University of Tennessee Press, 1971); Mechal Sobel, *The World They Made Together: Black and White Values in Eighteenth-Century Virginia* (Princeton, N.J.: Princeton University Press, 1987), chap. 14; and Calhoon, *Evangelicals and Conservatives*. On the transatlantic dimensions of eighteenth-century Christianity, see Mark A. Noll, David W. Bebbington, and George A. Rawlyk, *Evangelicalism: Comparative Studies of Popular Protestantism in North America, the British Isles, and Beyond, 1700–1900* (New York: Oxford University Press, 1994).

123. Donald G. Mathews, *Slavery and Methodism: A Chapter in American Morality, 1780–1845* (Princeton, N.J.: Princeton University Press, 1965), chap. 1; Cynthia Lynn Lyerly, *Methodism and the Southern Mind, 1770–1810* (New York: Oxford University Press, 1998), 122–24.

124. Alan Gallay, "The Origins of Slaveholders' Paternalism: George Whitefield, the Bryan Family, and the Great Awakening in the South," *Journal of Southern History* 53 (August 1987): 389. Bolzius, for his part, continued to oppose slavery in Georgia until the trustees changed their policy, a position that he acknowledged placed him in a tiny and unpopular minority of the colony's population. Once slavery became legal, however, Bolzius made his peace with it. See Young, *Domesticating Slavery*, 22; and Klaus G. Loewald, Beverly Starika, and Paul S. Taylor, eds., "Johann Martin Bolzius Answers a Questionnaire on Carolina and Georgia," *William and Mary Quarterly*, 3rd ser., 14 (April 1957): 220. On the Salzburger experience in Georgia, see P. A. Strobel, *The Sazlburgers and Their Descendents: Being a History of a Colony of German (Lutheran) Protestants . . .* (Baltimore: T. N. Kurtz, 1855); and George Fenwick Jones, *The Salzburger Saga: Religious Exiles and Other Germans along the Savannah* (Athens: University of Georgia Press, 1984).

125. Gallay, "Origins of Slaveholders' Paternalism," 372. The increasing significance attached by scholars to proslavery Christian theology is best seen in the works of Genovese and Fox-Genovese. Genovese's early works such as *The Political Economy of Slavery* commented hardly at all on the religious origins of the slaveholders' worldview. More recently, however, Genovese and Fox-Genovese have organized their interpretation of the slaveholders' worldview around religious sources. See Genovese, *A Consuming Fire: The Fall of the Confederacy in the Mind of the White Christian South* (Athens: University of Georgia Press, 1998); Genovese, *Slaveholders' Dilemma;* Genovese and Fox-Genovese, "The Religious Ideals of Southern Slave Society," *Georgia Historical Quarterly* 70 (Spring 1986): 1–16; and Genovese, *"Slavery Ordained of God": The Southern Slaveholders' View of Biblical History and Modern Politics* (Gettysburg: Gettysburg College, 1985).

126. Gallay, "Origins of Slaveholders' Paternalism," 371–72. Gallay maintained that James Oakes, in his desire to downplay the significance of paternalistic defenses of slavery, mistakenly marshaled James Habersham's life as evidence that racism precluded organic conceptions of the biracial plantation relationships.

127. *The Letters of Hon. James Habersham, 1756–1775* (Savannah: Savannah Morning News Print, 1904), 100, 242, 241.

128. Young, *Domesticating Slavery,* 46.

129. *Letters of Hon. James Habersham,* 39.

130. Ibid., 50; Henry Laurens to James Grant, November 1, 1765, in George C. Rogers et al., eds., *The Papers of Henry Laurens,* vol. 5, (Columbia: University of South Carolina Press, 1976), 40. In Laurens's case, the mob had invaded his house and threatened him with violence for allegedly holding the stamped papers in his possession. Significantly, each man registered his complaints to high-ranking imperial administrators. Habersham was corresponding with William Knox, the colonial agent for Georgia whom I discuss below. Laurens was writing to his friend James Grant, the royal governor of East Florida.

131. Gregory D. Massey, *John Laurens and the American Revolution* (Columbia: University of South Carolina Press, 2000), 18.

132. For Laurens, see ibid.; Robert Olwell, "'A Reckoning of Accounts': Patriarchy, Market Relations, and Control on Henry Laurens Lowcountry Plantations, 1762–1785," in *Working toward Freedom: Slave Society and Domestic Economy in the American South,* ed. Larry E. Hudson Jr., 33–52 (Rochester, N.Y.: University of Rochester Press, 1994). For Habersham, see *Letters of Hon. James Habersham.*

133. For Knox's role as an imperial administrator, see Theodore Draper, *A Struggle for Power: The American Revolution* (New York: Times Books, 1996), 217, 287, 308–10, 350–51.

134. In perhaps the most famous Tory quip to this effect, Samuel Johnson asked, "How is it that we hear the loudest yelps for liberty among the drivers of negroes?" Quoted in Jack P. Greene, "Slavery or Independence: Some Reflections on the Relationship among Liberty, Black Bondage, and Equality in Revolutionary South Carolina," *South Carolina Historical Magazine* 80 ( July 1980): 193–94.

135. Bernard Bailyn, *Ideological Origins of the American Revolution* (Cambridge, Mass.: Belknap Press, 1967); Greene, "Slavery or Independence"; and Robert M. Weir, "'The Harmony We Were Famous For': An Interpretation of Pre-Revolutionary South Carolina Politics," *William and Mary Quarterly* 3rd ser., 26 (October 1969): 473–501.

136. In recent years historians of the American North have demonstrated the decidedly piecemeal and gradual character of the northern states' disassociation with slavery. See Arthur Zilversmit, *The First Emancipation: The Abolition of Slavery in the North* (Chicago: University of Chicago Press, 1967); Shane White, *Somewhat More Independent: The End of Slavery in New York City, 1770–1810* (Athens: University of Georgia Press, 1991); Gary B. Nash and Jean R. Soderlund, *Freedom by Degrees: Emancipation in Pennsylvania and Its Aftermath* (New York: Oxford University Press, 1991). Still, as David Brion Davis has illustrated, this antislavery movement, however retarded in its implementation, nonetheless constituted the most radical political opposition to slavery in human history and paved the way to the institution's wholesale demise in the Western Hemisphere. *Problem of Slavery in the Age of Revolution.*

137. For Henry's recognition of slavery as a "lamentable evil" that contradicted the "rights of humanity" as "defined and understood in a country above all others fond of liberty," see Bailyn, *Ideological Origins,* 236. Merrill D. Peterson, ed., *Jefferson: Writings* (New York: Viking Press, 1984), 22.

138. Bailyn, *Ideological Origins,* 236.

139. Kenneth S. Greenberg, "Revolutionary Ideology and the Proslavery Argument: The Abolition of Slavery in Antebellum South Carolina," *Journal of Southern History* 42 (August

1976): 365–84; and Robert McColley, *Slavery and Jeffersonian Virginia* (Urbana: University of Illinois Press, 1964).

140. Patricia Bradley, *Slavery, Propaganda, and the American Revolution* ( Jackson: University Press of Mississippi, 1998).

141. Robert Olwell, "'Domestick Enemies': Slavery and Political Independence in South Carolina, May 1775–March 1776," *Journal of Southern History* 55 (February 1989): 21–48; Sylvia R. Frey, *Water from the Rock: Black Resistance in a Revolutionary Age* (Princeton, N.J.: Princeton University Press, 1991), chap. 2; and Woody Holton, *Forced Founders: Indians, Debtors, Slaves and the Making of the American Revolution in Virginia* (Chapel Hill: University of North Carolina Press, 1999).

142. However, at least a few colonial newspapers published pieces condemning the British recruitment of African American slaves, and these works sometimes expressed proslavery assumptions about the relatively favorable treatment of slaves by their American masters. Bradley, *Slavery,* chap. 7.

143. For the charge that the Anglican Church had become a vehicle for British tyranny over the colonies, see Patricia U. Bonomi, *Under the Cope of Heaven: Religion, Society, and Politics in Colonial America* (New York: Oxford University Press, 1986), chap. 7.

144. Anne Y. Zimmer, *Jonathan Boucher: Loyalist in Exile* (Detroit: Wayne State University Press, 1978), 57.

145. Ibid., 49, 297.

146. Ibid., 191–92.

147. Ibid., 295–98. Jonathan Boucher espoused these views in two major publications: *Reminiscences of an American Loyalist, 1738–1789* (repr., Boston: Houghton Mifflin, 1925); and *A View of the Causes and Consequences of the American Revolution; in Thirteen Discourse, Preached in North America between the Years 1763 and 1775* (London: G. G. and J. Robinson, 1797). By the end of the eighteenth century, Boucher did come to concede the moral problems of slavery in terms of its economic inefficiency and negative impact on the slaveholders' morals. But even then, he insisted that the institution could offer positive benefits to the slaves themselves.

148. Willie Lee Rose, "The Domestication of Domestic Slavery," in *Slavery and Freedom,* ed. William W. Freehling, 18–36 (New York: Oxford University Press, 1982), quotation 21. For more detailed analysis of the swirling relationship between revolutionary ideals and notions of slavery, see Duncan J. MacLeod, *Slavery, Race and the American Revolution* (London: Cambridge University Press, 1974).

149. Thomas Jefferson, *Notes on the State of Virginia,* in Peterson, *Jefferson: Writings,* 288–89.

150. Ibid., 264–65.

151. P. J. Staudenraus, *The African Colonization Movement, 1816–1865* (New York: Columbia University Press, 1961).

152. Thomas Jefferson to Edward Coles, August 25, 1814, in Peterson, *Jefferson: Writings,* 1346.

153. Thomas Jefferson to Thomas Cooper, September 10, 1814, in the Thomas Jefferson Papers, series 1, General Correspondence, Library of Congress, Online Collections in American Memory, http://www.loc.gov/rr/mss/ammem.html.

154. Mathews, *Slavery and Methodism,* chap. 1, (quotation) 20; Lyerly, *Methodism and the Southern Mind,* chap. 6.

155. Douglas Ambrose, "Of Stations and Relations: Proslavery Christianity in Early National Virginia," in *Religion and the Antebellum Debate over Slavery,* John R. McKivigan and Mitchell Snay, 35–67 (Athens: University of Georgia Press, 1998).

156. Devereux Jarratt, *Thoughts on Some Important Subjects in Divinity; in a Series of Letters to a Friend* (Baltimore: Warner and Hanna, 1806), 76–77; Ambrose, "Of Stations and Relations," 42.

157. Henry Pattillo, *The Plain Planter's Family Assistant* ( Wilmington, 1787); and William Graham, "Lecture 30: An Important Question Answered," Special Collections, Washington and Lee University, Lexington, Va. Reproduced in chapter 8 of this volume.

158. Pattillo, *Plain Planter's Family Assistant,* 22–23. For evidence of these trends in the Lower South, see Young, *Domesticating Slavery,* chap. 3.

159. Edmund Botsford, *Sambo and Toney: A Dialogue in Three* Parts (Georgetown, S.C.: Francis M. Baxter, 1808); and the "Dialogue" in *Sermons Addressed to Masters and Servants,* ed. William Meade, 140–56 ( Winchester, Va.: John Heiskell, ca. 1813). For the possibility that whites could be swayed toward Christianity by the positive example of slaves, see Young, *Domesticating Slavery,* chap. 4.

160. Max Farrand, ed., *The Records of the Federal Convention of 1787* (New Haven, Conn.: Yale University Press, 1937), 2:371.

161. Young, *Domesticating Slavery,* 111, 127. Historians have traditionally characterized the early national South as "unawakened" to the political uses of proslavery rhetoric. See, for example, Charles S. Sydnor, *The Development of Southern Sectionalism, 1819–1848* (Baton Rouge: Louisiana State University Press, 1948), chaps. 1–4.

162. Donald Robinson, *Slavery in the Structure of American Politics* (New York: Norton, 1979), 306–10.

163. Young, *Domesticating Slavery,* 95, 127.

164. *Annals of Congress,* 1820, pp. 259–78. The speech is reproduced in chapter 11 of this volume.

165. "Forum: The Making of a Slave Conspiracy, Part One," *William and Mary Quarterly,* 3rd ser., 58 (October 2001): 913–76; "Forum: The Making of a Slave Conspiracy, Part Two," *William and Mary Quarterly,* 3rd ser., 59 ( January 2002): 135–202.

166. Freehling, *Prelude to Civil War.*

167. Young, *Domesticating Slavery,* 168; Whitemarsh B. Seabrook, *A Concise View of the Critical Situation, and Future Prospects of the Slave-Holding States, in Relation to Their Coloured Population* (Charleston, S.C.: A. E. Miller, 1825), 10.

168. Young, *Domesticating Slavery,* 172–73; Daniel W. Stowell, ed., *Balancing Evils Judiciously: The Proslavery Writings of Zephaniah Kingsley* (Gainesville: University Press of Florida, 2000).

# CHAPTER I

# George Whitefield, 1740

THE FORMAL DEFENSE OF SLAVERY in the South first emerged under the shadow of a religious controversy stretching from England to America. In the late 1730s the Anglican minister George Whitefield traveled across the Western world and sparked a series of revivals that would forever reshape the Christian faith. His ministry revolved around the concept of the "New Birth"—the notion that worshippers needed to make a conscious decision to embrace God emotionally and spiritually. By the early 1740s Whitefield had established himself as the most famous revivalist in an era of "Great Awakening." Preaching to enormous crowds on both sides of the Atlantic, the charismatic preacher forged an international network of supporters that effectively publicized his sermons and promoted his doctrines. Along the way, however, Whitefield antagonized Anglican authorities who viewed his unorthodox style as a threat to religious order. Some Anglican churches went so far as to deny their pulpits to Whitefield when he passed through their communities.

The American South played a prominent role in this story of religious fervor and animosity. Whitefield had journeyed to Georgia in 1738. There he established an orphanage (at Bethesda) that became the focus of global fund-raising efforts. In many ways, Whitefield's philanthropic project in Georgia served as the focal point for his entire religious empire. The crowds that flocked to hear his preaching in cities like Philadelphia heard descriptions of the good works taking place in the Deep South and were encouraged to donate a portion of their own earnings to maintain the philanthropic campaign. To prick the conscience of the Western world, Whitefield elevated the Georgia experiment into the perfect symbol of humankind's ability to fulfill God's mandate for a caring society. Of course, as Whitefield's activities integrated the American South into a global religious dynamic, they also exposed the slaveholders to uncomfortable scrutiny.[1]

Like other Christian authorities, Whitefield did not reject slavery in the abstract; he merely wanted to Christianize the institution so that it would reflect church teachings about reciprocity. When the Georgia trustees initially outlawed slavery in the new colony, Whitefield sided with the proslavery faction seeking to overturn the stricture.[2] But Whitefield was appalled by the southern slaveholders' utter disregard for the humanity of their bondservants. In January 1740 he pub-lished his criticisms of the slaveholders in an open letter to the residents of Mary-land, Virginia, North Carolina, and South Carolina. Whitefield accused the slaveholders of working the slaves "as hard if not harder than the Horses whereon you ride" and described the sadistic punishments meted out by some inhumane masters. Although Whitefield claimed that he "heartily" prayed that the slaves would "never be permitted to get the upper Hand," he asserted that "should such a Thing be permitted by Providence, all good Men must acknowledge the Judg-ment would be just" given the mistreatment of the slaves by their southern own-ers.[3] Such commentary came dangerously close to an endorsement of revolutionary violence, and Whitefield could hardly have been surprised by the slaveholders' outraged response.

Still, Whitefield's letter did not advance an attack against slavery in the ab-stract. Instead, he offered reasoning that he hoped would convince the slavehold-ers of their slaves' capacity to be improved by Christian teachings. Affirming that Christianity required slaves to "be subject in all lawful Things, to their Masters," he likened African Americans to the slaveholders' own white children in terms of their capacity for moral growth.[4] This devastating attack against the slaveholders therefore gave voice to the central assumptions of Christian proslavery ideology. Far from advocating abolition, Whitefield wanted American slavery to become an organic institution that accorded with scriptural accounts of the master-slave rela-tionship. Elite members of South Carolina society, however, did not recognize this proslavery thrust to Whitefield's thought.

GEORGE WHITEFIELD, *Three Letters from the Reverend Mr. G.Whitefield: viz. . . . Letter III. To the Inhabitants of Maryland,Virginia, North and South-Carolina, Concerning Their Negroes* (Philadelphia: B. Franklin, 1740)[5]

As I lately passed through your Provinces in my Way hither, I was sensible touched with a Fellow-feeling of the Miseries of the poor Negroes. Could I have preached more frequently amongst you, I should have delivered my Thoughts in my publick Discourses; but as my Business here required me to stop as little as possible on the Road, I have no other Way to discharge the Concern which at present lies upon my Heart, than by sending you this Letter: How you will receive it I know not; whether you will accept it in Love, or be offended with me, as the Master of the Damsel was with *Paul,* for casting the Evil Spirit out of her, when he saw the Hope of his Gain was gone; I am uncertain.[6] Whatever be the Event, I must inform you in the Meekness and Gentleness of *Christ,* that I think God has a Quarrel with you for your Abuse of and Cruelty to the poor Negroes. Whether it be lawful for Christians to buy Slaves, and thereby encourage the Nations from whom they are bought, to be at perpetual War with each other, I shall not take upon me to determine; sure I am, it is sinful, when bought, to use them as bad, nay worse, than as though they were Brutes; and whatever particular Exceptions there may be (as I would charitably hope there are some) I fear the Generality of you that own Negroes, are liable to such a Charge; for your Slaves, I believe, work as hard if not harder than the Horses whereon you ride.

These, after they have done their Work, are fed and taken proper Care of; but many Negroes when wearied with Labour in your Plantations, have been obliged to grind their own Corn after they return home.

Your Dogs are caress'd and fondled at your Tables: But your Slaves, who are frequently stiled Dogs or Beasts, have not an equal Privilege. They are scarce permitted to pick up the Crumbs which fall from their Masters' Tables. Nay, some, as I have been informed by an Eye-Witness, have been, upon the most trifling Provocation, cut with Knives, and had Forks thrown into their Flesh—Not to mention what Numbers have been given up to the inhuman Usage of cruel Task Masters, who by their unrelenting Scourges have ploughed upon their Backs, and made long Furrows, and at length brought them even to Death itself.

It's true, I hope there are but few such Monsters of Barbarity suffered to subsist amongst you. Some, I hear, have been lately executed in *Virginia* for killing Slaves, and the Laws are very severe against such who at any Time murder them.[7]

And perhaps it might be better for the poor Creatures themselves, to be hurried out of Life, than to be made so miserable, as they generally are in it. And indeed, considering what Usage they commonly meet with, I have wondered, that we have not more Instances of Self-Murder among the Negroes, or that they have not more frequently rose up in Arms against their Owners. *Virginia* has once, and *Charlestown* more than once been threatened in this Way.[8]

And tho' I heartily pray God they may never be permitted to get the upper Hand; yet should such a Thing be permitted by Providence, all good Men must acknowledge the Judgment would be just.—For is it not the highest Ingratitude, as well as Cruelty, not to let your poor Slaves enjoy some Fruits of their Labour?

When, passing along, I have viewed your Plantations cleared and cultivated, many spacious Houses built, and the Owners of them faring sumptuously every Day, my Blood has frequently almost run cold within me, to consider how many of your Slaves had neither convenient Food to eat or proper Raiment to put on, notwithstanding most of the Comforts you enjoy were solely owing to their indefatigable Labours.—The Scripture says, *Thou should not muzzle the Ox that treadeth out the Corn.*[9] Does God take Care of Oxen? And will he not take care of the Negroes also? Undoubtedly he will.—*Go to now, ye rich Men, weep and howl for your*

*Miseries that shall come upon you!*[10] Behold the Provision of the poor Negroes, which have reaped down your Fields, which is by you denied them, crieth; and the Cries of them which reaped, are entered into the Ears of the Lord of *Sabaoth!*[11] We have a remarkable Instance of God's taking cognizance of, and avenging the Quarrel of poor Slaves, *2 Sam. 21. 1.* "*Then there was a Famine in the Days of David, three Years, Year after Year; and David enquired of the Lord. And the Lord answered, it is for Saul and his bloody House, because he slew the Gibeonites.*"—Two Things are here very remarkable.—First, that these *Gibeonites* were only Hewers of Wood and Drawers of Water, or in other Words, Slaves like yours. Secondly, That this Plague was sent by God many Years after the Injury, the Cause of the Plague, was committed.[12]—And for what End was this and such like Examples recorded in Holy Scripture? Without doubt, for our Learning, upon whom the Ends of the World are come—For God is the same Today as he was Yesterday; and will continue the same forever. He does not reject the Prayer of the poor and destitute, nor disregard the Cry of the meanest Negroes! The Blood of them spilt for these many Years in your respective Provinces, will ascend up to Heaven against you. I wish I could say, it would speak better Things than the Blood of *Abel.*[13] But this is not all—Enslaving or misusing their Bodies, would, comparatively speaking, be an inconsiderable Evil, was proper Care taken of their Souls. But I have great reason to believe, that most of you, on Purpose, keep your Negroes ignorant of Christianity; or otherwise, why are they permitted thro' your Provinces, openly to prophane the Lord's Day, by their Dancing, Piping and such like? I know the general Pretence for this Neglect of their Souls is, That teaching them Christianity would make them proud, and consequently unwilling to submit to Slavery: But what a dreadful Reflection is this on your Holy Religion? What blasphemous Notions must those that make such an Objection have of the Precepts of Christianity? Do you find any one Command in the Gospel, that has the least Tendency to make People forget their relative Duties? Do you not read that Servants, and as many as are under the Yoke of Bondage, are required to be subject, in all lawful Things, to their Masters; and that not only to the good and gentle, but also to the froward?[14] Nay, may I not appeal to your own Hearts, whether deviating from the Laws of Jesus Christ, is not the Cause of all the Evils and Miseries Mankind now universally groan under, and of all the Vices we find both in ourselves and others? Certainly it is.—And therefore, the Reason why Servants generally prove so bad is, because so little Care is taken to breed them up in the Nurture and Admonition of the Lord.—But some will be so bold perhaps as to reply, *That a few of the Negroes have been taught Christianity, and, notwithstanding, have been remarkably worse than others.*[15] But what Christianity were they taught? They were baptized and taught to read and write: and this they may do, and much more, and yet be far from the Kingdom of God; for there is a vast Difference between civilizing and Christianizing an Negroe. A Black as well

as a white Man may be civilized by outward Restraints, and afterwards break thro'
those Restraints again. But I challenge the whole World to produce a single
Instance of a Negroe's being made a thorough Christian, and thereby made a
worse Servant. It cannot be.—But farther, if teaching Slaves Christianity has such
a bad Influence upon their Lives, why are you generally desirous of having your
Children taught? Think you they are any way better by Nature than the poor
Negroes? No, in no wise. Blacks are just as much, and no more, conceived and
born in Sin, as White Men are. Both, if born and bred up here, I am persuaded,
are naturally capable of the same Improvement.—And as for the grown Negroes,
I am apt to think, whenever the Gospel is preach'd with Power amongst them, that
many will be brought effectually home to God. Your present and past bad Usage
of them, however ill-designed, may thus far do them good, as to break their Wills,
increase the Sense of their natural Misery, and consequently better dispose their
Minds to accept the Redemption wrought out for them, by the Death and Obedience of Jesus Christ. God has, not long since, been pleased to make some of the
Negroes in *New-England,* Vessels of Mercy; and some of them, I hear, have been
brought to cry out, *What shall we do to be saved?* in the Province of *Pennsylvania.*
Doubtless there is a Time, when the Fullness of the Gentiles will come in;[16] And
then I believe, if not before, these despised Slaves will find the Gospel of Christ
to be the Power of God to their Salvation, as well as we.—But I know all Arguments to prove the Necessity of taking Care of your Negroes' Souls, though never
so conclusive, will prove ineffectual, till you are convinced of the Necessity of
securing the Salvation of your own. That you yourselves are not effectually convinced of this, I think is too notorious to want Evidence.—A general Deadness as
to divine Things, and not to say a general Prophaneness, is discernible both in Pastors and People.

Most of you are without any teaching Priest.—And whatever Quantity of Rum
there may be, yet I fear but very few Bibles are annually imported into your different Provinces.—God has already begun to visit for this as well as other wicked
Things.—For near this two Years last past, he has been in a remarkable Manner
contending with the People of *South-Carolina.* Their Houses have been depopu-
lated with the Small Pox and Fever, and their own Slaves have rose up in Arms
against them.[17]—These Judgments are undoubtedly sent abroad, not only that the
Inhabitants of that, but of other Provinces, should learn Righteousness. And unless
you all repent, you all must in like Manner expect to perish.—God first generally corrects us with Whips; if that will not do, he must chastize us with Scorpi-
ons.—A foreign Enemy is now threatning to invade you, and nothing will more
provoke God, to give you up as a Prey into their Teeth, than Impenitence and
Unbelief.[18]—Let these be removed, and the Sons of Violence shall not be able to
hurt you;—No, your Oxen shall be strong to labour; there shall be no Decay of

your People by epidemical Sickness; no Leading away into Captivity from abroad, and no Complaining in your Streets at Home;—Your Sons shall grow up as young Plants, and your Daughters be as the polished Corners of the Temple; and to sum up all Blessings in one,[19]—Then shall the Lord be your God.—That you may be the People who are in such a happy Case, is the earnest Prayer of

Your sincere Well-Wisher and Servant in Christ,

G. Whitefield

Savannah, January 23, 1739,40.[20]

## Notes

1. Robert M. Calhoon, *Evangelicals and Conservatives in the Early South, 1740–1861* (Columbia: University of South Carolina Press, 1988), chap. 1; Harry S. Stout, *The Divine Dramatist: George Whitefield and the Rise of Modern Evangelicalism* (Grand Rapids, Mich.: W. B. Eerdmans, 1991); and Frank Lambert, *Pedlar in Divinity: George Whitefield and the Trans-atlantic Revivals, 1737–1770* (Princeton, N.J.: Princeton University Press, 1994).

2. Alfred O. Aldridge, "George Whitefield's Georgia Controversies," *Journal of Southern History* 9 (August 1943): 357–80; and Allan Gallay, *The Formation of a Planter Elite: Jonathan Bryan and the Southern Colonial Frontier* (Athens, 1989).

3. See page 70.

4. See page 71.

5. I transcribed the edition reproduced in *Early American Imprints*, series 1, no. 4651, pp. 13–16 of the sixteen-page text.

6. Acts 16:16–24. Here the slaveholders' desires for fiscal gain are presented as being in conflict with Christian salvation. The slave damsel in question had been a source of income for her owners because she was possessed by a "spirit of divination" and was therefore able to foresee the future. When Paul freed her from the spirit, her masters bemoaned the loss of income and had Paul imprisoned and beaten.

7. Actually, colonial slave codes and legal practices made it extremely unlikely that any white person would face prosecution let alone execution for murdering a slave. Of course, the legal codes dealing with slavery varied considerably from colony to colony and also changed over time. See Thomas D. Morris, *Southern Slavery and the Law, 1619–1860* (Chapel Hill: University of North Carolina Press, 1996), 165–71; Robert Olwell, *Masters, Slaves, and Subjects: The Culture of Power in the South Carolina Low Country, 1740–1790* (Ithaca, N.Y.: Cornell University Press, 1998), 62; Philip D. Morgan, *Slave Counterpoint: Black Culture in the Eighteenth-Century Chesapeake and Lowcountry* (Chapel Hill: University of North Carolina Press, 1998), 262–96.

8. Slaves committed suicide with enough frequency for some African groups to be considered at higher risk for this act. See Daniel C. Littlefield, *Rice and Slaves: Ethnicity and the Slave Trade in Colonial South Carolina* (Baton Rouge: Louisiana State University Press, 1981), 10–15.

9. 1 Corinthians 9:9.

10. James 5:1.

11. This sentence closely follows James 5:4.

12. The punishment for this abuse of power by a master was considerable. Moreover, it was ultimately directed at Saul's offspring because Saul was already deceased. Seven of his sons were "flung . . . from the mountain" to their deaths. As such, the episode presented to American slaveholders a dire warning as to the repercussions attending any disregard for their responsibilities as masters. 2 Samuel 21:1–9.

13. Genesis 4:10. After Cain murdered his brother Abel, Abel's blood cried out to God from the ground onto which it had been spilled.

14. 1 Peter 2:18.

15. The assumption that Christian slaves were more prone to resist white authority might have been reinforced by the Stono Slave Rebellion of 1739 (discussed in note 16 below). Many of these rebellious slaves were from Kongo—a kingdom that embraced Catholicism in the late fifteenth and sixteenth centuries—and likely identified themselves as Christians. See John K. Thornton, "On the Trail of Voodoo: African Christianity in Africa and the Americas," *The Americas* 44 (January 1988): 261–78; and "African Dimensions of the Stono Rebellion," *American Historical Review* 96 (October 1991): 1101–13.

16. Romans 11:25.

17. For evidence of the smallpox epidemic and for an account of the Stono slave rebellion of 1739, see Peter H. Wood, *Black Majority: Negroes in Colonial South Carolina from 1670 through the Stono Rebellion* (New York: Knopf, 1974), chap. 12. In September 1739 a group of approximately twenty slaves armed themselves and attacked white settlers. Moving south toward Spanish territory, they augmented their strength with additional recruits and managed to kill some twenty white men, women, and children before they were confronted by colonial authorities. In the ensuing battle, the main body of the slave army was defeated; however, a band of slaves managed to escape, and they continued to threaten white authority during the following winter.

18. England and Spain were at war from 1739 to 1742 (the War of Jenkins' Ear). This struggle carried over to their American colonies.

19. Psalms 144:12.

20. The year "1739,40" reflects the lack of agreement in England over when to begin the new calendar year. England's Julian calendar officially designated March 25 as New Year's Day. However, the Roman convention of starting the new year on January 1 remained widely in use in England and the colonies. To minimize confusion, documents and publications reflected both calendar conventions for dates between January 1 and March 25.

# CHAPTER 2

# Alexander Garden, 1740

THE MAN WHO STEPPED FORWARD to rebuke George Whitefield was the Anglican Church's foremost authority in the region. Alexander Garden arrived in South Carolina in 1720 and immediately rose to a position of religious leadership. By the middle of the decade, Garden was actively working to discipline clergymen who lapsed into vice. In 1728 Bishop Edmund Gibson appointed him commissary for the Carolinas. When Whitefield passed through the South in 1740, he found entrenched church authorities ready to confront him for deviating from (and criticizing) Anglican policies. Garden's assistant denied Whitefield access to the pulpit in St. Philip's Church, leading to a personal showdown between Garden and Whitefield in March of that year. After Whitefield dared to call Garden "ignorant" about crucial theological issues and promised to defy his authority, Garden kicked Whitefield out of his home (where the meeting took place). Garden believed that his office required him to guard "the People of my Charge against the fascinating gibberish" preached by Whitefield. Toward this end, Garden published a series of letters challenging Whitefield's theology. One of these letters specifically engaged Whitefield's remarks about slavery.[1]

Garden rejected Whitefield's charges of widespread slave abuse. The Anglican commissary insisted that southern masters treated their bondservants with humanity. The irony of this proslavery tract was that its author was attacking a man who actually harbored almost identical views about Christianity and slavery. Both men wanted to Christianize plantation slavery rather than abolish it. And Garden himself conceded in his publication that southern slaveholders had not exposed their slaves to Christian teachings. Unlike Whitefield, however, Garden denied that the slaveholders were actively opposed to opening their plantations to Christianity. Over the next fourteen years, Garden managed to open a school in Charleston for educating local slaves. But to his disappointment, the slaveholding elite never warmed to the plan, and the colonial period closed without any major shift in the slaveholders' attitude toward organic Christian thought. In life, Whitefield and Garden remained bitter enemies (with Garden taking the step to suspend Whitefield from his Anglican office in 1742). Yet their intellectual legacies are intertwined. Both worked tirelessly yet fruitlessly to make their organic proslavery creed the defining principle of the plantation South.

A~3@C~

Alexander Garden, *Six Letters to the Rev. Mr. George Whitefield. . . . The Sixth, Containing Remarks on Mr. Whitefield's . . . Letter Concerning the Negroes* (Boston: T. Fleet, 1740)[2]

In my humble Opinion, Sir, had you caused another *Edition* to be printed at *Philadelphia,* of the *Bishop of London's Letter to the Masters and Mistresses of Slaves* in these Parts, and dispersed the Copies on your Way, as you came through the several Provinces, you had done much more effectual Service, than by the Publication of your own.[3] But if you knew of any such Letter of his *Lordship's* being extant, I suppose you'll plead a special Call for the Publication of your own, and that answers all Objections.

*You must inform them* (the Inhabitants of *Maryland, &c.*) you say, *in the Meekness and Gentleness of Christ,* &c. the *Invective* is so apparent throughout this notable Epistle, that these can only be taken for some *Cant-Terms* you accustom yourself to in all your Scriblings. But what is it you must thus *inform* them of? Why, *that you* THINK *God has a Quarrel with them, &c.* Had God sent you charged with this *special Message* you might well say, that you must inform them of it; but as 'tis only a Matter of your own *Thoughts,* the *Necessity* does not so well appear. Your *Thoughts* in the Case may possibly be idle or ill grounded, and so better kept at Home. But God, you THINK has a Quarrel with them, and *for their Abuse of and Cruelty to the poor Negroes.* That God will have a *Quarrel* with any of the Human Race, for their *Abuse* of and *Cruelty* to others, is a very just Thought; and sinful out of all Doubt it is, for any of those Inhabitants *to use their Negroes as bad, nay worse, than as though they were Brutes.* But pray, Sir, on what Grounds do you bring *this Charge* against *the Generality* of those Inhabitants who own Negroes, of *using them as bad, nay worse, than as tho' they were Brutes?* Do you *know* this Charge to be just and honest? Or have you sufficient *Evidence* to support it? No; you only *think* it to be so, and *fear* it, and *believe* it. But on the contrary, I shall presume, and on much better Grounds, to *think, fear,* and *believe,* that your Charge is false and injurious! and that the very Reverse of it is true, *viz.* that what particular Exceptions soever there may be as to *good Usage* of Slaves (as some doubtless there are) yet that the *Generality* of Owners use their Slaves with all due Humanity, whether in respect of *Work,* of *Food,* or *Raiment.* And therefore I farther *think* and *believe,* that the *Generality* of Owners of Slaves in the respective Colonies, may bring their Actions of *Slander* against you; and that in a certain Country I know, you wou'd be *indicted* for meddling, as you have done in this Matter, which may endanger the Peace and Safety of the Community.

Hitherto we have only your *Thoughts,* your *Fears,* and your *Belief,* on the Matter; you advance a pace into *positive* Assertions. *And perhaps,* you say, *it might be better for the poor Creatures themselves to be hurried out of Life, than to be made* so miserable, *as* they generally *are in it. And indeed, considering what Usage they commonly meet with, &c.*—I suppress the remainder of this, and the next following *Paragraph* of your Epistle, as judging it both sinful, and dangerous to the publick Safety to reprint them. More Virulence and Falshood cannot be contained in so few Lines. For so far are the generality of Slaves in these Colonies, from being miserable, that I dare confidently vouch and affirm, and partly on my own Knowledge, that their Lives in general are more happy and comfortable in all temporal Respects (the Point of Liberty only excepted) than the Lives of three fourths of the hired *farming* Servants, and Day Labourers, either in *Scotland, Ireland,* or even many Parts of *England,* who not only labour *harder,* and fare *worse,* but have moreover the Care and Concern on their Minds how to provide for their Families; which *Slaves* are entirely exempted from, their Children being all provided for at the *Owner's* Charge.

Now, Sir, if this be really the Case with respect to the *generality* of Slaves in these Colonies, which can fully be proved it is; what *Apology* can suffice either for the Matter or Manner of your Letter, specially the two modest *Paragraphs* above mentioned? Will you plead *Hearsay* or *Report?* Alas, Sir, this Plea will never do! I have heard by *Report,* of your *Abuse and Cruelty* to the poor *Orphans* under your Care; not only in *Pinching* their Bellies, but giving them up also to Task-Masters or Mistresses, *who plow upon their Backs, and make long Furrows,* in a very inhuman Manner. And would you think it a fair and honest Thing in me, should I, on such *Hearsay* or *Report,* print and publish a *Letter* directed to you, pretending a Necessity of *informing* you, that *God had a Quarrel with you, for your Cruelty to the poor* Orphans;—that *perhaps they had better be hurried out of Life, than be made so miserable as they are in it;*—and that *I wondered, they did not either put an End to their own Lives or Yours, rather than bear such Usage:* Would you think this, I say, a fair and honest Proceeding in me, and not rather foul and injurious, and having no good Meaning, either towards *yourself* or the *Orphans?* And tho' it came prefaced *in the Meekness and Gentleness of Christ,* would you not regard it rather as a Burlesque of the Words?[4] No, Sir, I know there must be a due *Discipline,* or Rod of Correction exercis'd among Children; and this may be, and often is misrepresented for Cruelty and bad Usage. I know also, that like Discipline and Correction must be observed among every Parcel of Slaves; and which in like Manner, may be, and often is misrepresented in the same Light: And therefore no such Reports, in either Case, can justify a direct Accusation.

As to the little or no *proper Care taken by* Owners *of the Souls* of their *Slaves,* it is too sad a Truth; and I tremble to think, what Account they will give of it at the great Day! A sore Evil indeed! But for which, your Letter, I conceive, will afford but a poor Remedy. I cannot think so ill of *any,* as you do of *most* of them, *viz.* that *on Purpose,* they keep their Slaves ignorant of Christianity. I believe the Reason of their being so kept, is the want of one certain uniform Method of teaching them, and which I hope will soon be established with Success. I readily agree, that the Objection to teaching them Christianity, *viz.* that it would tend to make them less governable, or worse Slaves, is wild and extravagant: But wish you had a little explained, what you mean by the Phrases, *Christianizing;*—and MADE *thorough Christians;*—and *the Gospel preach'd with Power;*—whether, by these Phrases, you mean Things in the Power of Men? For sure I am, *that* Paul *may plant, and* Apollos *may water, but God Alone can give the Encrease.*[5] Men may teach *true Christianity,* but no Man can MAKE a *true Christian.*

Your Complement on *Pastors* and *People,* and apprehended Difference 'twixt the Importation of *Rum* and *Bibles,* are no *Exceptions* to the usual Stile, Modesty, or Manners of your Epistles, and particularly of this under Consideration, which I have now done with, and remain,

*Sir, Your very humble Servant,*

Alex. Garden.

*Charlestown, July 30th. 1740.*

Notes

1. S. Charles Bolton, *Southern Anglicanism: The Church of England in Colonial South Carolina* (Westport, Conn.: Greenwood Press, 1982); and Robert M. Calhoon, *Evangelicals and Conservatives in the Early South, 1740–1861* (Columbia: University of South Carolina Press, 1988), chap. 1.

2. I transcribed the edition reproduced in *Early American Imprints,* series 1, no. 4515, pp. 50–54 of the fifty-four-page tract.

3. Garden was referring to Edmund Gibson, *A Letter of the Lord Bishop of London to the Masters and Mistresses of Families in the English Plantations Abroad; Exhorting Them to Encourage and Promote the Instruction of Their Negroes in the Christian Faith* (London, 1727).

4. Whitefield's enemies did, in fact, circulate reports that the Bethesda orphans were being subjected to physical abuse. Stuart C. Henry, *George Whitefield: Wayfaring Witness* (New York: Abingdon Press, 1957), 149–50.

5. 1 Cor. 3:6.

# CHAPTER 3

# Thomas Bacon, 1749

THOMAS BACON'S BACKGROUND AND ACHIEVEMENTS were, in many ways, typical of the Anglican ministers who journeyed to the New World in the eighteenth century. Bacon was born ca. 1700 on the Isle of Man and came to intellectual maturity in Dublin (where he published his first work, a study of the English revenue system). After his ordination as a priest in 1745, he traveled to Maryland, and in 1746 he became rector of St. Peter's Parish in Talbot County. Soon after his arrival, Bacon began to concern himself with the religious education of the Maryland slave population. As early as 1749 he published several sermons that pushed for the inclusion of African Americans in church life. Over the next few years, Bacon published tracts pursuing this same theme. According to Bacon, masters and slaves owed responsibilities to each other and to God. At times the minister lectured the slaveholders about the benefits of extending religion to the slaves; in other instances he warned the slaveholders of the grave consequences awaiting them if they failed to fulfill their duties.[1]

Like Alexander Garden, Thomas Bacon attempted to open a school for the instruction of African Americans. The Anglican organization the Associates of Dr. Bray authorized the venture and sent Bacon schoolbooks in 1761. Maryland residents, however, did not appear to share the organization's enthusiasm for this project, and the school never opened. His contemporaries remarked favorably on his "sober" personality and his immense learning. Yet Bacon's greatest intellectual achievements were not creative endeavors. He was perhaps best known for compiling, over a period of seven years, Maryland's laws and publishing them in 1765, just three years before his death.

To make sense of Bacon's proslavery pronouncements, then, one need not search for any exceptional attributes on the part of this Maryland minister. Hierarchical conceptions of the moral universe had long since been articulated by Christian authorities, and (as we have seen) early-eighteenth-century Anglican figures such as the bishop of London had already pronounced the need to reform the master-slave relationship in the New World. Bacon's sermons presented an extended case on behalf of Christian proslavery logic—a mentality that had already taken root among the Anglican missionaries in the American South before the middle of the century. Bacon's cosmopolitan outlook made him a logical candidate for the pursuit of this reform, and his published sermons reveal that he possessed sufficient intellect for the challenge. As Bacon extended Christian teachings to the Maryland slave population, he obviously took great pains to articulate religious principles that upheld the earthly authority of masters over slaves. Like Garden and Whitefield before him, Bacon was seeking to reassure those slaveholders harboring, in his words, "groundless Jealousies about the Instruction of Slaves." Toward this end, Bacon emphasized the organic ties between the powerful and the weak, the rich and the poor, the white master and the black slave, all fulfilling the responsibilities associated with the particular station in life assigned to them by God.

Thomas Bacon, *Two Sermons, Preached to a Congregation of Black Slaves at the Parish Church of S. P. in the Province of Maryland* (London: John Oliver, 1749)[2]

Matt. XI.5.

—And the Poor have the Gospel preached to them.

To the Inhabitants of the Parish of [Saint Peter's] in the Province of Maryland.
My kind Neighbours, and Parishioners,
The two following Discourses, which had your general Approbation at the Time of Delivery, are now published, just as you heard them, for the following Reasons.

I.   That as many as had desired to borrow my Notes, either to refresh their Memories, or to take a Copy of them, might be furnished with them in an easier Manner.

II.   That such pious and well-disposed Persons, as are inclined to join with me in the necessary Work of bringing up their Slaves in the Knowledge of God (by giving them private Instruction, as well as sending them to be taught at Church) may receive some Assistance from the Heads, the Method, or the Hints herein laid down; the Whole being intended to take in a general View of a Christian Slave's Duty.

III. That such among you as have conceived groundless Jealousies about the Instruction of Slaves, may see plainly what Sort of Doctrines I do intend to teach them; the following Discourses being, as it were, the original Draught, or Foundation of all my future ones, which (excepting a few upon the first Principles of Christianity) will, for the most Part, be only larger Explanations of those practical Duties, which are little more than hinted here, and need often repeating, and much insisting upon, to such poor ignorant Creatures as they are well known to be at present.—I mention this Reason more particularly, because at the Conclusion of each Sermon, when you were retired into the Church-yard, your general Remark was,—"If these poor Creatures would but mind, and do as the Minister has told them Today, they would make *excellent* slaves."

IV.   That such as have made Objections to, and misrepresented some Passages in the following Discourses, upon Notions taken up at second Hand[3] . . . be convinced, that [there] is nothing so dangerous or impolitic in attempting to make good Christians of their Slaves, or in laying the Rewards, as well as the Duties of Religion, before them, as they seem fond of representing it at present.

V.    Because, it is possible, these plain Discourses may fall into other Hands, capable of improving well-meant, though poorly executed, Schemes of this Sort, to the noblest of Purposes;—It may raise a Spirit of Emulation among my Brethren the Clergy, to attempt something, in their respective Parishes, towards the bringing home so great a Number of wandering Souls to Christ; and prevail upon some of the Laity, in our neighbouring Parishes, to join with their Pastors for promoting so salutary an End; especially when they see that the direct Tendency of the Gospel-Doctrine is to make their Negroes the better Servants in Proportion as they become better Christians.

In setting this Scheme, for the better Instruction of the Negroes, on Foot in my Parish, I consulted nothing but Conscience, had no other View than the Discharge of that Duty I so solemnly took upon me at my being admitted into Holy Orders.—May God, of his infinite Mercy, enable me, by the Assistance of his Holy Spirit, to perform it as I ought to do, for yours and my own joint Benefit:—May this Grain of Mustard-seed take deep Root, and spread its Branches far and wide:[4]—May all pious Undertakings, for propagating the Gospel of Christ, and promoting Christian Knowledge at Home and Abroad, prosper under the Hands of the Labourers:—And may you, and I, my dear Parishioners, in our several Stations, so demean ourselves in the midst of a corrupt World, so strive to exalt the Kingdom of God upon Earth, and to promote his Service with our utmost Power and Influence, that after a truly Christian Life spent here, we may meet all together in his Paradise, there to wait for that joyful Resurrection, which shall complete the Happiness of all his Saints, and admit them to the full Enjoyment of that glorious, unspeakable Bliss, which he hath prepared for them from the Foundation of the World, through Jesus Christ our Lord. Amen.

This, my dear, well-beloved Parishioners, is the daily prayer of
Your faithful Pastor
And most affectionate Friend and Servant

## Sermon I.

Ephes. VI. 8.

> Knowing, that whatsoever good Thing any Man doth, the same
> shall he receive of the Lord, whether he be Bond or Free.

When I consider the Station in which the divine Providence hath been pleased to place me, and to how weighty an Office and Charge I am called, as Minister of this Parish;—that I am appointed a *Messenger, Watchman,* and *Steward* of the great Lord of Heaven and Earth, to teach, and to premonish, to feed and provide for the Lord's Family;—to seek for Christ's Sheep that are dispersed Abroad, and for his Children that are in the midst of this wicked World, that they may be saved through Christ for ever:—When I call to mind how great a Treasure is committed to my Charge, even those Sheep which Christ bought with his Death, and for whom he shed his most precious Blood;—and that I am to *watch for their Souls as one that must give Account,** I am struck with an awful Dread, and my Heart trembles within me, lest any one of these precious Souls, for which our Saviour died, should be lost through my Carelessness;—knowing, that if the Church of Christ, or any the least or poorest Member thereof, should take any Hurt or Hindrance by reason of my Negligence, how great a Crime I should have to answer for at the Judgment-Seat of Almighty God,—and how horrible a Punishment would fall upon my guilty Head, when not only my own Sins, which are many, but also the Blood of those unhappy Souls, which perished through my Fault, should be required at my Hands.

These Considerations, my dear Christian Brethren, have long employed my serious Thoughts, and put me upon various Methods of performing this great and important Duty, which I owe to the *poorest Slave,* as well as the *richest* and most *powerful* among my parishioners.—And indeed, in this Province, the Clergy are under a particular temporal Tie, as we are supported by a *Poll Tax,* in which every Slave, above Sixteen Years of Age, is rated as high, and pays as much as the Master he or she belongs to, and, consequently, have an equal Right to Instruction with their Owners.—But though the common Duties of Christianity, as Godliness, Righteousness, and Temperance, do belong to them, as much as to those of a higher Rank;—and though these, with their several Branches, are explained every Lord's Day at Church, whither they may, with their Masters' Leave, resort for Instruction; yet there are other Duties, peculiar to their State of Life, which need a particular Explanation.—Besides, their Ignorance of the first Principles of Religion is generally such, that Discourses, suited to those who are but indifferently acquainted with the Grounds of Christianity, and know but a little of the holy Scriptures, are no way suited to their Capacities and Understandings:—

*Heb. xiii. 7.

And most of them, from their Want of Skill in our Tongue, are not able to reap such Instruction from what they hear, as they would from Discourses framed on Purpose; wherein the Language is lowered as near as possible to their own Level, and the Christian Doctrine stoops, as it were, to meet them.——This I have attempted in *Exhortations,* as Opportunity offered; at their *Funerals* (several of which I have attended)——and to such small Congregations as their *Marriages* have brought together, as well as at my own House, on Sunday, and other Evenings, when those in the Neighbourhood come in.——But these occasional Instructions can reach but to a very few; and much the greatest Number, either from their Distance, which keeps them most Sundays from Church, or their understanding but little of what is said or done when they come there, are deprived of a great Part of the Benefit they might otherwise receive.——These Hindrances might, indeed, be in a great Measure removed, if their *Masters* and *Mistresses* would but take a little Pains with them at Home, by Reading, or causing some easy Portions of the holy Scriptures, particularly the Gospels, to be read to them in an Evening, together with such plain short Tracts, upon the Principles of Christianity, as are easily procured, and of which, Numbers have been distributed in the Parish since my coming into it.—— Some few Heads of Families do, from a Principle of Conscience, take pious Care in these Matters; and, it is to be hoped, that by the Blessing of God, their Numbers will increase:——But till that is the Case, other Methods must be taken, and particular Days be now and then appointed for the Instruction of these poor People, as this hath been:——In which, may Almighty God, of his great Mercy, assist me, his poor unworthy Servant, in the faithful Performance of my Part; and open their Hearts and Minds, that they may gladly receive, and truly understand the Things which belong to their Peace, through our Lord and Saviour Jesus Christ. *Amen.*

And now, *my dear Black Brethren and Sisters,* I beg that you will listen seriously to what I shall say.——You all know what Love and Affection I have for you, and I do believe that most of you have the like Love for me, as you have always found me ready to serve you, when you wanted my Help.——I doubt not therefore, that you will readily hearken to the good Advice I shall now give you, (as you know me to be your Friend and Well-wisher) and hope you will remember it hereafter, and think upon it at Home, and talk of it to your Fellow-Servants that are not here, that they may receive Advantage by it, as well as you, that hear it from my own Mouth.

I have chosen a Text of Scripture, which I could wish you all had by Heart, and would all remember;——because it shews you what a *Great Friend* you may have in Heaven, if you will but take any Pains to gain his Favour. For *St. Paul,* who wrote by the Direction of the Holy Spirit of God, assures you, that *whatsoever good Thing a Man* or *Woman doth,* they *shall receive the same,* that is, shall be rewarded for it by the Lord, *whether they be Bond or Free.*——And this cannot but give you great Comfort, to know, and be assured, that whatever good Thing you do, though you be Slaves, bound to serve Masters and Mistresses here upon Earth, for the Sake of a bare Maintenance;——yet, while you are doing what is right and good, you are, at the same Time, working for a just Master in Heaven, who will pay you good Wages for it, and will make no Difference between you, and the richest Freeman, upon the face of the Earth.——For God is no Respecter of Persons.——He values no Man for his Riches and Power, neither does he despise or overlook any one for his Rags and Poverty.——He loves none but those that are Good, and hates none but those that are Bad.——And our Lord and Saviour Jesus Christ hath given us an Account, from his own Mouth, of a certain great Man, who had Riches and Pleasures at Will, while he lived in this World, that was thrown into Hell at his Death, because he was not Good:——While a poor despised Beggar, all overrun with Sores and Filth, who died for Want at this great Man's Gate, was carried by Angels into Heaven, because he had been a good Man, and had served God, his heavenly Master, so far as he had Knowledge and Opportunity.[5]

That you may easier understand, and better carry away in your Memory what you shall hear, I shall endeavour, by God's Help, to lay before you, in the plainest Words,

I. Why you ought to serve God.
II. What Service, or what good Things God expects from you.
III. What Kind of Reward you may expect to receive from him.

I. And the first Reason why you ought to serve God, is,——BECAUSE THAT GOD MADE YOU;——and he *made* you, and all Men, to *serve* him.——You know that, when you were born, you did not come into the World by any Power or Help of your own:——Nay, you were so far from knowing any Thing about it, or how you came here;——whether you were found in the Woods, or grew out of the Ground,——that it was some Years before you could help yourselves, or had so much Sense as to know your right Hand from your left.——It was Almighty God, therefore, who made you, and all the World, that sent you here, as he had sent your Fathers and Mothers, your Masters and Mistresses before you, to take Care of you, and provide for you, while you could take no Care of, or help, or provide for yourselves.——And can you think that Almighty God, who is so wise and good himself, would send you into the World for any bad Purposes?——Can you be so silly as to fancy, that He, who made every Thing so good and useful in its Kind, sent you here to be Idle, to be Wicked, or to make a bad Use of any good Thing he hath made?—— No, my Brethren, the most ignorant among you has more Sense than to think any such Thing:——And there is none of you but knows, that you ought to be good;—— and whosoever is good, let him be ever so Poor and Mean, is serving God.——For this whole World is but one large Family, of which Almighty God is the Head and Master:—He takes Care of all, by causing the *Sun to shine, the Rains to fall, the Waters to spring, the Winds to blow, the Grass, the Trees, and the Herbs to spring, and the Corn, the Plants, and the Fruits to come in their due Season;* thus providing Food and Shelter for all living Creatures.—And to Mankind in particular, he hath given *Reason* and *Knowledge,* to teach them how to make use of, and turn all these Things to their own Comfort and Support, giving more or less of them to every one, according as he thinks fit, and as he knows to be best for them.—And this general Provision which God makes of all Things, and this particular Disposal of them, in giving *more* to some, and *less* to others,—together with his own secret Ways of bringing it about, is what we call his DIVINE PROVIDENCE.

Now, for carrying on these great and wonderful Ends, God hath appointed several *Offices* and *Degrees* in his Family, as they are dispersed and scattered all over the Face of the Earth.—Some he hath made *Kings* and *Rulers,* for giving Laws, and keeping the rest in Order:—Some he hath made *Masters* and *Mistresses,* for taking Care of their Children, and others that belong to them:—Some he hath made *Merchants* and *Seafaring men,* for supplying distant Countries with what they want from other Places:—Some he hath made *Tradesmen* and *Husbandmen, Planters* and *Labouring-Men,* to work for their own Living, and help to supply others with the Produce of their Trades and Crops:—Some he hath made *Servants* and *Slaves,* to assist and work for the *Masters* and *Mistresses* that provide for them;—and others he hath made *Ministers* and *Teachers,* to instruct the rest, to shew them what they ought to do, and put them in mind of their several Duties.—And as Almighty God hath sent each of us into the World for some or other of these Purposes;—so, from the King, who is his head Servant in a Country, to the poorest Slave, we are all obliged to do the Business he hath set us about, in that State of Life to which he hath been pleased to call us.—And while you, whom he hath made Slaves, are honestly and quietly doing your Business, and living as poor Christians ought to do, you are serving God, in your low Station, as much as the greatest Prince alive, and will be as much taken Notice of, and have as much Favour shewn you at the last Day.

2. A second Reason why you ought to serve God, is—BECAUSE YOU HAVE SOULS TO BE SAVED.—If you have nothing in this World but hard Labour, with your coarse Food and Clothing, you have a Place provided for you in Heaven, when you die, and go into the next World, if you will but be at the Pains of seeking for it while you stay here.—And there is no other Way of getting to Heaven, but by serving God upon Earth.—Besides, when People die, we know but of two Places they have to go to, and that is, *Heaven* or *Hell:*—so that whoever misses the one, must go to the other.—Now *Heaven* is a Place of great Happiness, which God hath prepared for all that are good, where they shall enjoy Rest from their Labours, and a

Blessedness which will never have an End:—And *Hell* is a Place of great Torment and Misery, where all wicked People will be shut up with the *Devil,* and *other evil Spirits,* and be punished for ever, because they will not serve God in this World.— It was to save you, and all Men, from that dreadful Punishment, that our blessed Lord Jesus Christ came down from Heaven,—was made a Man like us, and suffered a most shameful and bitter Death, his Hands and Feet being riveted with great Nails to a *cross Piece of Timber,* and his Side pierced through with a Spear, as he hung upon it in all that Pain and Agony.—And if he so loved our Souls that he gave himself up to so cruel a Death to redeem them from Hell, ought not we to have as much Regard for ourselves as he had, and take some Pains to save our own Souls?—Believe me, *my black Brethren and Sisters,* there was not a single Drop of his precious Blood spilled, in which the poorest and meanest of you hath not as great a Share, as the richest and most powerful Person upon the Face of the Earth.— And think, O think, what a sad Thing it must be, to lose any Soul which cost Almighty God so dear as the Life of his own well beloved Son!—But you must always remember, that though our Saviour died for the Sins of all Men, yet none shall have the Benefit of what he did for us, but such as will *serve* God:—For he made that the Condition of our Salvation, through him, that we should *love and fear God, and keep his Commandments.*—If, therefore, we would have our Souls saved by Christ, if we would escape *Hell,* and obtain *Heaven,* we must set about doing what he requires of us, and that is, to *serve* God.—Your own poor Circumstances in this Life ought to put you particularly upon this, and taking Care of your Souls:—For you cannot have the Pleasures and Enjoyments of this Life, like rich free People, who have Estates, and Money to lay out as they think fit.—If others will run the Hazard of their Souls, they have a Chance of getting Wealth and Power,—of heaping up Riches, and enjoying all the Ease, Luxury, and Pleasure, their Hearts should long after:—But you can have none of these Things.—So that if you sell your Souls for the Sake of what poor Matters you can get in this World, you have made a very foolish Bargain indeed.—Almighty God hath been pleased to make you Slaves here, and to give you nothing but Labour and Poverty in this World, which you are obliged to submit to, as it is his Will it should be so. And think within yourselves what a terrible Thing it would be, after all your Labours and Sufferings in this Life, to be turned into Hell in the next Life;—and after wearing out your Bodies in Service here, to go into a far worse Slavery when this is over, and your poor Souls be delivered over into the Possession of the Devil, to become his Slaves for ever in Hell, without any Hope of ever getting free from it.—If, therefore, you would be God's *Free-men* in Heaven, you must strive to be good, and serve him here on Earth.

Your Bodies, you know, are not your own, they are at the Disposal of those you belong to:—But your precious Souls are still your own, which nothing can take from you if it be not your own Fault. Consider well then, that if you lose your Souls by leading idle, wicked Lives here, you have got nothing by it in this World, and you have lost your All in the next.—For your Idleness and Wickedness is generally found out, and your Bodies suffer for it here, and, what is far worse, if you do not repent and amend, your unhappy Souls will suffer for it hereafter—And our blessed Saviour, who well knew the Value of a Soul, and paid so dear for putting them in the Way leading to Heaven, hath assured us in his holy Word, *that if a Man was to gain the whole World by it, it could not make him amends for the Loss of his Soul.*[6]—You see, then, how necessary it is for you to be *good,* and *serve* God, since that is the only Way by which your Souls can be saved, the only Means by which you can secure the Favour and Friendship of Almighty God, who, upon that Condition, will make you great Amends in the next World, for whatever you want, and whatever you suffer in this for his Sake.

3. Another Reason why you ought to serve God, is,—That *far the greatest Part of you have been Baptized,* and do profess yourselves to be *Christians.*—Many of you were baptized before my coming into the Parish, and since that Time, I have myself baptized, of Young and Old, near Two Hundred.

—Now, as many as call themselves Christians, do profess to serve the Lord Christ:—And as many as have been baptized, have made a solemn Promise and Vow,—*That they will obediently keep God's Commandments, and walk in the same all the Days of their Life.*—Such of you, therefore, as have been baptized, ought to consider that you are bound by a Promise and Vow, made before God and the Congregation, to *serve him;*—and that if you neglect it, you shall severely answer for it at the Judgment Seat of God; when your own Promise shall be brought to witness against you; and your Punishment in Hell will be the greater, because you mocked God, in making him a Promise, which you took no Care to perform, and because you knew your Duty and would not do it.

Having thus laid before you some Reasons why you ought to *serve God,*—I shall, in the next Place, endeavour to shew you,

II. What Service, or what good Things, God expects from you.

And here, you must not think that you can be of any Advantage or Benefit to Almighty God by *serving* him.—He, that hath Millions of glorious and powerful Angels waiting continually round his Throne in Heaven, and ready every Moment to perform his Commands, cannot want, or stand in need of any *Help* or *Service,* from the Hands of such poor mean Creatures as we are.—But when God made us, he intended that we should all be happy with him in Heaven, when we leave this World, if we would live in such a Manner *here,* as to be fit Company for his blessed Saints and Angels *hereafter.*—For he delights in the Happiness of all his Creatures, and his Holy Spirit is grieved when they, by their Wickedness, make themselves miserable.—To this great End, he hath given us Rules to walk by;—

which, if we follow, will prepare us for that happy State he hath provided for us in the next Life.—And whosoever observes these Rules, and ordereth his Behaviour according to their Directions, is said to *serve God;* though, in reality, he is then *serving himself* in the highest Degree.

Now these Rules of Behaviour relate to three Things; namely, how we ought to behave—*towards God*—*towards Mankind*—and towards Ourselves;—and these I shall endeavour to explain to you under the following Heads:

1.  Your Duty or Behaviour towards God.
2.  Your Duty or Behaviour towards your Masters and Mistresses.
3.  Your Duty or Behaviour towards your Fellow Servants, and others.
4.  Your Duty towards Yourselves.

1. And in the First Place, Your Duty towards God is to look upon him as *your Great and chief Master,* to whom you are accountable for all your Behaviour, either in Private or Publick;—both towards Himself, and to all Mankind.—You are to remember, that you can do nothing so secretly but he will know it, and that no Place is so dark and private, but his all-piercing Eye can see what you are doing in it:—*For the Darkness and the Light are both alike to him.*[7]—You are farther to consider, that his Eyes are continually upon you, and that it is impossible for you to conceal yourself a single Moment out of his Sight:—That he is *pleased* when he sees you doing what is right, and *angry* with you when he sees you doing any Thing that is bad.—And this will surely be a mighty Check upon you, when you are inclined to do any bad Thing, to think that Almighty God is that very Moment looking upon you, and taking an Account of your Behaviour.—So that if it should be done so secretly and artfully as never to be known in this World, yet your heavenly Master sees it, and knows it, and will not fail to punish you for it in the next World, for doing what he hath forbidden you to do.—This Consideration will also be of great Comfort and Encouragement to you, in doing what is Right and Good;—for if no Body else was to take Notice of it, you are sure that He will:—And if you meet with no Recompence for it here, you know that Almighty God, who is the best of Masters, will reward you for it hereafter.—For you are assured in the Text, that *whatsoever good Thing any Man doth, the same shall he receive of the Lord, whether he be Bond or Free.*

2. Another Duty you owe to God Almighty, is,—*To love him with all your Heart, with all your Mind, with all your Soul, and with all your Strength.*[8]—In short, you must love God above all Things.

And indeed, if you do but seriously think what God hath done, is every Day doing, and will do for you hereafter, if it be not your own Fault,—you cannot chuse but love him beyond the whole World.—Hath not God made you?—Hath he not given you all the Comforts you have enjoyed in Life?—Hath he not given you, along with the rest of Mankind, *Sense* and *Reason* beyond all the other Sorts of earthly Creatures?—Hath he not preserved and supported you to this very Hour?—And do not your very Lives this Moment depend upon his Goodness and Mercy?—These are great Obligations to Love and Thankfulness;—but what he hath done for your Souls is of far greater Value.—Hath he not given you *Souls to be saved?*—Hath he not brought you out of a Land of Darkness and Ignorance, where your Forefathers knew nothing of Him, to a Country where you may come to the Knowledge of the only true God, and learn a sure Way to Heaven?—Hath he not shewn such wonderful Love and Kindness for your Souls, as to send his only *Son, our Saviour* Jesus Christ, to suffer Death for your Sakes, and to leave *Rules* and *Directions* behind him, which, if you follow, will bring you to everlasting Happiness?—And hath he not so ordered it in his Providence, that you should be taught those Rules this Holy Day of his own appointment, and at other Times?—And will He not bestow Heaven itself upon you, if you will make good Use of the Opportunities he hath given you of learning his Laws, and living accordingly?—You see that Almighty God hath thought nothing too good for you, and surely, you cannot think any Love too great for Him.—Take good Heed therefore, that you do not let *Idleness* and *Vanity, Lust* and *Sin,* run away with those Hearts and Affections which you ought to bestow intirely upon so kind and good a God.—For while you desire to do any Thing which is not lawful and good, you love that Thing, whatever it is, better than you love God; and therefore, he will not love you:—and the Loss of God's Love is the dreadfulest Loss that can happen to you.

3. Another Duty you owe to God, is Fear.—Now there are two Sorts of *Fear,*—the one proceeding from *Love,*—and the other from *Terror.*—If we sincerely love any one, we are afraid of doing any Thing that will make him uneasy:—And if we love God sincerely, we shall be afraid of doing any ill Thing, because we know that his Holy Spirit is grieved at our Wickedness.—But if our *Love* to God be not strong enough to make us *afraid of grieving his Holy Spirit,* the *Dread of his terrible Judgments* will surely keep us in Awe.—When any of you have done something that deserves Correction, and you find that your Masters have come to the Knowledge of it, does not the Fear of a Whipping make you tremble?—Do not your Hearts fail you, and the Terror of the Lash make you wish you never had done it?—And while that *Fear,* and the *Thoughts of Correction* hang over you, does it not keep you from doing what may bring upon you such severe Punishments?—Alas, my Brethren, all this is a meer Trifle!—If Men for your Faults should be provoked to lash you immoderately,—if your Correction should be so severe as that you died under it,—there would be an End of that Suffering, and you could feel no more, if they were to cut your Body into Pieces, or throw it into the Fire.—But if you lead wicked Lives, and provoke God to Anger, he can not only, if he thinks proper, strike you dead upon the Spot, [or] cause you to die of some lingering,

painful Distemper, but can also plunge your Souls into Hell-fire, there to remain in Pain and Torment for ever.—Let this Thought be strongly fixed in your Hearts; —and when sinful Desires arise in your Minds, and evil Inclinations begin to get the better, then remember that the great God is looking at you, and say within your-selves, as *Joseph* said, when he was tempted to Sin by his wicked Mistress,—*How can I do this great Wickedness and Sin against God?*—Now *Joseph*, like you, was a *Slave* in a strange Land, and was sold by his wicked Brethren, as many of you, or your Fore-fathers, have been sold to Masters of Ships, by your Parents or Relations:—His Temptation was very great: He was a *Young Man* and a *Slave*:—But his *Fear* of God was such, that he rather chose to suffer the Consequences of his Mistress's Rage, and to go to Prison, where he remained several Years, than to displease God by commit-ting Sin.⁹—Our blessed Saviour, speaking of this holy *Fear* and *Dread* of offending Almighty God, saith—*Fear not to them which kill the Body, but are not able to kill the Soul: but rather fear him, which is able to destroy both Body and Soul in Hell.*¹⁰

4. Another Duty you owe to Almighty God, is—WORSHIP;—and this is of two Sorts,—PUBLICK and PRIVATE.—PUBLICK WORSHIP is that Devotion we pay to God at *Church*, on Sundays and other *Holy-Days*;—and PRIVATE WORSHIP is that Duty of *Prayer* and *Thanksgiving* which we offer up to God at Home.—It gives me great Satisfaction, and I bless God for it, that I see so many of you come here on Sundays:—It looks well, and seems as if your Inclinations were good, and I hope many of you will receive great Benefit by it.—But I cannot help saying, that many more might come if they would, who spend their Sundays in *Idling* and *Visiting, Drinking, Hunting,* and *Fishing,* and spending the *best* of Days to the *worst* of Pur-poses.—It is certain you cannot all be spared, and that some are at a great Dis-tance from Church.—But such of you as can be spared, to visit, trifle away your Time, and ride about, might spend this Time much better at Church, and do their Masters' Horses less Harm.—Others of you work on Sundays, which is a great Sin:—For those that will labour on the Lord's own Day, which he hath ordered to be set apart for his Worship, God will most certainly punish them either in this World or the next.

PRIVATE PRAYER is a Duty which God expects from you, as much as from People of a higher Rank.—It were indeed much to be wished, that we had more *praying Families* among us, where Servants would have an Opportunity of praying regularly every Day:—But there are few of you but can say the *Lord's Prayer;* and that, said over devoutly Morning and Evening upon your Knees, would bring down a Blessing upon you and the Family you belong to.—If you were to consider what PRAYER is,—that it is speaking to Almighty God, and asking freely from him a Supply of every Thing that is needful for you, you surely would be very fond of Praying.—And do not say that you want Words;—For if you want any Favour from your *Masters* or *Mistresses,* you can find Words plain enough to ask it from them.——Now Almighty God invites you to come to him, and tells you, that you need but *ask* of him, *and you shall have, seek and you shall find, knock and it shall be opened unto you.*[11]——If, therefore, you will not ask a Blessing from him in Prayer, you cannot expect to have it;——if you will not seek for his Favour, you cannot expect to find it;——and if you will not take the Trouble of knocking at the Gate of Heaven, you cannot hope to have it opened to let you in.——It is not long Prayers, nor a Set of fine Words, that God requires.——But if the *Heart* be desirous of obtaining any Request, the *Tongue* will find out Words to express it in;——and God who looks upon the *Heart* more than the *Tongue,* will grant whatever you ask of Him, if it be for your Good.——It is no Matter how short your Prayer is, if your Heart go along with it:——And any of you have Sense enough to pray in this manner.——"*Lord have Mercy upon me, I am a great Sinner: I have done such a Thing, which I ought not to have done, and I am sorry for it.——Spare me, good Lord, pardon me this once, for the Sake of my Saviour Jesus Christ, and, by the Blessing of God, I will do so no more.*"

"*Lord, give me Grace, and make me a good Man!*"

"*Lord, bless my Master and Mistress, and prosper the House I live in!*"

"*God bless me, and keep me from Sin and Danger!*"

"*Lord, make me truly thankful for thy great Goodness to me!*"

"*Lord, make me your Servant while I live, that when I die, I may remain in your House for ever!*"

You can never want *Time* for Prayers of this Sort:——You can think of your Souls, and pray thus, either in the *House* or the *Field,* whether you are *Up* or in *Bed,* or *Walking,* or *Working;* at the *Plough,* the *Axe,* the *Hough,*[12] or the *Spade.*——And God is always ready to hear you.——But remember this, that whenever you pray to God for *Grace,* you must strive *to be* what you pray for.——If you desire of God to make you good, or sober, or honest, or diligent, you must first of all strive to be that *good,* that *sober,* that *honest,* that *diligent* Servant you desire to be, and then God will help you with his Grace in making you so.

5. Another Duty you owe to God is Reverence and Honour.——But many of you are so far from shewing any *Honour* or *Respect* to God Almighty, that you will *curse* and *swear,* and *blaspheme* his Name upon every little Fit of Passion, at any silly Thing that crosses your Humour,——and sometimes out of meer Wantonness, when nothing disturbs you at all.——Take Care, my Brethren, it is very dangerous sporting with *the great and fearful Name of the Lord our God:*[13] And he hath threatned that he *will not hold that Person guiltless that taketh his Name in vain;*[14]——that is, that whosoever makes an irreverent Use of his holy Name by *vain Oaths,* and *Cursing* and *Swearing,* shall certainly be punished for it, either in this World, or in the World to come.

6. Another Duty you owe to Almighty God, is TRUTH.——For God is a God of Truth, and hates all *Lies* and *Liars.*——The HOLY SCRIPTURES are full of Texts to this

Purpose, of which, I shall repeat a few, to shew you what a sad Thing it is to tell Lies.——In one Place we are told by King *Solomon,* that *Lying Lips are an Abomination to the Lord.*[15]——Our Saviour himself tells us in another Place, that *the Devil is a Liar, and the Father of* it.[16]——And St. *John* tells us, that *all Liars shall have their Part in the Lake that burneth with Fire and Brimstone;*[17] that is in Hell.——Now many of you think there is little Harm in a Lie;——but you see what a sad Mistake it is.——For you see, by what has been said, that if you have a Mind to make yourselves hateful and abominable to God,——if you have a mind to become the Devil's own Children,—— if you want to plunge yourselves headlong into Hell, and walk to all Eternity in Fire and Brimstone, you need but get an Habit of Lying, and it will as surely destroy your Souls, as Murder, Fornication, Adultery, or any other Sin.

II. Having thus shewn you the chief Duties you owe to your great Master in Heaven, I now come to lay before you the Duties you owe to your *Masters* and *Mistresses* here upon Earth.

And for this, you have one general Rule, that you ought always to carry in your Minds;——and that is,——*to do all Service for Them, as if you did it for God himself.* ——Poor Creatures! you little consider, when you are idle and neglectful of your Master's Business,——when you *steal,* and *waste,* and *hurt* any of their Substance, ——when you are *saucy* and *impudent,*——when you are telling them *Lies,* and deceiving them,——or when you prove *stubborn* or *sullen,* and will not do the Work you are set about without Stripes and Vexation;——you do not consider, I say, that what Faults you are guilty of towards your Masters and Mistresses, are Faults done against God himself, who hath set your Masters and Mistresses over you, in his own Stead, and expects that you will do for them, just as you would do for Him.——And pray, do not think that I want to deceive you, when I tell you, that your *Masters* and *Mistresses* are God's OVERSEERS,——and that if you are faulty towards them, God himself will punish you severely for it in the next World, unless you repent of it, and strive to make amends, by your *Faithfulness* and *Diligence,* for the Time to come;——for God himself hath declared the same.——And you have, at the same Time, this Comfort, that if any of your OWNERS should prove WICKED OVERSEERS, and use you, who are his under Servants here, as they ought not to do;——though you must submit to it, and can have no Remedy in this World, yet, when God calls you and them together Face to Face before him in the next World, and examines into these Matters, He will do you strict Justice, and punish those that have been bad Stewards and Overseers over you with the greater Severity, as they had more of this World entrusted to their Care:——And that whatever you have suffered *unjustly* here, God will make you amends for it in Heaven.

——I will now read over to you the rules which God hath given you, in his own Words, that you may see what I say is Truth.——*Servants, be obedient to them that are your Masters according to the Flesh, with Fear and Trembling, in Singleness of your Heart,* as unto Christ:——*Not with Eye-service, as Men-pleasers, but as the Servants of Christ, doing the Will of God from the Heart.*——*With good will doing Service, as to the Lord and not to Men.*——*Knowing, that whatsoever good Thing any Man doeth, the same shall he receive of the Lord, whether he be Bond or Free.*——*And ye Masters, do the same Things unto them, for-bearing* (or moderating) *Threatning; knowing that your Master is also in Heaven; neither is there Respect of Persons with him.*

Now, from this great general Rule, namely, that you are to *do all Service for your Masters* and *Mistresses, as if you did it for God himself,* there arise several other Rules of Duty towards your *Masters* and *Mistresses,* which I shall endeavour to lay in order before you.

1. And in the First Place, *You are to be obedient and subject to your Masters in all Things.*——For the Rules which God hath left us in the Scriptures are these——*Servants, obey in all Things your Masters according to the Flesh, not with Eye-Service as Men-Pleasers, but in Singleness of Heart, fearing God:*——*And whatsoever ye do, do it heartily, as to the Lord, and not unto Men; knowing, that of the Lord ye shall receive the Reward of the Inheritance, for ye serve the Lord Christ*——*But he that doeth Wrong shall receive for the Wrong he hath done; and there is no Respect of Persons.*\*——*Servants, be subject to your Masters, with all Fear, not only to the good and gentle, but also to the froward.*†——And Christian Ministers are commanded to *exhort Servants to be obedient unto their own Masters, and to please them well in all Things, not answering again,* or murmuring, or gainsaying.‡——You see how strictly God requires this of you, that whatever your Masters and Mistresses order you to do, you must set about it immediately, and faithfully perform it, without any disputing or grumbling,——and take care to please them well in all Things.——And, for your Encouragement, he tells you, that he will reward you for it in Heaven, because, while you are honestly and faithfully doing your Master's Business here, you are serving your Lord and Master in Heaven. You see also, that you are not to take any Exceptions to the Behaviour of your Masters and Mistresses, and that you are to be subject and obedient, not only to such as are *good,* and *gentle,* and *mild* towards you, but also to such as may be *froward, peevish,* and *hard.*——For you are not at liberty to chuse your own Masters, but into whatever Hands God hath been pleased to put you, you must do your Duty, and God will reward you for it.——And if they neglect to do theirs, God will punish them for it:——For there is no Respect of Persons with him.——There is only *one Case* in which you may refuse Obedience to your Owners,——and that is, if they should command you to do any *sinful* Thing.——As *Joseph* would not hearken to his Mistress, when she tempted him to lie with her.——So that if any Master could be so wicked as to command you to *steal,* to *murder,* to *set a Neighbour's House on Fire,*

\*Col. iii. 22, 23, 24. 25.

†1 Pet. ii. 18.

‡Tit. ii. 9.

to *do Harm to any Body's Goods, or Cattle,* or to get *drunk,* or to *curse and swear,* or to *work on Sundays,* (unless it should be in a Case of great Necessity)——or to do any Thing that God hath forbidden, there it is your Duty to refuse them;——because God is your HEAD MASTER, and you must not do a Thing which you know is contrary to his Will.——But in every Thing else, you must obey your Owners, and God requires it of you.

2. You are *not* to be *Eye-Servants.*——Now *Eye-Servants* are such as will *work hard,* and seem mighty diligent, while they think that any Body is taking Notice of them; but when their Masters and Mistresses Backs are turned, they are idle, and neglect their Business.

——I am afraid that there are a great many such *Eye-Servants* among you,——and that you do not consider how great a Sin it is to be so, and how severely God will punish you for it.——You may easily deceive your Owners, and make them have an Opinion of you that you do not deserve, and get the Praise of Men by it.——But remember, that you cannot deceive Almighty God, who sees your Wickedness and Deceit, and will punish you accordingly.——For the Rule is, that you must *obey your Masters in all Things,* and do the Work they set you about *with Fear and Trembling, in Singleness of Heart, as unto Christ, not with Eye-Service, as Men-pleasers, but as the Servants of Christ, doing the Will of God from the Heart: With good Will doing Service as to the Lord, and not as to Men.*——If then, you would but think, and say within yourselves,——"My Master hath set me about this Work, and his Back is turned, so that I may loiter and idle if I please, for he does not see me.——But there is my GREAT MASTER in Heaven, whose Overseer my other Master is,——and his Eyes are always upon me, and taking Notice of me, and I cannot get any where out of his Sight, nor be idle without his knowing it, and what will become of me if I lose his good-Will, and make him angry with me."——If, I say, you would once get the Way of thinking and saying thus, upon all Occasions, you then would do what God commands you, and serve your Masters with SINGLENESS OF HEART,——that is, with *Honesty and Sincerity;* you would do the Work you are set about *with Fear and Trembling,* not for Fear of your Masters and Mistresses upon Earth (for you may easily cheat them, and make them believe you are doing their Business when you do not)——but *with Fear and Trembling,* lest God, your HEAVENLY MASTER, whom you cannot deceive, should call you to Account, and punish you in the next World, for your *Deceitfulness* and *Eye-Service* in this.

3. You are to be *faithful and honest to your Masters and Mistresses,*——not *purloining* \* (or wasting their Goods or Substance) *but shewing all good Fidelity in all Things.*

——If you were to *rob* or *steal* from others, you know that it would be a very bad Thing, and how severely the Law would punish you for it.——But if your Master is

---

\*Tit. ii. 10.

robb'd of what belongs to him by your Wastefulness or Negligence, do not you think it is as wicked and as bad as if you were to *steal* his Goods and *give* them to other People?—For, pray, what is the Difference to me, when my Substance is gone, whether a Thief took it away from me, or whether I am robbed of it by my Servants' Negligence?—The Loss is the same, and they will have it equally to answer for.—How then, can many of you be so careless about your Master's Business?—How can you be so unfaithful and wicked, as to see their Substance perish and be lost, when a little of your timely Care would prevent the Loss?—Is this not a very common Case among you?—And do not most Masters complain, with great Justice, that unless they happen to see into every Thing themselves, their Servants will take no Care?—Nay, even when they are told of it, and ordered to do it, they will still neglect, and let the Goods perish?—Do not your Masters, under God, provide for you?—And how shall they be able to do this, to *feed* and to *cloath* you, unless you take honest Care of every Thing that belongs to them?— Remember that God requires this of you, and if you are not afraid of suffering for it here, you cannot escape the Vengeance of Almighty God, who will judge between you and your Masters, and make you pay severely in *the next world* for all the Injustice you do them *here*.—And tho' you could manage so cunningly to escape the Eyes and Hands of Man, yet think what a dreadful Thing it is, to fall *into the Hands of the living God, who is able to cast both Soul and Body into Hell.*[18]

4. You are to *serve your Masters with Chearfulness, and Reverence, and Humility.*— You are to do your Masters Service *with good Will,* doing it as *the Will of God, from the Heart,* without any Sauciness or answering again.—How many of you do Things quite otherwise, and, instead of going about your Work with a good Will and a good Heart, *dispute* and *grumble,* give saucy Answers, and behave in a surly Manner?—There is something so becoming and ingaging in a modest, chearful, good-natur'd Behaviour, that a little Work, done in that Manner, seems better done, and gives far more Satisfaction, than a great deal more, that must be done with Fretting, Vexation, and the Lash always held over you.—It also gains the good Will and Love of those you belong to, and makes your own Life pass with more Ease and Pleasure.—Besides, you are to consider, that this *Grumbling* and *ill Will* does not affect your *Masters* and *Mistresses* only:—They have Ways and Means in their Hands of forcing you to do your Work, whether you are willing or not.— But your *Murmuring* and *Grumbling* is against God, who hath placed you in that Service, who will punish you severely in the next World for despising his Commands.

Thus I have endeavoured to shew you, why you ought to serve God, and what Duty in particular you owe to him:—I have also shewn you, that while you are serving your Masters and Mistresses, or doing any Thing that God hath commanded, you are, at the same Time, *serving* him; and have endeavoured to shew you what Duty or Service you owe to your Owners, in Obedience to God, and that in so plain a Manner, as, I hope, the greatest Part of you did well understand. —The other Parts of your Duty, and the Rewards which God hath promised to you (if you will honestly set about doing it) I shall endeavour to lay before you at our next Meeting here for that Purpose.—In the mean Time, consider well what hath been said.—Think upon it, and talk about it one with another, and strive to fix it on your Memories.—And may God, of his infinite Mercy, grant, that it may sink deep into your Hearts, and, taking Root there, may bring forth in you the Fruit of good Living, to the Honour and Praise of his holy Name, the Spreading abroad of his Gospel, and the eternal Salvation of your precious Souls, through our Lord and Saviour Jesus Christ, to whom, with the Father, and the Holy Spirit, be all Honour and Glory, World without End. *Amen.*

Notes

1. My portrait of Bacon is drawn from John C. Van Horne, ed., *Religious Philanthropy and Colonial Slavery: The American Correspondence of the Associates of Dr. Bray, 1717–1777* (Urbana: University of Illinois Press, 1985); Nelson Waite Rightmyer, *Maryland's Established Church* (Baltimore: Church Historical Society for the Diocese of Maryland, 1956); and Lawrence C. Wroth, "A Maryland Merchant and His Friends in 1750," *Maryland Historical Magazine* 6 (September 1911): 213–40.

2. This text is available through Eighteenth Century Collections Online. I transcribed the first sermon in this eighty-page tract, pp. 1–38.

3. Two lines—some twelve words—are illegible in the text.

4. Matthew 13:31–32; and 17:20.

5. Luke 16:19–25.

6. Luke 9:25.

7. Psalms 139:12.

8. Mark 12:30.

9. Genesis 39:6–23.

10. Matthew 10:28.

11. Matthew 7:7.

12. "Hough" is an antiquated alternative spelling for "hoe."

13. Deuteronomy 28:58.

14. Exodus 20:7.

15. Proverbs 12:22.

16. John 8:44.

17. Revelation 21:8.

18. Hebrews 10:31.

CHAPTER 4

# Samuel Davies, 1757

INTERDENOMINATIONAL RIVALRY LED TO BITTER religious disputes in mid-eighteenth-century America. Yet, insofar as religious activists were concerned about the morality of the master-slave relationship, their actions reflected a considerable proslavery consensus. Samuel Davies, one of the most prominent Presbyterians of his era, provides us with a dramatic case in point. Over the course of his career, he was deeply immersed in the fight for religious freedom for the newly emerging New Light evangelical wing of the Presbyterian Church. Born in 1723 in a Welsh settlement in Delaware, Davies grew up in a household that was steeped in religious dissent. In 1732 his mother Martha was expelled by the Baptist Church for her acceptance of Presbyterian doctrine. In his youth, Davies received instruction from the prominent New Light scholar Samuel Blair, who ran a "log college" in Chester County, Pennsylvania. Upon completion of his studies in 1746 and his ordination in 1747, Davies moved to Virginia, a colony then notorious for "profaneness and immorality."[1] Although some colonial officials such as the attorney general Peyton Randolph harassed Dissenters in general and Davies in particular, Davies was ultimately successful in obtaining a license to preach from the lieutenant governor William Gooch.

Overcoming the hostility of existing colonial authorities, Davies demonstrated a zeal for slave conversion that evoked the efforts of established ministers such as Alexander Garden in South Carolina and Thomas Bacon in Maryland. For Davies, the conversion of African American slaves played a major role in his responsibilities as a pastor. "Never have I been so struck with the appearance of an assembly," he recounted in 1755, "as when I have glanced my eye to that part of the meetinghouse where they usually sit . . . with so many black countenances eagerly attentive to every word they hear, and frequently bathed in tears."[2] Over the years his sense of mission toward the slave population enabled him to build alliances with Anglican institutions such as the Society for the Propagation of the Gospel, which sent him gifts of books as a means toward fulfilling their common goals.[3]

Davies's efforts to Christianize slavery did not push him to oppose the institution. A slaveholder himself, Davies counseled Virginia slaves to appreciate the relative benefits extended by the mastery of benevolent American slaveholders. Confronting the menace of French invasion in 1755, Davies urged the slaves to remain loyal to their masters, warning them that the French were "cruel, barbarous people" who punished disobedient slaves with "death in the most shocking manner."[4] In his sermons concerning the subject of slavery, Davies urged Virginia slaveholders to recognize their religious responsibilities to their bondservants— an appeal that flowed from his conviction that Christianity upheld the legality of slavery and promised to make the slaves more faithful and diligent workers. In 1759 Davies moved from Virginia to Princeton to accept the presidency of the College of New Jersey, a post he held until his death in 1761.

SAMUEL DAVIES, *The Duty of Christians to Propagate Their Religion among the Heathens, Earnestly Recommended to the Masters of Negroe Slaves in Virginia. A Sermon Preached in Hanover, January 8, 1757* (London, 1758)[5]

### Sermon.
Genesis 18:19.

> For I know him, that he will command his Children and his
> Household after him, and they shall keep the Way of the Lord,
> to do Justice and Judgment.

A Creature formed for *immortality,* and that must be happy or miserable through an *everlasting* duration, is certainly a being of vast importance, however mean and insignificant he may be in other respects. His immortality gives him a kind of *infinite* value. Let him be white or black, bond or free, a native or a foreigner, it is of no moment in this view: he is to live *forever!* to be forever *happy,* or forever *miserable!* happy or miserable in the *highest degree!* This places him upon a kind of equality with Kings and Princes; nay, with Angels and Arch-angels: for it is this that adds importance and dignity to the most exalted parts of the human, and even of the angelic nature.

In this view, the crowds of neglected Negro Slaves among us, have often appeared to me as creatures of the utmost importance. The *same* immortality is entailed upon them, as upon us. They are candidates for the *same* eternal State with us, and bound for the *same* Heaven or Hell. How awful and important a trust, then, is *the care of a Soul!* the Soul even of a poor Negro Slave! To be entrusted with the care of forming and educating an *immortal* for his everlasting State! to be instrumental in preparing him for eternal joys, or eternal torments! to be accountable for our management in this trust, to the Supreme Judge of the Universe, with whom there is no respect of persons! to be rewarded for our faithfulness; or punished for our negligence, as having promoted the happiness or been accessary to the ruin of an immortal Soul!—Pause, and think of these things, and they will certainly appear very solemn and weighty.

This solemn and important trust, I must tell you, brethren, is committed, not only to parents, with regard to their Children, those dear other selves, but to *Masters,* with regard to their Servants and Slaves, of whatever country or colour they are. And as this duty is most scandalously neglected in this Christian country; and the neglect is likely to be followed with the most dangerous and ruinous consequences to thousands both Masters and Slaves; permit me to address you upon this head, with the utmost plainness and solemnity. You are my witnesses, that I have looked upon the poor Negroes as part of my ministerial charge; and used various endeavors to bring them to the faith and practice of Christianity, not without promising appearances of success, in sundry instances. It affords me no small pleasure to reflect, and I mention it with gratitude to God and Man, that my endeavors of this kind have, of late, met with no opposition from the Masters, of whatever denomination, in any one instance that I can recollect. And it affords me a still greater pleasure to reflect, that sundry of you not only consent that your Negroes should receive instructions from me, but also zealously concur with me, and make conscience of your own duty to them, in this respect. But alas! are there not some among you, and are there not thousands in our country, who must be conscious of their wilful negligence; nay, who, perhaps, are rather instrumental in hardening their Slaves in sin, and confirming their prejudices against our holy religion, than in promoting their conversion to God? Were your Negroes but so many *Brutes,* you might treat them as you do your Horses, fodder them, and make them work for you, without once endeavouring to make them sharers with you in the glorious privileges of religion, the distinguishing prerogative of human nature. But I hope you have divinity and philosophy enough to know, this is not the case. Let me therefore plainly lay your duty before you, with regard to them, in order to engage you to the practice of it. For sure, you are not hardy enough to neglect the practice, in spite of conviction. Sure, you dare not sin on still, and continue your career to ruin with your eyes open.

*Abraham* is often proposed as a pattern to believers in general; and I may particularly recommend his example to your imitation, in your conduct towards your domestics. Here you have his character drawn by the all-knowing God himself. "I know him, that he will command his Children, and his Household after him, and they shall keep the Way of the Lord." He not only instructed, advised, persuaded, entreated; but he used his *authority;* he *commanded* not only his Children, but his Household; which included his Servants, *Slaves,* and all his Domestics of every order. *Abraham's* family was like the generality of ours, in this, that he had hereditary *Slaves* in it, who were his property during life. We repeatedly read of his "Servants *born in his House,* and *bought with money* of strangers:"\* both which were probably *Slaves.* And he had so numerous a family of them, that, when he went upon an expedition to rescue *Lot* from captivity, we are told, "he armed his trained Servants, *born in his own House,* three hundred and eighteen."† Where, by the by, it is remarkable, and the remark is very pertinent to the present state of our country, that by instilling good principles into them, and by humane treatment, this numerous crowd of Slaves were become so faithful to their Master, that he could safely confide in them, without fear of their deserting him in the engagement, and going over to the enemy, in hopes to recover their liberty.⁶ All these, as well as *Ishmael,* and his favorite *Isaac,* he had instructed in the true religion. He had laid his *commands* upon them to serve the Lord, not only during his life, but "*after him,*" i.e. after his decease. Though he was mortal, he endeavoured to make religion immortal to his family. He was solicitous to leave the world with the joyful hope, that his Domestics would retain and observe his pious instructions, when he should be no more their head.

It is sufficient to recommend this example to our imitation, that it is the example of *faithful Abraham.* But it is still more strongly enforced by the express approbation of God himself. "The Lord said, shall I hide from Abraham the things that I do?" No, I may trust him even with my secrets: "For I know him;" I approve of him; I have full proof of him, and therefore may safely trust him; "*because* he will command his Children and Household, and they shall keep the Way of the Lord:" being once entered in the Way of the Lord by his instructions, they will keep it. "Train up a Child in the way in which he should go, and when he is old, he will *not depart* from it."‡

It is not my present design to consider the general duty of family-religion and good education, though my text is a very proper foundation for it. But I intend only to inculcate *the particular duty of instructing Slaves* in the true religion, and using all proper means to enter them in the way of the Lord. To give you directions how to perform it, before you are convinced it is your duty, would be useless and preposterous. And therefore,

My first and principal business shall be, *to convince you, that this is really your duty, and that it is a duty of the utmost importance and necessity.*

Here, I take it for granted, you are, at least, professed *Christians* yourselves; i.e. you profess to believe that the Christian Religion is divine, and to embrace it as *your* religion. Otherwise, instead of persuading you to endeavor to Christianize your Negroes, I would persuade you to become Christians yourselves. I would then deal with you, as with your Heathen Negroes, and labour to convince you of

---

\*Gen. 17:12, 13, 23, 27.
†[Gen.] 14:14.
‡Prov. 22:6.

the truth and divinity of the religion of Jesus, from those numerous topics of argument, by which so clear and important a truth may be demonstrated.—But you are fond of wearing the Christian name; you present your Children to be initiated into the Christian Church by Baptism; you acknowledge the truth of the scriptures, by complying with the usual ceremony of kissing the Bible in taking an oath; you attend upon the forms of worship in the Christian Church, and externally conform to them. These things you do; and these things are certainly a strong profession, that you are Christians. And none of you, I presume, will dare to renounce it, rather than admit the conviction that I would now force upon your minds from this consideration.

Therefore, taking this for granted, I need no other principle to convince you of the duty I am now recommending. And I shall reason from the nature and design of Christianity—from the example of Christ and his Apostles—from the worth and importance of the Souls of your poor Slaves—from the happy influence Christianity would have upon them, even for your own interest—from the zeal and generosity of others in this affair—and from your relation to them as their Masters.

1. If you consider the *nature* and *design* of Christianity, you cannot but be convinced of this duty.

Christianity, in its own nature, is calculated to be a *catholic,* or *universal* religion, and is equally the concern of *all* the sons of men. It proposes *one* God, as the object of *universal* adoration to white and black, bond and free: *one* Lord Jesus Christ, as a *common* Saviour for Britons, Africans, and Americans: *one* Holy Spirit, by whom alone Sinners of *all* nations, colours and characters, can be sanctified: *one* faith to be embraced, *one* rule of morality to be observed, by Masters and Servants, rich and poor: *one* Heaven and *one* Hell, as the last mansions of *all* the millions of mankind; to which they shall be adjudged according to their moral character, and, if they have heard the Gospel, according to their acceptance or non-acceptance of it; and not according to the trifling distinctions of country, colour, liberty or slavery.—Christianity is a *Religion for Sinners;* for Sinners of *all* kindreds, and nations, and languages. They *all* need those instructions, which its heavenly light sheds upon a benighted world. They *all* need that pardon, which it offers; that grace, which it communicates; and that salvation, which it ensures. In short, *all* its doctrines intimately concern them: *all* its precepts are binding upon them: *all* its blessings are needed by them: *all* its promises and threatenings shall be accomplished upon them, according to their characters. And must it not then be the grand concern of *all?* Yes; as there is but one air for Whites and Blacks, Masters and Servants to breathe in; one earth for them to walk upon; so there is but *one common* Christian Religion for them *all,* by which they can please God, and obtain Salvation. To be a sinful creature of the race of man, under the Gospel, is sufficient alone to render it his greatest concern, and a matter of absolute necessity, to

be a Christian. And to be entrusted with the care of such a creature, is alone a sufficient foundation for the duty I am recommending; and strongly binds it upon
every one of us, to whom that trust is committed.

And as Christianity is, in its own nature, the common concern of all, and calculated to be the universal religion of mankind; so it is designed by its great author
to be propagated among all. No corner of our world was left out in the commission, which the gracious founder of our religion gave to the teachers of it. "Go ye
into all the world," says he, "and preach the Gospel to every creature; i.e. to every
creature of the human race."* The great God "now commandeth all men every
where to repent."† And when the Apostles went out to discharge their extensive
commission, the Holy Spirit concurred with them, and rendered their labors successful in Asia, Europe and Africa, without distinction. He put no difference
between Jews and Gentiles, but purified the hearts of both by the same faith!‡ The
doors of the church were thrown wide open, for the admission of all, that would
come in upon the terms of the Gospel. The Roman Centurion, the Æthiopian
Eunoch, Onesimus, a run-away Slave, were as welcome, as the Jews of Jerusalem.
—"All were one in Christ Jesus; in whom there is neither Greek nor Jew, Barbarian, Scythian, bond or free."§ A black skin, African birth or extract, or state of slavery, does not disqualify a man for the blessings of the Gospel; does not exclude
him from its invitations, nor cast him out of the charge of its ministers. If history
may be credited, the Gospel did once flourish in Africa, and penetrated far into
those inhospitable deserts, which are now the regions of Mahometism, or Heathen idolatry. And we have all the certainty which the sure word of prophecy can
afford, that it will yet visit that miserable country. Yes, brethren, "the earth shall
be full of the knowledge of the Lord, as the waters cover the sea."‖ "The kingdoms
of the world shall yet become the kingdoms of our Lord, and of his Christ."# And
"from the rising of the Sun unto the going down of the same, his name shall be
great among the Gentiles; and in every place incense shall be offered to his
name."** "Æthiopia," Guinea and Negro-land "shall yet stretch out their hands
unto God."†† Negroes and Slaves are included in that "Fulness of the Gentiles,"
which, St. Paul tells us, "shall come in."‡‡ And may the happy few, who in this land

*Mark 16:15.
†Acts 17:30.
‡Acts 15:9.
§Colos. 3:11.
‖Isai. 11:9.
#Rev. 11:15.
**Mal. 1:2.
††Psal. 68:31.
‡‡Rom. 11:25.

of their bondage, have been made partakers of "the glorious liberty of the Sons of God," be the first fruits of this blessed harvest to Christ in Africa!

And now, brethren, do you not begin to feel this argument conclude? Is Christianity adapted and intended to be the *universal* religion of mankind? And must it not then be the duty of Christians, to do their utmost to spread it through the world? Is it the design of Heaven, that it shall be propagated among all nations? And is not the duty of Christians, especially of masters, who have a command over others, to concur in this gracious design, and do all in their power to hasten that blessed period, which has been so long the eager wish and hope of believers? The man that can be inactive and indifferent in such an affair as this, must have a temper directly contrary to that religion which he professes; must be entirely careless about the glory of God and the Redeemer, and the happiness of his fellow-creatures, and disaffected to the great designs of providence towards them. Has he imbibed the spirit of the Christian Religion, who can keep, perhaps, half a score of Heathens under his roof, and oblige them to drudge and toil for him all their lives; and yet never labor to gain them to the faith of Christ? Alas! how can he keep his conscience easy in such a course? But,

2. The example of Christ and his Apostles obliges you to this duty.

The example of Christ must certainly be a law to his followers; and in vain do they pretend to that character, unless they conform themselves to it.——And what did Christ do in this case? Why, he felt all the glories of his native Heaven; he assumed human nature with all its common infirmities, and, in circumstances of uncommon abasement, he spent three and thirty tedious and painful years in this wretched world, and passed through an uninterrupted series of poverty, fatigue, ill-treatment and persecution; he at length died in ignominy and torture upon a cross. And what was all this for? It was for *Africans,* as well as Britons: it was for the contemptible *Negroes,* as well as Whites: it was for poor *Slaves,* as well as for their Masters. Yes, for poor *Negroes* and *Slaves,* he thought it worth his while to shed the blood of his heart. As "God would have *all* men to be saved, and to come to the knowledge of the truth," so Christ "gave himself a ransom for *all.*"*

I am sure, such of you as are lovers of Christ, begin already to feel the force of this argument. Did he live and die, to save poor Negroes? And shall not we use all the means in our power, to make them partakers of this salvation? Did he pour out the blood of his heart for them? And shall we begrudge a little labor and pains to instruct them? We are not called to agonize and die upon a cross for them: but Jesus was; and he did not refuse. And shall we refuse those easier endeavors for their salvation, which are required on our part? If we are capable of such a conduct, it is high time for us to renounce all pretensions of regard to him, and his example.

*1 Tim. 2:4, 6.

The example of the Apostles also, and the primitive ministers of the Gospel, binds us to the same duty. When they received their extensive commission, the love of Christ carried them through the world, to discharge it, among Jews and Gentiles, among Masters and Servants. Wherever they found a Sinner, they preached to him "repentance towards God, and faith towards the Lord Jesus Christ," without regard to the cutaneous distinction of colour, the humble state of a Servant, or a Slave. "The *poor* had the Gospel preached unto them;" and among such it was most successful. "Not many mighty, not many noble after the flesh, were called: but God chose the weak, the foolish, the base and despised things of the world—that no flesh should glory in his presence."* St. Paul, in particular, the Chief of the Apostles, and who was eminently the Apostle of the *Gentiles,* shunned no fatigues or dangers, to carry this joyful news to the remotest and most barbarbous parts of the world. For this end, he became a wandering pilgrim from country to country: he braved the dangers of sea and land, and all the terrors of persecution; and at last gloriously died in the attempt. Servants and Slaves were not beneath his care. Many parts of his writings are addressed to them; from whence we learn, that many of them had embraced the Gospel, which he had published in their ears. He thought it an object worthy of his apostolic office, to give them directions for their behaviour, and to exhort them to be cheerfully contented with their mortifying condition in life. "Let every man," says he, abide "in that calling, wherein he was called." Christianity makes no alterations in matters of property, in civil distinctions or employments. "Art thou called, being a *Servant?* Care not for it—for he that is called, being a Servant, is the Lord's free-man."† The Servants he here speaks to, were probably not indented Servants or Hirelings, but what we call *Slaves.* And in those times it was a much more common practice, than it is now among the civilized nations of Europe, to make *Slaves* of the prisoners taken in war. But even to these, St. Paul says, "If thou are called, being a Servant, or a Slave, *care not* for it:" a Christian may be happy, even in a state of slavery. Liberty, the sweetest and most valuable of all blessings, is not essential to his happiness: for if he is destitute of civil liberty, he enjoys a liberty still more noble and divine: "He is the Lord's free man." The Son hath made him free from the tyranny of Sin and Satan; and therefore he is free indeed. What a striking instance is this, both of apostolic zeal for the poor Slaves, and of the invaluable advantages of being a Christian, which can render the lowest and most laborious station in life so insignificant, that a man need *not care* for it, but continue in it with a generous indifferency!—I shall only add one instance more, and that is the case of Onesimus, Philemon's Servant. He had been once unprofitable to his Master, and run

---

*Cor. 1:26–29.
† Cor. 7:20–22.

away from him, as some of your Negroes do now. But in his ramblings, he happened to come in St. Paul's way, while a prisoner in Rome. The Apostle did not despise the unhappy *Runagade,* but esteemed his conversion to Christianity a prize worth laboring for. He therefore communicated the Gospel to him; and it pleased God to open his heart to receive it, and he became a sincere convert. Upon this, the Apostle wrote a letter to his Master in his favor, which is still preserved, among his immortal Epistles, for the benefit of the Church in all ages. He shews all the affection and concern of a Father for him, and does not disdain to call him *his Son,* dear to him as *his own bowels.* "I beseech thee," says he to his Master, "for *my Son* Onesiumus, whom I have begotten in my bonds: who in time past was unprofitable, but now is profitable to thee, and me: whom I have sent again: thou therefore receive him that is *mine own bowels*—for perhaps he therefore departed for a season, that thou shouldst receive him forever; not now as a Servant, but above a Servant, a *brother beloved,* especially to me; but how much more to thee, both in the flesh and in the Lord? If thou count me therefore a partner, receive him *as myself.* If he hath wronged thee, or oweth thee aught, put that on mine account. I Paul have written it with my own hand, I will repay it. Yea, brother, let me have joy of thee in the Lord: refresh my bowels in the Lord, by thy compliance."*—What fatherly affection and solicitude, what ardent zeal is here, for a poor run-away Slave! How different is this from the prevailing spirit of the Christians of our age? Had the Apostles and their fellow-labourers been as careless about propagating the Gospel among Heathens, as the generality among us are, Christianity would have soon died in that corner of the world, where it had its birth; and we and the rest of mankind would now have been as much Heathens, as the African Negroes?

But do these examples lay no obligation upon us to follow them? Did the Apostles discover such an ardent zeal for the salvation even of Servants and Slaves; and shall we be quite negligent and careless about it? Did they take so much pains, pass through such severe sufferings, risk their lives, and even lose them, in the generous attempt? And shall not we take the easier measures required of us for their conversion? Alas! Is the Spirit of primitive Christianity entirely lost upon earth? Or is Christianity declined with age, and become an insignificant thing, unworthy of zealous propagation? Or have the Souls of Slaves lost their value, so that it is no matter what becomes of them? How can you pretend to learn your religion from the Apostles; and yet have crowds of Negroes in your Houses or Quarters, as ignorant Heathens, as when they left the Wilds of Africa, without using any means for their conversion? Will ye not endeavour to be followers of the Apostles in this respect, as they also were of Christ? If their example has no weight,

---

* See the Epistle to Philemon.

methinks the conduct of the Jews, Heathens, and Mahometans may shame you. They are all zealous to gain proselytes to their religion, though antiquated, or false. And will not you labor to proselyte your Domestics to the divine religion of Jesus? Certainly, if you do not, even Jews, Heathens and Mahometans may rise up in judgment against you. But,

3. Your duty in this respect will appear, from the worth and importance of the Souls of your poor Slaves. This I have hinted at already; but it deserves a more full illustration.

The appointments of Providence, and the order of the world, not only admit, but require, that there should be civil distinctions among mankind; that some should rule, and some be subject; that some should be Masters, and some Servants. And Christianity does not blend or destroy these distinctions, but establishes and regulates them, and enjoins every man to conduct himself according to them. In this respect, there are many distinctions in the world.——But these distinctions are confined to this world, and do not reach beyond the grave. As to the affairs of religion and eternity, all men stand upon the same footing. The meanest Slave is as immortal as his Master; as capable of happiness or misery, in the highest degree, and of eternal duration; as much a candidate for Heaven or Hell. Now it is this that gives importance to a being. An angel, or the most exalted creature, if the being of a day, or a thousand years, would be but a trifle, a shadow. When his day, or his thousand years are past, he is as much nothing, as if he had never been. It is little matter what becomes of him; let him stand, or fall; let him be happy, or miserable; it is all one in a little time. But immortality is so important an attribute, that it adds a kind of infinite value to every being to which it belongs, however mean and insignificant in other respects. An IMMORTAL! a being that shall never cease to be! a being whose existence runs on forever in parallel lines, with that of the eternal Father of Spirits! a being whose powers of action, and whose capacities for pleasure or pain, shall never become decrepit or contracted, but ripen, improve and enlarge, through the revolutions of eternal ages! a being, that shall perpetually ascend, in an endless gradation, from glory to glory, from perfection to perfection, in the scale of blessedness; or that shall sink forever from deep to deep, from gulph to gulph, in Hell!——What an awful important being is this! a sharer with Angels, in their highest prerogative and dignity! a black skin, or a state of slavery for sixty or seventy years, is of no consideration at all, in our estimate of such a being.* To be entrusted with the care of such a being, in its state of

* "Immortal! ages past, yet nothing gone!
  Morn without eve! a race without a goal!
  Unshortened by progression infinite!
  Futurity forever future! Life

trial, to form it for its everlasting state!——How vast, how awful the trust! To be instrumental to render such a being happy, through its immortal duration! to "SAVE A SOUL FROM DEATH!" to save that precious immortal thing, the *Soul!* to save it from *Death!* from that *dreadful* kind of death, which a *Soul* can die!* How benevolent an act, how noble an exploit, how glorious a salvation is this! more benevolent, more noble, more glorious, than to deliver nations from slavery or famine, or the severest *temporal* distress. But to be accessary by negligence, or more *direct* means, to the ruin, the eternal ruin, of such a being! to render its immortality its curse, a meer capacity of immortal pain!——how horrid the crime! how deep the guilt! how shocking the thought! To be accessary to the murder of the body, to lay countries waste, and turn cities into ruinous heaps, were nothing, in comparison of this: for what are mortal bodies, perishable countries, and cities, when compared to an immortal Soul? Well, *such* a Soul, such a *precious immortal* Soul, has the meanest *Slave.*——Yes, those stupid despised black creatures, that many treat as if they were brutes, are, in this important respect, upon an equality with their haughty masters. And can you think it is no concern of yours, to endeavor to bring these immortals into the way of salvation, and save them from an endless duration of exquisite misery? God has communicated to you the *grand secret* of obtaining his favor, and eternal life; I mean the Revelation of Jesus Christ, which you have in your Bibles: "a mystery, which was hid from ages and generations." And he has communicated it to *you,* that you may communicate it to *others,* particularly your Domestics, who are your immediate care. And will you still reserve it to yourselves, when immortal Souls under your roof, are perishing for want of the knowledge of it? Is it nothing to you, that their blood should be upon your heads; or that the supreme Judge should condemn you, as accessary to their eternal

---

> Beginning still, where computation ends!
> 'Tis the description of a Deity!
> 'Tis the description of the meanest Slave!
> The meanest Slave, dares then Lorenzo scorn?
> The meanest Slave thy sovereign glory shares—
> Man's lawful pride includes humility;
> Stoops to the lowest; is too great to find
> Inferiors; all immortal! brothers all!
> Proprietors eternal of thy love."
> [Edward Young], "Night Thoughts, No. 6"

* This paraphrase seems to me to point out the striking emphasis of the Apostle's short expression. ( James 5:19, 20.) "Brethren, if any of you err from the truth, and one convert him; let him know" this for his encouragement, and he neither needs, nor can have a stronger, "that he which converteth the Sinner from the error of his way, shall save a Soul from Death." An illustrious self-rewarding exploit! a glorious salvation indeed!

destruction? What do you think of being shut up with them, in the same infernal prison, without any distinction or superiority; unless it be *distinguished* and *superior* misery, as having sinned in spite of clearer conviction, and stronger obligations? Are you proof against the terrors of such a thought? Or are you insensible to the generous pleasure, of being instrumental in rendering those happy forever, in the world to come, who have done you so much service in this; and in peopleing the Heavenly regions with inhabitants transplanted from the barbarous Wilds of Africa? I beseech you, have pity upon these miserable immortals. For God's sake, for their sakes, and for your own, do not let them sink into Hell from between your hands, for want of a little pains to instruct them. I hope you would by no means exercise barbarities upon their bodies; and will you be so barbarous, as to suffer their precious never-dying Souls to perish forever; when, through the divine blessing, you might be the means of saving them? Sure you are not capable of such inhuman cruelty.

4. The duty I am urging will appear, if you consider the happy influence your religious instructions might have upon your Negroes, even for your *own interest*.

Your own interest inclines you to wish, they would become good Servants; faithful, honest, diligent and laborious. Now there is no expedient in the world, that can so effectually render them such, as to make them *real Christians*. You cannot but own, that the *precepts* of Christianity, are a complete directory for the behaviour of Servants, and enjoin upon them every duty, that a Master can reasonably require of them: and that the *temper* and *spirit* of Christianity, is the most excellent and amiable, that can adorn human nature, in any station of life. There never was a good Christian yet, who was a bad Servant. To be a Christian, as it refers to man, is to be obedient to superiors, kind and benevolent to all, faithful in every trust, diligent in every calling.——And is not this the very character you wish your Servants to deserve? Well, endeavour to make them true Christians; and if God bless your endeavors, such they will be. Indeed, they may be baptized, and be Christians in *name,* and yet be as bad Servants, and as bad men, as if they were Heathens. But this is not the thing I am urging. Endeavour to make them Christians *indeed;* and then you will find, they will deserve the character I have described. This will make them better Servants, than the terror of the lash, and all the servile and mercenary measures you can use with them. Then they will be governed by a *principle of conscience* towards God: a principle, which will make them as honest and diligent in your absence, as while under your eye. Then, according to St. Paul's injunctions, they will "be obedient to their Masters in all *lawful* things; not with eye-service, as men-pleasers, but in singleness of heart, fearing God;" whose eye, they will be sensible, is always upon them. Then, "whatsoever they do, they will do it *heartily,* as to the Lord, and not to men: knowing, that of the Lord they shall receive the reward" of their fidelity; "for they serve the

Lord Christ," even in serving their earthly Masters; and he will reward the service, as done to himself.*—You see, therefore, that your *own interest* would be promoted by this means: In other cases, you are not insensible of the powerful influence of interest.—And shall it not prevail upon you, to use proper endeavors for the conversion of your poor Negroes? Did some spend that time in the use of such endeavors, which they spend in tying them up, and whipping them, they would probably receive more advantage from it. Resolve, at least, to make trial of this expedient; and pray for a divine blessing upon it: and you will probably see the happy effects of it.

5. The zeal and generosity of others may stir you up to the discharge of this duty.

Sundry good people in *England,* at the distance of near four thousand miles, who have no connection with your Slaves, but what they have with human nature in general, are much more zealous and active for their conversion, than, alas! thousands of their Masters among us. As reading is one important mean of acquiring religious knowledge, they are very solicitous the Negroes should learn to read; and that such of them as have learned, should be furnished with good books.[7] For this purpose, they have been at the expense of two hundred pounds sterling in books, which they have, at different times, sent over to be distributed among them. A most seasonable pious and disinterested charity! And may the God of all grace crown it with success! I solicit your prayers with my own, for this blessing; that our generous benefactors, though they should not receive the intelligence sooner, may meet in Heaven with many from Virginia, both whites and blacks, who were brought thither by means of this charity. And I cannot but hope, and even believe, that this, in some instances, will be the happy consequence. Such assistance from so remote a quarter is a new spring to my endeavors among you; and gives me some encouragement, that God has remarkably gracious designs towards this guilty land. It sometimes seems to me, as if the strongholds of Sin and Satan among us were attacked from all quarters; and therefore, that it is determined in Heaven, they shall fall. Oh! let your prayers contribute to the accomplishment of my *hope.*

Now, my brethren, I may leave yourselves to judge, whether the religious instruction of your Negroes, be not a duty incumbent upon *you.* Is this the concern of Christians on the other side of the vast ocean? And is it not much more yours, for whom these poor creatures labour and toil all their lives, and who receive the benefit of their labours? No creatures in the British dominions stand in greater need of such a charity from our British friends, than the poor Negroes among us. But yet, I must say, this necessity proceeds rather from the want of

*Colos. 3:22, 24.

pious zeal and generosity in their Masters, than from the want of ability. Certainly, he that can lay out forty or fifty pounds to purchase a Slave, is able to spare a few shillings to furnish him with a few books for his instruction.—This is undoubtedly the case in general, though there are some exceptions. And who so strongly obliged to furnish your Slaves with these, as yourselves, who reap the benefit of their labours? Methinks you might blush to receive assistance in this case. But waving this point at present, what I would inculcate upon you is, that you would at *least,* concur with the endeavors of the noble-spirited benefactors, to Christianize your own domestics. Let their example fire you with emulation, and engage you in this apostolic work. Some of you, I doubt not, will honestly make the attempt. But alas! I am afraid, others will continue negligent, even after these helps are put into their hands. If so, I warn you beforehand, that you must give an account to the great God for your criminal omission; and it is time for you to bethink yourselves, what defence or excuse you shall be able to make. To enforce this argument the more, let me add,

6. The relation you bear to your Negroes as their *Masters,* obliges you to instruct them in the Christian Religion.

Indeed, this duty is not yours *alone:* it is the duty of *every* Christian, according to his station, to do all in his power for the conversion of others: and there is no person so insignificant, but he may contribute something, through divine grace, to this benevolent design. The meanest member in a family may drop a word, or at least lead a life, that may tend to give favorable impressions of Christianity to those around him. The instruction of Negroes is particularly the duty of *Overseers,* who have the immediate care of them; and they will find it impossible to excuse themselves, by flinging the fault upon the Owners: especially if they are removed beyond the reach of the owner's inspection. Their Souls will be required of the Overseer's hand. And I tremble to think, what a terrible account many of them must give. But after all, the care originally and principally lies upon the masters and proprietors. It is as much their duty to feed their minds with sacred knowledge, as to feed and clothe their bodies. All the numerous and strong arguments for family-religion in general, are equally conclusive in favour of this particular branch of it. But I cannot now take time to mention them. Will the example of *Abraham* in my text, have no weight with you? Are not you under the same obligations with *Joshua,* to resolve, that, let others do what they please, "as for you and your *House,* you will serve the Lord?"* It is mentioned to the honor of the Roman Centurion, that he feared God *with all his House;* and some of his *household Servants* or Slaves, and the soldiers under him, were devout men.† And why should not you

*Jos. 24:15.
†Acts 10:1, 7.

endeavor to render your Slaves such? But I need not enlarge upon so plain a point. I will venture to leave it to your own consciences, to determine, whether God would place immortal Souls under your care, without obliging you to endeavour to educate them for a happy eternity? Shall they work and drudge for you all their lives? And are not you bound, in justice and gratitude, to retaliate them, by endeavoring to make them partakers of the rich blessings of the Gospel? Will you not labor to make this land of slavery, a land of spiritual liberty to them; and to bring them to share in the heavenly inheritance, in exchange for their liberty, and as a reward for the fruits of their labors, which you enjoy?

And now, upon a review of all these arguments together, I would have you come to some conclusion what you intend to do with regard to this duty, of which, I presume, you are now convinced. Brethren, what do you determine to do? I am sure, if you have any regard to the religion you profess, or the divine author of it; if you have any regard to the salvation of an immortal Soul, or to the laws of justice and gratitude; if you have the least spark of sincere piety towards God, or true benevolence to men you will honestly begin the attempt, and will not dare to live one week more, in the neglect of so plain and important a duty. But I know, those that are disaffected to the duty, will try to ward off the conviction, by various pleas and excuses. And were you now to speak your minds, I should probably hear you start a thousand objections.

Some of you perhaps, would object, "That your Negroes are such sullen perverse creatures, or stupid dunces, that it is impossible to teach them any thing that is good." This is undoubtedly the true character of some; and it must afford a great deal of grief to such of you, as are really concerned for their everlasting happiness. All you can do, in such a discouraging case, is to continue your endeavors; and earnestly pray for a blessing upon them, from that God, who alone can render them efficacious. And who knows what may be the issue? Do you wait patiently; and you may yet reap the fruits of your pious labors. Sullen, and perverse, and stupid as they are, divine grace can render them gentle, pliable, and teachable, as a little child. But should your endeavors always continue unsuccessful, as you may expect they will with regard to sundry; yet you have this solid consolation left you, that you are clear of their blood, and have delivered your own Soul, and your reward is with the Lord. He will accept and reward even *unsuccessful* fidelity. But I am apprehensive this objection, in many cases, is but an idle pretence. Your Negroes may be ignorant and stupid as to divine things, not for want of capacity, but for want of instruction; not through their perverseness, but through your negligence. From the many trials I have made, I have reason to conclude, that making allowance for their low and barbarous education, their imperfect acquaintance with our language, their having no opportunity for intellectual improvements, and the like, they are generally as capable of instruction, as the white people.

Besides, Christianity, as far as it is essential to Salvation, is not a difficult science; and if they do not learn it, the fault lies in the heart, rather than in the head. Some of them shew, that they have sense enough to love God, and hate Sin, though they are very ignorant in other respects. But to be short—be sure you make a thorough trial, before you start this objection. Take all proper means to reach them, before you conclude they are unteachable. And bear upon your minds a deep sense of the vanity of all human endeavors, without the concurrence of the Holy Spirit, for which, pray without ceasing.

Some of you, perhaps, will object, "That you can find no time to instruct your Negroes; nor can you allow them time to attend to instruction." I grant, that Religion should by no means be made a pretence for idleness in Masters or Servants; and that moderate industry in your lawful callings, is as much your duty, in its place, as the religious instruction to your Domestics. But granting this, there is no plausible ground for the objection after all. For are not the affairs of eternity of infinitely greater importance to you, than those of time? Should you not be much more solicitous how you and yours shall subsist thro' eternal ages, than how you shall subsist for a few years in this vanishing world? If a proper care of the one, be inconsistent with the other, to which should you give the preference? If you have not time enough to lay out upon both, which, do you think, should be neglected? Time or Eternity? Earth or Heaven? your perishing bodies, or your immortal Spirits? Can you hesitate a moment in so plain a case? Whatever become of yourselves or your families in this world, by no means neglect to provide for your and their happiness in the eternal world, which is just before you. Whatever be undone, let not the work of Salvation be undone. Rather be poor, yes, rather perish through hunger and nakedness in this world, than let your souls and bodies, and those of your Slaves, perish forever in the world to come. This is a sufficient answer to your objection, upon the worst supposition you can possibly make, viz: that the religious instruction of your Negroes is inconsistent with your temporal interest, and would rend them useless, or a burden to you. But this supposition is wholly groundless: for the discharge of your duty to them, would not take up so much time, as that the loss would be perceivable at a year's end. Let this duty take up your Sunday evenings, and other leisure hours, which both you and your Slaves now spend in trifling and sinning. And if you should set apart two or three stated hours in the week for this purpose, where would be the mighty loss? Will you begrudge this short space of time for the Salvation of those poor creatures, who spend their whole lives in your service? Besides, you may easily drop a word of instruction while you are looking after them in the field. Their ears are open, and their thoughts may be employed about divine things, with an Axe or a Hoe in their hands. In short, you will find, that this duty may be so managed, as to be no hindrance at all to your business: and in the issue, it may be a great advantage to it.

For if God should bless your pious diligence, it will render them much better Servants to you, as well as to him. Therefore, no longer think to excuse yourself with this frivolous pretence; but immediately attempt what is unquestionably your duty.

Will any of you farther object, "That Christianizing the Negroes makes them proud and saucy, and tempts them to imagine themselves upon an equality with the white people?" But is this the *native tendency* of real genuine Christianity? Is the true Christian spirit haughty and insolent? Do the doctrines or precepts of Christianity tend to cherish pride and disobedience? If you think so, why do you not renounce it yourselves? Will you profess a religion, which has a native tendency to make men worse, and cherishes and confirms their wicked dispositions? Will you initiate your Children into such a diabolical Religion? If you have such notions of Christianity, you are as rank Heathens at heart, as the rudest African Negro: and your Christian profession is a most glaring absurdity. But you cannot but know in your consciences, that *true* Christianity is quite another thing; that it tends to inspire its subjects with modesty, humility, meekness, faithfulness, and every grace and virtue; and that a *good Christian* will always be a *good Servant*. Recollect what I have said on this head already, and it will entirely remove your objection. I grant indeed, that there is nothing so excellent, but the depraved heart of man may be capable of abusing it to the vilest purposes. But this is no objection against the *thing*, but against the unnatural *abuse* of it. A man may be proud of his good sense, learning, estate, or any real or imaginary excellency. But will you hence infer, that you should keep yourselves or your children ignorant, illiterate, poor, and destitute of every good quality, in order to keep you humble and pliable, and to guard against pride and insolence? Upon this principle, you would leave human nature naked of every excellency, and, to prevent pride, make it a mere mass of deformity. In like manner, the holy Religion of Jesus may be abused as an occasion of vanity and self-conceit, by those that usurp the name and external badges of it, without imbibing its spirit. A Negro may desire to be baptized, merely that he may be in the fashion; and even from this base principle he may be prompted to make such a profession of his faith and repentance, as the Ministers of the Gospel, who cannot inspect the heart, may judge sufficient for his admission to the privileges of the visible church, though his profession was but gross hypocrisy in the sight of God, and may afterwards appear such to them. Baptism and the Christian name may indeed render such a wretched creature worse. But that is not because he *is* a Christian, but because he is *not* a Christian, that is, a Christian *indeed,* while he vainly *imagines* himself such. Nothing can be inferred from hence, but that great care should be taken in the admission of Catechumens to Baptism: And it is your duty to give all the information to Ministers on this point, which may help to direct them in so difficult and important an affair. I am sensible that the ordinance

of Baptism, learning the Creed, Ten Commandments and the Lord's Prayer, a confused desire to be admitted to Church privileges, and such superficial qualifications, are far from rendering them *true* Christians; and if they are admitted upon
no better evidence, they, as it were, receive a deadly blow from the hand that bap-
tizes them; & the Christian name will be of no service to *them;* & they are likely
to be a scandal to *it.* Let them first see their sins; let their hearts be broken with
penitential sorrows for them; let them long and cry after Jesus as the only Saviour; and receive him with all their hearts; let them, in short, give some hopeful
evidences, that they are Christians indeed; and then let them wear the Christian
name, and share in all the privileges of the Children of God. Some such, blessed
be God, are to be found among us; and to their lives I may refer you for the most
effectual confutation of your objection. Are not the Savages transformed into
Lambs and Doves? Are they not humble and meek, dutiful, faithful, diligent, and
the reverse of what they once were? Such would all the Negroes be, were they all
sincere Christians: and what can be a more striking evidence of the happy tendency and powerful efficacy of our holy Religion, to make men of all nations, &
in all stations, truly good?

But you will perhaps say, "Some, who once made a great profession of Religion,
and were baptized, have apostatized, & become as bad as ever." This, alas! is too
true as to some: and the Lord have mercy on the miserable backsliders, whose last
state is worse than their first! But you know, this is not the case of all, nor, I hope,
of the generality: and to find even a few chosen, among the many that are called,
is no unspeakable pleasure; and a sufficient encouragement to the duty I am recommending.—But were the ground of this complaint more general than it is,
what would you infer from it? That it is not the duty of Christians to propagate
their Religion, and particularly of Christian masters to propagate it among their
Domestics? This would be an extravagant inference indeed; and upon this principle, you would banish all Religion out of the world. Are there no apostates among
white people, among Britons and Virginians? Would to God there were not! but
the melancholy fact is too notorious to be denied. And shall all religious instructions be given up on this account; and the immortal Religion of Jesus suffered
to die with the present generation, without any farther endeavours to preserve
and spread it, lest some that have pretended to embrace it, should afterwards
renounce it in practice or profession? The truth [is that] offences must come; apos-
tasies must happen, in the present state of things. There have been apostates from
all the Religions that ever were in the world, whether true or false: Apostates
from Judaism, Mahometism, Heathenism, (if I may call them apostates) as well as
from Christianity. And if we must give over our attempts to propagate it on this
account, it is to consent to put an end to all Religion, whether natural or revealed,

whether true or false. The best remedy against this, is what I prescribed in answer to the last objection, viz: to take all possible care, that none be admitted to Baptism, and into the Christian Church, but such as give hopeful evidences of a thorough conversion. After all, it must, alas! be expected, that while Ministers can judge only by *external* appearances, and some even of the unpolished Negroes are artful enough to deceive, many will unavoidably be admitted, who, like the crowds of Christians among us of a *fairer* colour, are but hypocrites: and, notwithstanding all their privileges, will be condemned at last as workers of iniquity; or may, perhaps, even in this life, throw off the mask, and render it necessary to exclude them from the communion of Christians.

The dullest of mankind have generally a very ready invention to find out objections against a duty that is disagreeable to them: And it may be impossible for me to particularize them all. But I dare say your judgment is already convinced; and, however unwilling you may be to own it, your conscience is on my side. You may pretend this and that as the reason of your omission. But shall I tell you the plain truth?——The true reason is, your stupid carelessness about Religion, and about your own Souls, as well as those of your Slaves. Could this objection, not of your *reason,* but of a *wicked heart,* be once removed, we should hear no more of the rest. For this is a certain truth, that he that loves Religion himself, will endeavour to bring others to love it; he that is concerned about his own salvation, will be also concerned about that of others; and he, and only he, who is careless what becomes of his own Soul, can be careless about the Souls committed to his charge. And are you fit for Heaven, or likely to be admitted thither, while this temper is predominant in you? Are you prepared for the Region of Holiness, while you are thus disaffected to it? Alas! no; in your present condition, you are *fitted for destruction,* and nothing else. And is it not time for you to awake to the care of your *own* immortal Souls? When once you begin to take care of them, you will soon extend your care to the Souls of your poor Negroes.

And now, Sirs, may I not hope, you are determined to live in the willful neglect of this duty no longer? If not, will you not be self-condemned? Will you not carry an uneasy monitor in your own breasts, that will be perpetually urging you to your duty, and remonstrating against your omissions of it? And oh! what account will you give to the great God at last? Oh! that you may think of it in time: for I can assure you, it deserves your most serious thoughts.

What now remains is, to give you some directions for the right performance of this duty. And these shall refer both to the *qualifications* required in you, as the instructors of your Slaves, and the best *manner* of instructing them. I shall not enlarge upon either: for, I know, if you are zealously set upon the discharge of the duty, a few short hints as to the manner will be sufficient.

The directions with regard to *yourselves* are such as these.

Endeavour to furnish your own minds with religious knowledge; otherwise, it is impossible you should communicate religious knowledge to your domestics. For this purpose, read, hear, pray, meditate, and diligently attend upon all means of instruction. In this way, you may hope to remove an objection, which alas! has as much truth in it, as any of those I have answered, viz: "That you are so ignorant yourselves, that you are not capable of teaching others." How scandalous and criminal is this, to be ignorant of the Religion you profess! to be ignorant of it, with Bibles in your hands, and means of instruction all around you! How dangerous a state is this! Can you expect to *blunder* into Heaven at random, without knowing the way that leads to it? Alas! you may be destroyed for *lack of knowledge,* as well as by the grossest vice.* Therefore labour to furnish your minds with useful knowledge. Again;

Endeavour to maintain a deep sense of eternal things upon your spirits. Or, labour to get your hearts deeply impressed with the things you know.—This will at once excite you to use proper means for the conversion of those under your care, and make you serious and solemn in the use of them.

Let your example enforce your instructions, and exhibit to them a living pattern of practical Religion. The dullest Negro has sense enough to see the absurdity of a mere profession of Religion, without a correspondent practice. But if they see that your religion make you good men, and consequently good masters, it will be a strong presumption to them in its favour.

In a word, endeavour to be true Christians yourselves, in knowledge, in temper, and in practice, and then you are qualified to instruct your families. But without these qualifications, you will not either make the attempt; or are not likely to succeed in it.

Let me now add a few directions as to the *[manner and] ways* of instruction.

Encourage your Negroes to learn to read, and give them all the assistance in your power. Encourage your Children to teach them: or let one of themselves be taught either at home, or at school; and let him teach the rest.† There may be some of them so old, so stupid, or so ignorant of our language, that it may be almost impossible to teach them. But as to the young, especially those that are born in your houses; and as to those that are desirous to learn, though advanced in age, I

---

*Hos. 4:6.

†As I would earnestly recommend reading the Scriptures and singing the praises of God as parts of family-religion; so I would recommend it, as an easy and very useful expedient to improve the Negroes in reading, that, when they begin to read, they be ordered to bring their Bibles and Psalm-Books with them, when they attend upon family-worship, and to look over the Chapter or Psalm, as it is read by the master of the house. This I have found by experience to be a very good expedient.

have found by experience, this direction is very practicable. Let us zealously make the attempt with the present generation; and then they will be able to teach their Children themselves; and thus this useful branch of learning will be conveyed down to their posterity, with little trouble or expense to their owners.

Frequently speak seriously to them upon the great concerns of Religion.

Maintain the daily worship of God in your families. And endeavour to time it so, that your Slaves may have opportunity of attending. What can more familiarly teach them their wants and mercies, their duties and sins, than to hear you solemnly mention them every day in your prayers to God?

Restrain them from rambling about on the Lord's Day, the most proper time for them to get knowledge; and do not connive at their working upon it for themselves; much less oblige them to it, in order to furnish themselves with those necessaries, which it is your duty to provide for them. *Command* and oblige them to spend those sacred hours in public and private attendance upon divine worship; and endeavour to make them sensible of the ends and designs of it.[8]

Maintain a proper authority over them, and do not make yourselves contemptible to them, by excessive familiarity and indulgence. But, on the other hand, do not treat them with barbarity, as if they were dogs, and had no share in the same human nature with yourselves.

Finally; be always sensible, that the success of all your endeavours depends upon the concurrence of divine grace; and earnestly pray to God for the blessed spirit to make them effectual.

These short directions are easy to be understood by those that are disposed to practice them. And certainly, they are not impracticable, through the grace of God, to a Christian. The objections against them must arise not from reason or inability, but from a slothful disaffected heart. The omission will involve you in very dreadful guilt, and it is likely to occasion the eternal ruin of thousands of immortal Souls. The observance of them, through the divine blessing, might contribute to your satisfaction and interest in time and eternity, and advance a very miserable part of human nature to all the glory and happiness of the heavenly world. If any of you are proof against the energy of such considerations as these, I have none more weighty or affecting to propose to you. But some of you, I doubt not, have already felt their force, and others will, I hope, submit to it, for the future. Which may God grant for Jesus' sake. *Amen.*

Notes

1. George William Pilcher, *Samuel Davies: Apostle of Dissent in Colonial Virginia* (Knoxville: University of Tennessee Press, 1971), 13 (quotation).

2. Ibid., 108.

3. Davies, *Letters from the Rev. Samuel Davies, &c. Shewing the State of Religion in Virginia, Particularly among the Negroes* (London, 1757), 9–10.

4. Pilcher, *Samuel Davies,* 113.

5. My transcription is based on the edition reprinted by William Spencer, *The Duty of Masters to Their Servants in a Sermon, by the Late Reverent, Pious, and Learned, Samuel Davies, of Hanover County, Virginia* (Lynchburg[, Va.]: William W. Gray, 1809).

6. Virginia was at this point engaged in the French and Indian War (1754–63).

7. The prospect of slave literacy would eventually be associated with increased risk for slave flight and rebellion; by the antebellum era, laws were passed restricting slave education. See Janet Duitsman Cornelius, *"When I Can Read My Title Clear": Literacy, Slavery, and Religion in the Antebellum South* (Columbia: University of South Carolina Press, 1991).

8. Throughout the British plantation system in the New World, the commonly accepted work schedule afforded slaves considerable control over their own time on the Sabbath. To the frustration of many ministers, enterprising slaves often took advantage of the day to tend to their own gardens. This was a means to supplement their diets and, also, to pursue their own profit in an "internal" slave economy that has attracted recent scholarly attention. See, for example, Betty Wood, *Women's Work, Men's Work: The Informal Slave Economies of Lowcountry Georgia* (Athens: University of Georgia Press, 1995); and Larry E. Hudson Jr., *To Have and to Hold: Slave Work and Family Life in Antebellum South Carolina* (Athens: University of Georgia Press, 1997).

# CHAPTER 5

# William Knox, 1768

Born in Ireland in 1732, William Knox rose from a modest family to a position of political significance within the expanding British Empire. His life story illustrates the cosmopolitan implications of organic Christian thought in the eighteenth century. Knox came of age during an era when notions of British superiority over "uncivilized" peoples were hardening into cultural orthodoxy. After spending several years studying at Trinity College in the early 1750s, Knox made political contact with Henry Ellis, the newly appointed Georgia governor who hailed from Knox's hometown of Monaghan. In October 1756 Knox received an appointment as provost marshal for the recently settled colony.[1]

When the two men arrived in Savannah in February 1757, they found a local government paralyzed by factional strife. From the beginning of his tenure in Georgia, Knox maintained that executive power had to be strengthened for the colony to function smoothly. Over the ensuing half-decade, Knox campaigned to increase the power of the governor and the Governor's Council (which acted as the upper house in the colonial assembly). During this period he also managed to become one of the largest planters in Georgia, accumulating thousands of acres and more than 120 slaves. Accordingly, Knox's hierarchical social principles informed his agenda as both a planter and a politician. He believed that firm authority would reform troublesome colonists just as firm mastery would enlighten African slaves.

When Knox returned to England in 1762, he left behind a colonial political order that was about to become unglued. Financial pressures created by the French and Indian War pushed British officials to search for new sources of revenue. During the 1760s they would seek to more closely supervise the colonial economy, a decision that antagonized American settlers. Having been appointed Georgia's lobbying agent in England, Knox argued against the Stamp Act on the grounds that the legislation placed too onerous a burden on the colonists. However, Knox's deep commitment to organic principles led him to uphold Parliament's right to levy taxes on the colonial economy. On matters of policy, Knox attempted to chart a middle course between the colonial claims for autonomy from British regulation and the tyranny of a Parliament that, at times, seemed to care little for colonial welfare. In his mind, American settlers owed obedience to a mother country that served their needs even as it tended to the interests of the entire empire. Ultimately, Knox could not remain true to his hierarchical principles and to continue to please the Georgia Assembly. Although the Governor's Council supported him, he was dismissed from his position as colonial agent in 1768.

It was no coincidence that Knox published two important pamphlets during this period. At the very moment when he was composing an enthusiastic defense of British imperial authority, he was also penning his proslavery sermons. In the former, he asked, "Is the British empire to be suffered to be rent in pieces, and each member of it exposed to become a prey to its powerful neighbour, from a vain imagination that there is no supreme power in the state, which has authority to command the strength, the riches, and the swords of all the subjects of the realm, to defend every part of its dominions, and to protect the rights and possessions of every individual who lives under it?"[2] In the latter, he detailed his organic vision of the master-slave relationship, insisting that American masters "would be much better served" by "Negroes instructed in religion and taught to serve their masters for conscience sake." Sadly for Knox, the ideal of a just government that ruled by consent of the governed failed to materialize in either context. Rising to the position of undersecretary in the Colonial Office American Department, he witnessed the colonists' increasing radicalism and bemoaned their eventual decision to break from the empire. As the absentee owner of some 120 Georgia slaves, he fruitlessly struggled to establish a formal Anglican mission to service their religious needs.[3] Following the Revolution, he removed many of his slaves to Jamaica only to realize, in 1785, that they were suffering terribly from a want of supplies and shelter. His writings on slavery proceeded from coherent Christian logic about the social and spiritual benefits of organic hierarchy. Yet Knox's experiences as a slaveholder and as a British official demonstrate the limited appeal that this logic carried for the planter elite in the colonial American South.

⚜

WILLIAM KNOX, *Three Tracts Respecting the Conversion and Instruction of the Free Indians and Negroe Slaves in the Colonies. Addressed to the Venerable Society for Propagation of the Gospel in Foreign Parts* (no listed publisher, ca. 1768)[4]

### Tract the Second.
*Of the Negroe Slaves in the Colonies.*

The difficulties attending a plan for the instruction of the negroe slaves in our colonies are very different from the obstacles which present themselves to the conversion of the North American Indians. The quick sagacity of the Indian keeps him aloof from every attempt to convert him. The dull stupidity of the Negroe leaves him without any desire for instruction. Whether the creator originally formed these black people a little lower than other men, or that they have lost their intellectual powers through disuse, I will not assume the province of determining; but certain it is, that a *new Negroe,* (as those lately imported from Africa are called,) is a complete definition of indolent stupidity, nor could a more forcible means be employed for the conversion of a deist, than setting one of these creatures before him as an example of man in a state of nature *unbiased* by revelation or education.[5] Their stupidity does not however authorize us to consider them as beasts for our use, much less to deny them all knowledge of the common salvation. The Negroes born in our colonies are undoubtedly capable of receiving instruction, and those who are born among the French are instructed in the Roman Catholic religion; but our planters are generally averse to their Negroes being taught any thing but labour, and yet the generality of our North American planters have a regard for religion, and are punctual in the discharge of its duties as far as they think themselves obliged by them. How this comes to pass must be our first enquiry, for unless the planter can be prevailed on to give his assistance, it will be in vain to propose any method for instructing his slaves.

Our planters' objection to their Negroes being instructed is simply this, that instruction renders them less fit or less willing to labour. Experience justifies their opinion, and a little reflection will convince us that such must be the consequence.

The British laws disown perpetual servitude, and the people of these islands have a general antipathy to slavery. The right of the planter to his Negroe is only founded on the acts of his provincial assembly, and beyond their jurisdiction he has no power over him. If he teaches his Negroe to read one book, he will of himself read another, and such has been the imprudence of some ill informed writers, that books are not wanting to exhort the Negroes to rebel against their masters. Were the Negroes universally taught to read, and *a late publication* which out of respect I forbear to name, put into their hands and circulated among them, there would be little doubt that the next ships informed us of a general insurrection of the Negroes, and the massacre of their owners; and yet the writer's intention was certainly to engage the planter to have his Negroes instructed![6]

The case is very different with the French planter and his Negroes. The perpetual servitude of the Negroes is not only consented to by that nation, but is expressly authorized by the king's edict. "De clarons les esclaves estre meubles & commetels entrent en la communaute, les en fans qui naistront de marriage entre esclaves seront esclaves, & appartiendront aux maistres des semmes esclaves," are the terms of the perpetual edict of March, 1687.[7] The French planter can therefore have no apprehension of losing his slave by giving him instruction, nor will the slave's being instructed make him less willing to obey his master. There are no books to be given them to read which charge their masters with *infringing both divine and human laws* by retaining them in slavery; nor are such doctrines transmitted to them under the sanction of a religious society composed of the governors of the national church. Here then is the true source of the evil, and the remedy is obvious. If the purchasing a Negroe for a slave to be an *infringement of divine and human laws,* in God's name, why is such a trade permitted? A few words in an act of parliament prohibiting the importation or sale of Negroes in our colonies will destroy the practice in the future.——And a few words more declaring the offspring of Negroes already imported to be free, will prevent slavery extending to the next generation. This method is certainly the most proper, and the only one which can have efficacy; nor does it seem very consistent in any member of either house of parliament to declaim without doors against the integrity of this transaction, and bear no testimony against its encroachment within. Even the last session of parliament, 1766, furnished an occasion for asserting the rights of the Negroes, and displaying the infamy of trading in them. The act for opening free ports in the West-Indies, declares Negroes a *lawful commodity* and to be imported and sold there upon paying a certain duty, but neither upon the passing that act, nor upon the passing any former one for the encouragement of the African trade, does there appear a single protest in abhorrence of that trade, or *of treating rational creatures as property.* But, besides, the perpetual servitude of the Negroes in our colonies is not the act of their masters, nor is it the mere effect of their power over those wretches. In every colony the right of the owner is fixed by a law of the colony framed under the king's instructions, and afterwards transmitted for his approbation in his privy council: It is therefore in the discretion of the privy council to repeal all these acts of the colonies, and if that were done every Negroe born in the colonies would become entitled to all the privileges and franchises of the natural born subjects of this realm. How then does it happen, that these acts, so *repugnant to all divine and human laws* are suffered to exist? Are there no lords of the council sufficiently zealous in the cause of liberty and religion to procure their repeal? Or, are there none others to make application to the council for that purpose? If therefore the purchasing Negroes for slaves be a *violation of the laws of nature and humanity,* it is pretty evident that the American planters do not *alone* bear the weight of that iniquity, nor are they only to be called upon to remove the evil. If however on the other hand the purchasing Negroes for slaves be consistent with divine and human obligations, care should be taken to secure the property of the slave to his owner under all circumstances, and such a plan of instruction should be digested, as might best conduce to the Negroes eternal welfare, without making them uneasy in their present condition, or encouraging them to revolt against their owners. As the first thing to be done therefore is to determine the lawfulness of purchasing Negroes for slaves, it may be proper to state the fact fully, that those whose high office it is to expound the divine will as far as it has been revealed, may be the better able to judge of the conformity or repugnance of this transaction to it.

The African states on the west coast of that vast peninsula are all, except the Fantees, purely monarchical, and the sovereign claims the absolute disposal of the persons as well as effects of his subjects. There is no individual over whom the sovereign does not claim this right, unless such individual has obtained his freedom by the grant of the sovereign. Those whom the sovereign has permitted to have property, invest it in slaves which they purchase either of their sovereign or from the rich men of other states, or their own; These great men consider the offspring of their slaves as their annual income, and sell the children or parents as their convenience or necessity directs. Throughout Africa, as well among the Fantees as other nations, not only a man's slaves, but his wife, children, and even himself are all liable to his debts, and the fines set on him by the sovereign or the supreme council. The monarchs by this means frequently repossess themselves of their manumitted subjects and his slaves and children, and the Fantees by this means rid the state of any dangerous individual. That such should be the policy of the African states will not appear strange to any one who is acquainted with what passes or has past in more enlightened parts of the world. 'Tis a good speculative position that no man ought to be bound by conditions to which he never personally consented, yet we shall find no government existing where the child would not be punished for refusing submission to the constitution handed down to him by his ancestor; and indeed the permanency of all government rests upon the acknowledged right in the parent to decide the political condition of his offspring. In Ireland more than two-thirds of the inhabitants are not only denied a right to give their personal consent to the laws by which they and their children are bound, but they are made incapable of acquiring that sort of property which might give them influence with those who make the laws. It is still the case in Poland, and was the case in some parts of Britain not many years since, to transfer the service of the inhabitants and the power over their lives, with the titles to the lands: And it was the universal practice among the Asiatic nations, the jews only excepted, to consider a man's wife and children as his effects, and to sell them for the satisfaction of his creditors, as appears from all history ancient and modern, but most authentically from the parable of debtor and creditor, recorded by St. Matthew.[8]

These things are not mentioned either to excuse the policy of the African states by their example, or to censure those who have done them; but in order to obviate a vulgar reflection upon the African traders, which is, that the slavery of the people on that continent is owing to the demand their princes have found for slaves from the American colonies: Whereas men have sold one another from the very earliest ages of the world, and wherever sovereign authority has been lodged, it has assumed a right to dispose of the lives and properties of the subjects. From the coast of Guinea to the extremity of Abyssinia there is not a state, the Fantees only excepted, where the people are not, and as far as we know of them, always were, slaves; and their princes and great men traded with one another in slaves long before America was discovered. The demand which the American colonies have occasioned, has probably given rise to many acts of tyranny and oppression in the sovereigns, in order to possess themselves of the slaves of their great men, but on the other hand it may have made them more careful of the lives of their own slaves or subjects, because of the profit they made by selling them. A captain of an English ship who had offered the King of Dormi or Dehouma less than he had asked for five hundred of his slaves, was invited by him to dinner the following day; they dined in a tent, and when they were rising from table, the king of Dormi said to the captain, you would not give me my price for my five hundred slaves, did you think I valued them too high? You may have them for half the money. And ordering the back of the tent to be drawn up, the five hundred heads were shewn to him piled upon one another. This story, which is indubitably attested, is a shocking proof of the despotism of the African princes, and it also serves to shew how ill founded another vulgar notion is, that the Negroes annually brought to our colonies from Africa, are stolen by our traders from thence. Indeed it is astonishing, that such a notion should ever have been entertained by any one, who ever thought about trade. To suppose that the several European states should settle forts and factories upon that coast, in order to protect their subjects in stealing away the inhabitants: That the same ships and captains should return annually to the same places, and among them steal away near forty thousand people each voyage, is so monstrous, that the bare stating it is a sufficient confutation. The manner in which that trade is carried on is this: The return of our ships to the coast of Africa being regular, the Negroe factors bring down the slaves they have purchased in the interior parts of the country at the time the ships are expected, and sell or barter them to our captains for the best price they can get; some of these factors bring slaves even from the interior parts of Abyssinia, if their own accounts may be credited, and others are brought from an equal distance to the sea coast of Barbary to supply the Turks. The princes and great men who reside near the coast, or upon the navigable rivers, make their own bargains with our ships' captains, or the governors of our forts, so that instances are very rare, of even single Negroes being clandestinely carried off by any of our people. Whenever such a thing has been done, the captain who did it has never dared to return there again; and very fatal revenge has been taken upon some of his countrymen.

The Negroes being arrived in our colonies, are put up to sale by their owners, and the planters purchase them. The Fantees are generally carried to Jamaica, where they are greatly valued on account of their hardiness and high spirit. But as they were freemen in their own country, they are very difficult to be managed as slaves, and this is the principal reason of the frequent insurrections in that island; while upon the continent especially, insurrections are seldom heard of.[9]

The other Negroes having been always slaves, submit to their new masters willingly enough, when they know how they are to be employed: At first indeed they are under great terrors of being eat[en] by the white people, and so strong have been the apprehensions of many of them upon their arrival, that no entreaties could prevail on them to take any sustenance, lest they should become fat and fitter for food, until some of their countrymen who had resided some time in the colony were brought to them, and convinced them of the folly of their suspicions.

From this account of the trade, the plain state of the question seems to be whether it be lawful in the captains of our ships to purchase Negroes in Africa, from those of that country, who by the nature of their government, consider them as their property, and keep them in actual servitude? And whether it be lawful for the British subjects in the colonies to purchase those Negroes of those captains, and to continue them and their offspring in a state of servitude?

If the reverend members of the society should be of opinion that this trade is contrary to divine laws, it will surely be proper to apply to government for an act of parliament to prohibit it, and at the same time to apply for lands to be given to such Negroes as their masters, influenced by that opinion, may release from servitude; for such will be its effect upon many of the North American planters. But if on the contrary the opinion should be, that the trade is not a violation of the divine laws, it will be highly proper to transmit that opinion to the colonies, for the satisfaction of conscientious planters, as well as to encourage them to give their Negroes instruction, thereby to avail themselves of such authority for making them contented with their condition.

No planter is so grossly barbarous as not to wish to have his Negroe do his work with a good will; and very few would be so brutal or ignorant as not to perceive, that were their Negroes instructed in religion, and taught to serve their masters for conscience sake, that they would be much better served by them; but it is surely the height of folly to expect of any owner of Negroes to permit them to be told, that he violates all divine and human laws by retaining them in his service, or to allow them to have any notions of a religion, whose sanctions he must appear to them condemn, by making them his slaves. Until therefore the lawfulness of continuing these people in perpetual servitude be determined, it will be in vain to expect that our American planters will permit their Negroes to be instructed, much less contribute towards their instruction.

Many regulations are wanting for securing good usage to these unhappy people which no authority, but that of parliament, can enforce, and it is most reproachful to this country, that there are more than five hundred thousand of its subjects, for whom the legislature has never shewn the least regard. All regulation, 'tis true, would be preposterous if the servitude of these people be unlawful; but then it is still more reproachful to this country, that so great a number of its subjects are unlawfully made slaves. On all accounts therefore the lawfulness of the thing must first be determined. When the lords the bishops have declared their opinion of the divine law, an act of parliament will be sufficient to decide what shall be human law, and until the first is declared, it would be presumption to offer any regulations to be made by the other.

APPENDIX.

Sometime after the foregoing tracts were written, and were presented to the late most reverend and learned president of the society for propagating the gospel in foreign parts, the opinion of the society respecting the lawfulness of purchasing or keeping Negroe slaves was called for in order to frame an answer to a letter received by the society from Mr. Benezet of Philadelphia.[10] With permission of the venerable society, I subjoin a copy of the answer written by their secretary, as containing their opinion.

Copy of a letter sent by the reverend Doctor Burton, secretary of the society for the propagation of the gospel in foreign parts, to Mr. Anthony Benezet at Philadelphia. Dated the 6th of February, 1768.[11]

Sir,

Your letter to the society for propagating the gospel in foreign parts, of the 26th of April last hath been considered by them with all due attention. And I am directed to assure you that they have a great esteem for you, on account of the tenderness and humanity which you express for the Negroe slaves, and are extremely desirous that they should be treated with the utmost care and kindness, both with regard to temporals and spirituals. That their labour should be made easy to them in all respects. That they should be provided with conveniences and accommodations to render their situation comfortable, and especially that they should be regularly instructed in the principles of the Christian religion. The society have for many years past uniformly given directions to their agents in Barbadoes, agreeable to these sentiments, which they believe have been observed in a good degree: However they have lately sent to make more particular enquiries into this matter with full purpose of transmitting, in the strongest terms, such further orders as may be found necessary, and of watching over the execution of them with all possible attention; hoping that the good effects of their example will have a proper, and by degrees a general influence on other owners of slaves in America. But they cannot condemn the practice of keeping slaves as unlawful, finding the contrary very plainly implied in the precepts given by the apostles, both to masters and servants, which last were then for the most part slaves. And if the doctrine of the unlawfulness of slavery should be taught in our colonies, the society apprehend, that masters instead of being convinced of it will grow more suspicious and cruel, and much more unwilling to let their slaves learn Christianity; and that the poor creatures themselves, if they come to look on this doctrine as true, will be so strongly tempted by it to rebel against their masters, that the most dreadful consequences to both will be likely to follow, and therefore, though the society is fully satisfied that your intention in this matter is perfectly good, yet they most earnestly beg you not to go further in publishing your notions, but rather to retract them if you shall see cause, which they hope you may on further consideration.

### Tract the Third.
*Of the Negroe Slaves in the Colonies.*

The lawfulness of purchasing negroe slaves, and continuing them and their posterity in perpetual servitude, having been admitted by the venerable society for propagating the gospel in foreign parts, in their letter to Mr. Benezet, at Philadelphia, dated the 6th of February, 1768; I shall now, in pursuance of my former purpose, endeavour to engage the attention of the society to some considerations which may lead to a humane and Christian system, for the civil government and religious instruction of those unhappy people.

The term slave having no legal signification in Great Britain, and being generally used for describing the subjects of the most despotic tyrants, it is commonly understood to denote, one who has no rights, his labour, property and life being at the discretion of his master. This definition of the term is far from being a true one in respect to the Negroe slaves in the British colonies; their owners have no other than a legal property in them, and legal authority over them, and the same laws which make them slaves give them rights.

In no British colony is the life of the slave left in the power of the owner, and for cruel usage, or insufficient nourishment, the slave has a remedy similar to that of apprentices in England, though from the ignorance of the Negroe, and the partiality of the magistrates, who are too frequently *Socii Criminis,*[12] the tyranny of the planter is much seldomer punished in America, than is the rigour of a master in England.

If then the slavery of the Negroes in our colonies be no more than a legal, perpetual servitude, or hereditary apprenticeship; those people are surely to be deemed subjects of Great Britain in their particular capacity and circumstance, nor ought the laws of the several colonies respecting them, to pass *sub silentio,*[13] and without examination by the king's privy council, as matters with which the supreme magistrate has nothing to do; neither should those laws be permitted to sleep after they have been enacted, or what is still worse, suffered to be carried into execution by those they deem parties, and between whom and the Negroes, they create reciprocal duties.—The influence of the venerable society may perhaps obtain for these people, what it has been the disgrace of every administration since the revolution to have neglected, an impartial dispensation of the laws, nor has any patriot in all that time been found disinterested enough to take their cause in hand; the Negroes indeed can do nothing either to further them in their pursuit of power, or to secure their elections in the country; they can only recommend them by their prayers, to a seat in a kingdom where no modern patriot chuses to take his entire reward. We are now blessed with a prince upon the throne, whose heart, warmed by religious benevolence, wishes the felicity of all mankind;[14] would he then suffer, if he were informed of it, so vast a multitude of his own subjects to be inhumanely scourged, lacerated by whips, nourishment denied, and the talk of labour exacted, racked by every species of torture the most wanton tyranny can invent, and either forced to expire under them, or their lives shortened by their severity: And all this in the teeth of laws, to which his majesty, by his representative, has assented?

Were his majesty moved to give directions to his ministers, in this interval of war throughout the world, to take under consideration the several colony acts for the government of slaves, and to require the several governors and chief justices to report the manner of their execution; the legal rights of the Negroes would then be known, and the defects in the dispensation of justice towards them, be pointed out. It would then appear, that notwithstanding the provincial laws enjoin rest to the slaves on the Sabbath, the most humane planters in the islands allow the Negroes that day to work in for themselves, as their best way of employing their time, while others contrive to share with the Negroe in the profits of his labour, by either abridging him of his ordinary weekly allowance of provisions, or obliging him to find part of his cloathing on account of giving him *all Sunday to himself.* I take particular notice of this evasion of divine and statute laws, because of its rendering all religious instruction impracticable, and to shew that the civil and religious regulations respecting these wretches must go together; indeed until the planters are made to know that their property in their Negroes is legal, not absolute and unconditional, but that their Negroes have rights as well as they, nothing can ever be done for their civil comfort, or their religious instruction. The colony laws universally prohibit the teaching Negroes to write, a caution which the planters think necessary to prevent conspiracies, and communication of ill designs, nor is writing at all requisite for their religious instruction, even reading does not seem indispensably necessary for that purpose; How few among the Jews, or in any nation of antiquity, understood letters? And until the Reformation the people of this country were generally illiterate; will it then be said, that none in those circumstances were capable of being taught all that was necessary for their salvation? Or that they could not know and believe what was for their souls' health? On the other hand, the knowledge of letters even in the lowest degree, is too often supposed to carry with it a sort of qualification for an easy life, and an exemption from a laborious one; and the latter being the Negroes' lot, they might perhaps bear it with more unwillingness, or seek some desperate means for ridding themselves of it. The stated service of our church cannot indeed be joined in throughout, by those who cannot read; but I should hope to see a more simple mode of religious worship and instruction, presented to the Negroes, one in which they should bear a less share than is given by our liturgy to the people, and therefore better adapted to their capacities and condition. Too much must not be attempted at once, *men's meat must not be given to babes.* These creatures are even ignorant that there is a God, they must then be taught a maker before they can comprehend a redeemer. It has been too much our way to tell them of both in a breath, and if they could be got to gabber over the apostles' creed without understanding the meaning of a single term, then to throw some water in their face, and tell all the world how many Christians we had made, and thus expose the interests of the church and the honour of the society, to the ridicule of those who were acquainted with the mummery[15] of those vain boastings. Teaching the Negroes the Church of England's catechism, is the general employment of the society's missionaries, but besides its being much above their comprehension, it is too long and too difficult to be got by heart by the Negroes in the little time the missionary can spare to each, or their owners can be without their service, for the owners of slaves will not suffer them to assemble together in large bodies, nor to have much intercourse with one another; indeed few owners of Negroes will suffer them to go to the catechist at all, because of his house being a sort of general rendezvous for them, where they are more apt to teach each other mischief than to profit by the catechist's instructions. In those colonies where the Negroes out-number the white inhabitants, such rendezvous would be highly dangerous, even in the towns, and the planters in the country would never consent to let their several gangs meet together. The truth is, that all instruction intended for these people while they are slaves, must be given them within their owners' precincts.

Itinerant missionaries will therefore best serve this purpose, and as the missionary's attendance at each plantation would, after some time, be only necessary for an hour on Sundays, he might visit several the same day, for if the planters approved of the plan, either themselves or their overseers would carry it on in the absence of the missionary.

Lay men would probably be more zealous in this business than ordained missionaries, as they might hope by a faithful discharge of it, to recommend themselves to the society for Orders and less laborious missions. Besides, the capacity of a Negroe is so mean, and the things he knows so very few and of so ordinary a sort, that a man of a liberal education never could stoop to make use of such low, not to say absurd imagery, as would be necessary to convey his ideas to them. Indeed I am afraid there would be something impious in the representations he would be obliged to make of the almighty in order to bring him down to their understandings, nor would it be easy to frame any thing like a creed or catechism for these poor creatures that would not be either shocking or ridiculous.

There is a dialect peculiar to those Negroes who have been born in our colonies, or who have been long there, that the missionary must adopt, in order to make himself understood, than which nothing could be more uncouth, to the pronunciation of a man of science; nor would it be less difficult for him to bring himself to study what they said to him.[16] Enthusiasm is only equal to such undertakings, and none could be fitter for the employment than those lay preachers who are now in such numbers offering themselves to the society. Might I be permitted to hint at the instructions which would be proper for these missionaries: I would confine them to a very short summary of religion. That there is one God in heaven who never dies, and who sees and knows every thing. That he made all people both whites and blacks. That he punishes all roguery, mischief, and lying either before death or after it. That he punishes them for it before they die, by putting it into their masters' hearts to correct them, and after death by giving them to the Devil to burn in his own place. That he will put it into their masters' hearts to be kind to those who do their work without knavery or murmuring. To take care of them in old age and sickness, and not to plague them with too much work, or to chastise them when they are not able to do it. That in the other world, after they die, he will give all good Negroes, rest from all labour, and plenty of all good things. That it was God Almighty who put it into their masters' heads to give them Sunday for a holiday, and for that reason they ought to say prayers to him, and sing songs to him on that day. That the missionary was come to them to tell them what God Almighty would have them do, that they might deserve his kindness for them, and that they would anger him if they did not mind what he told them. The heads of such a discourse being thrown into a sort of catechism for the Negroes to get by heart, it would be fixed in their memories, and those of them who could reason upon it would acquire an appetite to know somewhat more. To such, the doctrine of the satisfaction might then be opened, by simply telling them, that every body black and white had done so many bad things, that God Almighty was very angry with all the world, and said he would kill them all, and that none of them should be happy after their death. Upon which Jesus Christ, God's only son, said he would take their faults upon himself, and that God might punish him for them; and accordingly Jesus Christ came down from heaven and suffered himself to be whipped and tortured, and at last killed, and so made it up between his father and the world. That he left the bible behind him for directions to the world what they should do to please his father and him, and that he promised to stand up for all those who should do what that book told them, and would help them when they prayed to him for his assistance.

The Negroes in general have an ear for musick, and might without much trouble be taught to sing hymns, which would be the pleasantest method of instructing them, and bringing them speedily to offer praise to God. They should be taught short prayers for morning and evening, and grace to say at meals.

To engage the planters to second the endeavours of the missionaries, it would be highly necessary to preface the directory, which may be thought fit to be composed for the use of the missionaries, and to be dispersed among the planters with a discourse addressed to the owners of Negroes in the colonies, in which the lawfulness of retaining the Negroe slaves in perpetual servitude, should be set forth as the opinion of the society, and the obligation to bring those into the knowledge of the truth whom God Almighty permits to be subject to their direction, and to labour for their benefit, pressed home upon their consciences.

Care being thus taken for an impartial administration of civil justice to these unhappy people, and the sabbath allowed them for the purposes of religion: Their owners being also freed from all apprehensions of losing their Negroes' service by suffering them to be instructed in religious duties, and a mode of instruction being adapted to their capacities and conditions; much might be hoped through the divine favour and assistance, and the ignorance and cruel treatment of these creatures would no longer be a reproach to the wisdom and humanity of our civil and ecclesiastical rulers. The stupid obstinacy of the Negroes may indeed make it always necessary to subject them to severe discipline from their masters, but in no other circumstance does their condition of perpetual servitude, require that their treatment should be different from that of hired servants, especially if they had the same restraints from religion and morality to bind them, that the others have. But whilst the civil authority overlooks them, and they are left without other motives for action, and hardly more knowledge of their duty, than is common to them with domestic animals, it is no wonder that they are treated like brute beasts, or that it should be almost necessary to treat them as such. If they are incapable of feeling mentally, they will the more frequently be made to feel in their flesh. To those therefore who have the power or influence to redress the grievances of these poor wretches, is their case committed, and from those, who, through indolence, or by feigning ignorance, or pretending an abhorrence of their condition, turn away from considering it, will the impartial judge of all the earth, one day require an account of the misery of these fellow creatures.

Notes

1. For the biographical background on Knox, I have relied on Rena Vassar, "William Knox's Defense of Slavery (1768)," *Proceedings of the American Philosophical Society* 114 (August 1970): 310–26, which also offers a transcription of the source. Also, see Leland J. Bellot, *William Knox: The Life and Thought of an Eighteenth-Century Imperialist* (Austin: University of Texas Press, 1977); Bellot, "Evangelicals and the Defense of Slavery in Britain's Old Colonial Empire," *Journal of Southern History* 37 (February 1971): 19–40; and W. W. Abbot, *The Royal Governors of Georgia, 1754–1775* (Chapel Hill: University of North Carolina Press, 1959).

2. Knox, *The Controversy between Great-Britain and Her Colonies Reviewed* (London, 1769), 4.

3. Jeffrey Robert Young, *Domesticating Slavery: The Master Class in Georgia and South Carolina, 1670–1837* (Chapel Hill: University of North Carolina Press, 1999), 64–65.

4. Of the three sermons in this thirty-eight-page work, I have transcribed the second and third, pp. 16–38.

5. Deism was an eighteenth-century intellectual tradition that associated nature with divine purpose. Here Knox is scoffing at some deists' contentions that organized religion tended to distort the sacred truth inscribed by God into the primitive state of nature. See Roy Porter, *The Creation of the Modern World: The Untold Story of the British Enlightenment* (New York: W. W. Norton, 2000), chap. 5.

6. Knox was most likely referring to William Warburton, *A Sermon Preached before the Incorporated Society for the Propagation of the Gospel in Foreign Parts* (London, 1766), a work that harshly criticized American slavery as an abusive, irreligious institution (pp. 25–30).

7. The *Code Noir,* the French statutes dealing with colonial slavery, was issued by Louis XIV in 1685. See Robin Blackburn, *The Making of New World Slavery: From the Baroque to the Modern, 1492–1800* (London: Verso: 1997), 290–91. Knox's transcription of the passage in French obviously contains errors; it translates as follows: "We declare the slaves chattel, and they enter the community in this condition; the children born to marriages between slaves will be slaves and will belong to the masters owning the parents."

8. Matthew 18:23–35.

9. For modern scholarship on this question, see Eugene D. Genovese, *From Rebellion to Revolution: Afro-American Slave Revolts in the Making of the New World* (New York: Vintage Books, 1981).

10. Anthony Benezet, a prominent Quaker educator who resided in Philadelphia, sharply criticized slavery in a series of published works in the 1760s and 1770s. George S. Brookes, *Friend Anthony Benezet* (Philadelphia: University of Pennsylvania Press, 1937).

11. Daniel Burton was rector of St. Peter-le-Poer in London prior to becoming secretary of the SPG. See John C. Van Horne, ed., *Religious Philanthropy and Colonial Slavery: The American Correspondence of the Associates of Dr. Bray, 1717–1777* (Urbana: University of Illinois Press, 1985), 214n5.

12. Accomplices in crime.

13. In silence.

14. George III.

15. Meaningless ceremony.

16. The development of a distinct slave dialect was especially pronounced in the low-country of South Carolina and Georgia. See Margaret Washington Creel, *"A Peculiar People": Slave Religion and Community-Culture among the Gullahs* (New York: New York University Press, 1988), prologue.

# CHAPTER 6

## *Petition to the Virginia Assembly, 1785*

———————— ❧✦❧ ————————

IN THE YEARS IMMEDIATELY FOLLOWING the American Revolution, politicians wrestled with the great moral question of slavery. They did so, however, in piece-meal fashion rather than in grandiose debate in the American Congress. Even during the midst of war, the national government had seldom been able to exert meaningful influence over the individual states; by the mid-1780s, its stature was sinking to new lows.[1] Hence, when American statesmen charted new policies concerning the institution of slavery, they did so at the level of state government. In the North, the states made considerable strides toward equating white republican liberties with the gradual emancipation of African American slaves. Proceeding on constitutional, judicial, and statutory grounds, states such as Vermont, Massachusetts, and Pennsylvania managed to set slavery on the path to extinction by the end of the eighteenth century. Conversely, in the Lower South, white politicians never hesitated in their campaign to rebuild a plantation system hinging on perpetually enslaved black labor.[2]

In the Upper South, a brief but charged debate on the morality of slavery captivated the post-Revolutionary political scene. Prominent politicians such as Thomas Jefferson, St. George Tucker, and George Mason willingly conceded the abstract evils attending the institution of slavery. And a number of slaveholders —a minority to be sure, but a nonetheless noticeable amount—took the dramatic step of emancipating their own slaves. No less a figure than George Washington was included in this group of reformers who anticipated an era when the American South would rid itself of slavery. In his final will, Washington made a concerted effort to manumit those slaves under his legal control. And yet, notwithstanding the evidence of at least some genuine antislavery reform in the Upper South, recent scholarship has characterized these efforts as exceptional in nature and relatively limited in impact.[3] When the Virginia delegates arrived at the Constitutional Convention in Philadelphia in 1787, some of them were still prepared to concede the moral problems associated with slavery. In terms of their concrete political agenda, however, these delegates already recognized that slavery would have to remain a central feature of southern society.[4] By the early nineteenth century, southern legislatures were denying individual slaveholders the opportunity even to free their own slaves as Washington had elected to do.[5]

During the brief period of open debate about slavery in the Upper South, the vast majority of white southerners worked to protect their prerogatives as masters or potential masters of black slaves. When, for example, the Virginia legislature formally considered a petition calling for a general emancipation in 1785, the response was unanimously negative. When citizens in heavily slaveholding Virginia counties petitioned their legislature in 1784 and 1785, they were able to make a positive case for slavery built on the conservative logic articulated by proslavery missionaries during the colonial era. To the evidence offered by Christian theology, the petitioners added the element of potential racial Armageddon should slavery be disrupted—a specter of widespread violence orchestrated by freed slaves. With the hideous wartime experiences of de facto anarchy overtaking the plantation order still fresh in the slaveholders' minds, the images of black unrest carried special rhetorical force. Emancipation could now be associated with the outrages inflicted on the Virginia countryside by the despised English enemy. In a marked departure from colonial patterns, the slaveholders themselves for the first time found good reason to elaborate their defense of human bondage. For the first time, they understood that they were living in an age of Revolutionary freedom that raised significant questions about the fate of slavery in the American republic.[6]

---

To the Honourable the General Assembly of Virginia the Remonstrance and Petition of the Free Inhabitants of Halifax County.

Gentlemen,

When the British Parliament usurped a Right to dispose of our Property without our Consent, we dissolved the Union with our Parent Country, and established a Constitution and Form of Government of our own, that our Property might be secure in Future. In Order to effect this, we risked our Lives and Fortunes, and waded through Seas of Blood. Divine Providence smiled on our Enterprise, and crowned it with Success. And our Rights of Liberty and Property are now as well secured to us, as they can be by any human Constitution and Form of Government.

But notwithstanding this, we understand, a very subtle and daring Attempt is on Foot to deprive us of a very important Part of our Property. An Attempt carried on by the Enemies of our Country, Tools of the British Administration, and supported by a Number of deluded Men among us, to wrest from us our Slaves by an Act of the Legislature for a general Emancipation of them. They have the Address, indeed to cover their Design, with the Veil of Piety and Liberality of Sentiment. But it is unsupported by the Word of God, and will be ruinous to Individuals and to the Public.

It is unsupported by the Word of God. Under the Old Testament Dispensation, Slavery was permitted by the Deity himself. Thus it is recorded, Levit. Chap. 25. Ver. 44, 45, 46. "Both thy Bond-men and Bond-maids, which thou shall have, shall be of the Heathens that are round about you; of them shall ye buy Bond-men and Bond-maids.—Moreover, of the Children of the Strangers, that do sojourn among you of them shall ye buy, and of their Families that are with you, which they beget in your Land, and they shall be your Possession, and ye shall take them, as an Inheritance for your Children after you, to inherit them for a Possession; they shall be your Bond-men forever."—This Permission to possess and inherit Bond Servants, we have Reason to conclude, was continued through all the Revolutions of the Jewish Government, down to the Advent of our Lord. And we do not find, that either he or his Apostles abridged it. On the Contrary, the Freedom which the Followers of Jesus were taught to expect, was a Freedom from the Bondage of Sin and Satan, and from the Dominion of their Lust and Passions; but as to their outward Condition, whatever that was, whether Bond or Free, when they embraced Christianity, it was to remain the same afterwards. This Saint Paul hath expressly told us 1 Cor. Chap. 7. Ver. 20th where he is speaking directly to this very Point; "Let every Man abide in the same Calling, wherein he is called"; and at Ver. 24 "Let every Man wherein he is called therein abide with God."—Thus it is evident the above Attempt is unsupported by the Divine Word.

It is also ruinous to Individuals and to the Public. For it involves in it, and is productive of Want, Poverty, Distress, and Ruin to the Free Citizen;—Neglect, Famine, and Death to the helpless black Infant and superannuated Parent;—the Horrors of all the Rapes, Murders, and Outrages, which a vast Multitude of unprincipled, unpropertied, vindictive, and remorseless Banditti are capable of perpetrating;—inevitable Bankruptcy to the Revenue, and consequently Breach of public Faith, and Loss of Credit with foreign Nations;—and lastly Ruin to this now free and flourishing Country.

We therefore your Remonstrants and Petitioners do solemnly adjure and humbly pray you, that you will discountenance and utterly reject every Motion and Proposal for emancipating our Slaves; that as the Act lately made, empowering the Owners of Slaves to liberate them, has been and is still productive, in some Measure, of sundry of the above pernicious Effects, you will immediately and totally repeal it;[7]—and that as many of the Slaves, liberated by the said Act, have been guilty of Thefts and Outrages, Insolences and Violences destructive to the Peace, Safety, and Happiness of Society, you will make effectual Provision for the due Government of them.

And your Remonstrants and Petitioners shall ever pray, etc.

[November 10, 1785]

Notes

1. Robert Middlekauff, *The Glorious Cause: The American Revolution, 1763–1789* (New York: Oxford University Press, 1982), chap. 25; and Lance Banning, *The Sacred Fire of Liberty: James Madison and the Founding of the Federal Republic* (Ithaca, N.Y.: Cornell University Press, 1995), chap. 2.

2. Shane White, *Somewhat More Independent: The End of Slavery in New York City, 1770–1810* (Athens: University of Georgia Press, 1991); Gary B. Nash and Jean R. Soderlund, *Freedom by Degrees: Emancipation in Pennsylvania and Its Aftermath* (New York: Oxford University Press, 1991); and Jeffrey Robert Young, *Domesticating Slavery: The Master Class in Georgia and South Carolina, 1670–1837* (Chapel Hill: University of North Carolina Press, 1999), chap. 3.

3. Winthrop Jordan, *White over Black: American Attitudes toward the Negro, 1550–1812* (Chapel Hill: University of North Carolina Press, 1968), chap. 12; Robert McColley, *Slavery and Jeffersonian Virginia* (Urbana: University of Illinois Press, 1977); Fritz Hirschfeld, ed., *George Washington and Slavery: A Documentary Portrayal* (Columbia: University of Missouri Press, 1997); and Henry Wiencek, *An Imperfect God: George Washington, His Slaves, and the Creation of America* (New York: Farrar, Straus and Giroux, 2003).

4. Young, *Domesticating Slavery*, 91–98.

5. Douglas R. Egerton, *Gabriel's Rebellion: The Virginia Slave Conspiracies of 1800 and 1802* (Chapel Hill: University of North Carolina Press, 1993), chap. 11.

6. For the historical circumstances surrounding the Virginia proslavery petitions, see Frederika Teute Schmidt and Barbara Ripel Wilhelm, eds., "Early Proslavery Petitions in Virginia," *William and Mary Quarterly,* 3rd ser., 30 ( January 1973): 133–46. I learned of the existence of these petitions from this work of scholarship. My own transcription of the Halifax County Petition differs from theirs only in my editorial approach to matters of punctuation. The original documents are cataloged by date and are available on microfilm at the Library of Virginia, Richmond, and I would like to thank the library staff for their assistance with this research and for granting permission to publish this document. For a sampling of other evidence of this kind from across the American South, see Loren Schweninger, ed., *The Southern Debate over Slavery,* vol. 1, *Petitions to Southern Legislatures, 1778–1864* (Urbana: University of Illinois Press, 2001).

7. The Manumission Act of 1782.

# CHAPTER 7

# Henry Pattillo, 1787

HENRY PATTILLO'S CAREER AS A PRESBYTERIAN minister and a proslavery author illustrates the ongoing relationship between Christian activism and the defense of slavery in the American South. Born in Scotland in 1726, Pattillo emigrated to America while a teenager and eventually settled in Virginia. Initially embarking on a career as a merchant, Pattillo was swept up by the religious enthusiasm characterizing the era of the First Great Awakening. By 1750 he had resolved to devote his life to the ministry. Having made plans to pursue his religious training in Philadelphia, Pattillo embarked for the North. His travels, however, were interrupted almost immediately by sickness that led to his finding shelter with no less a figure than the venerable Presbyterian authority (and proslavery thinker) Samuel Davies. Pattillo ended up residing and studying with Davies for significant portions of the next seven years. In 1758, having obtained his license as a minister, he began to preach to far-flung Presbyterian communities in North Carolina and Virginia. By the early 1760s he had earned a reputation as a prominent religious authority in the North Carolina Piedmont.

During the Revolution, Pattillo settled into the role of pastor of several churches in Granville County, the locale in which he would reside and preach until his death in 1801. In addition to publishing several works, he also operated one of the better schools in North Carolina. Like his mentor Samuel Davies before him, Pattillo interpreted Christian theology as a blueprint for organic hierarchy in human society. Whereas Davies had argued for a paternalistic master-slave relationship in the context of the British colonial system, Pattillo contemplated slavery in the setting of early national America. An enthusiastic patriot during the war, Pattillo experienced little trouble reconciling traditional organic notions of power with the new enthusiasm for republican political liberties. The extended plantation household was the foundation of Pattillo's social vision—one fixated on American liberty and Christian morality as opposed to the pursuit of material wealth. In the end, Pattillo sought to measure the success of American family life by the degree to which love informed the ties between husband and wife, parent and child, and master and slave. And he believed that this happy

American family would ensure the survival of the young republic that seemed to be floundering in the 1780s.[1]

⚜⚜

HENRY PATTILLO, *The Plain Planter's Family Assistant; Containing an Address to Husbands and Wives, Children and Servants* ( Wilmington, Del.: James Adams, 1787)[2]

### Preface.

A Short preface is necessary.——At a time when the state of our public affairs engages the anxious attention of the whole continent; and when complaints and disorders arise, on account of debts and taxes; I judged it a duty I owed my country, briefly to set before my fellow-citizens their comparative happiness; and if possible reconcile them to their own advantageous situation. How must our virtuous rulers feel, who employ all their powers for the interest and honor of their country, to be requited with discontent and ingratitude? And what encouragement has divine providence to continue or increase our happiness, if we are disobedient and unthankful? If at so early a period of our political existence, we are arrived at an awful resemblance to those nations whose vices and luxury have brought on them old age and decripitude, and are hastning their dissolution; we must not expect that our infancy can preserve us from their fate. The *Babylonish* empire took its rise, attained its glory and splendor; and by the weight of its own crimes, fell into final ruin; and all within less than a single century. In vain does the curious traveller enquire, Where stood *Babylon,* the glory of the *Chaldee's* excellency? though it never had its equal under the sun.

O my country-men! *Righteousness exalteth a nation; but sin is a reproach to any people.*[3] The worst foe a country has, is that inhabitant who does the most evil, and the least good; and the best friend of a nation, is he who does the most good, and prevents the most evil.

In the Address to husbands and wives, children and servants, my aim was to be honest and pertinent. A man who knows he can do nothing well, is not surprized at discovering his own deficiencies in every paragraph. But if I have traced, to their proper sources, some of our most dangerous and prevalent vices, viz. The profaneness and infidelity of our youth; and the heinous, and universal sin of Sabbath-breaking; may it excite a suitable emulation in all, to arise and apply the proper remedy: For *America* is infamous for that vice, as the *Sybarites* were for effeminacy; the *Cretans* for lying; or the *Germans* for drunkenness. The means prescribed in the address, might go far towards the cure of this national evil. But alas! How discouraging the prospect; when at the houses of many professors, you cannot enjoy five minutes on that day for reading, devotion, or conversation, without being disturbed and interrupted with the noise and play of children of all sizes and colours, within doors and without. O professors! the cure must begin with you. Sinners will not attempt it. Hypocrites will tire and faint. If the green be barren, what can be expected from the dry? And if the feed of the godly are as uncultivated, as the off-spring of sinners, what shall the next generation be?

I expected to find the composition of original catechisms a work of difficulty, and was not deceived. Some may judge them too long; while others can mention important truths that are wholly omitted. The length of some of the answers is a real objection, which I know not how to remedy but by the assistance that 1st. 2d. 3d: &c. may afford, unless I had left out some necessary parts of the answer; or had divided it into a number of questions, proposed in nearly the same words. Such as they are, I commit to God's blessing, and to an indulgent public. If my *Plain Planter,* and his family, discover in them a number of important questions asked, and answered with any propriety, may he and his profit by them, and know the truth as it is in JESUS. I am well satisfied, that a youth, of any memory and application, may be able, in one month, to answer every question in this cate-chism, by spending half an hour daily upon it; and I flatter myself it will richly reward his pains. He will not only have a little treasure of useful knowledge, for enlightening his mind, and regulating his practice; but as far as he can trust to their orthodoxy, may be able, by them, to judge of the truth or falsehood of doctrines when he hears them. Shall *American* youth despair of committing to memory, a lit-tle system of religious knowledge, when an actor on the stage shall retain, and with accuracy pronounce, a large part of fifty different plays? And if the memory is so weak, that it cannot retain the whole; yet the very attempt will imprint the substance of the answer on the mind. In composing the Negroes' catechism, I had fresh proofs of my own incapacity to make truth plain to the meanest understand-ing; and yet I hope there is nothing but what they can comprehend, if frequently inculcated. That little composition is not so peculiarly appropriated to Negroes, but that it may properly enough be learned by whites, as an additional introduc-tion to the youth's catechism. The world will consider these compositions, so far from being intended to supersede the Assembly's catechism, that I would have them considered as an introduction to it. For that little system of divinity contains a greater variety of divine truths than the longest of mine; though I handle some subjects more largely than it does.

In the prayers, I have studied the utmost plainness, in imitation of the language of worshippers given us by inspiration. Nothing can more stronger indicate human pride, or consist less with the spirit of a humble worshipper, than a studied elo-quence in our addresses to God. I have laboured to avoid such odious bombast on the one hand, and a slovenly disregard to elegant plainness on the other. And I bless God, upon viewing them, that I was led to mix so much of the divine oracles with them, perhaps not so few as twenty sentences of holy writ, in each prayer. No language, like that of inspiration, can equally affect the human heart, animate devotion, or, perhaps, find acceptance with God. Thus far have I laboured for your good:—now, my dear reader, comes your part. What I have been often applied to do for particular families, is here done for the common benefit. No longer can you plead your incapacity to lead the devotion of your families. You are left without excuse, if you longer neglect the very important duty of family religion. One of these prayers can be distinctly pronounced in about seven minutes. To read a moderate chapter, and sing four or five stanzas of a psalm or hymn, will employ about ten or twelve minutes more. If this be really too much to devote to the service of God in your houses twice a day, you must tell your maker and judge at last, that you was a man so given up to the world, that you had not time nor heart for religion; and Satan himself cannot bring a worse charge against you.

As to the short paraphrase on the Lord's Prayer, I would observe, that this portion of sacred writ, claims the preeminence, in the social worship of Christians, whether considered as a model, to be literally followed, or as a general direction for devotion. But either way, I fear it is more used than understood; and this part of devotion, which requires closer attention, and greater steadiness of thought than, perhaps, any thing we ever attempted, there is reason to apprehend is worse performed than any other part of divine worship. The paraphrase, will in some measure, shew its vast extent, and comprehensiveness. I beg leave to make a few observations. 1. This prayer is intended for social worship; as all the pronouns are plural, and cannot properly be said by one alone. 2. It is a family prayer, taught by Christ to his household the apostles, and to be daily presented, if we daily need our bread. 3. It is a trial, and test of character, and requires true piety in those who use it, of which every sentence is a proof. 4. CHRIST dictated this prayer, before he taught his church to pray in HIS NAME. In this respect, therefore, it is an imperfect model for Christian worship since that command was given. 5. This prayer should be pronounced with a slow solemnity, that the worshippers may include as much of the matter it contains in their mind as possible. 6. The improper word *which,* in the first sentence, as it makes Almighty of the neuter gender, I have changed into the proper pronoun *who,* agreeable to all our ideas of the supreme being, and to the well known sense of the Greek article *ho,* in this very place. How so many learned men as translated the Bible, came to be so careless of grammar, as to make God, angels and men, of the neuter gender, so often as they have, is hard to account for. In the third of Luke, the English reader must pronounce *which,* for *who,* about sixty times in fourteen verses. Let all grammarians, at least, read their Bibles with propriety. A little care and attention will render it easy and natural. I know a man who has read thus these for twenty years, and, perhaps, has not missed the proper pronoun thrice in that space of time. 7. I have followed the true and emphatical reading, in the fifth petition, *debts,* and *debtors,* as every scholar knows to be the exact and literal sense of our Saviour's words, instead of the comparatively trifling, and unemphatical words, *trespass,* and *trespasses.* How they found their way into that prayer in the prayer book, I never could conjecture.—I commit my book and reader to God's blessing. Farewell.

## To Heads of Families.

*My Friends and Brethren,*

I CONSIDER the station in which Providence has placed you, as one of the most important in life. I consider you as either a husband, a father, a master; or as all these in one; and he who acts these several parts well, *hath purchased to himself a good degree,* and is one of the most useful members of civil society.[4] A family is a little community within itself; of which smaller bodies, states and kingdoms are composed. Out of your families are to arise the future citizens of these States. Cast back your eyes to the *American revolution.* Never forget the wonders God hath wrought for your country. The acknowledged *independence of America,* is an event that engages the eager attention of all *Christendom.* It has, to a vast extent of continent, secured those civil and religious liberties, which are unknown in any other part of the globe. For you are thereby, not only delivered from the tyranny of kings, the rapacity of courtiers, and the dominion of lords spiritual and temporal; but you can elect or be elected into any office of your country. *You* make the laws by which you are governed; and *you* only, have a negative on those laws, if they are found inconvenient. Your *religious* liberties are still more surprizing. Here, *The Lord hath created a new thing in the earth.*[5] You have the honour to possess that soil, and breathe that air, where legislators have, for the first time, declared, that they have nothing to do with religion but to protect its professors; and that God alone is the Lord of conscience. This was always true, and always plead by suffering Christians. But kings, princes, law-givers, popes, and lord-bishops, *combined against the Lord and against his Anointed;*[6] and to this hour deny it all the world over. O my country-men! If you are not the most thankful people under heaven, you are, of all men, the most inexcusable; and betray your ignorance of the state of mankind in all other nations. *Britain* is confessedly the most friendly to human liberty of any kingdom on earth: Yet in that favoured land, not one man in many hundreds, has a vote in their elections for commons. Their national debt overwhelms the imagination:* to pay the interest of which, and supply the national expence in time of

---

*To give the Plain Planter some idea of the annual expences, and national debt of Britain, I would observe, that a pint of melted gold will weigh about nineteen pounds and

peace, requires fifteen millions sterling; and renders their taxes enormous, when about eight millions of inhabitants are to pay it yearly, or ruin and bankruptcy await them. The tenth of every thing their fields produce, goes to support the clergy of the established church; no distinction being made betwixt the field of the church-man, and the dissenter. Almost every thing they eat, drink and wear, is taxed. They pay for liberty to ride the road, and for the light of heaven that shines through their windows. There the Test Act rears its impious head, and reigns in defiance of all the laws of holiness. I shall risk my reputation with my *Plain Planter,* when I acquaint him, that above an hundred years ago, in the reign of Charles II who lived a libertine, and died a papist, the English parliament, with a professed design to keep Roman-catholicks out of office, passed an act, enjoining all who should bear any office, civil or military, to receive the sacrament of the Lord's supper, in the church of England, before they could act in their office. This degrades one of the most solemn rites of the Christian religion, to an engine of state; and prostitutes this holy ordinance of Christ, enjoined on his followers, *in remembrance of him,*[7] to the abuse of every powdered fop, and graceless infidel, who can, by favour or purchase, procure a commission in the army, the navy, excise, customs, &c. In the magistracy, from the lord chancellor to the under sheriff, they shall all thus qualify. When the office of mayor, sheriff, alderman, &c. comes in course to a dissenter, he shall comply with this act, in defiance of conscience, or shall pay a heavy fine for delinquency. This act has stood all former and latter attempts of men of decency and generous spirits, to have it blotted from the *English* code. *Imprisonment for debt,* is only an impeachment of *British,* (and, alas! I may add of *American*) justice and humanity. But the Test Act insults heaven itself, "and laughs at gods and men." High-church bishops and a tory parliament, prop up their idol, at a time when the popish sovereigns of *Germany, France,* and even of *Spain,* have given some noble proofs of liberality of sentiment.

If this be a true draught of some of the features of the freest kingdom in *Europe,* what a shocking picture must other nations exhibit? Could you travel through *Portugal, Spain, France, Italy, Germany, Poland* and *Russia,* how would you long for an angel's wing to bear you to *America,* the only residence of liberty, and hide you from such complicated scenes of wretchedness, as would every where strike your

---

an half. Let us suppose a pint of guineas to weigh 15 or 16 pounds, and to be in value £.1000 sterling. Sixty-four thousand pounds, then, will make a bushel of guineas. Now if you divide 15 millions, the annual tax, by 64000, it quotients 234 bushels of gold, or about 11 or 12 tobacco hogsheads full of guineas, for their annual expence in time of peace. And if you suppose the collection made in silver, the bulk will be about twenty times as great. It is easy to apply this calculation to the whole national debt, which is about 250 millions, and would fill 100 hogsheads of gold; and nearly 4000 of silver.

eyes. Should you take *England* in your way, you would then be in a country, where the names so dear to your hearts, your *Franklins,* your *Washingtons,* your *Hancocks,* your *Adamses, Henrys, Dickinsons, Paines, Jeffersons,* and many others, whose wisdom and valour God made use of for the salvation of your country—in *England,* I say, those names, so venerable with you, would not be permitted to fill the meanest office, unless they would divest themselves of honour and conscience, and make religion a ladder to preferment.

Your country, indeed, labours under the weight of a foreign and domestic debt; and heavier taxes must ensue, than could befall you, before you was an independent nation: yet still, by comparison with the two most flourishing kingdoms in *Europe,* viz. *France* and *England,* the balance of happiness turns in your favour. For although you have not their trade, nor numbers, yet your national debt is, to theirs, scarcely in the proportion of one to thirty. Remember, that seven years ago, you would gladly have agreed, not to be a shilling richer at the end of twenty years on condition your country could enjoy peace, liberty and independence; and that in those twenty years, you could pay off your whole national debt, and leave your children the sons and daughters of FREE AMERICA. Divine providence granted your wishes sooner and more amply than you dared to expect. *America* was declared a free and independent nation, by all the powers on earth. And this country, at its first existence, owes a two-fold debt: The first of gratitude and praise to God, to be paid with every morning light and evening shades, for the wonders he hath wrought for you and your country. The second a national debt, to be sunk by taxes, for all the expences of a seven years war, particularly for clothing, pay, arms, ammunition, and provisions, furnished to our brave officers and hardy soldiers during the conflict; in which they had to oppose generals bred in the military school, and armies greatly their superiours in discipline, and all the apparatus of war. These debts are acknowledged on all hands to be justly due. Good manners, we say, is one of the cheapest and most commendable things a man can carry about with him. This is eminently true, of gratitude to God. The payment of this debt, does not depend on kindly seasons and plentiful crops. A thankful sense of divine goodness, and a tongue to express it, though it pays not the debt, is yet all that God requires. Your *great Creditor,* your own heart, your family and friends, know how you acquit yourself, in paying this debt. If it stands in full force against you, *sin lies at your door.*[8] And you ought to be ashamed of future expectations, if you requite past kindness with ingratitude. Your taxes are a debt you owe for your protection, and for your rights as citizens: but it requires the united wisdom and authority of your country to secure the payment of it. The public debts of your country are as justly due, as those you owe by private bargain. Every pound you discharge, is so much put out at interest for your posterity; who must otherways pay a larger sum at any future day, and the longer it is deferred, the heavier it must fall. If Christians are commanded to pay their taxes, with chearful readiness, to those pagan princes who ruled the earth when the *New Testament* was written; though most of them were monsters of lust and cruelty, and would waste at a single entertainment the taxes of a whole province—will you, my friends, grudge to pay your proportion of the national expence, when you know it is applied by the men of your own choice, to the sinking of the public debt; the support of government among you; and to maintain the credit of your country? You have fewer temptations to hunt after riches than formerly. The purchase of slaves is now no object with wise Americans. Virtuous republicans aim not at great wealth, but a decent competency, acquired by the union of industry and frugality. We have no kings' companions among us; no lords or princes, to own half a county, and to let out their lands at high rents to a thousand drudges. You generally possess farms, from the cultivation, preservation, and improvement of which you are to draw what you eat and drink; and if you are what I wish you, far the greatest part of your clothing. What you can raise for exportation, will be sufficient to pay your proportion of the national debt, and procure you some necessary articles which your farms will not produce.

But my dear friends, though I earnestly wish you that moderate competency, unincumbered with riches, which has been the aim of the wise and virtuous in all ages; yet I am still more solicitous respecting your happiness as candidates for eternity, than as citizens of *America.* You are the inhabitants of the happiest country under heaven, could you resist the temptation of riches; and avoid debts and foreign frippery—but are you securing *a better country, that is an heavenly?*[9] Come, my beloved country-men; a friend of yours is come to enquire after your spiritual health, and religious prosperity; and you must allow him to be as particular as the prophet of old—*Is it well with thee? Is it well with thy wife? Is it well with thy children? Is it well with thy servants?*[10]

1. *Is it well with thyself?* Thou hast a dwelling in this land of liberty; but hast thou secured a residence *in the house not made with hands?*[11] Thou ownest a farm within these states; but art thou not like the sons of *Reuben* and *Gad,* so captivated with the balsam groves of *Gilead,* the pools of *Heshbon,* and the rich pastures of *Bashan,* that thou hast no lot in the promised land beyond the flood?[12] It may be thou hast a balance in thy favour, when thou settlest accounts with mankind; but God *the judge of all,*[13] has a private account against thee of ten thousand talents. If of silver, it is between four and five millions sterling; if of gold, it is more than seventy. To this enormous sum does he compare thy sins, who only knows the evil of them. Thou hast, and deservest the character of an honest man; an obliging neighbour; a useful member of society; the poor man's friend, and no man's foe. Well, Sir, thou are just fit to live *in this world:*[14] such worthy members does human society need, for its support and ornament, and *America* owns you for a son—but, my

fellow-immortal, thou mayest be as unfit for the society and employments of heaven, as thou art to preside at a college, head an army, or rule a kingdom. The enjoyments of that world, may be as disgusting to you, as a well-furnished table to a stomach sick unto death; and you may be found at last wholly a man of this world, and totally unqualified for a better. If temporal death put an end to your whole existence, your present character, as a worthy member of civil society, would be your highest praise. But you expect to out-live sun, moon and stars; and you know your own interest calls on you to be fit for that station which God hath promised, and good men look for, when they die. To be a *man of the world,* can no more qualify us for the heavenly state, than spending our youth at the plough could qualify us to teach law, physic or divinity. Until you can prove, then, that to pay your public and private debts, is *rendering to God the glory due unto his name*[15]— That to cultivate your field is *to work out your own salvation*[16]—That to fill your barns with plenty, is *lay up treasure in heaven*[17]—That to love your country, family, friends and neighbours, *is to love the Lord your God with all your heart*[18]—That to do no harm, is doing all the good you can—That to teach your son to keep accounts, is *to number your days*[19]—To teach your daughter to spin, weave and make up, is to secure *the wedding garment*[20]—That to see your family early at work, is *paying your morning sacrifice*[21] to God with them; and following them to the field, is *praying to your FATHER who seeth in secret*[22]—That to close the day as you began it, and no devotion among you, is *to pray without ceasing*[23]—And that to enjoy your fortune with credit and liberality, is to *deny yourself, take up your cross, and follow JESUS CHRIST:*[24] Until, I say, you can prove that the *one* of these is the *other,* you must never believe that the man of the world is the man of God; or that creditably to fill our station on earth, certainly fits us for *the glory that shall be revealed.*[25] It may be then, my friend, that it is *not well with thee;*[26] and that thou art fit for no world but this. Thy first care, then, thy great concern, is to be on terms of friendship with thy Maker, and on sure grounds for eternity. Death and judgment will discover to you, that to be a man of the world, and a man of God, are vastly different things. That the *friendship of the world, is enmity with God;*[27] and if any man love the world, *the love of the Father is not in him.*[28] The *one thing needful*[29] for thee, then, is personal piety; the power of religion on thy heart; the temper of heaven in thy soul; and the practice of godliness in thy whole deportment. If thou wouldst not sink forever, be now on *the rock of ages.*[30] If thou wouldst be safe, be in the hands of CHRIST. If thou wouldst be a son of heaven, be *born again.*[31] If thou wouldst be in the way to heaven, enter on it through *the strait gate:*[32] and if thou wouldst go *through the gates into the city*[33] at last, it must be by self-denial, and *following JESUS in the way.*[34] Before you either eat or sleep, set to work, and try what God may do for you. And as you are pleading for more than life, you must not give up your suit: YOU MUST SEEK, TILL YOU FIND. Read on your knees the parable of the widow and

the unjust judge, Luke xviii. 2–8; and if you would prevail with God, you must persist as she does, till you obtain the blessing. See this importunate spirit illustrated in another widow, Matthew xv. 22–28. With our Lord's proper titles in her mouth, she cries to him for mercy. He seems to take no notice of her. The disciples intercede for her. He tells them, he was sent to work miracles only for the *Jews.* The poor woman is not discouraged; she breaks through the company, and falls at his feet with a *Lord help me.* He calls her a Gentile dog, that had no right to the bread of God's children. The humble creature acknowledges her character and unworthiness; but begs a dog's portion, a crumb under the children's table. Having exercised her patience thus far, and given her faith full scope to display itself, the glory of JESUS breaks in upon her with these transporting words, *O woman, great is thy faith! Be it unto thee even as thou wilt.*[35] Get thou, my friend, the spirit of importunate widows; wrestling *Jacobs;* penitent *Ephraims;* humble publicans, and praying *Sauls;* and resolve not to leave the place without a blessing. And if thou attainest to this, JESUS will also say to thee, *Be it unto thee even as thou wilt.* Then it shall be *well with thee* indeed: thou shall be a penitent, a believer, a true convert, and a son of God. Thou shalt glorify him on earth, and enjoy him through all eternity. This brings on the second question.

2. *Is it well with thy wife?* She is the woman of thy choice, whom thou hast singled out from all the daughters of thy people. She preferred thee to all others; forsook her natural relations for thy sake; put herself under thy care and protection; and entered with thee the nearest and dearest relation upon earth. She is the painful mother, and careful nurse of thy children. Is it thy constant endeavour to promote her happiness? Do *her two breasts always delight thee?* Is she indeed, thy *other-self,* and dear to thy heart as the blood that flows there? Darest thou utter one harsh sentence, or wear a frown, when *that* form appears? Look on her again: her very weakness is amiable. That is the feeble vine, which demands you, the stronger tree, for its support; and it richly repays thee, with its shade and its fruit. American wives are worthy of double honour, with all men of sense and reflection. They nobly gave up husbands and sons, to go forth in defence of their country. And while the whole weight of care at home, lay on their weak hands, by their national virtue, and amazing industry, they convinced the world, for seven years together, that foreign trade is not essential to the subsistence of *America.* Those grey hairs are as lovely as they are honourable. Canst thou reckon up the labours of those two hands? Numbers were not made for that purpose. My sister; my daughter; *how is it with thee?* Are thou indeed what my fond wishes suppose thee? Can *the heart of thy husband* safely *trust in thee?* Art thou indeed, *an help meet for him?*[36] Can he lean his honour, fortune, and reputation, on thy faithful bosom? When treated with contempt or insult abroad, can he return home, and find his world in thee? Does thy winning sweetness smooth the rugged parts of his disposition? And

dost thou smile, or weep down the rising storm? Thy husband, I must hope, takes especial care, that children and servants shall pay thee all possible respect and obedience. Thou are therefore every creature's friend; and the powerful bond that binds the whole family together, with the golden chains of love. Be then thy principal ornament, *a meek and quiet spirit*[37] and let thy benevolence stand as a reproach on those daughters of fury, whom we should conjecture to be women only by the female dress, the smooth face, and the shrill voice. Wretched the man who calls her wife! He wedded a lamb; she became a tigress in his bosom. He hoped for a sweet companion through life, to share all its pleasures, and all its cares with him. But she is a grief to his heart; thunder to his ears; a tyrant to his servants, and ruin to his children, by excessive severity or partial indulgence. But I hope my picture has few originals; and I return with pleasure to the more amiable character of the most amiable sex, as I have long considered you. Your softness and delicacy are a constant check on the rougher temper of the other sex; who, without this restraint, would degenerate into brutal savages. To your abhorrence of vice and cruelty, it is chiefly to be ascribed, that men are not more vicious, and more cruel. And to conciliate your favour, and recommend themselves to your approbation, is the motive and source of perhaps half the good, the brave and generous actions of mankind. The good you do then, and the good you are the occasion of being done; with the evils which you prevent, preserve on earth a large proportion of the virtue it possesses. The happy man who calls you wife, feels his heart often saying, what your modesty forbids his tongue to utter. *Many daughters have done virtuously, but thou excellest them all.*[38] Thou art then, my sister, a worthy daughter of *America,* and a woman fit to live in *this world.*——But permit your friend and admirer to ask, How is it with thee *for eternity?* Thou hast, I hope a loving husband on earth; but is *thy Maker thy husband?*[39] Art thou married to the Lord Jesus, the glorious bride-groom of his church and people? Pause—and ask, whether his transcendent worth has won your heart; and whether you have given as chearful a consent to be his faithful spouse, as you did to the man in whose bosom you lie? I know your sex are tempted to trust to that sweetness of temper you often possess. But I pray you remember, that is not a *heavenly* temper. Your greatest danger, however, arises from the trust you have in your being innocent of many crimes, into which many of our sex fall. On what a broken reed are you leaning for eternity! As if exemption from crimes was that life of *holiness, without which none shall see the Lord.*[40] Thou couldst not survive the guilt of prostituting thy body to the adulterer. But dost thou not know, that *the body is for the Lord, and the Lord for the body?*[41] Thou darest not take the name of the Lord thy God in vain; nor talk the language of hell, like the sons of perdition. But dost thou glorify, worship and adore, *that great and dreadful name, The Lord thy God?*[42] Nothing could induce thee to drink to intoxication: but dost thou daily ask of jesus, and is he giving to drink

of the well of the water of life? Thou wouldst not bruise the face, wound the skin, or tear the clothes of thy female acquaintance: but art thou fighting *the good fight of faith*,[43] against *the sins of the flesh, the lusts of the eye, and the pride of life?*[44] Thou are a daughter of *Eve,* and exactly in the same circumstances to which her fall and apostacy reduced herself: to the loss of her true glory and innocence; exclusion from the tree of life; expulsion from paradise; and the curse of God upon her, and all she should conceive; unless He who was preached to her, as the *Seed of the woman,*[45] shall restore her and you to your lost station; and produce in you a divine life. O my dear creatures; let not your own hearts, not the tongue of the flatterer deceive you, as if you were angels in human form. Your sex is sure of an advocate in me, when virtue, decency, and comparative innocence are the topics. For many of you have every thing, but the *one thing needful.* But I must not conceal from you, what thirty years preaching to both sexes has confirmed me in,—That you are as much disaffected to God, and as destitute of true religion, as the other sex is. How often is the preacher's heart grieved, when his eye informs him, that the irreligious of your sex, is the most careless and giddy part of his audience? For neither the devotional, nor instructive part of public worship, can fix your attention for three minutes together, in two hours time. Alas! my daughters, what must this be ascribed to, but the want of love to God, and an awful disaffection to religion. Good heaven! Are you not horribly afraid of dying, and going to that world where there is nothing but religion? What a drudgery, what a hell, must heaven be to the irreligious! If a little of it be so disgusting to the vain and thoughtless part of womankind, how completely miserable must they be in that world, where there is nothing but the perfection of religion, to all eternity? And if you take up your residence in that world where there is *no* religion, you do not expect happiness there: *that* God rendered impossible, when he created that world as a proper residence of pain, misery and desperation. You can never taste of happiness, then, until you find it in religion; that is, in loving, glorifying and serving God. This gives the only heaven upon earth: it is all the furniture you can carry to heaven with you; and all the happiness you will find, when you arrive there. God Almighty awaken you to a sense and knowledge of these things! What an everlasting lamentation will it be, after filling your station on earth with so much credit, to be shut out of heaven at last, for want of religion. If you would be lovely in God's sight, and safe and happy, whatever shall befall you, observe the directions given to husbands; and put them instantly in practice. The ear of JESUS is accustomed to the cries of importunate and weeping women. His glory will shine forth upon them at last, when he says, O woman, great is thy faith, vehement thy desires, numerous thy tears; be it unto thee even as thou wilt. Then heaven breaks into thy soul, and CHRIST is formed within thee. Now your darkness is turned into the light of the morning, when *the sun of righteousness ariseth upon you.*[46] Now you anoint his head with your best ointment of praise and glory; and wash his feet with your joyful tears, and press them into your very soul. Now you will be an help meet for your husband, and travel again in birth for your children till Christ be formed within them. Turn to one of the prayers in this book, and by your loving endearments, engage him to the immediate use of it. He must rejoice, that he has a wife who encourages him to religion. He must not, will not, dare not refuse; while all the eyes of heaven are upon him; a weeping wife by his side, and a house-hold perhaps longing to have a God among them. Precious souls! Sleep no longer with a curse of God on your prayerless habitation. Gather your family around you. Read a portion of the sacred scriptures—sing the praises of God—then fall on your knees, or reverently stand, and pronounce one of these prayers with solemnity and devotion; or use any other you may prefer before them, until you can, to your own comfort, and the edification of your family, perform this great duty without such assistance. And let no company nor business, divert you from your course. May I now hope, that you have a God in your house, and in your closet; in your heart, and in your life? Then *blessed are you of the Lord.*[47] Go on in his ways; grow in grace; and as true yoke-fellows, mutually encourage each other *to love and to good works.*[48] You have now a friend in heaven; *a refuge from the storm; a very present help in trouble*[49] a God to whom you can look, and on whom you can trust, for all you need for time and eternity. A God who has promised he will *never leave you, nor forsake you,*[50] but *will be your guide even unto death.*[51] Now you are anxiously concerned for the glory of God; the honour of JESUS; and for the prevalence of religion all around you. And now too, what church you shall join, will become a matter of serious consideration with you. And though I tell you, that if you are truly pious, you cannot chuse much amiss, whatever church you join; yet I wish you not too precipitate. Give yourselves time to read your Bibles, and to get acquainted with the Articles and Confessions of the several denominations among us. How many are hurried into a profession, on the bare supposition that every thing must be right there, where *they* have received some religious impressions; and that there is neither truth nor piety any where else. In the mean time, they are so extremely ignorant, that they know not the difference betwixt the covenant of works, and the covenant of grace: the difference betwixt conviction, and repentance; betwixt regeneration, and conversion—What saving faith is, and wherein it differs from the faith of assurance. They know not that many have saving faith, that is not grown up to assurance; and that many have assurance, who have not saving faith at all. And this must be the case with many unhappy souls, who are taught to believe, that their safety depends, rather on the good opinion they have of themselves, than on the approbation of their maker; and if they can be brought to an assurance that their sins are pardoned, it shall be sufficient proof that they really are so. O my dear creatures, what dangers await you, on every hand! How many dangerous rocks of error threaten you with ship-wreck, before you are safe on *the rock of ages?*[52] How many floods of false joy may break upon you, before God, by his SPIRIT, give you *joy and peace in believing?*[53] And how many of the deeps of Satan's policy must you pass through, before you are safely lodged in the hands of CHRIST. *O be not deceived!*[54] The great concern is, to be a true Christian. When you have read for instruction, and frequently prayed for direction, you will be better qualified to chuse a profession. And it will be for the promotion of love and harmony among you, if the whole family go together: for different professions in the same house, you will feel and regret, as long as you live together. And now your household will become a special object of your care and solicitude; which brings on the next question.

3. *Is it well with your children?* If you are living without God in the world, what becomes of them? If worldly pursuits and conversation be all they see and hear about their father's house, they will naturally conclude, that they were made for no other purpose but to laugh and play while they are children; and to make crops and clothes when they are men and women. If my *Plain Planter* has made dancing a part of his children's education; the dear young creatures have been taught to believe, that to enter a house gracefully, and to walk a minute with ease, is of much greater importance, than to learn the doctrines and duties of religion and morality: for they well know there have been twenty times more pains and expence bestowed on the one, than on the other. From the manner of spending the sabbath, in these middle and southern States, children are led to believe, that the command, *Remember the sabbath day, to keep it holy,* signifies, that people are to put on clean clothes; the children to play the day out; the Negroes to walk about idle, or to work for themselves; and that their parents are obliged to go abroad, or to entertain their neighbours, and to talk on every subject but religion and their duty. When they see the Bible so totally neglected, they must conclude, that the use of it is to teach children to read, and to get disagreeable talks out of; but to be totally disused when they grow up. They see the duties there commanded so generally neglected; and the vices there forbidden so commonly practised, that they are sure that book was made to vex and restrain children; and they long to be grown out of its way, that they may talk and act like other people, without reproof or correction. But I fear the bulk of our inhabitants dare neither reprove nor correct their children; but have forfeited their right to both. Such the examples you have given them, and such the conversation they learn from your own lips, that should your unhappy ruined child use the language of fallen angels in your hearing, you are so fallen from dignity and innocence, that you cannot reprove, correct and weep over him. Guilt, conscious guilt, stops your mouth, and arrests your arm. The miserable lost youth, grows up a confirmed reprobate. All good men will avoid his conversation. No pious family can encourage his visits;

but must be alarmed to see him among their children. No good woman can think of marrying him, to be the mother of *a brood of vipers,*[55] who would hiss against the heavens, and taint with their poisonous breath whoever comes near them. His head is so empty of sense, and his conversation so barren, that if he may not swear, he knows not what to say. He deems himself such a liar, that his word is not to be taken, without his oath. Unhappy, mistaken mortal! It is a rule with people of sense, never to believe what needs an oath; for honest truth will forever stand without it. But his case is not wholly desperate, on the *Christian* plan. There may be hopes of him still, while he believes the Bible. Its truths may some day reach him with mighty power, and make him a wonderful penitent, and a glorious convert to righteousness. But alas! The ungodly lives of parents, have been laying in him the seeds of infidelity from his infancy; and they cannot be surprised to hear, that, before he is twenty-five years of age, he has given up his Bible, and is a confirmed DEIST. He is now to deny *the Lord that bought him,*[56] as long as he lives; and JESUS CHRIST denies him before his FATHER and his Angels. Luke xii. 8, 9. O parents! Let me give you the observation of a heathen poet. "What reverence is due to a child?"[57] With what awe should the eye and presence of a child strike the heart, seal the lips, and stop the hand of a wicked parent. If such powerful monitors admonish in vain, remember, you are sanctifying vice, and recommending it to your children's practice, by your own example. You are inflicting a wound that never may be healed; and planting a tree which will produce fruit unto death. Your children must either despise you for your wickedness, or imitate your conduct. O parents! If you must be wicked, let it suffice, that heaven and earth are witnesses; but studiously conceal it from your children.* Here, at last, hypocrisy is a virtue. Retire far from the sight and hearing of your children, before your tongue insults the heavens; or your actions set at defiance all the laws of holiness; unless it be a very blessed and desirable thing with you, to have them as bad as yourselves. In vain would men and angels preach to them the evil of wicked actions, and profane language, while they are recommended to them, by the practice of their parents. But let me indulge brighter hopes. It may be better with your children than my

---

*Would it not be a good expedient, for such parents, whose corruptions are too strong for their resolution, but who possess for their children some of that reverence which *Juvenal* recommends, to take a child with them wherever they go; and let the presence of the child be a constant check on the words and actions of the parents, should the eye and ear of God and man fail of their effect. The child will naturally consider itself as taken out to learn a proper behaviour and conversation, from the example of their parent: and it might have a happy effect upon both, while the design was remembered. True it is, the infallible cure of vice, is divine grace, and to watch, pray and fight against it. Still, if parents will sin, let it be any where on earth rather than in the sight or hearing of their families.

fears suggest. They may be the children of prayer, before they saw the light. And for every year they count, you have lodged a thousand petitions at the throne of grace for each of them. Whenever you have remembered the death of CHRIST, you have given them all up by name to the Lord, at his holy table. You have instructed them in the doctrines and duties of religion. You have reproved and warned them, as the case required. You have strengthened all your precepts, by your own examples. You have mourned over their fallen state; and felt the pangs of a labouring woman, till they should be born into the new world of grace. Perhaps *it is well* with some of them;[58] and you *no more remember the anguish, for joy that a child* of yours is born an heir of glory.[59] This was to you, as the day of your own espousals to CHRIST; and was a mighty revival to your own soul. O my dear youth! Here is true pleasure. JESUS would be far sweeter to you than the honeycomb, could you but taste him. Here is safety: the wings of divine mercy would be over you, *and underneath the everlasting arms.*[60] Here, in religion, you will find a treasure past all computation; an eternal inheritance. You will secure a set of new friends, God, angels, and good men; who will own and take care of you, when father and mother must forsake you. Let a mother's tears, a father's prayers; the invitations of JESUS, and the calls of God, prevail with you to *hear, and your soul shall live;* to obey and be happy.[61] The devil will tell you, there is no pleasure in religion. There is none for *him,* indeed; for it is the want of religion that makes him a devil. But if you would have the testimony of proper judges, all the good men on earth; the spirits of the just in heaven, and all the angels of glory, will testify, that religion furnishes all their happiness. Could religion be shut out of heaven, all their happiness goes with it. And could the damned in hell see the beauty, and feel the force of religion; that moment they forget their pangs, and the joys of heaven are all their own. O come, and taste her pleasant ways. Feed no longer on the husks of sinful pleasure, when thou mayst *feast on fat things, full of marrow, and wines on the lees well refined:*[62] when thou mayst have JESUS, *the guide of thy youth, and thy portion forever.*[63] Then it shall be *well with thee;* and thou shalt know what heaven is: heaven must consist in an endless and unlimited degree of the happiness you will then enjoy. I now ask,

4. *Is it well with your servants?* I must flatter myself, that my country increases in humanity. The slaves you own, generally grew up with yourselves, or have been raised with your children. You feel, then, a kind of brotherly or parental affection for them. They have so often fed from your hand; played at your door, and shewn such a willingness to please and oblige you, that you consider them as your *humble friends,* and perhaps the best you have. The severities of former times, are known only by report. Unreasonable tasks; inhuman corrections; naked backs, and starved bellies, are known no more; except among a few tyrants, who are known over a whole county; and from whose brutality the unhappy creatures

must fly; and seek a precarious sustenance where they can find it.* But the slaves of my *Plain Planter,* are among the happiest of human beings. Well clothed, and well fed; a warm cabbin, and comfortable bedding; with their hearty thriving children, growing up under their eye. Their daily labour they scarcely feel, being void of all the distressing cares of life; such as educating, and settling out children; procuring food and raiment for a family; paying taxes, and a thousand other cares, that never disturb their solid sleep, nor rack their waking thoughts. I wish the Negroes to be put in remembrance,—That their bodily labour is all the compensation they make, for the whole of their keeping—That they can look round them and see many white families, whose rented land, or barren fields will not furnish them with that solid and wholesome food, the want of which has turned their children's blood to a mass of corruption, while their backs are covered with cotton rags. I wish them to know, that they are by no means their friends, who put freedom into their heads. This is an event, that all the wisdom of *America* seems at present unequal to; but which divine providence will accomplish in due time: and then, how to provide for them, and what to do with them, will be questions easily solvable, though neither you nor I can answer them at this time.

The avarice of the *British* merchants, sent them, or their fathers to *America.* This wicked branch of trade, found ready encouragement with the planters, while the country was a boundless forest; and the labour of the slaves was deemed necessary to clear and subdue it. But conscientious or prudential motives, have pretty generally prevailed among us, to discourage the importation of slaves; and the bulk of our inhabitants consider them as a formidable encumbrance, rather than

---

* Query, Whether it is friendly to the interest of virtue and humanity, for owners to be paid by the community, for slaves that are executed, or die in a state of outlawry? While the public are to pay their value, some masters may be tempted to breed them less virtuously; and rather promote than discourage their villanies, while only others are to suffer by them. A public execution is the worst that can happen; and the master secures a good price for a bad servant. The laws of humanity are equally sacrificed. Cruel treatment drives the miserable creature to the woods. He must live by plunder, for no one dares to employ him. An outlawry is procured. A hue and cry follows. Poor solitary wretch! the whole world are his enemies; and men and dogs beset him round. Whither shall he flee? To return to that inhuman, who, from the relation of a master, should be his protection, is to suffer forty deaths without dying. For I shall not easily believe that the pang of death is equal to a severe stroke with a hickory or cow-hide, on the naked human skin. Instead of protecting, he increases his wretchedness. He publishes £. 10 the price of his head; and ten dollars, if taken alive. In this last case, his trial is hurried on. Friendless, and without defence, he falls a victim to public justice, for the crimes which severity drove him to perpetrate. A good price, however, is secured, and the public pay it. Were it not so, some more care would have been taken, to instill virtuous, if not religious principles into these poor neglected creatures.

an advantage to the country, in the present exhausted state of the soil, and en-creasing difficulty of seasons. Is it really true, what many assert, That the slaves are the occasion of more guilt to our country, than any, or all other sources of evil? If this be true, what an awful, and lamentable reflection is it, that we have guilt in common with all other nations, and an additional, and enormous burden peculiar to ourselves! I readily acknowledge, that whoever has had the management of half a dozen Negroes, for as many years, has had his patience put to severe trials; per-haps too great for his philosophy and piety both united. Their real, or pretended ignorance; their obstinacy and laziness; their endeavours to evade, or flight their work, under his very eye; the universal practice of lying, to conceal or lessen their offences; their provoking or petulant answers, when reproved, or moderately cor-rected; with a countless train of other faults and deficiencies, are doubtless made the occasions of very great guilt by many. The poor worm rises into instant fury. Whatever comes to hand, is used as a rod. The tongue, that unruly evil, spits forth its deadly poison; and the prisoners of the pit listen with horrid pleasure, to hear their language so properly spoken on earth. Whatever is done, is all wrong together. Nothing can be right, where passion rules and dictates. And thus the vicious part of our country-men, may storm and rage, and act the incarnate fury; and then blame the Negroes as the cause of their wickedness. But *God, the judge of all,* will form a very different estimate; and find the cause of their vices in their own depraved natures, and ungoverned passions.[64] Something might be said for persons of this unhappy turn, if they could prove two things. 1. That every person who is offended with his slave, must of necessity act this wicked, weak, and shameful part. And 2. Because you are offended with your slave, that shall be suf-ficient reason for breaking the commands of God, and all the laws of decency and humanity. The first can never be proved; because I trust, a great majority of mas-ters act a very different part, and reason thus: My servant has offended me; but my master is in heaven, whom I offend every day of my life: Should he now sit in Judgment on my soul, and his displeasure wax hot against me, how could I stand when God ariseth, *or answer to him for one of a thousand.*[65] What is the duty and obe-dience my servant owes to me, when compared with the strength of my obliga-tions to God my owner, and Christ my master? I gave to my servant neither breath nor being; nor can I preserve these to him a single moment, when his and my mas-ter calls him. What proportion can there be, then, betwixt his offence against me, and my sins against God? My orders are sometimes weak, passionate, contradic-tory or impossible; and my expectations beyond the strength or skill of my ser-vant: but the commands of my master are all perfectly wise and holy; fit for him to command, and me to obey; and yet I have refused obedience to this universal owner, as well by neglecting commanded duty, as by wilful and known disobedi-ence. Shall I then seize my fellow-servant by the throat, for his trivial debt to me, when I owe to my master, a sum of such magnitude? God forbid! I will therefore pass it by with reproof; or I will use *soft* blows, and *hard* arguments, that we may be able to pray together, *Forgive us our debts, as we forgive our debtors.*[66]

The second case is still less capable of proof. Your servant offending you, can never furnish a reason, why you should fly in the face of heaven, and offend God ten times more than it is possible for any creature to offend you. Remember, God has done you no injury; and no reason can be given, why he should suffer insult from your caprice, or the delinquency of your servant. Try this conduct in any other case. Your slave has offended; and you turn round and strike your father, or spit in the face of your governor—Or you rush into the house, insult and curse the court, and drive them from the bench of justice. To plead that you was offended beyond the power of flesh and blood to bear, will not preserve you from the resentment of your country, and the sentence of its laws. We know, the flesh and blood that sinners carry about with them can bear very little. But what is grace for, if not to subdue flesh and blood? *If ye live after the flesh, ye shall die; for flesh and blood cannot inherit the kingdom of God.*[67] If this plea will not screen you from present suffering, can you imagine, that God is less wise to judge, and less just to punish? If you, with a breeding and education much superior to that of your slave, are yet a worse servant to God than he is to you, what would you have been with his education? Or what might he have been with yours? Perhaps, then, my friend, the truth is, that much of your servant's wickedness and deficiency is to be ascribed to your own negligence of the duties you owe to God and your household. Can you expect him to be virtuous and dutiful, without instruction, and example? Or that he should serve you from principle, when perhaps neither of you have the fear of God before your eyes. The praise of good men is, *That they will teach their children, and their household, to serve the Lord.*[68] I readily grant, that the omission of this duty of religious instruction to the slaves, is a great national evil; and the source of numerous others to society. Many of them are as much in a state of heathenism, as they could have been in the unenlightened regions of *Africa.* The language, the manners, and the ideas of your children, receive such a tincture from being bred up with so many pagans, that discerning people must feel and lament it through life.

It is a question highly worthy the enquiry of the Divine, the Philosopher, and the Legislator, whether the awful breach, and general disregard to the Sabbath-day, among all ranks, in these middle and southern states, is not chiefly to be ascribed to the influence of the heathen slaves over the inhabitants in their younger days. And so deeply rooted is this national evil, that even a profession of religion is found inadequate to remove it: some professors paying little more regard to the instruction and behaviour of their children and servants, on that holy day, than they did while confessedly living without God in the world. Whoever reads the fourth commandment, the 58th of *Isaiah,* and many other parts of sacred writ, will see the strictness enjoyned on the ancient church. And should any pretending to Christianity insist, that we are not bound to keep that sacred day with the same veneration, they must first prove, that New Testament saints are not to be as holy as Old Testament believers. In vain will any plead the example of our blessed SAVIOUR. I know he is often, by the Jews, charged with, and is in frequent danger of being stoned for, sabbath-breaking. But does our heavenly teacher plead for graceless omissions, or sinful indulgences? Far from it: he only insists that it was lawful to *do more good* on that day than their contracted views admitted. He is for healing the sick, relieving the distressed, and for shewing the same compassion to the bodies of men, that themselves allowed to the herds of the stall. Let carnal professors know, that JESUS was otherways employed than to sleep away the hours of that day, and wake to talk on worldly things. Every true Christian knows, that the service of God, and the business of their own, and their family's salvation, requires every hour of that sacred day; and leaves no room for trifling and dissipation. How easy, and how much in your power is the cure of this crying evil, as far as it depends on human activity? Would you start early from the bed of sloth; enter your closet for secret devotion, and there spend one quarter of any hour at least in earnest prayer to God for yourself and your family; for church and state; and particularly for grace to keep holy that Sabbath day; and that God would prosper you in the government and instruction of your family, and in your attendance on public ordinances: Would you then convene your household for the solemn worship of God, and charge all under your roof, to remember the day, and keep it holy to the Lord; strictly forbidding all secular labour, vain conversation, play, dissipation, and idle visits; taking care to see your own orders obeyed, by reading, or having read, the scriptures, sermons, and other good books; And then, instead of the Negroes corrupting your children, let your children be employed in teaching your Negroes psalms, hymns, catechisms, prayers, and the art of reading; whether or not, you make conscience of sending your young Negroes to school, or take a teacher in your family. If it be a day of public worship, enjoyn the decent attendance of all your household; and remember, your cook has as good a claim to the holy rest of that day, as your other domestics, and cannot be deprived of it without injustice and oppression.* So better a cold dinner, than an offended God, an angry conscience, and an oppressed servant. In the evening convene your whole family; briefly repeat to them what you have been reading or hearing; exhort them to a practical improvement of the doctrines and duties recommended; know what advances they have made that day, and how they have spent it. And then, after the

---

*If on any extraordinary occasion cooks should be employed on the Lord's day, they ought to have Monday, or some succeeding day of the week to themselves.

public worship of God as a family, let each conclude the day with praying to *their Father who sees in secret.*[69] Surely, surely, my dear *Planter,* this looks more like keeping holy the Sabbath-day, than the present graceless practice of our country. If people who are destitute of religion will intrude their unwelcome company upon you, shall it be a question, whether they shall *keep* the day with you, or you *break* it with them? A steady perseverance in the course of your duty, would speak at once your piety and your courage, and soon rid your family of such pernicious visitants. I am far from wishing the legislature to meddle with religion; CHRIST is king of his church, and has given us his laws in the Bible: but I humbly think they might make Lord's day visiting as penal as Lord's day labour. If the stroller pleads that he has business, still he is a Sabbath breaker; for no business is to be transacted or spoken of on that day, but that of piety, necessity, and mercy. Such a law in our country, and such a conduct among serious people, would oblige such empty creatures to sleep out the day at home, as the men of the world do, to whom the Sabbath is a weariness. Alas! my friend, you need no hindrance from abroad. To keep your children in proper bounds, and religiously employed, will require great steadiness and watchfulness too. And if you can secure the regular attendance of your slaves, on divine worship in your family, you are happier than many of my acquaintance, who often find it a very perplexing difficulty, arising from their brutal disregard to religion, or from their low attachment to some other profession. Many of them, however, would exceedingly rejoice, if their master had a religious family, and would give their regular attendance, with pleasure and profit. But no disposition in your children or servants, will excuse your neglecting the duties you owe to God and to them. They must have instruction, whether they hear or forbear; and God must be worshipped, though all the hearts in your family do not concur in it. Reading the sacred scriptures; singing the praises of God, and sending up your united prayers to heaven, may prove a happy mean to win the attention, and gain the hearts of the most backward among you at last. *Wait, I say, upon the Lord, and he shall give thee the desires of thine heart.*[70] And *though it tarry long, yet wait for it.*[71] Though you *sow in tears* and disappointment, you may yet reap a joyful harvest:[72] and you and your household meet at last with joy unspeakable before your judge and Saviour; and you be able to say, *Here, Lord, I am, and the family thou gavest me.*[73] Amen.

### The Negroes' CATECHISM.

*Question 1. Do you know who made the Negroes?*
*Answer.* The same God that made all things.

*Q. 2. Do you think white folks and negroes all come from one father?*
*A.* Yes: The book says, God hath made of one blood all nations of men, on all the face of the earth. Acts xvii. 26. And I should think they were so myself.

*Q. 3. What makes you think so?*

A. Because, except the black skin, and the curled head, their bodies, I believe, are just alike, within and without.

*Q. 4. Have you any other reason to believe they are from one father and mother?*

A. Yes: they are more alike in their souls, than in their bodies.

*Q. 5. How do you know you have a soul?*

A. Because I can think and understand—I can be glad and be sorry—I can wish for what I like, and be afraid of what will hurt me; and I feel pleasure and pain;—but the body can do none of these; for without the soul it is a dead carcase.

*Q. 6. Why do you think the souls of whites and blacks are related?*

A. Because we all seem to think alike. We all love and hate the same things; and what gives pain or pleasure to the one, does to the other.

*Q. 7. Do they shew their relations any other way?*

A. Yes: they seem to have hearts alike, and all bad together. The same sins that the one loves, the other loves too. The one talks and lives as wickedly as the other. It is as hard for one to turn to God, as for the other: and when they get God's grace, it works the same way upon both.

*Q. 8. By this you believe that all are sinners: did God make them so?*

A. No surely: God made all things good; and nothing bad can come from him.

*Q. 9. How came all men to be bad then?*

A. God gave our father and mother a thousand blessings; but strongly forbid them to eat or touch the fruit of one particular tree; for if they did, it would poison their whole body and soul, and bring diseases and death on the one; and blindness and sin, and a curse on the other, and on all his children, and every thing about him.

*Q. 10. And did they disobey and eat after all?*

A. They did.

*Q. 11. What followed this great crime?*

A. All that God had told them. They were directly stripped of all their beauty, and glory, and holiness; and sin, and death, and the devil took possession of them.

*Q. 12. Did God leave Adam and his children in their ruined state?*

A. God of his mercy promised to fallen man a Saviour, who should overcome their enemy, and restore their fallen nature.

*Q. 13. Who is the Saviour of fallen man?*

A. Jesus Christ.

*Q. 14. Who is Jesus Christ?*

A. He is true God in one nature; real man in another; produced by the power of the eternal Father, and born of a virgin.

*Q. 15. Did Christ come as soon as man fell?*

A. No: he gave the world great notice of his coming; for he did not really come in the flesh till 4000 years after Adam's fall.

*Q. 16. Why must Jesus Christ be God?*

A. That he might be able to go through his undertaking, and give sufficient worth to what he did and suffered.

*Q. 17. Why must Jesus Christ be man?*

A. That he might be capable of suffering, which he could not be as God; and that he might be the *second Adam,* to fulfil all righteousness.

*Q. 18. Why must he be God and man in one person?*

A. That he might bring God and man to a friendly agreement.

*Q. 19. What did Jesus Christ do for us?*

A. He paid a perfect obedience to the whole law of God; and he set us an example of all holy living.

*Q. 20. What did Christ suffer for the salvation of man?*

A. He suffered the miseries of life; the opposition of men and devils; the pains of death in his body, and the pains of hell in his soul.

*Q. 21. How are we to be any better for what Christ did and suffered?*

A. We must repent of sin; believe in Christ; be born again, and turn to God.

*Q. 22. Are negroes allowed to hope for the gospel salvation?*

A. I thank God they are. Jesus tells his disciples, Go ye into all the world, and preach the gospel to every creature.

*Q. 23. You say we must repent; what is repentance?*

A. It is being grieved and ashamed for our past sins; turning from them, and sinning no more.

*Q. 24. What is believing in Christ?*

A. It is really believing him to be the son of God, and Saviour of men. It is coming to him, and trusting in him for the favour of God, and for complete salvation.

*Q. 25. What is being born again?*

A. It is that great work of God, by which a humbled sinner is made a child of God, and is renewed after his holy image.

*Q. 26. What do you mean by turning to God?*
A. This is called conversion; and is a turning away from all known sin, and turning to the ways of God and holiness.

*Q. 27. What should a poor negroe do to get a share in the gospel salvation?*
A. They should learn to know God, and Christ; and their own dangerous and lost condition.

*Q. 28. What must they do when they see their danger?*
A. They must cry day and night to God for mercy.

*Q. 29. Will not temptations be very busy, when a negroe thinks of being religious?*
A. Yes: the Devil will tell them it is too soon, or too late. Their own wicked heart will strive against them. Their old sins will seek to hold them fast; and their wicked acquaintance will be a great weight upon them.

*Q. 30. How must they do, if they would be safe and right?*
A. They must hear Christ their friend, and look on all that would hinder them as their worst enemies. They must cry, day and night, God be merciful to me a sinner. They must break through all that is in their way, and never stop, till the door is opened for them, and they find Christ and the great salvation.

*Q. 31. How will it be with them then?*
A. Then it will be well with them. God is their Father and portion; Christ their friend and Saviour, who dwells in them by his Holy Spirit. They are pardoned and justified by his merit and righteousness, and shall never come into condemnation.

*Q. 32. Well, now they are Christians, and safe, they may sin without fear, may they not?*
A. God never made them Christians to set them a sinning; they could do that fast enough before.

*Q. 33. What do you think of those that say, now they are converted, sin cannot hurt them?*
A. If they mean that grace keeps them from sin I think very well of them; but if they mean that their sins would not be as bad as other people's, I think them very wrong, and no Christians at all. For the grace that bringeth salvation teaches all who have it, to deny all ungodliness, and worldly lust; and to live soberly, righteously, and godly in the world.

*Q. 34. But they say sin is no sin in them, for it will not be imputed to them, but to Christ: what would you say to such professors?*
A. I did not think there were any such people in the world. But I am sure they make Christ *the minister of sin;* and would *continue in sin, that grace may abound.* God forbid, we should be evil, because he is good. Grace makes us good trees, and our

fruit is to shew it. It was worse for *David* and *Peter* to do what they did, than for any two men then in the world; and so they thought by their bitter repentance.[74] *He that committeth sin is of the Devil,* if he had an hundred conversions.[75]

*Q. 35. Do you speak from experience?*
A. I hope I do. Since I had reason to hope, that God had mercy on my soul, I know not how to please and serve him enough; but often ask, what shall I render to God, for all his goodness to me. When my master treats me well, it brings a hell to my conscience if I offend him, or neglect his business; and Christians feel thus towards God.

*Q. 36. How then do you think Christians should behave?*
A. They should walk as Christ walked. They should be in the fear of the Lord all day long. They should shew the world the difference betwixt the sons of God, and the children of the wicked one; and that they whom Christ has made free, will not be the servants of sin.

*Q. 37. When negroes become religious, how must they behave to their masters?*
A. The scriptures in many places command them, to be honest, diligent and faithful in all things, and not to give saucy answers; and even when they are whipt for doing well, to take it patiently, and look to God for their reward.

*Q. 38. Do not masters owe their slaves great duties too?*
A. Yes: masters should teach their slaves the doctrines and duties of religion—call them daily to the worship of God with them—set them all good examples—provide them with every thing necessary; require nothing but what is reasonable; and keep them from being abused by other people.

*Q. 39. Which do you think the happiest person, the master or the slave?*
A. When I rise on a cold morning to make a fire, and my master in bed; or when I labour in the sun, on a hot day, and my master in the shade; then I think him happier than I am.

*Q. 40. Do you ever think you are happier than he?*
A. Yes: when I come in from my work; eat my hearty supper, worship my maker; lie down without care on my mind; sleep sound; get up in the morning strong and fresh; and hear that my master could not sleep, for thinking on his debts, and his taxes; and how he shall provide victuals and clothes for his family, or what he shall do for them when they are sick—then I bless God that he has placed me in my humble station; I pity my master, and feel myself happier than he is.

*Q. 41. Then it seems every body is best, just where God has placed them?*
A. Yes: The Scriptures say, if I am called, being a slave, I am not to care for it; for every true Christian, is Christ's free man, whether he be bond or free in this world.

*Q. 42. How can you be free and bound both?*

A. If Jesus Christ broke the chain of sin, and freed me from the curse of the law, and the slavery of the devil, I am free indeed, although my body and services may be at the command of another.

*Q. 43. Do Negroes owe their children no duties?*

A. Yes: they must teach their children the doctrines of religion, and all the duties they owe to God and man. They must set them good examples in all things; and correct them when they transgress.

*Q. 44. What do you do when you fall into any sin?*

A. I lament, I mourn, I confess my sin; I lie at Christ's feet for pardon; I turn me from my evil ways; and resolve to sin no more.

*Q. 45. Will not masters and servants meet another day?*

A. Yes: we shall all appear before the judgment seat of Christ, and give an account of all our conduct.

*Q. 46. How dare any body appear there, when all are sinners, and come short of our duty?*

A. Every body must appear there, whether they will or not. And though all have sinned, and deserve condemnation, yet some will stand there with joy and safety.

*Q. 47. How can that be?*

A. Those that were God's people, and Christ's servants in this world, he will own as his, and acknowledge them before all present.

*Q. 48. Is there the same heaven and hell for white and black?*

A. Yes: there will be no difference there, but what more holiness or more sin makes.

*Q. 49. What will become of those that live and die in their sinful state?*

A. If they were in heaven, they could not love God; therefore they sink to hell with the weight of their sins, and the curse of the Judge; for they are fit for nothing else.

*Q. 50. How are regenerate and holy persons disposed of then?*

A. If they were in hell, they would love God; and therefore the Judge invites them to the joys of their Lord. They are fit for heaven, and nothing else, and they enter through the pearly gates, and serve their God and Saviour through all eternity. Amen.

### Prayer for a Negroe.

O Thou great God, the Maker and Lord of all creatures, I, a poor sinner, black in body, and still blacker with sin, would humbly try to worship thee, and glorify thy name, that I am allowed to pray to thee, and to hope for thy mercy, through the Lord Jesus Christ. Blessed be God that I ever heard of that glorious saviour, who invites all sinners to come unto him, that they may find rest to their souls. Lord I am a sinner. I was born a sinner. Many days and nights have I sinned against thee, and heaped ruin and destruction on my own head. I am so wicked that I have not loved God; and such a fool as to destroy myself with sin. I am all over a sinner. I feel it in every part of me, and if thou bring me to trial, my mouth is stopped, and I am gone forever. But, O God of mercies, I throw myself in the dust before thee. I abhor and condemn myself, and heartily hate all my wicked ways: Turn me, O Lord God, turn me from them; and let them no longer rule over me. And O take this wicked, foolish hard heart, and break, and melt and make it a new heart. Lord take me into thy powerful hand, and make me every thing that thou wouldst have me be. Give me Jesus Christ, and mercy and pardon through his blood; and put thy Holy Spirit within me, that I may go and sin no more. Lord give me grace to love thee, and thy dear Son, and thy blessed ways, and thy holy law, and to love all that love God; and make the land of my slavery, the place of my true freedom. Lord pity poor Negroes, that are living without God in the world, and turn and convert them to thee. Bless my master, and all that are his. Make me a faithful servant; and teach me to remember, that what good thing soever any man doth; the same shall he receive of the Lord, whether he is bound or free. And God grant that I may see religion and goodness every where growing, and may have a heart to rejoice in it. Good Lord, keep me watching, and praying against every sin. May I daily grow in grace, and in the knowledge of my blessed Saviour; and may I be willing to suffer any thing, rather than to grieve and offend him. Lord fit me to die, and prepare me for that better world, where all thy servants meet, and can be as holy as their souls desire. May I finish my course with joy, and at last enter in through the gates into the city, and love thee, and serve thee, and worship and glorify thee, Father, Son, and Holy Spirit, one God, through all eternity. Amen.

## Notes

1. Durward T. Stokes, "Henry Pattillo in North Carolina," *North Carolina Historical Review* 44 (October 1967): 373–91.

2. The sixty-three-page tract is available in *Early American Imprints,* series 1, no. 49801 (digital supplement). I have not included "A Short Introduction to the Youth's Catechism," "Dr. Watt's First Catechism, for Children from Three to Seven Years of Age," "A Prayer for a Little Child," "The Youth's Catechism," and "A Youth's Prayer"—material covering pp. 28–46. I have also not transcribed "Family Prayer, for a Week-day Morning"; "Family Prayer for a Week-day Evening"; "Family Prayer for Lord's-day Morning"; "Family Prayer for Lord's-day Evening"; and "The Lord's Prayer Paraphrased" (pp. 52–63).

3. Proverbs 14:34.

4. 1 Timothy 3:13.

5. Jeremiah 31:22.

6. Acts 4:27.

7. 1 Corinthians 11:23–25.

8. Genesis 4:7.

9. Hebrews 11:16.

10. 2 Kings 4:26.

11. 2 Corinthians 5:1.

12. Joshua 22.

13. Hebrews 7:23.

14. Titus 2:12.

15. Psalms 29:2.

16. Philippians 2:12.

17. Matthew 6:20.

18. Matthew 22:37.

19. Psalms 90:12.

20. Matthew 22:11–14.

21. Numbers 28:8.

22. Matthew 6:4.

23. 1 Thessalonians 5:17.

24. Mark 8:34.

25. Romans 8:18.

26. Thomas à Kempis, *The Imitation of Christ,* 30:1.

27. James 4:4.

28. 1 John 2:15.

29. Luke 10:42.

30. 1 Corinthians 3:11.

31. John 3:3–7.

32. Luke 13:24.

33. Revelation 22:14.

34. Mark 10:52.

35. Matthew 15:28.

36. Genesis 2:20.

37. 1 Peter 3:4.

38. Proverbs 31:29.

39. Isaiah 54:5.

40. Hebrews 12:14.

41. 1 Corinthians 6:13.

42. Malachi 1:14.

43. 1 Timothy 6:12.

44. 1 John 2:16.

45. Genesis 3:15.

46. Malachi 4:2.

47. 1 Samuel 15:13.

48. Hebrews 10:24.

49. Isaiah 25:4; Psalms 46:1.

50. Hebrews 13:5.

51. Psalms 48:14.

52. Isaiah 26:4.

53. Romans 15:13.
54. Galatians 6:7.
55. Luke 3:7.
56. 2 Peter 2:1.
57. Juvenal, *The Satires,* xiv, 47.
58. Genesis 29:6.
59. John 16:21.
60. Deuteronomy 33:27.
61. Isaiah 55:3.
62. Isaiah 25:6.
63. Psalms 73:26.
64. Hebrews 12:23.
65. Job 9:3.
66. Matthew 6:12.
67. Romans 8:13; 1 Corinthians 15:50.
68. Joshua 24:15.
69. Matthew 6:4.
70. Psalms 37:4.
71. Habbakkuk 2:3.
72. Psalms 126:5.
73. Genesis 22:11.
74. Acts 2:38; 2 Samuel 12:13.
75. 1 John 3:8.

# CHAPTER 8

# William Graham, 1796

—————————— ⚜ ——————————

BORN IN PENNSYLVANIA IN 1745, William Graham grew up in a Scots-Irish farming household—the kind of family that filled the ranks of the congregations to which ministers such as Samuel Davies and Henry Pattillo preached. Graham, in fact, graduated from the College of New Jersey in 1773, just a little more than a decade after Samuel Davies's presidency of that institution. Moving to Virginia on the eve of the Revolution, Graham obtained his license as a minister and also took charge of a classical academy in Augusta County.[1] During the war Graham served as a captain in the militia and also published patriotic writings that led Presbyterian authorities to censure him for his political activism. Graham also struggled to keep his school—renamed Liberty Hall Academy—in operation. He moved the academy to a location just outside Lexington in 1779 and successfully appealed to the state legislature for a new charter in 1782. After years of financial uncertainty, the academy finally achieved a measure of stability in 1796 when George Washington made a considerable financial contribution.[2] Graham resigned from the academy that same year and moved to Richmond, where he resided until his death in 1799.

Reflecting his embrace of the American cause of independence and his ongoing commitment to Christian teachings, Graham's post-Revolutionary thought blended democratic rhetoric (and an aversion to centralized power) with a fervent desire to hold society to strict moral standards. Involved in a fruitless effort to organize a new state—to be named Franklin—out of the territory that eventually became Tennessee, Graham went so far as to draft a state constitution that called for universal white male suffrage and electoral review of all legislation passed by the assembly. During the debate over ratification of the federal Constitution in 1787, he espoused the antifederalist position that Virginia should guard its sovereignty from interference from a strengthened national government. And he denounced the federal government's use of troops to quell the Whiskey Rebellion of 1794—a brief uprising of Pennsylvania farmers against a despised federal tax. Yet, for all his suspicions about centralized political power, Graham decried anarchy as the greatest threat to the new republic. In a tract published in 1786, he mocked "that silly farcical notion of some half thinking . . . people" who believed "that Liberty consists in an exemption from paying their money, and a freedom from an obligation to obey any laws." Such doctrines, he cautioned, "must be wholly rejected. Such people should not pretend to live in regular society; but join themselves to the Cherokees at once."[3] In his consideration of slavery, Graham not surprisingly turned to organic Christian doctrine to defend the institution.

WILLIAM GRAHAM, Lecture 30th: An Important Question Answered, 1796[4]

We shall in this Lecture endeavor to answer the question is it just to continue those in Slavery who are found in that State? That this question merits an accurate and full investigation will not be doubted by any one who lives in America and is acquainted in the least with the Disputes and contention that have been and still are made about it. There are not a few most zealous Declaimers for universal Emancipation without regard to the Habits, Customs and mental improvement of the Slaves. But these men call themselves the Philosophers of the Age, the great Supporters and friends of human happiness and some of the Teachers of the new Testament. But if we act as Philosophers and make a fair induction of their several dispositions from what we see of their conduct in their respective Stations we shall be obliged to conclude very differently—That Ignorance and Froth form one class of them—Infidelity and the most raging Fanaticism another; while Superstition and [blank space] form a 3[rd] Class. It is not easy to tell whether the 1[st] Class merits pity or contempt. The 2d Class cry out against those who have Slaves because they have none themselves—and the 3[rd] Class are Infidels in a practical as well as in a Scriptural Sense.

It is a clear Induction that mankind are depraved and prone to injure one another. But these men suppose they are as pure and harmless as when they came from the hands of their Creator—that their Depravity or Disposition to injure one another is owing altogether to Priest Craft, and evil Priests. But let us attend a little to the Arguments used to maintain their Doctrine.

The 1st set of them is drawn from Religion. They tell us we should do to others as we would they should do to us. When this is rightly understood it is one of the finest moral precepts that is any where to be met with. But when it is applied to a change of State it is easily perverted to make the caprice of men the Rule of Duty. For instance if I were a Servant I must desire my master's Estate and even his Wife or his Daughter. Now according to the use they make of this as an argument it is my Duty to give what ever my servant may request because were I in his situation I might desire the same. But the plain meaning of the precept is this: that supposing our Status were exchanged, then in that situation what ever I had a right to expect from my master it is my duty to bestow as a Master to my Servant—then instead of this proving any thing in their favor it rather proves the contrary.

Again they take it for granted it is wrong to keep Slaves—and from thence infer that he who lives in the known practice of injustice cannot be a Christian. But whence do they derive this political maxim? It must either be from the common Sense of mankind or Revelation. The 1st is not true for more than [4]/5ths of mankind have thought Slavery to [be] right. Is it from Revelation? That can hardly be or we might have known it as well as themselves. I would here observe that it is a great abuse of Christianity to drag it into this Service. Christianity was never designed to alter the political or civil Status of men but only to bring them to the Love of God—and inculcate the performance of the Duties of their several Stations whether Magistrate or People, Husband or Wife, Parent or Child, Master or Servant. That Christianity was not designed to change men's Civil Relations is evident from the 7th Chapter of 1 Corinthians. The apostle in this place undertakes a Solution of several Difficulties concerning which the Christians of the Church of Corinth had written to him. Let it here be observed that whatever he says with regard to the dissolution of any Relation, he gives it only as his opinion, but when he speaks of the violation of any Relation he declares that he speaks by the command of the Lord—An Example of the former we have in the 5th and 6th verses. In the 6th verse he says: But I speak this by permission and not of commandment. An Example of the latter we have in the 10th verse in these words: And unto the married I command, yet not I but the Lord.[5]

Having said so much of the Design of the Gospel we come now to the question before us which was one of those proposed to the apostle by the Corinthians—and let us hear what he says upon it. In the 20, 21 and 22nd verses he speaks to the very point in question: Let every man abide in the same calling wherein he was called—art thou called being a Servant? Care not for it but if thou mayest be made free use it rather[6]—For he that is called in the Lord being a Servant is the Lord's free man, likewise also he that is called being free is Christ's Servant; and in the 24th: Brethren let every man wherein he is called therein abide with God. We shall select 2 or 3 passages more on this head. The 1st is from the 6th Chap. of the apostle to the Ephesians: Servants be obedient to them that are your Masters according to the flesh with fear and trembling in singleness of heart as unto Christ—not with Eye Service as Men pleasers but as the Servants of Christ doing the Will of God from the heart knowing that whatsoever good thing any man doeth the same shall he receive of the Lord whether he be bond or free.[7] The 2nd is from the 20th of Paul's Epistle to Titus: Exhort Servants to be obedient to their own masters and to please them well in all things, not answering again—not purloining but shewing all good fidelity that they may adorn the Doctrine of God our Saviour in all things. The 3rd is a part of the 6th Chap. of Paul's 1st Epistle to Timothy, where we have these remarkable words: Let as many Servants as are under the yoke count their own Masters worthy of all honor; that the name of God and his Doctrine be not blasphemed and they that have believing masters let them not despise them because they are Brethrens but rather do them honor because they are faithful and beloved partakers of the Benefit. These things teach and exhort. If any man teach other wise and consent not to wholesome words even to the words of our Lord Jesus Christ and to the Doctrine which is according to Godliness; He is proud knowing nothing but doling about questions and strifes of words whereof cometh Envy, Strife, Railings, evil Surmisings—perverse disputings of men of corrupt minds and destitute of the truth—supposing that gain is Godliness—from such turn away thyself. And it should be noted that where he writes to Masters he never intimates any thing like it being a Duty to set [free] their Servants—but always exhorts them to treat their Servants with gentleness and good usage which becomes Masters as Christians and which Servants have a right to expect.

I would only observe here that the word *Doulos* used in all these passages always signifies a Slave and not a hired Servant. These persons were therefore all Slaves and as Christianity found them so it has left them with regard to their civil Relations. It does not point out any mode of their Emancipation nor even suggest the propriety of it but only directs them diligently and faithfully to perform the Duties of their Station as doing the Lord Service and therefore performing his Will.[8]

Let us now examine the arguments our opponents would insinuate are drawn from Reason. They tell us it is cruel and unjust to take and sell the innocent Africans as Slaves who never have done us any Injury. When we say we did neither take nor sell them they reply that we purchased them and the purchaser of Stolen Goods is as bad as the Thief. But to this we may answer that thief and purchaser are both dead. The property is here on our hands and what shall we do with it? It is a fact that none are imported now, [nor] do I attempt to defend the justice or propriety of importing them at first—but thousands have been imported and are here in our Country and the question is would it be right and safe to emancipate them? If I would not be right to emancipate them it follows it is just and right to keep them in their present Situation for no man was ever under a necessity to commit a moral Evil.

Then how does it appear that they are either fit to enjoy civil Liberty or that it would be safe to trust them with it? If they are unfit for Liberty it would do them an injury to set them free and our opponents say we must not do them an injury. But how can we avoid it and do as they tell us? It is to be considered that they are Savages whose dispositions prompt them to act as Savages in Opposition to every principle of humanity and such persons cannot be fit for civil Liberty when it requires the rigor of civil authority to restrain them. If then you set the Savage free he must have such a Law to govern him as the wisdom of the wisest men could form and execute—but he is to make his own Laws and have the execution of them as his own will so he will do as he pleas[es] and remain a Savage still. How can our Safety be trusted to people of such a Disposition? It is fully acknowledged on the other part that it cannot—and this they advance as an argument for Emancipation. But whether would there be more danger in freeing the Negroes and thereby putting it in their Power of uniting in one Body against us or to continue them in their present Situation where such a combination is wholly impracticable? It is granted that in their present State they may do injury in a particular place or Neighbourhood but if I am afraid of being injured by the strength of one man I would not double his strength to put such an Injury out of his Power.

It may be said that the Slave will feel himself obligated to [the] person who gives him his freedom and therefore not be disposed to do him an injury. But the caprice of Man was never made the Rule of Safety, and supposing the Slave has a right to demand his Liberty, the ground of such gratitude is taken away. If he [has] not this Right the question is given up. We are told that one rational Being cannot be the property of another. Property is something that is my own. The Slave is the property of no one, therefore he is not mine etc.[9]

Notes

1. For a more detailed biography of Graham (as well as an alternate transcription of Graham's proslavery text), see David W. Robson, "'An Important Question Answered': William Graham's Defense of Slavery in Post-Revolutionary Virginia," *William and Mary Quarterly,* 3rd ser., 37 (October 1980): 644–52.

2. In 1797 the grateful trustees renamed the school Washington Academy; it is now known as Washington and Lee University.

3. Graham, *An Essay on Government* (Philadelphia, 1786), 7.

4. This lecture was part of a larger series delivered by Graham in a class on "Human Nature." My transcription is from manuscript lecture notes in the Zechariah Johnston Papers, Special Collections, Leyburn Library, Washington and Lee University. My thanks to the library staff for their assistance with this research and for granting permission to republish this document.

5. This chapter of 1 Corinthians actually deals with relations between husbands and wives. The instructions delivered in terms of "permission" rather than "commandment" pertain to the need for husbands and wives to remain sexually available to each other. The command issued directly from the Lord forbids wives to leave their husbands.

6. The ambiguity of this verse (in 1 Corinthians 7:21) poses a problem for modern translators. The Revised English Bible offers two possible and opposing readings of the passage: "though if a chance of freedom should come, by all means take it"; and "but even if a chance of freedom should come, choose rather to make good use of your servitude."

7. Ephesians 6:5–8.

8. Scholars have debated this point of translation. "Doúlos" can be taken to mean slave or servant depending on the context; however, there is little doubt that the New Testament frequently refers to slaves without calling for their liberation. According to J. Albert Harrill, "Slavery was taken for granted in that period." See his "Slave," in *Eerdmans Dictionary of the Bible,* David Noel Freedman, ed. (Grand Rapids, Mich.: W. B. Eerdmans, 2000), 1232.

9. Indicating that the note taker had run out of time, the manuscript ends abruptly without presenting Graham's proslavery response to these criticisms against slavery.

# CHAPTER 9

# Edmund Botsford, 1808

THE YEARS FOLLOWING THE REVOLUTION were troubled times for American religion, but they were also times of tremendous growth. The political break from England had thrown American churches into turmoil. Due to its association with British imperial tyranny, the Anglican Church not surprisingly suffered the greatest misfortune. Baptist, Methodist, and other evangelical ministers, by contrast, often managed to associate themselves with the patriotic cause. Yet they too labored amid the hardships engendered by years of war. Hence, ministers of every denomination tended, in the 1780s and 1790s, to complain about the "languishing state" of religion, particularly in the southern states.[1] Still, notwithstanding these troubles, southern churches were expanding their membership rolls in the decades following the war. A good number of well-educated ministers spent these years busily establishing a religious infrastructure that would eventually support the wave of revivals initiated in 1800. Edmund Botsford was an influential member of a group of capable, well-connected Baptist ministers that included Oliver Hart, Richard Furman, and Henry Holcombe. Botsford's campaign to build a biracial church in South Carolina revealed the slaveholding elite's changing attitude toward Christian proslavery thought.

Botsford was born in Wooburn, England, in 1745, the son of a moderately successful merchant who passed away when Botsford was seven years old. Raised by a Baptist aunt, Botsford received regular exposure to the denomination's teachings. At the age of twenty-one, he immigrated to Charleston, where he came under the influence of the Baptist minister Oliver Hart. In 1771 he received his license to preach, and one year later he was ordained as a minister. In the years preceding the war, he traveled through Georgia and South Carolina, where he gained a reputation as a successful itinerant minister. His vigorous support for American independence led to his exile in Virginia following the fall of Charleston to the British in 1780. With the termination of the war, he returned to South Carolina to serve the Welsh Neck Baptist Church and eventually was named the pastor of the Baptist church in Georgetown.[2]

Botsford campaigned to Christianize plantation society—a mission that hinged on recognizing the humanity of African American slaves. Black membership in his Baptist church swelled considerably during the 1780s, in no small part due to

Botsford's efforts to welcome African American worshippers into the same holy space managed by whites. By 1790 Botsford was reporting that "a great number of rich planters" had converted and had subsequently recognized that "their slaves are of increasing value to them when they become religious." His tract, *Sambo and Toney,* presented in fictive form the religious ideals to which he devoted his life. Certain that the paternal care of religious white masters would lead to the spiritual improvement of African Americans, Botsford set about convincing both slaveholders and slaves of the need to recognize their reciprocal responsibilities. Appearing in 1808, Botsford's work was one of the earliest publications to associate Christian slaves with the "Sambo" persona (and, for that matter, may have played a role in associating that name with this particular racial stereotype). His tract presented a proslavery Christian message tailored not only to African American slaves but also to a generation of southern masters who were finally ready to justify slavery in Christian terms.

<hr />

EDMUND BOTSFORD, *Sambo and Toney: A Dialogue between Two Africans in South Carolina* (1808; repr., Philadelphia: A. Walker, 1816)

[READER! the salvation of thy Immortal Soul is the subject of this book. Prepare to meet thy Judge, O Man! for I who write, and you who read, may be in eternity before the rising of another Sun.]

A DIALOGUE

*Sambo*

HOWDY, brother Toney, I am glad too much for see you, I no see you for long time, I hope you well.

*Toney.* Is this Sambo? Oh I glad for see you too brother, how you done this long time?

*Sambo.* Thank God, brother, I been well all the time I live up the country; and that I believe been five six year.

*Toney.* Yes, I believe, old Master been dead more than five year, and after that you went up there soon. Well, brother, how you like living up the country, how you like cotton planting, you got a good master Sambo?

*Sambo.* Yes, thank God, brother Toney, my Master good, and I like up the country and cotton planting very well—you got a good master, Toney?

*Toney.* So, so, he do, he give us victuals enough and good clothes, but he make us work devilish hard.

*Sambo.* Devilish hard! what sort a talk is that, Toney, what you mean by such word, that no good.

*Toney.* Why what harm, Sambo, I hope you no one them religious sort a praying negroes?

*Sambo.* I hope you no think it hard for work, Toney, when you say your Master use you well, every body ought to work that can, and I suppose you no work harder than your fellow servants.

*Toney.* I can't say I do.

*Sambo.* Well then, why you complain and say devilish hard, you know what devilish mean, Toney? devilish is something wicked, I fear you use such words, you wicked too, Toney.

*Toney.* What you call wicked, Sambo?

*Sambo.* Why brother Toney, you know well enough what I mean, you know that be wicked for tell lie, curse and swear, thieve and such like things, you know it's sin against God. I hoped God had changed your heart, and you had been one good man, and as I heard too, that many black people near you had been converted, baptised and joined the church.

*Toney.* O yes, Sambo, we have praying and singing, exhorting and preaching all around us, and some on our plantation, but I like none on it. I think I'm as good as them that make such a noise, many that pray and all that, be no better than we who make no pretence, they do bad things too with all their religion.

*Sambo.* I'm very sorry to hear that them that been baptised do as bad as them that make no pretence to religion. Do they curse and wear, tell lie and steal, be they idle and ramble about for mischief?

*Toney.* I no like them, they be hypocrites, by and by they will all turn back again. This religion for white men, not for negro.

*Sambo.* Who tell you so, Toney?

*Toney.* Our overseer, he say all black people will go to the devil.

*Sambo.* So they will, and the white people too if they no repent, and believe the gospel. The word of the Lord say, except ye repent, ye shall all perish.[3] May be your people give the overseer a heap a trouble, stealing and no doing their work, and may be some pretend for be religious when they no be so, and the overseer find them out in some of their bad tricks, and he thinks as you, that they be all alike; if he wicked himself then he think so for true.

*Toney.* Hey Sambo, where you learn all this 'bout the gospel and repent, who make you so wise, do you have preaching and praying and all that up the country where you live?

*Sambo.* Yes, Toney, we have preaching, and the Lord he bless the preaching to many black people, as well as the white; several of my fellow-servants, I hope, are converted and be good and faithful servants now.

*Toney.* What you call converted, Sambo, I know nothing about it.

*Sambo.* I am afraid, Toney, you no want for know. I am very sorry for you, I loved you always, Toney. When we came out of the ship I been glad that one gentleman buy us both, and when old master die and we been parted I very sorry. I should be glad for see you become serious and thoughtful about your soul, you no live always, and when you die 'twill be dreadful if you die in your sins.

*Toney.* Die, I know I must die some time or other, but while I live I wish for joy all the pleasure I can, time enough for talk about repent and die when I am old man.

*Sambo.* But suppose you no live till you old, how then, do you see many men on your plantation that be old? and should you live old, you may then be hardened in sin; you no see old men very wicked? Suppose now, Toney, you should run away from your master, and no come back again till you be old, and no strong for work, do you think your master would care for you then? If you should be that master, you would say, what you come to me for now? when you strong for work you keep out, now you sick and old you come home. Go again, you are no worth, begone. Well now, if you serve the devil all the best of your days, and when you can't serve him longer, then you come and call upon God for mercy; he may then say to you begone; I send my ministers, they tell you, I give you my gospel that call you, you no come; you loved sin and all bad things; now I will not hear you. So God say in his word. I tell you Toney you had better think on your poor soul, now, before it be too late.

*Toney.* Why Sambo, do you want me for leave off dance and sing and frolic; hey, Sambo, I cant leave them off, I love them too much; besides, Sambo, I know nothing 'bout this gospel and praying and all these things.

*Sambo.* I am so sorry for you Toney, I don't know what I can say—you make my heart ache, I can't help crying; poor Toney, I am afraid you will harden your heart in sin so much, that God Almighty will some day strike you dead in the midst of your wickedness, then your poor soul will be lost, and you will be sent to hell with devils and damned spirits, then you will see your folly when it will be too late, then there will be no mercy for you. O think of these things now, while mercy may be had, before you drop into hell.

*Toney.* What you cry for, Sambo, I am no such bad man as you think, I never kill any body, I no swear, only when I am vex. I never steal only a little now and then from master. True I love dance and frolic; sure Sambo, it's no harm for make merry now and then.

*Sambo.* I can't help crying when I think on the danger you're in. Suppose you no so bad as some very wicked wretches, yet as you talk, you not only bad, but what worse, you no see any need for turning to God, and you have no love for good things and good people.

*Toney.* Is no body good but them praying sort a people?

*Sambo.* No body who allow themselves in such things as you plead for can be good. Is it good for tell lie, steal, swear, and keep bad company?

*Toney.* I tell you, Sambo, I never steal from any body but master, and that no harm, if he no find it out; and I never swear only when I vex; as for frolic and dance I love them for true. I no tell lie about it, but I don't love this praying and going to meeting. What have we black people for do with that, the minister, no never say any thing to us.

*Sambo.* So Toney, you think it no harm when you steal from your master; now I think it more harm than from most any body else, and I will tell you why. Now, Toney, mind what I say. In the first place your master give a great price for you; next place, he find you in victuals and clothes, and then he give you land for plant, and most every day you have time for work for yourself, and then he trusts you with his things, who can he trust but his servants, so if you steal, you deceive him, and then you tell lie for hide it, and may be after all the fault is laid on your fellow servants, and so they get punished for your fault, and get the ill will of your master; and more than all, the word of the Lord say, "Thou shalt not steal, and that a thief cannot enter the kingdom of heaven." Now Toney, if your master be a bad man and used you ill, yet you must no steal from him; the word of the Lord no say, if your master be a bad man you may steal; no, good or bad, you must not steal, no thief can go to heaven.

*Toney.* I no understand 'bout this book. I never heard such things as these.

*Sambo.* Do you never go to meeting for hear the minister preach?

*Toney.* Yes, I go sometimes, but the minister never preach to we black people.

*Sambo.* Why Toney, the minister preach to every body; may be you think he no preach to the black people, because he no call upon you and say, black people I speak to you. The word of the Lord speak to every body alike, white people, black people, rich man, poor man, old man, and young man, and it say, repent every one of you.

*Toney.* Hey Sambo! I believe you be Parson, do you preach Sambo?

*Sambo.* I am very sorry, Toney, for see you so hardened and so careless 'bout your poor soul; no, Toney, I no parson; I no preach, but my mind be quite changed from what it been when you and I live with old master, then I thought much as you do now; I loved frolic and dance and such bad things; but I thank God I have seen my folly; and though I don't go to frolic and dance I am much more happy than when I used for go with you to such places.

*Toney.* You talk like some of our people, they say now they be religious, they hate frolic and dance, as much as they once loved it, and talk about being happy and all that, but I no understand 'bout all these things.

*Sambo.* Suppose you can't understand how all this be, some things you can understand; and should you give your mind to these things, and pray God, the Lord would enlighten your mind and make you see and understand, and should you once see your danger, you could no rest till you believe in Jesus Christ, and find peace and comfort in your soul.

*Toney.* Some of our people tell a great deal 'bout their danger, and 'bout the Lord enlightening their hearts, and 'bout believing in Jesus Christ, and a heap such things.

*Sambo.* Will you answer me two three questions Toney?

*Toney.* Yes, Sambo, I will.

*Sambo.* Well now, Toney, suppose you should die just now this minute; do you think you are prepared for that?

*Toney.* I hope I shall live many years yet, Sambo.

*Sambo.* But you no answer my question.

*Toney.* I don't know what I can say to that, I don't know if I be prepared to die; my heart feel strange at such talk, Sambo; I no like it.

*Sambo.* You say you don't know if you be prepared to die, nor do you intend thinking 'bout it till you be old man. Now Toney, I will tell you why you have such thoughts. You never seriously consider what a dreadful thing it be for sin against God, you no been much troubled about it. Some time you think, well, I must die some time or other, that make you uneasy; so you put such thoughts away; when any your people die, that trouble you but little while, cause you young and strong, and think you will not die yet, so you go dance and sing again. Then you think you can repent when you please, and that many worse than you. Now, Toney, mind what I tell you, so long as you think you can repent when you please, so long will you go on in your old ways; 'tis the devil that puts such thoughts in your heart, and keep you from repenting and turning to God.

*Toney.* Why Sambo, how you know my thoughts, for true I thought just as you say.

*Sambo.* Again, Toney you know very well that life is uncertain, you see young people die as well as old, and some die very suddenly, and you may die as well as any other young man, and suddenly too, and might have no time for say so much as Lord have mercy, and so drop into hell at once. I once had such thoughts as you have now; and if God had left me to myself, I should to this day been serving the devil. But thank the Lord for his goodness, he was pleased for bless the preaching of the gospel to my poor soul, which brought me for see that I had been doing wrong all my days, and that if I died in such a state I should certainly go to hell.

*Toney.* Why, Sambo, you talk so serious; and seem so sorry for me it make me feel strange. I never feel so in my life before; I most wish I was like you, can't you tell me what I must do?

*Sambo.* I am but a poor creature for give advice; but I love you Toney, and should be glad for see you become a good man.

*Toney.* I believe you do love me, and I always loved you, Sambo. I remember when old master die and we been parted, my heart trouble me a long time. I wish, Sambo, you would tell me how I must pray and how I must repent and believe the gospel; for I never think upon these things in my life before.

*Sambo.* I have no much time now for talk with you Toney; I must go to the boat and see about unloading the cotton. But I would advise you Toney, for pray the Lord for direction, and as for how you must pray, just pray as you can, and the Lord will hear you when you pray with all your heart. I can stay no longer, but I beg you for think seriously upon what I have said to you. Sit down, Toney, and think over your whole life, and think which the best that you go on in sin and so at last go to hell, or turn to God and believe in the Lord Jesus Christ, and so be happy in your soul while you live, and be prepared for heaven when you die.

*Toney.* I thank you, Sambo, I will try and do as you say, and I hope you will pray the Lord for me. Farewell.

*Sambo.* I hope I shall pray for you. Farewell.

PART II.

*Toney.*

HOWDY, brother Sambo, I glad for see you once more.

   *Sambo.* I thank you, brother Toney, I am very well, bless God; I am very glad for see you too, I hope you're well.

*Toney.* Thank God brother, I am very well.

*Sambo.* Well brother, have you been think upon the things we talked about when we met last?

*Toney.* O Sambo! I hope I have reason to remember that talk while I live, and to thank God for putting into your heart for talk to me.

*Sambo.* If it been of service to you I am very thankful. Now, Toney, tell me how it's been with you, for ever since we parted my heart been strangely drawn out in prayer for you.

*Toney.* Well brother, as you wish for know I will tell you, but some my thoughts been so foolish and some been so bad, I most shamed for tell you.

*Sambo.* Never mind, tell me all, and tell me first what you think while I talk to you; then how you feel after that.

*Toney.* O Sambo! I never feel so in all my life before. When you first began for talk to me, my heart most rise up against you, I think you turn fool you talk such nonsense; by and by when you seem so sorry for me, and tell me what I think, I feel sham'd I talk so foolish to you, and been most think you been right, and if you been right, I know I must been wrong, and when you ask me suppose I die that minute, my heart tremble. I think upon my fellow servant, Joe, I dare say you remember him.

*Sambo.* Yes, very well, he used been very wild then.

*Toney.* Yes, he been very wild for true, him and me been to many frolic together. When some body talk to him about religion, he always make game, he would say, its enough for white people to mind religion, he no care bout it. One day as we been work together in the rice field, he been taken very sick and been obliged for leave his work and go to his house. When I done my task, I went for see him; soon as he see me he cry out, O Toney, I shall die and go to hell; sure enough Joe die that night; his death trouble me a little while, but it soon wear off again; I hardly ever think upon Joe, till you talk to me, then it came fresh in my mind, and I think who know but I may die like Joe; well, soon after I leave you, wicked thoughts come in my mind, I say, I don't care, I will dance and sing, I will take pleasure, God Almighty no expect black man should be like white man; beside, don't white man dance, and sing; yes, and curse and swear too, and he no fear going to hell, I am no worse than other people.

*Sambo.* These been bad thoughts indeed, the devil put these thoughts into your head.

*Toney.* Yes I know that now, but I no think so then. However that night, I had a dream which frighten me most to death. I dream I was very sick and thought I was dying. I thought a man come to me and call, Toney; I say, sir; he say I am come for you, are you ready to go? I say, go where, sir? He say, go with me into tother world. I say, no sir, I no ready, I cant go; but the man say, you must go and that directly, God Almighty send for you. My heart strike me with such terror, I never feel in all my life before. I say to myself this is death. I must now die like poor Joe, in all my sins, and go to hell. Now all your talk come into my mind. I now remember every bad thing I did in all my life, I feel so confounded I could not pray so much as Lord have mercy upon me. I saw I must be damned, and I think God so angry with me that the moment I die he would strike me down headlong into hell. I so frighten, I cry out, O Sambo, what shall I do? This woke me and my heart tremble a long time, at last I found it had been a dream.

*Sambo.* Well, Toney, how did this dream make you feel?

*Toney.* I feel like a condemned man, I did not know what to do; it seem like something say to me, Toney, you have lost your soul, you can't repent, you need not pray, God wont hear such a wicked man, you may as well go on your old way and get all the pleasure you can; soon as you get home, go dance and sing and shake off this foolish nonsense, it been only dream.

*Sambo.* O how cunning Satan is, first he tell us, time enough to repent and turn to God, then if we get uneasy, he tell us now too late to pray, God will not hear; Satan mean by this to make us despair. He serve me just so; but if God take hold of the heart, you can't find pleasure in such things as you did once, you no see them like you used to do. Well, how you make out?

*Toney.* O brother I can hardly tell; my heart been so troubled, I can hardly eat, or work, or know what I been about. You know we came to town in a big flat with rice; well, before we got home, no being so careful as we should been, some how the flat got aground, so we lost most one tide; this make the overseer who been with us so vex that he curse every body. I never mind any body's cursing before, but now it frighten me. I never think cursing so ugly before, it make me feel strange all over. Well, I think, go to heaven or hell, I will never curse again long as I live, my heart rise up against it. We loss so much time it been in the night before we got home, when I been going up to the negro houses, I hear the fiddle, they been dance in the driver's house. O brother, you can't tell how I been feel. Before when I hear fiddle, I feel good, now my heart turn 'gainst it. I say to myself, Ah poor people! you're dancing to hell: I go by fast as I could; when I come by Uncle Davy's house, I think I hear him pray, I go softly and listen, and O brother Sambo, I never hear such prayers in my life. Uncle Davy pray for master and mistress and children, he pray the Lord for convert young master, and he thank the Lord that he open master's heart for let the minister come and preach to we black people, and he pray the Lord for bless the gospel to his fellow servants, that they may be converted, and then he thank the Lord for revealing Jesus Christ to him, such a poor sinner, then he prays so heartily that he and them that been baptised might be kept from evil, and that they might live peaceably and quiet; and then he pray very earnest, if any poor creature upon the plantation be in trouble for his sins, Lord carry on the work in his soul, till he find rest in Christ Jesus, and a good deal more like that. All this time my heart trouble me for true. It make me love uncle Davy, and wish I may be like him.

*Sambo.* Did you never hear Davy pray before?

*Toney.* O yes, many time, but I no mind it, I no understand it, I made game at his praying; but I being going to tell you, soon as uncle Davy had done prayers I went home, and my wife been out and the children asleep. I sit down and lament my case. I now seed myself the worst man in the world. O I thought I must be lost, my sins seem'd too great for God to pardon. By and by, Fanny my wife come home. I ask her where she been; she say she been to uncle Davy's house to prayers; she say, I wish Toney, you been there; I say, why? she say, uncle Davy pray the Lord for us all, for master and all; O Toney, I wish you been like uncle Davy, he is one good man; when he done pray for us, then he talk so good to us 'bout our souls it make me love him true. I tell her I heard uncle Davy too, and never been so troubled in my life before, and that I now been determine, I would never live as I have done, but I being such a poor miserable sinner I could not pray, and what to do I did not know. My wife advised me for go and talk with uncle Davy and tell him how I feel, and he would tell me what for do.

*Sambo.* That been good advice, Toney, that Fanny give you, what a mercy she did not oppose you. Well did you go to Davy?

*Toney.* I had just been laughing at uncle Davy's praying and talking, before we went to town, I been shame for go. I think I will leave some my bad ways first, and be more serious, then I go for tell him.

*Sambo.* Poor Toney, you did not know what a deceitful heart you had, you would first make yourself good, and then go to Davy for make you so; see brother, what a deceitful thing sin be, how it deceive us. Well how you go on?

*Toney.* Why, Sambo, it seem to me I get worse and worse, I see myself so bad I wonder God did not strike me dead; I see so plain that I deserve it. I think God would do right to send me to hell. Every day it come to my mind what you say to me; I try for pray, sometime I can say a little, sometime I am afraid to speak, sometime my heart so hard and wicked I cant pray; one day I think why don't God kill me like poor Joe? who know may be he mind to spare me; then again it came in my mind, he only let me live, for sin more and more, that it might be worse with me, cause I make game of the gospel, and do every bad thing more than any body. Then again I think upon God, that he make every body and every thing, the rice, the corn, the grass, and all the good things, what make me so wicked? O I wish hundred times I never been born, I sin so much gainst the Lord who been so good. Well, I go to uncle Davy and tell him all these things.

*Sambo.* And what did Davy say to you?

*Toney.* Uncle Davy see me in such trouble he pity and pray for me. Uncle Davy one fine man, he know my case, and he talk so good and so kind, and ask me this thing and tother thing, till he make me tell every thing, all my heart, then he say he glad for see me in this trouble, he say, God at work with my heart, he bid me go to meeting and pray God for direct the minister to my case.

*Sambo.* Well, and did you go to meeting?

*Toney.* O yes, I go to meeting next Sunday; but I feel so bad as I been going, I most half mind turn back and go home again. However I go, and I would not miss that sermon for all things in the world. Such a sermon I never heard before. The minister take his text from these words—*God be merciful to me a sinner.*[4] When the minister take his text he look so hard upon me, I sure he know what a sinner I been. I shall never forget that sermon. First, he shew what heart and what conduct a sinner have; then he shew how God can be merciful to sinners, and then what that mercy be. O Sambo, it been such a day to me, as never been before.

*Sambo.* Well, how did the minister tell you sinners get their wicked heart, which make all their conduct wicked?

*Toney.* I will tell you as well as I remember. He say God make the first man, I think he say he name been Adam. Well, he say, he make him very good and holy, he have no sin; now, God tell the man, he must mind and be very good and he

would be very happy; but he tell him if he dont mind what he say, but break
the law he give him, he should die, and as all men would come from him, if he
break the law, then he bring all men should die. Well, sure enough, he break
the law, and now every body, said the minister, that is born into the world be
born sinners, with a wicked heart, and as soon as they begin to talk and so on,
they love do wrong, 'tis their very nature to do so, their choice. Now then he
say, a sinner is one that has broken the law of God. And as a sinner he is under
the curse of God; and as we are all sinners, we are all under the curse of God.
O how my heart ache when he say that, for I feel myself under the curse of
God. Well now he say, how come God not to condemn and send every body to
hell? How can God save poor man and keep his word? For God said the soul
that sins shall die, not only the body die, but the soul be sent to hell. I declare,
Sambo, my heart tremble, when he say that, for I could see no way how God
could keep his word and save poor sinner. Well now, the minister say, I will tell
you, and I pray the Lord you may understand, and particularly you poor black
people. I will speak as plain as I can, but you must pray to God that he make
you understand it. Now when there was found no one that could save poor
man, the Lord Jesus Christ, the Son of God say, Father, send me, and I will save
poor man; well, how will he save him? He say, I will become man, I will be
born of a virgin, so I will have no sin, then, I will be both God and man; then
I will keep the law that man broke, and as man must die for breaking the law,
I will die for him, in his place. Now, Jesus Christ, being equal to his Father, all
that he did was of more worth than all the men in the world could do. Well,
Jesus Christ was born of a virgin, and so did not come into the world a sinner;
he kept the law of God, and he suffered and died, the just for the unjust, and
as he was God as well as man, he raised up himself from the dead to be our Saviour, and justify us, and deliver us from punishment. Now, said the minister,
what Jesus Christ did and suffered, make God willing to forgive poor man;
now in this way God can keep his word and the poor sinner be saved. Well, now
God send his ministers to tell the people, he can pardon and forgive the poor
sinner, and keep his word, his justice and truth. Then you will say why are not
all poor sinners saved? I will tell you, before they can be saved, they must come
to the Lord Jesus Christ; this they will never do while they love sin, nor till
they feel themselves in a lost ruined state, and this they will never see till the
Spirit of God shew them their sin, and this he does many ways, sometime by
preaching, sometime by a godly friend talking, sometime one way and sometime another; but I will tell you how you may know if the Spirit of God is at
work with you—if you feel sorry for sin and hate it, if your hearts are full of
trouble about your souls, full of guilt and shame, and fear, and like the poor man
in the text are smiting your breast and crying God be merciful to me a sinner.

*Sambo.* Well, Toney, you have a good memory to remember all this, it must have reached your heart.

*Toney.* O yes, Sambo, it reached my heart for true.

*Sambo.* Well, how this sermon make you feel.

*Toney.* O Sambo, it would be hard to tell. However it make me love the minister, tho' I no understand all he say, and I encourage still for pray.

*Sambo.* And did you now believe you must be saved by what Jesus Christ had done?

*Toney.* O yes, the minister tell us there could be no pardon only for what my Lord had done, and as soon as we believe with all the heart, we should cast ourselves on him, trust our souls with him, and he would make himself known to us, and we should find peace, and the minister charge us to go pray the Lord to have mercy on us for Christ sake.

*Sambo.* And did you do as the minister tell you?

*Toney.* Yes, over and over again.

*Sambo.* And did you find peace?

*Toney.* No, I no find for twenty times.

*Sambo.* Well, what you do den? Had you no mind for leave off prayer?

*Toney.* Yes an hundred times.

*Sambo.* And how come you no leave it off?

*Toney.* O Sambo, I cant leave it off, because I believe the word the minister tell me, he say, without faith or believing in Christ all the world could not save me. So I think with myself, if I leave off prayer I loss for true, and I can but be loss if I pray. I go to uncle Davy and tell him all my trouble, and beg him to pray for me.

*Sambo.* And what did Davy say to you?

*Toney.* He tell me that no body could help me, that I must believe in Jesus Christ, or I would be damned; but he say, the word of the Lord is in your favour, for it say, "come unto me all ye that labour and are heavy laden and I will give you rest."[5]

*Sambo.* Well, what you do then?

*Toney.* Do, I know not what for do. I looked upon myself as a poor loss sinner. I had no body for blame but myself, and I often think I should drop into hell. However, I continue for pray and begging for mercy, till one day the Lord enable me to believe in Jesus Christ, and give me peace in my soul.

*Sambo.* And how was that?

*Toney.* I think it been the day we begin for plant rice. That day I felt bad too much, my heart too hard, my sin look more worse than ever, I think that day no body such a big sinner like me, O I dont know what for do. By and by, I think like some body speak and say, "believe in the Lord Jesus Christ and thou shalt be saved."[6] I say, Lord, I can't believe, Lord give me faith, then I hear this word, "cast thy burthen on the Lord,"[7] and that word in the hymn come in my mind —"come hither, all ye weary souls, ye heavy laden sinners come."[8] O Sambo, these last words never seem so sweet before; they make me feel like I never feel in my life before. I now been see when my Lord die, he no die for himself, for him own sin, but for poor sinners; then I cry, Lord, here been one poor sinner, had more than any sinner in the world. Lord save me or I perish. It seem like I now believe that Jesus was able and willing for save just such a sinner as I been. I now think I see my Lord has done every thing for the poor sinner. O now I see how much I deserve hell, I say Lord if you send me to hell, I no say one word, but if you save me I will praise my Lord for ever and ever. O now my heart feel light, my trouble all gone; O now I love my Lord, I love the good people, I love every thing but sin, my heart rise up against that, I think I will never sin no more as long as I live. When I think now my Lord suffer for sinners, I say, if my sin been so great, what must my Lord suffer for all them he save. O my heart sorry for my Lord when I think how it save poor sinners. O I been wish I could always feel so, for now I been thank and praise my God for sending Jesus Christ to die for poor sinner would come to this precious Saviour. O Sambo, I been too happy, I say glory; glory to my God for ever and ever.

*Sambo.* Well brother, you been happy for true, you no tell Davy of this?

*Toney.* O Sambo, I tell most every body. I go to my master, I fall down on my knees, I say O my master, Toney been one bad negro, I been curse and lie and steal and done every bad thing; O my master forgive me, I hope I never do the like again, I hope I been see my folly, I hope the Lord pardon my sin.

*Sambo.* And what did your master say?

*Toney.* Master say, Toney, I am glad to see this change in you, I hope it is the work of the Lord; I freely forgive you any thing in which you may have wronged me. However, Toney, take care, the heart is very deceitful, watch and pray that you fall not into temptation, and a good deal more: he talk so good, it make me love him for true. I wish every poor negro been have such a good master.

*Sambo.* Suppose you tell Davy too, what he say to you?

*Toney.* What brother Sambo, uncle Davy been most as glad as myself. He thanks and bless the Lord that he answer his prayer for me and tell me, now Toney, you have began a new life, the life of a Christian. Now you must be on your guard, the devil will try to trouble you every way he can, you must therefore try and live near to God, by prayer and faith; watch your heart, that you do not backslide from God, constantly pray to him to keep you by his grace from sinful thoughts, words and actions, and help you to walk by faith and not trust to your own strength, and a good deal more like that.

*Sambo.* Blessed be God for his goodness to you my brother, I praise God too, for hearing my prayer for you. When we were boys together I loved you, but now I love you with another sort a love, I now love you cause you love my Lord. Well, my brother, we been now Christ's soldiers, we must fight the good fight of faith 'gainst every sin, and be careful for do every thing our Lord say in the book, then we have peace and comfort in our soul. Well now, brother Toney, I want you for answer two questions.

*Toney.* With all my heart, brother, if I can.

*Sambo.* Well, Toney, tell me, do you now think it no harm to steal from your master?

*Toney.* O, no talk, brother Sambo, steal from master no harm! that man no Christian, his heart no changed, who can think it no harm for steal from master or any body.

*Sambo.* Very true, Toney, but I hear some black people say, though it been harm to steal from stranger, it been no harm to steal from master.

*Toney.* I never can think them people been converted who plead for stealing; before I converted I been think it no harm to steal from master; but now, bless the Lord, my mind quite changed. Stealing be one great sin, for you know the word of the Lord say, no thief can go to heaven; now, if I steal, no matter it from master or stranger, my heart no right with God.

*Sambo.* You been right, Toney, I 'gree with you, Christian man no thief. Well, Toney, tother question is, do prayers make you good and carry you to heaven?

*Toney.* Hey, Sambo, what you mean? I never hear such thing before! I thank God he been help me for pray, and I pray the Lord every day for keep me, and lead me, and never leave me, for I still find myself one poor sinner, my heart sometime have bad thought, sometime devil tempt me, sometime I feel so bad I think no Christian like me, then I go to my Lord. I tell you Sambo, I love my Lord, I love good people, I love good thing, but it all been come from my Lord. I hope God Almighty save me, and at last take me to heaven, but not for my prayers, but for what the Lord Jesus Christ been do for me, upon him I trust, he my Lord and my God.

*Sambo.* Bless the Lord, my brother, you been understand these things so well, by and by your mind will be more enlightened; beside, Toney, you must learn to read, then you will understand these things more better. Well, Toney, what reason have we for praise the Lord. We two poor African negro, & both been wicked together a good while, and now God meet with us in love and mercy. I hope God will be with us and bless us, and help us to live for his glory, then by and by he will take us to heaven, there we shall live with the blessed Lord Jesus Christ, and all his saints for ever and ever.

*Toney.* O Sambo, I often think, if after all, I get to heaven, I shall have most reason of any body for praise God for his goodness for bringing such a poor sinner to salvation. Well, Sambo, I must go, but I hope it no be long before I see you gen; I wish you could come at Christmas time for see us; uncle Davy, my wife and the brethren would all be glad too much for see you.

*Sambo.* Thank you, Toney, I will try for come. I hope you will pray for me; remember me to Davy, your wife and all the brethren. Farewell.

*Toney.* You will pray for me, and remember me to all your brethren. Farewell.

PART III.

*Sambo.*

WELL, brother Toney, you see I keep my word, I have come for see you, and brought brother Titus with me; I hope you well.

*Toney.* I am very well brother, and very glad for see you, and more so as you bring a brother with you. I hope you well brother Titus.

*Titus.* Thank God, brother, I am very well. Brother Sambo, when he return from town, tell me of you, as one, who the grace of God wonderfully meet when you been going on in sin; this make me wish for see you, as I hope I love all good people.

*Toney.* Well brother, I hope we been known one another more better before we part. Brother Sambo, I have good news for tell you; since I see you in town, some of our people I hope been converted.

*Sambo.* That good news for true.

*Toney.* Well brethren, let us go to the house, Fanny will be might glad for see you, Sambo—Fanny, this brother Sambo you hear me talk so much about.

*Fanny.* Howdy, brother Sambo, I am very glad for see you for true, my husband tell me 'twas you talk to him that first set him for seek the Lord; I been very thankful to you, brother, ever since, for that same night he come home the Lord been take hold of my heart; if Toney no been taken hold on too, I dont know how I would made out.

*Sambo.* Bless God, sister, then I hope you go hand in hand in the way of the Lord, 'tis a blessed thing when husband and wife both seek the Lord together.

*Toney.* Here is uncle Davy, Sambo, 'tis so long since you see him, I suppose you hardly know him.

*Sambo.* O brother Davy, how you do, I sure if I been meet you when I no expect, I would not know you, how you do my brother?

*Davy.* Why, bless the Lord I am in good health, and right glad to see you.

*Sambo.* This brother Titus, one of my fellow servants.

*Davy.* I am glad to see you brother.

*Titus.* I am glad to see you too brother, I often heard of you as one that God been bless in wakening some young men on this plantation.

*Davy.* Why, thank God brother, I have been trying to stand by our minister, and sometime talking a little and praying with our people, and bless the Lord, at that time, some be enquiring about Jesus Christ, and I hope a few have found him.

*Titus.* That good news, brother, it make my heart glad.

*Fanny.* When I used for talk to Toney bout repenting and serving the Lord, Toney say, time enough, by and by, when I old man. Now the work of the Lord been come I see old men no care for it; tis young people that think most about it.

*Davy.* Tis most always so, sister. Last Sunday our minister tell us of some great minister in England, who had been preach a great many years, and see a great many converted, and he say the most were young people.

*Sambo.* Yes, I believe when the Lord bless young people with the gospel, and they no get converted, the Lord leave them for grow hard in sin.

*Toney.* I been see under some sermons most every body take notice but a few old men, they no mind it.

*Sambo.* You no remember, Toney, when I talk to you, you say by and by when I old man?

*Toney.* Yes, I remember very well, I then love sin and no want for part with it, then I think there be no pleasure in religion, beside I think I can repent when I please.

*Titus.* But when you make trial, you no find it so easy as you think.

*Toney.* No no, nor I never make trial, if I no find myself a poor loss sinner.

*Fanny.* I sure I bless the Lord he take hold of your heart, for my sake well as your own, for your heart been set gainst uncle Davy and all the good people, so you no let me go to sermon and prayers and such like.

*Titus.* I dare say, brother Toney been glad too that the Lord take hold of your heart, for now he wife go with him and help him.

*Toney.* I always loved my wife, and now I been love her more than ever.

*Sambo.* Well, brother Davy, you be most old man, and you been converted good many year, and you read the word of the Lord, and you often been talk with ministers, we then expect you will teach us; I feel happy when I think I shall hear some good things from you.

*Davy.* I am glad you come to see us with so good intention, I hope then you prayed the Lord to be with us; as for teaching you, brother, I need teaching myself; however, I shall be willing to talk with you on spiritual things, and tell you every thing I can.

*Sambo.* That very kind, brother; then I hope we been have a good Chrismus, for I love for talk bout Jesus Christ; as we come long, brother Titus and me both pray the Lord be with us when we come to the brethren.

*Titus.* I should be very glad for hear brother Davy talk upon one thing. I mean bout some people who seem to be awakened, and for some time seem engaged a good deal, they pray and talk bout religion, leave off bad ways, go every Sunday to meeting, and seem like they would soon join the church, aye, and some do join the church; then by and by they turn right back into sin, make game and laugh at every thing serious. Now, brother Davy, I wish you would tell us bout such people.

*Sambo.* Aye, brother Davy, I join brother Titus for beg you for talk upon that.

*Toney.* I should be glad to hear uncle Davy too.

*Fanny.* And I sure I should, for many time I fear I shall turn back, I find so many wicked thought in my heart, and sometime I cant pray my heart so hard. I wonder many time if any Christian be like me.

*Davy.* Well, my brothers and sister, as you desire it, I will try and tell you something about these sort of people, for alas! there be too many. One sort be they who as soon as they hear the gospel, particularly that part which tells about the goodness of God in sending Jesus Christ to die for sinners; and also to preserve the law and word of God, that God may be holy and just when he pardon the sinner, that God may appear opposed to sin while he forgive sinners, I say when those sort of people hear all this, and a good deal about heaven and the joys of the saints there, and all this being new to them, their hearts are made glad, and some how they get a notion, because they feel their hearts light that they going to heaven. They sing and pray and talk with every body they meet, and think all is well with them. These be the people that say, Lord, Lord, but do not do the will of God.

*Sambo.* Yes, and for a while deceive many.

*Davy.* Yes, but the worst is they deceive themselves, for all this time their hearts are bad, they never had a right sense of sin; then by and by when they lose their comforts as they call them, that is, when these things be no longer new, their hearts lean after their old ways again, and not finding the same good feeling in prayer, nor in hearing sermons, they by degrees leave off prayer, and find more pleasure in their old ways, and so go back again.

*Titus.* That time when they been seem most religious, they no been very serious, only at sermon; other time they been laugh and talk foolish; this show their heart no been right.

*Davy.* True my brother, they never know their hearts were deceitful, all they think upon was to feel good and happy; when they cant feel so any longer, then they get tired of religion and go back again to sin. Then some people say they fall from grace, when poor things they never know any thing about grace.

*Sambo.* Very true, brother, these people never know their heart wicked, that make they never go to Jesus Christ for pardon, they satisfy with feeling good when minister preach, that been all their religion.

*Fanny.* Well, uncle Davy, I do no like these people, my heart no so, I no spec for always for feel good, cant you tell us of nother sort who go back?

*Davy.* My dear sister, there be many sorts that go back, and but few that go right. We had need watch and pray lest Satan, or our own hearts, deceive us. The word of the Lord say, "Let him that think he stand take heed, lest he fall."[9] I will now tell you of another sort who turn back. They be them who believe if they go on in wickedness they will be lost, they believe God is just and will send them to hell, except they repent; this give them trouble, make them very fraid, now they leave off telling lie, cursing and swearing, stealing and all such bad thing, they pray, go to sermon and seem very earnest, all the while this trouble last, but by and by when this trouble for fear of hell be gone, then they turn again to folly and sin. Now, brother Sambo, I dare say you can tell us why they turn back, and how they go from one thing to another, till they get as bad as before they begin to pray.

*Sambo.* Why brother, I think I know a little bout it; but as you begin, I shall be glad you go on and tell us all about it, for you more old in religion than me, and so know more better about these things.

*Davy.* Well, brother, I will go on then: now the main reason why such turn back, their heart never been changed. With all their trouble and fear of hell, their heart never been right with God. They be like a man at the court, when tried for his life; he fear he will be hanged, this make him sorry and repent; but if he get clear he goes to stealing again. This shews he was not sorry for the sin, but his fear and trouble was about the punishment. Now then, when this fear and trouble leave them, they leave off prayer; then by and by they leave off going to sermon; they then begin to find fault with their brethren, and leave their company; then they go among the wicked and laugh and joke with them; then they go little furder, till they harden their heart so much that they no shame to do as bad as before trouble come upon them, and some time much worse, for they make game at the Christians and try to bring them into trouble with their master or overseer.

*Toney.* I hope the Lord will keep us from turning back, for as the minister say last Sunday, the end of such men will be dreadful.

*Sambo.* Well, brother Davy, I been think you lay off all these people very right, for I been think if they been truly converted they never been love sin again: if the heart no been change by the grace of God it will love sin, nothing but that grace can cure the heart of sin; they may talk and talk bout the love of God, and such things; but if the heart no change, by and by something come to try them; they been shew they be still in the bond of sin; but him whose heart been right with God, tho' sometime all been seem wrong with him, and the wicked ones been bring him into trouble, aye, and for suffer too, will that been make him leave the Lord? no no, it been make him look bout him, look into his heart, look upon his conduct for see if all right; trouble make him go more earnest to the Lord for direct him and help him, he no run away into sin.

*Davy.* Very true, brother, you talk like a Christian; this bring my mind to think what happen to one of my fellow servants, in old master's time. I will tell you how it was. Soon after we begin to hear about religion, the Lord take hold of

Simon and me, I think it was the first sermon we hear. Well, we leave off our bad ways, and pray and talk to some of our people; this make most every body gainst us; now first one then another would go to overseer with some tale to make mischief, and try to set the overseer gainst us. He was wicked and dont mind religion, otherwise he very clever man. These tales make him watch we two very close; well, we be upon our guard too; I believe it was for our good; but the wicked ones no mean it so.

*Titus.* I suppose it make you stick more closer together and pray more earnest for the Lord for help you.

*Davy.* Yes it did so. However by and by some body steal rice. I am sure no body could steal for want of rice, for we then had our lowance in small rice; beside most every body have rice of their own, for we all had land to plant, and most every day we done our task time enough to work for ourselves. However the rice was stole, and some thought Simon steal it, and some things look like it might be Simon, but Simon tell me he no steal it, and beg me to pray for him. Well, Simon was confined, and the overseer try hard to find the thief. At last, some of the rice was found in Simon's house. The overseer dont know what to make of it, sometime he think it cant be Simon; then agen the rice was found in his house, and some of the wicked ones say something to make overseer think it must be him. I go to Simon and tell him if he steal the rice, he better tell all about it. Simon say, he no steal the rice for true, the Lord know I no steal it, I know nothing bout it. Well, the overseer punish Simon. When he done, Simon say, overseer will you hear me talk? Overseer say, yes; Simon say, sir, you punish me for stealing rice; as you find it in my house, it look like I steal it, but I sure you I no steal it, I know nothing bout it, my wife honest woman too, she no steal it, I never steal from any body since that time I begin for pray; you no see, sir, ever since that time, brother Davy and me mind our work for master, and work for ourselves, and trouble no body? and every time you call us, when we been work for ourselves we go, we never grumble; we never ramble about for mischief, we never go no where without ticket. I very sure some body put the rice in my house for bring all this upon me. I sorry for them, one day I hope the thief will be found, the Lord send this for try me—Simon talk so good and so humble to the overseer, it touch his heart. Well, did this make Simon turn back? No no, he pray for his enemy, he pray the Lord to give him repentance; and sure enough, in two or three month, Tom come one day to Simon and fall upon his knees and say, Simon, can you forgive me? Simon say for what? Tom say, O Simon! I been steal the rice, and put some in your house when you been at meeting. The devil got in my heart and help me to contrive all bout it. Yesterday, when the minister preach, he look upon me so hard when he tell us bout the devil tempting the black people for make mischief mong their fellow servants, I sure he know I steal the rice. My heart trouble me till I most dead, I spec God Almighty would strike me into hell. By and by, like some body say to me, Tom, go tell Simon, he one good man, he forgive you, and tell you how for repent and then to God. Now, Simon, what shall I do? Simon talk to him so good, till his heart melt. Then he take him to master, and Tom tell master all bout it; and Simon beg master not to punish Tom this time, cause his conscience trouble him so much.

*Titus.* Well, Simon do like a Christian for true. I believe very few would done so, and did your master punish Tom?

*Davy.* No, he let him go this time for Simon's begging for him, and sure enough, Tom become a sober honest man, and I hope a true Christian. I shall never forget what old master say about it.

*Sambo.* What he say?

*Davy.* Say? Why he say, Simon was too good for live long in this world, and that Tom ought to pray for Simon as long as he live. After this old master used to say, he wished all his servants were like Simon, Tom, and Davy.

*Titus.* Well brother Davy, Simon been one fine Christian, I wish we all had such a heart to forgive like him.

*Sambo.* I wish so too, and we all ought for have such heart. Every Christian prays God would forgive his sins as he forgives them that do wrong against him. If we no forgive, how can we spec we shall be forgiven?

*Davy.* I will tell you of another man; but he no like Simon. The minister tell me about him. The minister say, there was one man who run before every body for a while; he was for praying at every meeting, and he talk to every body; he talk to white men like they were his fellow servants, and hardly any body good enough for him; this one no pray to please him, tother one no talk enough! he find fault with minister, this one proud, tother one no half strick enough in preaching; this man seem to be going fast to heaven, that is, he think so himself. Now the minister no like his conduct, so he have his eye upon him. Well, by and by he miss meeting; the minister after missing him two or three times, ask some of the Christian people where is Peter? but nobody could tell; at last the minister hear about him. Peter one day went to hear a grave old minister preach, and after sermon, Peter talk to the old minister, and he run on talking as if he knew every thing. The old minister soon find out his religion, and like him he was afraid all his religion was in his tongue; and he ask Peter some close questions that puzzle him, and he begin for be ashamed. Peter would no mind this if the minister had not talk before some of the brethren; but the good, old gentleman let him know before the brethren that he thought little of his religion, and begged him to pray the Lord to change his heart; for say the minister, I am fraid you be a stranger to heart religion. Now this faithful talk no humble him and send him to the Lord, but Peter fended a heap, and from that time he begin to give way, and soon went back to his old ways and companions, and now laughs at every thing good.

*Sambo.* Well, brother, we need pray the Lord for keep us humble, 'tis sad thing when we think too much of ourselves, it give the devil great vantage of us.

*Davy.* Yes, brother, very true. The word of the Lord say, "be not high-minded but fear, the true fear the Lord is the beginning of wisdom."[10] What a humble man St. Paul was, he say, "I am less than the least of all saints."[11] Again the word says, "Pride goeth before destruction, and a haughty spirit before a fall. God resisteth the proud, but giveth grace to the humble."[12]

*Fanny.* What a blessed book be the word of the Lord. O I love for hear uncle Davy read in it; sometime it fill my heart full of love to my Lord; sometime it make me hate sin. When uncle Davy read how Christ die for sin, and how God angry for sin, and how some good men fight gainst sin, O I feel like I wish for be free from every sinful thought; this make me pray my Lord for keep me from all evil.

*Davy.* That's right, sister, the word of God is best of all, that tell us every thing, it tell we poor servants how to trust the Lord, and to do our duty to God and our master, it tell us how to be content and not murmur, and be honest, and how we should love our wives and take care of our children and try to live in love and peace with one another, and as much as we can with every body. And when the Lord enable us to do so, how much better 'tis than to wrangle and quarrel and murmur. Why what signify if we do have hard trial in this world: the Lord every now and then comfort our hearts, and by and by we shall be done with all trouble and sorrow.

*Toney.* Aye, and sin too brother. Suppose we been ever so rich and great, we must been have trouble too, and if we no been have grace, we should no be half so happy as we be now, and then agen when we come for die and no grace, O how dreadful! For my part I thank God for the gospel more than ever, when I think how many poor souls no hear nothing bout it.

*Davy.* Yes, brother, we ought to be very thankful to God for sending his gospel among us. When I was a boy, there was hardly any such thing among we black people, but now, bless God, most every plantation hear the word of the Lord; and I am sure we on this plantation ought to be more thankful than most any people; our master and mistress both good people, and I am sure would be glad if all we black people was converted.

*Sambo.* Our master also been very good in this thing, he sometimes been ask the minister for come to him house, and stay all night; ah! then we have good time for true; the minister pray and exhort we black people, and tell us how we must serve the Lord, and how the devil tempt the Christian, and how we must

fight gainst him, and tell us all bout our wicked heart, and how we must watch
and pray, and pray for our fellow servants, and all these things; why, brother
Davy, sometime it most like heaven.

Davy. I think most every master would encourage religion among his people, was
it not for the bad conduct of some professors. You know my brother, every
master is not like; some be good men, and some bad, but good or bad they all
wish to have their work done. And if I was master I should want my work done
too; well, if master good man and the servant pretend to be religious, the master expect he will be faithful and honest, no steal himself, and watch gainst
other stealing, and be quiet and peaceable and not grumble and murmur at
every thing; so if master a bad man what so likely to make him better, as to see
his servants honest and faithful in their business and living peaceable among
themselves; by and by he may see religion a good thing, and he may love it, and
if not, he must be very bad for true, if he use his servants worse for being faithful and honest.

Titus. I think, brother Davy, we should some time put ourselves in master's place,
then we soon been see what we expect from our servants.

Sambo. I think so too, brother. If I been master be sure I expect professors be very
careful and do every thing right, and mind their wife and children, and on Sunday look clean and go to meeting; I would say, well done, I glad for see you
behave well, I glad for find you honest, that my good negro. This make them do
more better and love master.

Titus. You know, Sambo, that the way our master been do, he no love for see any
body idle, he no idle himself. He love for see the man's clothes mended, he
then say that man got good wife. A Sunday when he see the wife and children
clean and behave well, he please too much, he say howdy, how your children,
you love for go to meeting; this make them feel good and love master. I often
hear master say, them negro who no take care of themselves will never serve
God.

Sambo. Brother Davy, you been a professor good many year and must be more better acquainted with the temptation of Satan than we, cant you tell us bout how
for manage him? I wish you talk little upon that.

Davy. Why, brother, the devil is so cunning and he have so many sorts of temptations, that it pretty hard to be a match for him, but I will tell you how you must
do; in the first place, live much in prayer; in the next place never be idle; when
you have done working for your master if you be not too tired, work some for
yourself; the devil always put some mischief in our heads when we be idle; then
learn to be content with your state, never mind if some of your fellow servants
seem better off than you, you will always see some that be worse, and remember you have more than you deserve; and again take care of pride; pride is one

bad sin, always pray for humility, but take care dont try to make people think you be more humble than you are; and be sure keep a good clean conscience; never tell lie, but stand by truth at all time, God almighty love truth, and devil love lie; never steal the least thing from any body, and mind your own business, and never trouble any body; and every day pray for more faith in God and Christ, and that you may better understand the gospel; now, brother, if you mind these things well, Satan cant hurt you much.

*Titus.* Brother Davy, you been talk very well, I think if we been mind these things well as you say, the devil no hurt us much.

*Davy.* However, Satan always busy, so our Lord say we must watch and pray that we enter not into temptation, and again the word of the Lord, "Resist the devil and he will fly from you."[13] Now, brother, we must be very careful that we no trust to our own strength, for when we done all, we be unprofitable servants, every thing God do for us he do for Christ's sake, Christ live for us, Christ die for us, by grace we be saved, and by his grace only can we be a match for Satan.

*Titus.* O that blessed book that tell us so much bout Jesus Christ. I wish I been able to read it.

*Davy.* Brother Titus, you no too old to learn; I have learned older men than you be; if you set your mind to it, you will soon learn; Toney and his wife are both learning and will soon be able to read the word of the Lord.

*Sambo.* Well, brother Davy, there be one thing more I wish you for talk a little upon.

*Davy.* What is that brother?

*Sambo.* Suppose one the brethren do something I think been wrong, and nobody but him and me know any thing about it; what must I been do? must I tell the minister?

*Davy.* No brother, you must tell nobody, before you talk with the brother himself. Now I will read to you what the word of the Lord say upon it, for that tell us very plain how to do. It is in the 18th chapter of St. Matthew; and now mind the words; "Moreover, if thy brother shall trespass against thee, go and tell him his fault, between him and thee alone; if he shall hear thee thou hast gained thy brother. But if he will not hear thee, then take with thee one or two more, that in the mouth of two or three witnesses every word may be established, and if he shall neglect to hear them, tell it unto the church." Now you see, my brother, this very plain. If thy brother offend thee, you must not tell any body about it, you must not wait for his coming to you, but you must go to him, and tell him his fault, by your two selves; if he confess his fault, why not forgive him and no talk of it to any body. If he no satisfy you, then you take one or two with you, then you tell him his fault before them two brothers; well if he humble and confess, then you forgive him, then you no talk any more about it to any body; but if he stout and no confess, then go to the minister, and he will tell you what to do; now do you understand?

*Sambo.* Thank you, brother, I been understand very well. I hope the Lord will enable me to mind it.

*Toney.* Well my brethren, tomorrow our minister preach, and brother Davy and me will beg him for come pray with us and give us some advice before we been part, he one very good man and love for teach we black people.

*Fanny.* Our minister been one good man for true; all the black people love him too much, he talk so plain we poor black people understand most every word he say, and some time he talk to the children and tell them for pray, and no tell lie, nor say bad words; but mind what their father and mother been say to them, and he talk so good and so loving that the children love him most as much as we do.

*Sambo.* Then I sure you ought to be very thankful and mind what he say, and pray God for bless his word among you.

At the desire of Davy and Toney the minister came in the evening, when some of those who had lately made a profession, and the brethren who came to visit Toney were waiting to hear him exhort them. He spoke to them in the following manner:

Your brethren Davy and Toney, desired me to come and pray with you, and drop a word of advice to you; my time is short. I cannot at present say much; I would observe, it gives me pleasure to see you so desirous of instruction. You, my brethren, have made a profession of religion. You will ever remember the eyes of the world will be upon you to wait for your halting and turning back into sin. The eyes of the church will also be upon you to observe your conduct, and watch for your souls; but what above all should make you fear to do wrong and wicked is the eyes of God are continually on you. You will therefore always try to act as in his awful presence; ever strive to keep a good conscience, giving no offence neither to God nor man. Let your whole conduct be sober and steady as becometh men professing godliness. Learn to be content with such things as you have, and guard against a murmuring discontented spirit. Live a life of prayer and dependence on God. Let your master, the people of the world, and your fellow-servants, see that you endeavour to live a pious godly life, agreeable to your profession in all honesty and sobriety. When you have an opportunity, talk to your fellow-servants about their souls' concerns and pray daily for their conversion. Guard against pride and self-conceit; humility is a lovely grace, and shines no where more than in a servant. Be careful to attend publick worship when you have opportunity, and be regular and strict in secret and family prayer. Live in love with your wives and keep to them only. Be careful of your children, that they do not tell lies and use bad words, and let them know how wicked it is to steal. Learn to make home the most agree[a]ble of any place to you, then you will not want to ramble from one plantation to another, and so be preserved from many temptations and hurtful snares. Try and learn to read, that you may know for yourselves what the word of the Lord contains. Mind your master's business, and be obedient to him in all things, pray daily for him and his family. Learn to live by faith on the Son of God, who loved us, and gave himself for us. Let your whole lives be such as you will wish they had been when you come to die. Thus you will grow in piety as you grow in years, and grow in grace and in the knowledge of our Lord and Saviour Jesus Christ. Then, when you come to die, the Lord will receive you into that world of joy and peace, where sin and sorrow will for ever cease, and where all tears will be wiped from your eyes, where you will see your Jesus, and be made like him, and with all the redeemed of the Lord, will sing the song of Moses and the Lamb. Amen.

Notes

1. The quotation is from Richard Furman, "On the Languishing State of Religion in the Southern States," 1799, repr. in the *Greenville Baptist Courier,* May 3, 1934.

2. Richard Furman, *Sketch of the Life of the Rev. E. Botsford* (Charleston, 1828); Sylvia Frey, *Water from the Rock: Black Resistance in a Revolutionary Age* (Princeton, N.J.: Princeton University Press, 1991), chaps. 8–9; Anne C. Loveland, *Southern Evangelicals and the Social Order, 1800–1860* (Baton Rouge: Louisiana State University Press, 1980).

3. Luke 13:5.

4. Luke 18:13.

5. Matthew 11:28.

6. Acts 16:31.

7. Psalms 55:22.

8. Isaac Watts, Hymn 127.

9. 1 Corinthians 10:12.

10. Romans 11:20; Psalms 111:10.

11. Ephesians 3:8.

12. Proverbs 16:18; James 4:6.

13. James 4:7.

# CHAPTER 10

# William Meade, 1813

DURING THE SAME PERIOD THAT the evangelical churches were rapidly expanding their influence over southern culture, the Episcopalian Church was struggling to rebuild. As representatives of the established faith during the colonial period, Anglican ministers could take at least some comfort from the fact that most elite planters were nominally associated with their church, even if these slaveholders tended to ignore the ministers' pronouncements about the need to Christianize plantation life. The Revolution, however, had forced many of the brightest Anglican ministers to flee the colonies and had shattered the financial and social base on which the church traditionally rested. The late eighteenth century was therefore a challenging era for the religious activists struggling to advance the fortunes of the American Episcopal Church. Its influence in Virginia was perhaps at its lowest point when William Meade was ordained as a minister in 1811. Born in 1789 into an aristocratic family (with ties to the most respected names in the state), Meade emerged as one of the most influential Episcopalian clergymen of his era. From his role as minister of Christ Church in Alexandria, he rose to the position of county minister of Frederick Parish and eventually became the bishop of Virginia and, finally, presiding bishop of the Protestant Episcopal Church in the Confederate States of America.[1]

As a young man, Meade maintained an uneasy attitude toward human bondage in the South. In 1816, for example, he joined the American Colonization Society as a charter member and even traveled through the slaveholding states as the society's general agent in 1819 to campaign for the removal of African American slaves from the South.[2] And yet, although Meade believed that slavery hindered the economic growth of his native state, he also insisted that the master-slave relationship could reflect the principles of Christianity. In 1813 he made the effort to compile for publication a series of Christian proslavery tracts by various authors. Demonstrating the convergence of proslavery thought in the early republic, Meade included in his volume not only the works of the Anglican minister Thomas Bacon but also a tract composed by the Baptist author Edmund Botsford.[3] Pursuing his goal of a plantation society united in its devotion to Christian principle, Meade saw no need to recognize denominational boundaries. As he discussed in his brief introduction, he also saw little need to contribute his own proslavery perspective, since he was so pleased by what he saw in the works of the authors whom he included in his volume.

By the late antebellum period, Meade had purged himself of his doubts about slavery's future in the plantation states. As he wrote in 1857, "While we admit and maintain that slavery has its evils, we must also affirm that some of the finest traits in the character of man are to be found in active connection with it. The very dependence of the slave upon his master is a continual and effective appeal to his justice and humanity. . . . If the evil passions are sometimes called into exercise, the milder virtues are much more frequently drawn forth."[4] But even before Meade fully committed himself to the protection of slavery as a southern institution, he had felt enough at peace with organic doctrines concerning slavery to publish Christian proslavery tracts under his own name. Certainly, here was evidence that reciprocal notions of the master-slave relationship were attracting a growing audience during the Early National period. When slaveholders read these works, they encountered the idealized image of the happy and faithful slave who preferred bondage to the morally suspect world of freedom. Such imagery would become the focal point of the regional identity forged by southern statesmen and intellectuals in the following decades.

***

WILLIAM MEADE, ed., *Sermons Addressed to Masters and Servants, and Published in the Year 1743, by the Rev. Thomas Bacon, Minister of the Protestant Episcopal Church in Maryland. Now Republished with Other Tracts and Dialogues on the Same Subject, and Recommended to All Masters and Mistresses to Be Used in Their Families* (Winchester, Va.: John Heiskell, [1813])

### Preface.

The Editor of this volume offers it to all Masters and Mistresses in our Southern States, with the anxious wish and devout prayer, that it may prove a blessing to them and their household.——He considers himself most happy in having met with the several pieces which compose it, and could not with a quiet conscience refrain from affording to others the opportunity of profiting thereby.

The subject treated of must be acknowledged, by all Christians, to be of great importance, and I hope it will seem to them also, that it is handled in a manner worthy of the theme.

It was the first intention of the Editor to have prefixed an introduction of some length, and in it to have urged the great importance of affording religious instruction to our slaves, by some, out of those many and powerful considerations, which ought to compel us to this duty; and also to have answered some of those vain objections, which even good people, as an excuse for their neglect, raise up against this charitable work; but a perusal of the volume itself, particularly of the sermons addressed to masters, satisfied him that it was quite needless and might even weaken the cause. In those sermons it was found, that every argument which was likely to convince and persuade, was so forcibly exerted, and every objection that could possibly be made, so fully answered,—and, in fine, every thing that ought to be said, so well said, and the same things so happily confirmed, by the interesting stories and dialogues which follow, that it was deemed best to refer the reader for the true nature and object of the book, to the book itself.—It is the earnest request of the Editor, that all who take it up will give it a careful examination throughout, before they form an opinion or pass sentence.—Let all whom it may concern, lay the subject before GOD and their consciences, and, after mature deliberation, determine upon the course they will pursue.

The Editor invites the attention of Christians of all denominations, to a subject in which they are all equally concerned; and especially beseeches the ministers of the gospel to take it into serious consideration, as a matter for which they also will have to give an account; for did not Christ die for these poor creatures as well as any other? and is it not given in charge to his ministers to gather his sheep into the fold?

The Editor thinks proper to mention, that this volume is only the promise and forerunner of others, on the same subject, which, by the blessing of heaven, will follow at proper intervals.[5]—In this present work, little else is attempted, than to state the duty and persuade to the performance of it; it is hoped that a desire will be kindled within the breasts of many, to do something in behalf of these our ignorant fellow-creatures. To enable them to put this wish into execution, it will be desirable to have in each family some books beside the Bible, which contain tracts addressed particularly to persons in their station, which may be read to them on proper occasions by any member of the family.—The Editor is now engaged in collecting such pieces; but in the mean time, let all who feel the duty, begin at once, and, out of the holy Bible, read to them the words of everlasting life, and pray with them and for them, to that GOD to whom sincere prayers are never addressed in vain.

To that GOD he commends them, himself, and this work.

*The following very interesting and simple Dialogue was written by a gentleman of our own Country and deserves to be read with attention.*[6]

The following dialogue took place between Mr. Jackson the master of a family, and the slave of one of his neighbours who lived adjoining the town, on this occasion. Mr. Jackson was walking through the common and came to a field of this person's farm. He there saw the slave leaning against the fence with a book in his hand, which he seemed to be very intent upon; after a little time he closed the book, and clasping it with both his hands, looked upwards as if engaged in mental prayer; after this, he put the book in his bosom, and walked along the fence near where Mr. Jackson was standing. Surprised at seeing a person of his colour engaged with a book, and still more by the animation and delight that he observed in his countenance; he determines to enquire about it, and calls to him as he passes.

*Mr. J.* So I see you have been reading, my lad?

*Slave.* Yes Sir.

*Mr. J.* Well, I have a great curiosity to see what you were reading so earnestly; will you shew me your book?

*Slave.* To be sure sir. (And he presented it to him very respectfully.)

*Mr. J.* The Bible!—Pray when did you get this book? And who taught you to read it?

*Slave.* I thank GOD sir, for the book. I do not know the good gentleman who gave it to me, but I am sure GOD sent it to me. I was learning to read in town at nights, and one morning a gentleman met me in the road as I had my spelling book open in my hand: he asked me if I could read, I told him a little, and he gave me this book and told me to make haste and learn to read it, and to ask GOD to help me, and that it would make me as happy as any body in the world.

*Mr. J.* Well did you do so?

*Slave.* I thought about it for some time, and I wondered that any body should give me a book or care about me; and I wondered what that could be which could make a poor slave like me so happy; and so I thought more and more of it, and I said I would try and do as the gentleman bid me, and blessed be GOD! he told me nothing but the truth.

*Mr. J.* Who is your master?

*Slave.* Mr. Wilkins sir, who lives in that house.

*Mr. J.* I know him; he is a very good man; but what does he say to your leaving his work to read your book in the field?

*Slave.* I was not leaving his work, sir. This book does not teach me to neglect my master's work. I could not be happy if I did that.—I have done my breakfast sir, and am waiting till the horses are done eating.

*Mr. J.* Well, what does that book teach you?

*Slave.* Oh sir! every thing that I want to know—all I am to do, this book tells me, and so plain. It shew me first that I was a wretched, ruined sinner, and what would become of me if I died in that state, and then when I was day and night in dread of GOD's calling me to account for my wickedness, and did not know which way to look for my deliverance, reading over and over again those dreadful words, "depart from me ye cursed into everlasting fire," then it revealed to me how JESUS CHRIST had consented to come and suffer punishment for us in our stead, and bought pardon for us by his blood, and how by believing on him and serving him, I might become a child of GOD, so that I need be no more terrified by the thoughts of GOD's anger but sure of his forgiveness and love.[7] O sir, when I learned all this, and found that GOD loved such a poor creature as me, that JESUS CHRIST died for me, it filled me with such love to GOD and such a desire to know and serve him, that I could think or care for nothing else. And though I was ignorant how I was to serve GOD, and often thought what could I do for GOD, yet I was sure I was willing to know what I should do, and all such, GOD promises, in his book, that he will teach.

And sure enough I now see that it is no strange and great thing that I am to do to be saved; I am to trust in JESUS CHRIST and do his commands.—I am a slave and have to work for my master; I am to do his work considering it as GOD's work, and what he has ordered me to do; and in this state I am to be content, and do all the duties of it cheerfully and faithfully, and GOD will reward me; and indeed I have good reason to be content and thankful, and I sometimes think more so than if I was free and ever so rich and great; for then I might be tempted to love and serve myself more than GOD, as rich and great people are apt to do; and besides, even if I wished to serve GOD in such a state as that, I might not know how to do it;—I might not know very often how I was to act, what things I should do and what I should avoid. But now I can't help knowing my duty. I am to serve GOD in that state in which he has placed me. I am to do what my master orders me;—my work is already appointed for me, and whatever it is, I am to do it as well as ever I can without my master's looking after me, and always remembering that my great master in Heaven sees me, and that I am serving him when I am serving my master: and sometimes, and while I am at work these thoughts make me so happy that I think I can scarcely love GOD well enough for making me what is in this blessed book.

*Mr. J.* Well, this book has done great things for you indeed, and if you give a true account of it, it has done for you all the gentleman promised when he gave it to you. But did you not find it very difficult to bear this new way of life and give up your old sins?

*Slave.* Master, GOD made it easy to me when I saw that he would stoop to think of such a poor creature as me, and that JESUS CHRIST was not above dying for me, it so filled me with love that every thing seemed easy to me.

*Mr. J.* I see your horses are coming out, but I shall be glad to talk with you further some other time—I hope you will continue in your present mind.

*Slave.* I thank you master; GOD bless you.

[Here Mr. J. pursued his walk; but soon reflecting on what he had heard, he resolved to walk by Mr. Wilkins's house and enquire into this affair from him. This he did, and finding him the following conversation took place between them.]

*Mr. J.* Sir, I have been talking with a man of yours in that field, who was engaged, while his horses were eating, in reading a book; which I asked him to shew me and found it was the Bible; thereupon I asked him some questions and his answers, and the account he gave of himself have surprized me greatly.

*Mr. W.* I presume it was Will—and though I do not know what he may have told you, yet I will undertake to say that he told you nothing but the truth. I am always safe in believing him, and do not believe he would tell me an untruth for any thing that could be offered him.

*Mr. J.* I thought his manner indicated as much and so no reason to doubt him—It is an instance of GOD's grace that affects me strongly, and I would be glad to know how he attained his present state, and that clear view of his religious duties which he seems to have, whether by your assistance and advice or otherwise.

*Mr. W.* Alas sir, he has been (I must own) a far greater help to me than I have ever been to him.—For when I saw what religion had done for him, it excited me to reflect more seriously on the importance of that which my worldly cares had made me quite negligent of.

This man sir, strange as it may seem, was among the worst among my people; he was always idle when my eyes were not upon him; I could not trust him to market with my things, for he was neither sober nor honest, and though often chastised, he grew worse and I had almost resolved to sell him that I might be no more plagued with him; this continued to be the case till about four years ago;—I then thought I remarked that he was grave and serious; I should have thought it sullenness, but he was more complaisant and obedient than usual; in a little time I saw that he was greatly changed, that his work was well done, that he was always in place, and seemed at all times anxious to receive my orders which were sure to be faithfully attended to. I thought him entitled to commendation and one day told him I was pleased to see him do so well—He replied, master, I have been a wicked good for nothing servant; I hope you will forgive me, and that I shall never do amiss again. I had observed that some how or other, without my knowledge, he had been learning to read; but I did not know what had produced his reformation, till I found he was always reading the book you saw him with at his leisure times, either by himself or to the other servants. I talked with him and was as much surprised, as you have been, at what he told me.

*Mr. J.* No doubt you gave him encouragement.

*Mr. W.* Yes, that I could not help but doing; and it set me to thinking how strange it was that he of all that belong to my family, should become religious; and that without either instruction or example from me. I had never even recommended religion to him,—I had never worshiped God in my family, I went to town on Sabbath-days to church, and thought that was all a Christian need do. What my blacks did on the Sabbath, I cared nothing about; they commonly worked in their patches, or went to town to sell their things. But I need not trouble you sir, with telling you how these thoughts preyed on my mind and what they set me upon.

*Mr. J.* That my dear sir, is what I chiefly wish to learn; for I feel that I have been sadly wanting in what I now begin to perceive is no small part of my duty.

*Mr. W.* Why, sir, as I was telling you, I weighed all these things, and thought more and more upon them, as I observed the increasing diligence and fidelity of this man; and as I moreover saw how happy and contented he had become. GOD was merciful to me, and led me on step by step, to know my own guilt and his goodness. I determined that I would reform that in which I had first seen my sinfulness, and that I would not only pray myself, but make my house a house of prayer. I spoke to Will and told him one Sunday morning, to desire the people all come to me, that I had something to say to them. When they came I told them in a few words, that I had neglected what I now considered a great duty; that we had not worshipped GOD together as I should have called on them to do: that perhaps many of them were ignorant of GOD, and what they must do to gain his favour; that I wished such as needed instruction to come to me at proper times, and I would read to them and talk to them. That hereafter every night and morning, we should join in family prayer, and hear some portion of the bible read, and that on Sundays they should no more employ their time in work or in selling their goods; that I would allow them other times for such things, and that on every Sabbath morning I should read to them and pray with them, and that then such as could leave home should go into town, where I would expect to see them at church; and at night we should meet together again for reading and prayer, and that none must be absent without leave, or a sufficient excuse. I then selected a chapter of the New Testament, and read a suitable prayer which I had promised. They were all attentive, though I perceived many of them much surprised.

*Mr. J.* Well sir, you have seen I trust in your family, good fruits from this beginning.

*Mr. W.* Yes indeed, sir, and that man was most instrumental in reconciling and encouraging all my people to the change. From that time I have regarded him as more a friend and assistant, than as a slave. He has taught the younger ones to read, and by his kindness and example, has been a great benefit to all. I have told them that I would do what I could to instruct and improve them; and that if I found any so vicious, that they would not receive it and strive to amend, I would not keep them; that I hoped to have a religious, praying family, and that none would be obstinately bent upon their own ruin. And from time to time, I endeavoured to convince them that I was aiming at their own good. I cannot tell you all the happiness of the change, that GOD has been pleased to make among us, all by these means. And I have been benefitted both temporally and spiritually by it; for my work is better done, and my people are more faithful, contented, and obedient than before; and I have the comfort of thinking that when my Lord and master shall call me to account for those committed to my charge, I shall not be ashamed to present them.

*Mr. J.* You have given me great satisfaction, and I hope to profit by your example. I too, have been introducing religion into my family after myself neglecting it all my life. But I had not before thought of what I owed to my slaves, or what it was practicable to do for them. It seems now plain to me that I have been greatly guilty, and in more things than I had supposed. I never looked on it in this light; but surely if GOD has put these poor creatures in our power, he will require at our hands what good we have done for them; whether we have used them merely for our profit or pleasure in this world, or taught them to serve him and fitted them for the world to come.

*Mr. W.* I am glad that what I have communicated should lead to such just thoughts. The word of GOD is plain—The Christian should be the teacher and pattern of his family; and we are as much, aye indeed, more bound to provide for the everlasting welfare of our slaves, than for their present necessities. All men agree that, that master is cruel who starves the bodies of his slaves, and yet this is kindness compared with his cruelty who starves their souls, who brings them up in utter ignorance, giving them no more instruction than he does to his beasts. Do masters remember that they and their slaves are one day to stand together before the judgment seat of CHRIST, that all are then to be judged by the word of GOD in the bible?

Most of my people can now read; I encourage them to learn and give them a bible when they can. When one or two have learned, it is quite easy to have the others, particularly the younger ones, taught.

*Mr. J.* Well sir, as I said, I hope I shall begin to do my duty in this respect. I shall think over what has passed between us, and, I hope, see you again.

*Mr. W.* I will be most happy at all times to render you any service in this way, by communicating my own experiments and continuances to further this design.

[After returning home, the following conversation took place between Mr. J. and his wife, his mind still dwelling on what had occurred during his walk.]

*Husb.* My dear! I have discovered, I think, another great duty in which we have both been sadly wanting. We have great need to implore GOD's forgiveness of the unchristian life we have been leading.

*Wife.* Well my dear what is it? Let us not be discouraged; you know we have prayed GOD to shew us whatever is amiss in us.

*Husb.* Yes, I trust it is in answer to our prayers that I have been led to what has happened this day.

*Wife.* Do not fear, you know we have also prayed that GOD would give us grace and strength faithfully to fulfil whatever duty he enabled us to perceive. That prayer will also be answered.

*Husb.* You are indeed a help-mate to me. I had been almost desponding; you shall hear what I have learned this morning.

[Hereupon he relates the matter of the aforegoing dialogues.]

*Wife.* Mr. Wilkins has done right, and why may not we hope to succeed in the same way. I will gladly join you with all the help I can give. These things seem harder than they are found when we set about them.

*Husb.* I hope we shall not be discouraged, be it ever so difficult. GOD has helped us hitherto in the discharge of our duties. So little had I thought of this that ever since we have had family prayer, we have not called in our slaves to join us. Hereafter let us be particular, that at those occasions none shall be absent without evident necessity. We will both take opportunities of reading to them, and give them the means of regular attendance at church. GOD will open a way for us in the mean time to do more; means may be had for teaching the younger ones and such others as wish it, to read; we can also by frequently reading over the catechism to them, fix it in their memories, and we can also explain it to them where it may not be plain enough for them.

*Wife.* It would be well also to obtain Mr. Wilkins's consent that this man whom you talked with, should come and see our people and gain their acquaintance. He would set them upon wishing to read and might perhaps have spare time enough to teach them. I would also myself help in this, and our daughter— would not object in being so engaged.

*Husb.* You have already done much to encourage me—Let us resolve to begin without delay, and trust that GOD will contrive to teach us his will and strengthen us in his ways—Let us now join in our prayers to him for this purpose.[8]

Notes

1. David Lynn Holmes Jr., "William Meade and the Church of Virginia, 1789–1829" (Ph.D. diss., Princeton University, 1971); William Meade, *Old Churches, Ministers, and Families of Virginia,* 2 vols. (1857; repr., Baltimore: Genealogical Publishing, 1966); Larry E. Tise, *Proslavery: A History of the Defense of Slavery in America, 1701–1840* (Athens: University of Georgia Press, 1987), 53–54, 294–99.

2. Holmes, "William Meade," 204.

3. These authors' works are reproduced in chapters 3 and 9 of this anthology.

4. Meade, *Old Churches,* vol. 1, 91 n.

5. Meade did not follow through on this promise. No further collections of this type appeared under his name.

6. I have not been able to identify the author.

7. Matthew 25:41.

8. I have not included the remaining 1,250 words of the dialogue. These passages present a prayer for guidance in domestic duties and relate Mr. Jackson's rejoinder to a slaveholder who was troubled by the campaign to instruct the slaves in religion.

# CHAPTER 11

# William Smith, 1818, 1820

---

EVEN DURING THE AGE OF REPUBLICAN ascendancy, when southern politicians wielded disproportionate power over the nation's political path, a few slaveholding statesmen nonetheless perceived an impending threat to the unfree labor system. William Smith, a senator from South Carolina, was one of the earliest and most forceful defenders of southern society in Congress. In the years following the War of 1812, Smith championed the cause of state rights, an agenda that placed him at odds with influential countrymen such as John C. Calhoun (who was then a fierce nationalist). Smith's feud with Calhoun prevented him from entering the first rank of Carolina politicians. Nevertheless, his speeches wedding proslavery thought to a state rights political agenda were enormously influential in their day. When Calhoun eventually abandoned his nationalist philosophy to help lead the nullification movement in South Carolina, he adopted views that Smith, Calhoun's old enemy, had articulated years earlier.[1]

Smith was born ca. 1762 and grew up in York County, South Carolina, where he formed boyhood relationships with Andrew Jackson and William Crawford, later a prominent Georgia state rights politician. Smith served in the South Carolina State Senate from 1802 to 1808, at which point he became an appellate court judge. In 1816 the assembly selected him to fill a vacant seat in the U.S. Senate, a position he held until his defeat for reelection in 1823. It was during this period that Smith emerged as one of the most prominent and aggressive defenders of slavery, as a man who championed slavery as the principal pillar of an ostensibly moral southern society. Smith was best known for his proslavery speech in 1820, in the midst of the Missouri controversy. However, as early as 1818, he was already giving voice to a proslavery philosophy during congressional debate over fugitive slaves. His troubled relationship with Calhoun prevented him from returning to the Senate until 1826, when increasing sectional agitation over the tariff brought him newfound popularity. Ironically, Smith could never bring himself to embrace the nullification movement. Although the nullifiers proceeded from assumptions about slavery and state rights that were at the core of Smith's philosophy as a statesman, his distaste for the movement's leaders—his old enemies—pushed him into the unionist camp. Realizing that his future as a Carolina politician was limited by these personal issues, Smith moved in 1833 to Louisiana and later resettled in Huntsville, Alabama. Turning down several opportunities to become a Supreme Court justice, Smith ended his life in relative obscurity. He died in 1840, at the end of a decade that witnessed the South's widespread embrace of principles that he had spent his lifetime advancing in both state and federal office.

Smith's proslavery speeches in the Senate advanced doctrines made familiar by the previous century's proslavery intellectuals. Like Alexander Garden, Thomas Bacon, and William Knox, the South Carolina senator presented human bondage as an institution that could be reconciled with Christian principles. The humane slaveholders of the South, he argued, rewarded their slaves with working and living conditions superior to those of the laboring poor in free countries. Smith claimed that, as a result, strong personal ties had been established between masters and slaves, leading to a greater degree of social stability than could be found in the northern states. Smith voiced these ideas during the very period when southern evangelical churches were popularizing organic conceptions of the master-slave relationship. Although Smith's rivals (both northern and southern) portrayed him as the isolated author of bizarre doctrines, Smith was actually giving voice to ideas that were gaining broad acceptance across the South. Unlike his proslavery predecessors in the colonial era, Smith could rightly anticipate that southern slaveowners as a group would respond favorably to these concepts. For unlike the colonial ministers preaching proslavery doctrines, Smith was tying organic notions to a defiantly sectional conception of southern identity. Whereas colonial ministers preached proslavery principles to better bind the colonies into one empire, politicians such as Smith appealed to organic doctrine to support their reading of the Constitution—a reading that granted to the individual states (and the South as a whole) tremendous latitude in managing the institution of unfree labor. To achieve this goal, Smith and the host of southern authors following suit were ready, by 1820, to disavow the antislavery rhetoric of no less an authority than Thomas Jefferson. Time-honored ideas about organic hierarchy, rather than the prestige of the Founding Fathers themselves, were the bedrock on which subsequent generations of slaveholders would construct their identity as a ruling elite.

<hr />

WILLIAM SMITH, Speech on Fugitive Slaves, *Annals of the Congress of the United States,* 15th Cong., 1st sess., March 6, 1818, pp. 231–39

Mr. Smith, of South Carolina, said, when this subject was first brought before the Senate, he had determined to take no part in the debate. But, as it had assumed such a complexion, both as it respects the constitutionality of the provisions of the bill itself and the subject matter upon which it is founded, as well as the severity of the remarks used by gentlemen opposed to its passage, he considered it his duty to make some reply. The gentleman from Rhode Island (Mr. Burrill) insists that the privilege of the writ of habeas corpus, secured by the ninth section of the first article of the Constitution, will be infringed by this bill, because a person of color taken under it cannot have the right to his freedom tried by the judge before whom the return of the writ of habeas corpus is made.[2] Mr. S. said he pretended to no law knowledge beyond that of the other gentlemen, yet he did most unequivocally deny the construction of the Constitution as given by that gentleman. The writ of habeas corpus was never intended to give a right of trial. It merely gives the right to the person confined to demand an inquiry whether he is held in custody upon a ground warranted by law; and if the judge before whom he is brought finds he is detained by legal authority and upon legal grounds, he cannot discharge him, but he is obliged to remand him. If the authority by which he is held appears to be legal, it is perfectly immaterial whether the cause is a just one or not. And when a fugitive from labor has been taken under this law, the cause of his detention will be fully set forth in the certificate by the judge before whom he is to be taken, whose duty it is specially made to do so. Then can it be pretended, after you pass a law prescribing expressly under what proofs a fugitive shall be taken, and that the fugitive shall be specially described by the judge in the order he is to give for his removal, and that the proofs have been satisfactorily made before him the person therein described is a fugitive slave, and belongs to the person who holds him in custody, that another judge has a right to question all this, and take upon himself alone to try his right to freedom, and discharge him? It is impossible. The writ of habeas corpus was never intended to give any such right.

This would give a judge the sole power of deciding the right of property the master claims in his slave, instead of trying that right by jury, as prescribed by the Constitution. He would be judge of matters of law and matters of fact; clothed with all the powers of a jury as well as the powers of a court. Such a principle is unknown in your system of jurisprudence. Your Constitution has forbid it. It preserves the right of trial by jury in all cases where the value in controversy exceeds twenty dollars. The gentleman has said, if this bill should pass it will enable the Southern planters to take and carry away, not only their own fugitive slaves, but any other person of color, whether he be a free man or a slave. It would enable them to carry off a free white man, and even one of the members of this Senate. Sir, the gentleman from Rhode Island may consider himself as perfectly safe from any such hazard; for, however much we may respect our Northern friends as gentlemen, as lawyers, and as statesmen, we should have no sort of use for them in our cotton fields. Nor should we admire their political instructions to our slaves if they should carry with them their recent impressions.

The honorable gentleman has spoken of the practice of the Southern people in kidnapping their free negroes, and calls them man stealers. And the gentleman from Pennsylvania (Mr. Roberts) has called them *kidnappers, men stealers,* and *soul drivers;* and he asks, in a very emphatic manner, who drew this bill, and upon what authority?[3] Or if it was brought in upon the application of any of the abolition societies? And then he answers these questions himself, and says it was not, but that it had been drawn by a cunning lawyer, and was supported by lawyers. Sir, this language does not comport with the moderation which that gentleman expressed a desire should prevail in this discussion when he addressed the Senate on the subject early in this debate. Is this the language we are to meet when we are suing for our Constitutional rights? The Constitution of the United States has guarantied to the master a right to pursue his fugitive slave, and has enjoined to the State to which he shall fly to deliver him up. It has not left it optional with the State to which he flies, but has made it imperative that he *shall* be delivered up. And has it come to this, that we must wait for the permission of the abolition societies before a law can be offered to secure the recovery of just rights? This was not more novel than strange.

Mr. S. said, it had been a practice in monarchical governments to discredit lawyers, where they had often been foremost in checking a high-handed tyranny; but he had not expected to hear it practised in the Senate of the United States. The lawyers of this country had nothing to fear upon an investigation of their general character. They had been wanting in no public duty. During the Revolutionary war, as well as the late war, many of them had displayed as much gallantry in the field, and as much ability in the councils, as any men in the nation, whilst these abolition societies were in ease and security at home, following their domestic pursuits, and leaving it to others to fight their battles. Mr. S. said, he was sorry to make these remarks, but they were just, and were forced from him. He admired the moderation and virtue of these people; he thought them worthy of imitation in many respects, but he did not admire their constant efforts to alienate the affections of the people of color from their masters, with whom they lived happy, and by whom they were better provided for than the peasantry of any other country upon earth; or, indeed, in some portions of this country, if the facts given by their writers be correct. Mr. Melish, of Philadelphia, in an essay published only a few days ago, states, that there are in the city and county of Philadelphia at least fifteen thousand people, all able and willing to work, who are either idle or occupied in unproductive labor, and says, that melancholy picture pervades the country throughout.[4] This place is the very centre of emancipation; and if unable to furnish employment for their own population, is there any reason why they should add to this picture of growing distress, by an accumulation of free negroes?

Notwithstanding all that has been said by our northern brethren against us for keeping slaves, they employ their free blacks in all their drudgery, and obtain their labor on better terms than masters do. And although it does not apply to that body generally, yet it is a fact, susceptible of proof, that some who profess to promote this principle of abolition, have seduced the slaves from neighboring States under promises to secure their emancipation, instead of which they put them to work, and treat them with so much more severity and injustice than their masters, that the slaves either made it known where they were, or run away from these new tyrants and went back to their former state of slavery, as a better and more desirable condition.

With all this boast about freedom and emancipation, there are only four States that have no slaves. Even the magnificent State of Pennsylvania is a slaveholding State; so is the State of Rhode Island. Those which are non-slaveholding States, with the exception of Ohio, have not long since got rid of them. Rhode Island, New York, and Pennsylvania, previous to taking steps to abolish slavery, furnished the Southern markets with considerable numbers. And the very moment the African trade was opened in South Carolina, in the year 1803, these very States furnished their full proportion of shipping to carry it on. Even our friends in Boston, and other New England States were willing to help with the shipping; besides, it furnished a market for their surplus rum. So we perceive, whenever interest is concerned, and a little profit to be made, all this delicacy about slavery is laid aside.

Whilst it was in their interest to hold slaves, so long they kept them. Whenever the interest coupled with it ceased, slavery ceased, but not before. After the war, trade revived, especially in the Eastern States; it was found that a negro capital must give way to a commercial capital; which was infinitely more profitable. So it is now with banking capital. Even in the States where slavery exists to the greatest extent, we find many selling off their negroes and vesting the proceeds in bank stock; and especially those who live in the towns and cities. This capital, being so much more profitable than the other, it is constantly increasing. And there are no persons more apt to remonstrate against that crying sin slavery, than such as have just sold off their stock of negroes, and vested the price in bank stock. Slavery, then, becomes very odious. They wish to see it abolished—they do not like this traffic in human flesh. But it is because they have got its precious price in a stock that will yield them a three or four-fold profit; not till then can they see its enormity. It is a very convenient thing to be receiving a large profit upon his stock, which is going on under the fostering hand of bank directors, whilst the owner is asleep or taking his pleasure. We have lately seen it published, that some banks have divided as much as thirty per cent upon their capital, whilst the most successful planter will not receive more than ten, and, very many years, not half that amount. This banking system is what will form the ground-work for overthrowing this species of property, by gradually diminishing the number of its holders, and increasing the bank-stock influence. Look how slavery has diminished in the public estimation, as the other system has grown. The States which have taken measures to abolish slavery, have become perfectly bank mad. New York has abolished slavery after ten years, and she is convulsed with banks, and not yet satisfied. There was a late attempt to establish one with a capital of six millions, but it was checked by the Executive. The State of Pennsylvania, already abounding in banks, incorporated forty-seven by one law—they climbed over the Executive veto to do so; two-thirds of the Senate, and about three-fourths of the House of Representatives supporting it. Many of these banks, without a farthing of capital, drawing a large income from the hard earnings of the honest and unwary part of the community, and absolutely refusing to redeem their paper, without one compunction for the misery and ruin it brings with it. When these very frauds were practising to an enormous degree, without a murmur, except from those who were sinking under it, the feelings of that country were bleeding for the supposed distress of the slaves of the South.

The famous article in the Treaty of Ghent, by which we have guarantied to England our cooperation in abolishing the African slave trade, is worth notice.[5] Our Commissioners, friendly to banks and opposed to slavery, had no instructions to enter into any such stipulation. Great Britain had not long before abolished that trade; and our Government had done so forty years before, by an ordinance of the First Congress, in 1774, and which had been rendered more complete by a law of 1807. It was totally unconnected with the subject of negotiation. We were at war upon other grounds entirely. Not even a question of commerce had ever arisen between the two nations upon it; yet it found its way, an isolated article, into a Treaty of Peace!

The Colonizing society is another step in this grand scheme.[6] This society intends to send the free negroes, and other persons of color, into the wilds of Africa; by which they are to be torn from the land of their nativity, and everything to which they are attached by friendship and habit, and the advantages of civilized life, and left to sink again into all the miserable barbarity of their ancestors. But it is said it will pave the way to a general emancipation.

We do by no means suppose that any honorable member of Congress would think of such a thing as a general emancipation; because, independently of interfering with private rights, they know too well that such a measure could not take place without involving the whole of the United States in an awful situation. But, that a general emancipation is intended there can be no doubt, by the Eastern and Northern States, if they can find means to effect it. The abolition societies are avowedly for it; what else can the very name itself indicate? Although their numerous petitions, now before Congress, purport to extend no further than to prevent kidnapping, yet, look at the language of the petitions. If they had applied directly for emancipation, they could not speak plainer. Connected with these petitions, now in the possession and under the consideration of Congress, is the resolution of the gentleman from Rhode Island (Mr. Burrill,) to inquire "into the expediency of the United States taking measures, in concert with other nations, for the entire abolition of said trade." As this resolution had been once before the Senate, and had been referred by a majority to a committee to report with what nations, and under what regulations we should connect ourselves to effect this project, Mr. S. said, it would not be out of the way to advert to it, and inquire what hopes we had of a fortunate result. With whom is this Government to connect itself in this desirable work? It would seem that it ought to be with nations whose general policy is favorable to emancipation, and whose subjects enjoy the blessings of civil liberty at home, before we could expect much beneficial aid from their co-operation. We are not to hope for this from Russia, Prussia, and Austria, whose subjects are borne down by the iron hand of tyranny. Their peasantry are bought and sold at home like slaves, and are suffered to be sent to this country and sold in our markets. Nor is it to be hoped for from England, if her policy should dictate to her a different course. She is now riding foremost in this career, because it promises to extend and promote her commercial interest, whilst her millions of paupers at home are dying in garrets, or falling by the way side, and if they assemble, to raise their cry to their rulers for bread, the riot act is read, and then the military is ordered to fire on them. Three of these nations, assisted by the ships of the other, have spread their sceptre over the destinies of Europe, and formed an holy league against its dawning liberties. These are the nations with whom you are to associate to abolish slavery. It is not to be wondered at, under all this influence, with a total want of knowledge of the comfortable condition of the slaves, that our northern neighbors should feel unfavorable to slavery. But most of the northern gentlemen, when they remove to the southward, and when they can see and judge for themselves, have no hesitation in buying slaves. General Greene, to whom the State of Georgia gave a plantation that cost five thousand guineas, and South Carolina ten thousand pounds sterling, for his services during the Revolutionary war, had no hesitation in purchasing a large gang of negroes to cultivate this plantation, notwithstanding he had been raised to the northward, and had been brought up a quaker.[7]

But, there is another perpetual source of misrepresentation, which serves to place it in an odious light to strangers: it is the number of catch-penny prints and pamphlets that are published by persons who know no more of the condition of the slaves than they do of the man in the moon. Go to a bookstore, and you meet prints hung up in some conspicuous place, in large capital letters, "Portraiture of Domestic Slavery," published in Philadelphia; or the "Horrors of Slavery," published in Cambridge, and sold in Boston.[8] These pamphlets contain all the extraordinary cases collected on the high seas, in the West Indies, or United States, together with such inflammatory speeches of travellers, who have no other means of giving to their writings interest, than by dealing in the marvellous; or of fanatic preachers, or speeches in the British Parliament, calculated to inflame without being able to instruct, and suited more to promote a particular policy than to promote the rights of humanity.

. . . But, we are told by these pamphlet writers, that slavery is "a violation of the Divine laws."[9] And the gentleman from New York, (Mr. King,) in discussing this subject, has told us, "it is contrary to our holy religion."[10] And the gentleman from New Hampshire (Mr. Morril) has told us, that in New England, they believe, "all men are born equally free and independent;" that "every *human affection* recoils at their bondage."[11] The gentleman has said, "the Bible is our moral guide;" and says it was for dealing "in gold and silver and precious stones and pearls and chariots and slaves and souls of men, that produced the downfall of the great Babylon." And he seems to think, that, unless we abolish slavery, we shall provoke the wrath of Heaven, and that we shall go next. The gentleman has forgot one of the great offences of that people: it was for taking of usury. The same Bible which he has adopted for his moral guide says: "Take thou no usury of him, or increase; but fear thy God." This part of the Bible must have become obsolete in New England since the introduction of banks. It must now be pleasing in the sight of Heaven to see a dividend as large as twenty per cent to each bank share. There are as many chariots, as many pears, as much gold and silver, perhaps, in New England, as there was in Babylon, at the time of its fall; yet they are in no danger till the vengeance of Heaven has fallen on the slaveholding States first, the gentleman seems to think.

Upon this great question, sir, notwithstanding the opinion of honorable gentlemen to the contrary, there have been some very respectable opinions as the Divine authority in favor of slavery. We all know that *Ham* sinned against his God and against his father, for which Noah the inspired patriarch cursed Canaan the son of *Ham,* and said, "A servant of servants shall he be unto his brethren." Newton, who was perhaps as great a divine as any in New England, and as profound a scholar, in a book of great celebrity called his *Prophecies,* in which he endeavors to prove the divinity of the Bible by the many prophecies that are now fulfilling, says that this very African race are the descendants of Canaan, and have been the slaves of many nations, and are still expiating in bondage the curse upon themselves and their progenitors.[12] But it may be said that this is only an *opinion* of Mr. Newton, and that we can see no reason in it. Mr. S. said, if the gentleman was unwilling to believe Mr. Newton, he would surely believe Moses and the prophets. And if the Senate would indulge him, he would show from the Bible itself that slavery was permitted by Divine authority; and for that purpose he would open to the xxvth chapter of Leviticus, and read as follows: "And the Lord spake unto Moses in Mount Sinai, saying, Speak unto the children of Israel, and say unto them," &c. 39[th verse: "]And if thy brother that dwelleth by thee be waxen poor, and be sold unto thee; thou shalt not compel him to serve as a bond-servant[. 40th verse]: But as an hired servant, and as a sojourner, he shall be with thee, and shall serve thee unto the year of jubilee. 44[th verse:] Both thy bond-men and thy bond-maids, which thou shalt have, shall be of the heathen that are round about you: and of them shall ye buy bond-men and bond-maids. 45[th verse:] Moreover, of the children of the strangers that do sojourn among you, of them shall ye buy, and of their families that are with you, which they begat in your land: and they shall be your possession[. 46th verse]: And ye shall take them as an inheritance for your children after you, to inherit them for a possession; they shall be your bond-men for ever," &c.

This, Mr. President, is the word of God, as given to us in the Holy Bible, delivered by the Lord himself to his chosen servant Moses. It might be hoped this would satisfy the scruples of all who believe in the divinity of the Bible; as the honorable gentleman from New Hampshire certainly does, as he has referred to that sacred volume for his creed. It might satisfy the scruples of Mr. Kenrick, and the divines who appear so shocked at seeing a father dispose of his slaves to his children by his last will and testament, as they will perceive the scriptures direct them to go as an inheritance. The honorable gentleman says, he speaks not only his own, but the universal sentiments of all those he represents. If he and his friends of New Hampshire have not turned aside after strange gods, it is hoped the authority I have quoted might satisfy them.

~⊃

William Smith, Speech on the Admission of Maine and Missouri, *Annals of Congress,* 16th Cong., 1st sess., 266–75

The subject of slavery, as it now presented itself, was one of serious import to the Southern and Western States. It was a matter of mere calculation with the Eastern States, since they had pressed their own to the South. Gentlemen had different feelings on it. Since this question had been agitated, he had looked into the history of slavery, and he found it had been the lot of man, in this shape or that, to serve one another from all time. At least, slavery has prevailed in every country on the globe, ever since the flood. All the nations of the East held slaves in abundance. The Greeks and the Romans, at the most enlightened periods of those republics. Athens, the seat of the Muses, held slaves. They were often chained at the gates of the rich, as porters, and were treated very different from ours; yet Demosthenes is made to say, "that the condition of a slave at Athens was preferable to that of a free man in many other countries."[13] The Spartans approached nearer to a pure democracy than any other people ever did; yet they held slaves in abundance too. It prevailed all over the Roman Empire. Julius Cæsar sold at one time fifty thousand slaves, yet Cæsar was never held to be a cruel or barbarous man. He would, no doubt, be thought a great sinner by the Eastern States, who hold but a few: for even the States of Pennsylvania and Rhode Island had their slaves yet. This was a small sin, and could be repented of after these few should die off.

In the course of this debate our attention had been called by the honorable gentlemen (Mr. Roberts, of Pennsylvania, and Mr. Mellen, of Massachusetts,) to what was going on abroad.[14] He, Mr. S., had not been inattentive to what was going on abroad; but he found it all confined to the Northern and Eastern States. He had read several pamphlets and dissertations on the subject of inhibiting slavery in Missouri, couched in the most bitter and dishonorable terms of reproach to slaveholders. They were subscribed by fictitious names. One subscribed himself as Marcus. This was a great name among the Romans. Another subscribed himself as Colbert. This was the name of another great man, of modern times. If their plot succeeds, and Missouri should not be admitted into the Union, they can then throw off the veil, give their true names, and come out as the champions of the enterprise. If their plot fails, they can remain Marcus and Colbert; and trace them if you can. Marcus may have further views for concealing his true name. He has, in his pamphlet, taken as much care to point out to this species of population the best means of procuring firearms, and munitions of war, and how they can arrange their forces. &c., as he could have done if he had been appointed by Government to marshal them to cut out throats; and when he shall find the train which he has laid ready for explosion, like the midnight assassin, may apply the match, and blow us up; that he may revel in the spoils. In this he was happy to say this man Marcus would be mistaken, as well as many others who had supposed we were not only in a constant state of alarm, but that we were also in constant danger, from an insurrection of this part of our population. This people are so domesticated, or so kindly treated by their masters, and their situations so improved, that Marcus and all his host cannot excite one among twenty to insurrection. They are able to compare their comforts and their labor, and are fully sensible that their comforts are as great, and their labor not more arduous, than any other class of laboring people. The owners of these people can place arms in their hands, if necessary. In the late war they played a manly part in defence of their masters, in many instances. They were among the defenders of the country at Orleans, as well as at other places; they are the shield of their masters, instead of their deadly enemy, all the apprehensions of Marcus and our Eastern friends to the contrary, notwithstanding.

One gentleman has wrote a long pamphlet, and given his name: this is Daniel Raymond, Esq., as he has called himself.[15] Mr. S. said he had ascertained this Esquire

Raymond to be an honest lawyer, who was under pay of the Abolition Society, and who was measuring his conscience and his humanity by the length of his fee. He has ascertained, as he says in his pamphlet, that the slaves increase not only much faster than the free people of color, but that they increase in a ratio of nearly double the free white population. This is represented as an evil of great magnitude. The great ground of complaint of these Abolition Societies, on former occasions, was the severe and cruel treatment of masters. Now, the objection is, they are treated so humanely that they will shortly overspread the whole land. If these people increase to the extent supposed, it is an incontrovertible evidence that they are well fed, well clothed, and supremely happy. There is no class of laboring people in any country upon the globe, except the United States, that are better clothed, better fed, or are more cheerful, or labor less, or who are more happy, or, indeed, who have more liberty and indulgence, than the slaves of the Southern and Western States. This Mr. Raymond, and some gentlemen who have spoken on the question, (Mr. Morril, from New Hampshire, and Mr. Otis, from Massachusetts,) had all concurred in the same opinion, that it was better to condense these people within the limited space of the old States, and by that means reduce their numbers by a state of starvation and oppression.[16] Heap Cruelties on them to destroy the race. The Greeks confined their slaves in cells; the Spartans suffered the Lacedemonian youth to fall upon them, when laboring in the fields, by stratagem, and massacre them in gangs, for the purpose of training their youth to feats of arms; the Romans threw them into the arena, where they cut one another down, for the amusement of their rich masters. But this was despatching them at once. The mode prescribed by our modern philanthropists is to kill by piecemeal—for a state of starvation is no better. If one mode of killing is more cruel than that of another, it is that which is brought on by the tortures of hunger and oppression.

It has been sung in every town and village of the States which call themselves non-slaveholding States, that slavery is opposed to our holy religion. The honorable gentleman from New Hampshire (Mr. Morril) had inculcated this doctrine in his address to the Senate. He would not hazard too much in calling the master a despot, and a violator of the laws of God. To prove his position, he had read sundry passages from Mr. Jefferson's Notes; the most prominent were the following:

"The whole commerce between master and slave is a perpetual exercise of the most boisterous passions. Our children see this, and learn to imitate it. I tremble for my country, when I reflect that God is just. The Almighty has no attribute which can take side with us in such a contest."[17]

Mr. S. Said he had the highest regard for that venerable patriot; he was a great philosopher and a statesman of the first order. He knew no words more appropriate in pronouncing his eulogy, than those used by himself in delineating the character of the immortal Washington: "His memory will be adored while liberty shall have votaries; his name will triumph over time, and will, in future ages, assume its just station among the most celebrated worthies of the world." With all this tribute, and with all the veneration which he felt for that great man, he did not hesitate to contradict him, in the most unequivocal terms. The master has no motive for this boisterous hostility. It is at war with his interest, and it is at war with his comfort. The whole commerce between master and slave is patriarchal. The master has every motive to impel him to it. As to the effect on children, it is quite the reverse. The black children are the constant associates of the white children; they eat together, they play together, and their affections are often times so strongly formed in early life, as never to be forgotten; so much so, that in thousands of instances there is nothing but the shadow of slavery left. These observations of Mr. Jefferson could not have been founded on facts. They were wrote to gratify a foreigner, at his own request, when every American was filled with enthusiasm. They are the effusions of the speculative philosophy of his young and ardent mind, and which his riper years have corrected. He wrote these Notes near forty years ago; since which his life has been devoted to that sort of practical philosophy which enlarges the sphere of human happiness, and to the promotion of civil liberty; and, during the whole time, his principal fortune has been in slaves, and he still continues to hold them. It is impossible, when his mind became enlarged by reflection and informed by observation, that he could entertain such sentiments, and hold slaves at the same time.

Mr. S. said he had taken the liberty, two years ago, to admonish his honorable friend from New Hampshire, (Mr. Morrill,) on this subject, as it respected our religion. This gentleman then declared, in plain terms, that slavery was forbidden by God, in his Holy Bible. He had now reinforced himself by Jefferson's Notes. The Bible would give the gentleman no support. . . .[18] Mr. S. said the holy book of our religion taught us that God was unchangeable; that he had no respect of persons; that he was without variation or shadow of turning; the same yesterday, to-day, and forever. But it is said that slavery is against the spirit of the Christian religion. When, and by what authority, were we taught to separate the positive laws of God from the Christian religion? Christ himself gave a sanction to slavery. He admonished them to be obedient to their masters; and there is not a word in the whole of his life which forbids it. Slavery was known to a great extent among all the nations of the earth. Christ came to fulfil the law, not to destroy it. Christ came to do the will of his heavenly father who sent him; he came to take away the sins of the world, and to turn men from their wicked ways. Some who are desirous to fix the character of irreligion on the practice of slavery, have said that Christ tolerated slavery, lest he should disturb the tranquillity of the world by exciting the numerous slaves to insurrection. This is a doctrine for you, sir!—that

God should send his only son to redeem the world, and yet that he should be afraid to do his duty, and suffer so crying a sin as slavery is represented to be, by our modern politicians, to go unnoticed, lest he should interfere with a principle of civil policy. And some of them had had the effrontery to charge the slaveholders with impiety, for alleging the Scriptures justified slavery.

If such enthusiasts will not believe Moses and the Prophets, they would not believe one even if he were sent from the dead.

Mr. S. said he would not be astonished if they were to attempt a new version of the Old and New Testaments, and new model them to suit the policy of the times. Throw off such parts as were uncongenial to their interests, and leave the residue to God. They had already given the Scriptures an implied construction, as different from its literal sense, as they had that of the Constitution of the United States. He hoped none of the holy fathers of the church, whose duty it was to teach the Holy Scriptures as God himself had given them, and not as they would model them to suit the frailty of their nature, had given in to this ungodly opinion, that they could pare down the Old and New Testaments, so as to make a convenient religion of them, instead of an unerring one.

Mr. President, the Scriptures teach us that slavery was universally indulged among the holy fathers. The chosen people of God were slaves; and that, by His divine permission, Joseph was sold by his brethren to the Egyptian merchants, who carried him into slavery. There was no vengeance of Heaven upon this people for holding them in slavery. They were not relieved until God in his wisdom saw fit. Pharaoh was, for his temerity, drowned in the Red Sea, in pursuing them contrary to God's express will; but our Northern friends have not been afraid even of that, in their zeal to furnish the Southern States with Africans. They are better seamen than Pharaoh, and calculate by that means to elude the vigilance of Heaven; which they seem to disregard, if they can but elude the violated laws of their country.

The gentleman from New Hampshire, (Mr. Morril) in the plenitude of his religion and humanity, has told us this is a fine country, and that we have imported a new breed of sheep. Here is fine pasture ground, and better starve the negroes than abandon the sheep. He has told us his ancestors came to Plymouth in 1620. He could tell the gentleman that, very shortly after, they began to import slaves from Africa, and continued it until the Revolutionary war took place. . . .[19]

There was but one more view which he would take of this case. Much had been said of the effects of slavery upon society. He would compare the morality of the slaveholding States with that of the non-slaveholding States. He did not mean the morality of individuals, but he would compare the political morality of the States. South of the State of Pennsylvania you had heard of no rebellions, no insurrections, no delays in performing all the requisitions of the State and General Governments.

The State of Massachusetts had emancipated what slaves she had left, shortly after the Treaty of Paris in 1783. In three years after, they had a rebellion which shook the State to its centre. The courts of justice were broken up throughout the State.[20] The civil authority was put down. Recourse was had to arms, from one end of the State to the other. Battles ensued; some were killed, others wounded, others taken prisoners, and some hanged, or rather condemned, and pardoned by the Executive. It raged to such a degree, that the principal citizens had at one time determined to make no efforts to check it, that the imbecility of a republican government might be fully manifested, and some government of greater energy resorted to. What that Government would have been, he knew not; but he supposes they would have chosen a King. This statement was contained in Minot's history of that transaction, which he had then before him, and which had been furnished him from the public library.[21]

The State of Pennsylvania had freed her slaves in 1780. In January, 1791, the Congress of the United States had under consideration the subject of excise. The Legislature of Pennsylvania were then in session. They took up the subject with the same temper—with the same enthusiasm and heat—which they have so lately manifested on the Missouri question, and passed the following resolutions for instructing their members of the Senate to oppose the measure:

"House of Representatives, January 22, 1791.

The Legislature of the Commonwealth, ever attentive to the rights of their constituents, and conceiving it a duty incumbent on them to express their sentiments on such matters of a public nature as, in their opinion, have a tendency to destroy their rights, agree to the following resolutions:

*Resolved,* That any proceedings on the part of the United States tending to the collection of a revenue by means of excise, established upon principles subversive of the peace, liberty, and rights, of the citizens, ought to attract the attention of this House.

*Resolved,* That no public exigency within the knowledge or contemplation of this House, can, in their opinion, warrant the adoption of any species of taxation which shall violate those rights which are the basis of our Government, and which would exhibit the singular spectacle of a nation resolutely opposing the oppression of others, in order to enslave itself.

*Resolved,* That these sentiments be communicated to the Senators representing the State of Pennsylvania in the Senate of the United States, with a hope that they will oppose every part of the excise bill, now before the Congress, which shall militate against the just rights and liberties of the people."

This was a high-handed measure, to oppose the constituted authorities in this bold and menacing form, because they were about to lay a small duty on whiskey, that delicious beverage. This law was passed by Congress, and, the year following,

Mr. Neville, the inspector of the revenue, was often menaced. At length they broke out into an open insurrection in the neighborhood of Pittsburg. The public mind was much agitated. Companies armed themselves, and marched into the neighborhood of the inspector. *Brackenridge,* in his history of that insurrection, which Mr. S. had in his hand, gives the following account:

"The next morning, after day-break, the inspector, having just got out of bed and opened the door, discovered a number of armed men about the house, and, demanding of them who they were and whence they came, the answer was such as induced him to consider their intentions to be hostile; and, on refusing to disperse, he fired on them. The fire was returned, and a contest ensued. The negroes, from some adjoining small buildings, fired on the flank of the assailants, and they were repulsed with six wounded, one mortally."[22]

He wished to call the attention of gentlemen to this faithful attachment of the slaves; they repelled the insurgents, without an order even from the master. They wounded six, one mortally. This all passed in Pittsburg, and not a white man even approached the scene. The inspector's houses were all burned down the next day, and no man attempted to oppose them. These slaves have presented an example of fidelity and bravery in defence of their master, while the whole population of Pittsburg were terrified into submission. He presented this for the view of Marcus and his associates. It may serve them as a beacon.

This insurrection extended itself over a great part of the western section of Pennsylvania.[23] It required the strong arm of the General Government to quell it. A regular armed force was called out before its impetuosity could be checked; an impetuosity which threatened to overwhelm the State, if not the whole Union. Does Pennsylvania and Massachusetts wish those feelings and those scenes renewed? If they do, the course they have taken may lead them directly to it. The American people, of whom it was his pride and his glory that was one, were as honest as any other people in the world, and only wanted to be correctly informed, to do justice to every policy and every measure. But if, under the misguided influence of fanaticism and humanity, the impetuous torrent is once put in motion, what hand short of Omnipotence can stay it?

New York has been a slaveholding State, until very lately, in the strictest sense of the word. The Governor of New York recommended to the Legislature of that State, only three years ago, to take measures for the emancipation of their slaves. Two years ago these measures were taken; and at the next session of Congress thereafter, their Representatives and Senators came out upon this very Missouri question, as the champions of freedom; and that State has given as hopeful signs of a turbulent temper as either Pennsylvania or Massachusetts, for the time that she has had after emancipation. What progress she will make in revolutions time will develop.

Notes

1. "William Smith," *Dictionary of American Biography,* ed. Dumas Malone, 359–61 (New York: Charles Scribner's Sons, 1964); William W. Freehling, *Prelude to Civil War: The Nullification Controversy in South Carolina, 1816–1836* (New York: Harper and Row, 1968).

2. James Burrill Jr. was a Federalist senator representing Rhode Island from 1817 to 1820. *Habeas corpus* is a legal writ that protects individuals from unwarranted imprisonment by preventing the government from arresting and holding people without presenting formal charges to a judge.

3. Jonathan Roberts represented Pennsylvania as a Democratic-Republican senator from 1814 to 1821.

4. John Melish was a noted cartographer and travel writer from England who relocated to Philadelphia in 1811. He published *Travels through the United States of America, in the Years 1806 & 1807, and 1809, 1810, & 1811* (Philadelphia, 1818).

5. The Treaty of Ghent ended the War of 1812. It was signed on December 24, 1814. The tenth article of the treaty stated, "Whereas the Traffic in Slaves is irreconcilable with the principles of humanity and Justice, and whereas both His Majesty and the United States are desirous of continuing their efforts to promote its entire abolition, it is hereby agreed that both the contracting parties shall use their best endeavours to accomplish so desirable an object."

6. The American Colonization Society was established in 1816–17. See P. J. Staudenraus, *The African Colonization Movement, 1816–1865* (New York: Columbia University Press, 1961).

7. Nathanael Greene, a prominent general in the American campaign for independence, did in fact acquire a slave plantation in coastal Georgia to which he relocated in 1785. Terry Golway, *Washington's General: Nathanael Greene and the Triumph of the American Revolution* (New York: H. Holt, 2005).

8. Jesse Torrey, *A Portraiture of Domestic Slavery, in the United States* (Philadelphia, 1817); and John Kenrick, *Horrors of Slavery, in Two Parts . . . Demonstrating That Slavery Is Impolitic, Antirepublican, Unchristian, and Highly Criminal . . .* (Cambridge, Mass., 1817). For scholarship on pro- and antislavery political rhetoric in the early national era, see Matthew Mason, "The Battle of the Slaveholding Liberators: Great Britain, the United States, and Slavery in the Early Nineteenth Century," *William and Mary Quarterly,* 3rd. ser., 59 (July 2002): 665–96.

9. I have not included several paragraphs of Smith's speech (some 750 words). The deleted material developed the theme of the hypocrisy of northerners and Englishmen denouncing southern slavery.

10. Rufus King served as a Federalist senator for New York from 1789 to 1796 and again from 1813 to 1825.

11. David Lawrence Morril represented New Hampshire as a Democratic-Republican senator from 1817 to 1823.

12. Thomas Newton, *Dissertations on the Prophecies, Which Have Remarkably Been Fulfilled, and at This Time Are Fulfilling in the World,* 2nd ed., vol. 1 (London, 1759).

13. Demosthenes was a noted orator in Athens in the fourth century B.C.E.

14. Jonathan Roberts, a Democratic-Republican senator, represented Pennsylvania from 1814 to 1821; Prentiss Mellen was a Federalist senator from Massachusetts from 1818 to 1820.

15. Daniel Raymond was the author of *Thoughts on Political Economy* (Baltimore: F. Lucas Jr., 1820).

16. Harrison Gray Otis was a Federalist senator from Massachusetts from 1817 to 1822.

17. Thomas Jefferson, *Notes on the State of Virginia,* ed. David Waldstreicher (New York: Palgrave, 2002), query 18, 195–96.

18. Smith's summary of his 1818 speech—some 250 words—is not included in my transcript.

19. I have not included a section of the speech developing the accusation that northern congressmen opposed territorial expansion into the Louisiana territory (some fifteen hundred words).

20. The Treaty of Paris formally brought the Revolutionary War to an end. Shays's Rebellion was an uprising of western farmers in Massachusetts who were protesting the taxation policies enacted by the state legislature.

21. George Richards Minot, *The History of the Insurrections, in Massachusetts, in the Year 1786, and the Rebellion Consequent Thereon* ( Worcester, 1788).

22. Hugh Henry Brackenridge, *Incidents of the Insurrection in the Western Parts of Pennsylvania, in the Year 1794* (Philadelphia, 1795).

23. In the Whiskey Rebellion of 1794, Pennsylvania farmers in the western portions of the state organized an armed resistance against federal taxes levied against whiskey distilleries.

# CHAPTER 12

# Richard Furman, 1823

DURING A DECADE OF MOUNTING slaveholder fears about abolitionism and insurrection, South Carolina authors led the way toward a sectional defense of slavery. During the Missouri Controversy, South Carolina statesmen had already exhibited a willingness to pursue a stridently proslavery agenda in a public forum. In 1822, when Charleston slaveholders discovered what they believed to be a wide-scale insurrection plot involving perhaps thousands of slaves, many white residents of South Carolina determined that they must directly affirm the righteousness of their labor system or else risk losing their slaves altogether.[1] Into this charged atmosphere entered several well-established religious authorities. Following the trials of Denmark Vesey and his fellow accused conspirators, ministers such as the Baptist Richard Furman and the Episcopalian Frederick Dalcho published tracts that defended slavery as an integral ingredient of a moral slaveholding society.[2]

Well before the 1820s Furman had already emerged as a leading authority within the Baptist Church. Born in 1755, Furman came to maturity during the Revolutionary era. He converted to the Baptist faith in 1772 after listening to the sermons of a charismatic itinerant preacher. Over the next two years, Furman preached regularly in South Carolina churches and was ordained as a minister in May 1774, the same year that he started his own family. During the contest with England, Furman devoted himself to the patriotic cause. When Charleston fell to the British in 1780, he fled with his family to North Carolina, where he spent the remainder of the war. Following the war, Furman established himself as a successful minister and planter, acquiring substantial holdings in land and slaves and gaining the pulpit at the Charleston Baptist Church. Ministers such as Furman were largely responsible for moving the Baptist Church into the realm of respectability by the early nineteenth century. The denomination that had once been associated with radical antislavery sentiment had, by the turn of the century, become the chosen faith of many elite slaveholders. As an educated man with numerous friends occupying the first ranks of southern society, Furman was in an excellent position to establish the proslavery credentials of his denomination.

Although some Charleston residents argued against any public acknowledgment of Vesey's aborted insurrection, Furman insisted that the plot had provided slaveholders with a perfect opportunity to affirm the morality of slavery. In private correspondence with the South Carolina governor Thomas Bennett, the Baptist minister declared that the "lawfulness" of slavery was "positively stated in the Old Testament" and was "clearly re[c]ognised in the New." Urging the governor not to blame the insurrection on slave religion, Furman appealed to longstanding Christian doctrines that "the Sentiments & correspondent Dispositions of the religious Negroes, which they derive from the Bible" is "one of the best Securities we have to the domestic Peace & Safety of the State." During most of the eighteenth century, such reasoning had failed to sway southern planters. By the 1820s, however, white authorities had learned to recognize the advantages of a ruling identity grounded in organic Christian thought. Bennett's successor, Governor John L. Wilson, enthusiastically supported the publication of Furman's proslavery tract. In subsequent years southern authors could well expect to be embraced by their region for presenting ideas that had once been a quick ticket for persecution at the hands of the slaveholding community.

Furman, for his part, had no illusions that he was advancing creative doctrines about Christianity and human bondage. Decades before the Vesey controversy, Furman was already using his sermons to sketch out the contours of his organic vision of the master-slave relationship. Within his own household, he had long since adopted the posture of the benevolent Christian steward—an identity that enabled him to justify his ownership of slaves even as he profited from their exploitation and sale. Although Furman's work signaled the onset of a new wave of proslavery sectional publications in the South, Furman should be characterized less as a pioneer and more as a shepherd. Rather than entering new ideological territory, the prominent minister was pushing centuries-old doctrine in a useful political direction. Proslavery thought had finally entered the vocabulary of mainstream slaveholding society in the South.

⁂

*Rev. Dr. Richard Furman's Exposition of the Views of the Baptists Relative to the Coloured Population of the United States, in Communication to the Governor of South-Carolina* (Charleston: A. E. Miller, 1823)

Charleston, May 28th, 1823

Dear Sir,

Several of your fellow-citizens who have perused the Rev. Dr. Furman's communication, submitting the propriety of your recommending a *Day of Thanksgiving and Humiliation,* think the dissemination of it might be beneficial, and ask your sanction to have it published.

With regard, yours,
B. Elliott[3]

*His Excellency* Gov. Wilson

My Dear Sir,

The request made by you, in behalf of yourself and several of your fellow-citizens, is most readily granted. There can be no doubt that such doctrines, from such a source, will produce the best of consequences in our mixed population, and tend to make our servants not only more contented with their lot, but more useful to their owners. The great piety and learning of DOCTOR FURMAN, his long established character with the religious of every denomination throughout our State, will at once command the respectful attention of every reader.

Receive the assurances of my respect and regard.

John L. Wilson

Benjamin Elliott, Esq.
*Charleston*

Charleston, 24th December, 1822
Sir,

When I had, lately, the honour of delivering to your Excellency an Address, from the Baptist Convention in this State, requesting that a Day of Public Humiliation and Thanksgiving might be appointed by you, as our Chief Magistrate, to be observed by the Citizens of the State at large, in reference to two important recent events, in which the interposition of Divine Providence has been conspicuous, and in which the interests and feelings of our Citizens have been greatly concerned—viz: The protection afforded them from the horrors of an intended Insurrection; and the affliction they have suffered from the ravages of a dreadful Hurricane.—I took the liberty to suggest, that I had a further communication to make on behalf of the Convention, in which their sentiments would be disclosed respecting the policy of the measure proposed; and on the lawfulness of holding slaves—the subject being considered in a moral and religious point of view.

You were pleased, sir, to signify, that it would be agreeable to you to receive such a communication. And as it is incumbent on me, in faithfulness to the trust reposed in me, to make it, I now take the liberty of laying it before you.

The Political propriety of bringing the intended Insurrection into view by publicly acknowledging its prevention to be an instance of the Divine Goodness, manifested by a providential, gracious interposition, is a subject, which has employed the serious attention of the Convention; and, if they have erred in the judgment they have formed upon it, the error is, at least, not owing to a want of consideration, or of serious concern. They cannot view the subject but as one of great magnitude, and intimately connected with the interests of the whole State. The Divine Interposition has been conspicuous; and our obligations to be thankful are unspeakably great. And, as principles of the wisest and best policy lead nations, as well as individuals, to consider and acknowledge the government of the Deity, to feel their dependence on him and trust in him, to be thankful for his mercies, and to be humbled under his chastening rod; so, not only moral and religious duty, but also a regard to the best interests of the community appear to require of us, on the present occasion, that humiliation and thanksgiving, which are proposed by the Convention in their request. For a sense of the Divine Government has a meliorating influence on the minds of men, restraining them from crime, and disposing them to virtuous action. To those also, who are humbled before the Heavenly Majesty for their sins, and learn to be thankful for his mercies, the Divine Favour is manifested. From them judgments are averted, and on them blessings are bestowed.

The Convention are aware, that very respectable Citizens have been averse to the proposal under consideration; the proposal for appointing a Day of Public Thanksgiving for our preservation from the intended Insurrection, on account of the influence it might be supposed to have on the Black Population—by giving publicity to the subject *in their view,* and by affording them excitements to attempt something further of the same nature. These objections, however, the Convention view as either not substantial, or overbalanced by higher considerations. As to publicity, perhaps no fact is more generally known by the persons referred to; for the knowledge of it has been communicated by almost every channel of information, public and private, even by documents under the stamp of Public Authority; and has extended to every part of the State. But with the knowledge of the conspiracy is united the knowledge of its frustration; and of that, which Devotion and Gratitude should set in a strong light, *the merciful Interposition of Providence,* which produced that frustration. The more rational among that class of men, as well as others, know also, that our preservation from the evil intended by the conspirators, is a subject, which should induce us to render thanksgivings to the Almighty; and it is hoped and believed, that the truly enlightened and religiously disposed among them, of which there appear to be many, are ready to unite in those thanksgivings, from a regard to their own true interests; if therefore it is apprehended, that an undue importance would be given to the subject in their view, by making it the matter of public thanksgiving; that this would induce the designing and wicked to infer our fear and sense of weakness from the fact, and thus induce them to form some other scheme of mischief: Would not our silence, and the omission of an important religious duty, under these circumstances, undergo, at least, as unfavourable a construction, and with more reason?

But the Convention are persuaded, that publicity, rather than secrecy is the true policy to be pursued on this occasion; especially, when the subject is taken into view, in connexion with other truths, of high importance and certainty, which relate to it, and is placed in a just light; the evidence and force of which truths, thousands of this people, when informed, can clearly discern and estimate. It is proper, the Convention conceives, that the Negroes should know, that however numerous they are in some parts of these Southern States, they, yet, are not, even including all descriptions, bond and free, in the United States, but little more than one sixth part of the whole number of Inhabitants, estimating that number which it probably now is, at Ten Millions; and the Black and Coloured Population, according to returns made at 1,780,000; That their destitution in respect to arms, and the knowledge of using them, with other disabilities, would render their physical force, were they all united in a common effort, less than a tenth part of that, with which they would have to contend: That there are multitudes of the best informed and truly religious among them, who, from principle, as well as from prudence, would not unite with them, nor fail to disclose their machinations, when it should be in their power to do it: That, however in some parts of our Union there are Citizens, who favour the idea of general emancipation; yet, were they to see slaves in our Country, in arms, wading through blood and carnage to effect their purpose, they would do what both their duty and interest would require; unite under the government with their fellow-citizens at large to suppress the rebellion, and bring the authors of it to condign punishment: that it may be expected, in every attempt to raise an insurrection (should other attempts be made) as well as it was in that defeated here, that the prime movers in such a nefarious scheme, will so form their plan, that in a case of exigency, they may flee with their plunder and leave their deluded followers to suffer the punishment, which law and justice may inflict: and that, therefore, there is reason to conclude, on the most rational and just principles, that whatever partial success might at any time attend such a measure at the onset, yet, in this country, it must finally result in the discomfiture and ruin of the perpetrators; and in many instances pull down on the heads of the innocent as well as the guilty, an undistinguishing ruin.

On the lawfulness of holding slaves, considering it in a moral and religious view, the Convention think it their duty to exhibit their sentiments, on the present occasion, before your Excellency, because they consider their duty to God, the peace of the State, the satisfaction of scrupulous consciences, and the welfare of the slaves themselves, as intimately connected with a right view of the subject. The rather, because certain writers on politics, morals and religion, and some of them highly respectable, have advanced positions, and inculcated sentiments, very unfriendly to the principle and practice of holding slaves; and by some these sentiments have been advanced among us, tending in their nature, *directly* to disturb the domestic peace of the State, to produce insubordination and rebellion among the slaves, and to infringe the rights of our citizens; and *indirectly*, to deprive the slaves of religious privileges, by awakening in the minds of their masters a fear, that acquaintance with the Scriptures, and the enjoyment of these privileges would naturally produce the aforementioned effects; because the sentiments in opposition to the holding of slaves have been attributed, by their advocates, to the Holy Scriptures, and to the genius of Christianity. These sentiments, the Convention, on whose behalf I address your Excellency, cannot think just, or well founded: for the right of holding slaves is clearly established in the Holy Scriptures, both by precept and example. In the Old Testament, the Israelites were directed to purchase their bond-men and bond-maids of the Heathen nations: except they were of the Canaanites, for these were to be destroyed. And it is declared, that the persons purchased were to be their "bond-men forever;" and an "inheritance for them and their children." They were not to go out free in the year of jubilee, as the Hebrews, who had been purchased, were; the line being clearly drawn between them.* In example, they are presented to our view as existing in the families of the Hebrews as servants, or slaves, born in the house, or bought with money: so that the children born of slaves are here considered slaves as well as their parents.⁴ And to this well known state of things, as to its reason and order, as well as to special privileges, St. Paul appears to refer, when he says, "But I was free born."⁵

In the New Testament, the Gospel History, or representation of facts, presents us with a view correspondent with that, which is furnished by other authentic ancient histories of the state of the world at the commencement of Christianity. The powerful Romans, had succeeded in empire, the polished Greeks; and, under both empires, the countries they possessed and governed were full of slaves. Many of these with their masters, were converted to the Christian Faith, and received, together with them into the Christian Church, while it was yet under the ministry of the inspired Apostles. In things purely spiritual, they appear to have enjoyed equal privileges; but their relationship, as masters and slaves, was not dissolved. Their respective duties are strictly enjoined. The masters are not required to emancipate their slaves; but to give them the things that are just and equal, forbearing threatening; and to remember, they also have a master in Heaven. The "servants under the yoke"† (bond-servants or slaves) mentioned by Paul to Timothy, as having "believing masters," are not authorized by him to demand of them

---

*See Leviticus, xxv.44.45.46. &c.

†*Upo zugon Douloi;* bond-servants, or slaves. *Doulos* is the proper term for slaves; it is here in the plural and rendered more expressive by being connected with yoke—UNDER THE YOKE.

emancipation, or to employ violent means to obtain it; but are directed to "account their masters worthy of all honour," and "not to despise them, because they were brethren" in religion; "but the rather to do them service, because they were faithful and beloved partakers of the Christian benefit."[6] Similar directions are given by him in other places, and by other Apostles. And it gives great weight to the argument, that in this place, Paul follows his directions concerning servants with a charge to Timothy, as an Evangelist, to teach and exhort men to observe this doctrine.

Had the holding of slaves been a moral evil, it cannot be supposed, that the inspired Apostles, who feared not the faces of men, and were ready to lay down their lives in the cause of their God, would have tolerated it, for a moment, in the Christian Church. If they had done so on a principle of accommodation, in cases where the masters remained heathen, to avoid offences and civil commotion; yet, surely, where both master and servant were Christian, as in the case before us, they would have enforced the law of Christ, and required, that the master should liberate his slave in the first instance. But, instead of this, they let the relationship remain untouched, as being lawful and right, and insist on the relative duties.

In proving this subject justifiable by Scriptural authority, its morality is also proved; for the Divine Law never sanctions immoral actions.

The Christian golden rule, of doing to others, as we would they should do to us, has been urged as an unanswerable argument against holding slaves. But surely this rule is never to be urged against that order of things, which the Divine government has established; nor do our desires become a standard to us, under this rule, unless they have a due regard to justice, propriety and the general good.

A father may very naturally desire, that his son should be obedient to his orders: Is he, therefore, to obey the orders of his son? A man might be pleased to be exonerated from his debts by the generosity of his creditors; or, that his rich neighbour should equally divide his property with him; and in certain circumstances might desire these to be done: Would the mere existence of this desire, oblige him to exonerate *his* debtors, and to make such division of his property? Consistency and generosity, indeed, might require it of him, if he were in circumstances, which would justify the act of generosity; but, otherwise, either action might be considered as the effect of folly and extravagance.

If the holding of slaves is lawful, or according to the Scriptures; then this Scriptural rule can be considered as requiring no more of the master, in respect of justice (whatever it may do in point of generosity) than what he, if a slave, could, consistently, wish to be done to himself, while the relationship between master and servant should be still continued.

In this argument, the advocates for emancipation blend the ideas of injustice and cruelty with those, which respect the existence of slavery, and consider them as inseparable. But, surely, they may be separated. A bond-servant may be treated with justice and humanity as a servant; and a master may, in an important sense, be the guardian and even father of his slaves.

They become a part of his family, (the whole, forming under him a little community) and the care of ordering it, and of providing for its welfare, devolves on him. The children, the aged, the sick, the disabled, and the unruly, as well as those, who are capable of service and orderly, are the objects of his care: The labour of these, is applied to the benefit of those, and to their own support, as well as to that of the master. Thus, what is effected, and often at a great public expense, in a free community, by taxes, benevolent institutions, bettering houses, and penitentiaries, lies here on the master, to be performed by him, whatever contingencies may happen; and often occasions much expense, care and trouble, from which the servants are free. Cruelty, is, certainly, inadmissible; but servitude may be consistent with such degrees of happiness as men usually attain in this imperfect state of things.

Some difficulties arise with respect to bringing a man, or class of men, into a state of bondage. For crime, it is generally agreed, a man may be deprived of his liberty. But, may he not be divested of it by his own consent, directly, or indirectly given; And, especially, when this assent, though indirect, is connected with an attempt to take away the liberty, if not the lives of others? The Jewish law favors the former idea: And, if the inquiry on the latter be taken in the affirmative, which appears to be reasonable, it will establish a principle, by which it will appear, that the Africans brought to America were, in general, slaves, by their own consent, before they came from their own country, or fell into the hands of white men. Their law of nations, or general usage, having, by common consent the force of law, justified them, while carrying on their petty wars, in killing their prisoners or reducing them to slavery; consequently, in selling them, and these ends they appear to have proposed to themselves; the nation, therefore, or individual, which was overcome, reduced to slavery, and sold, would have done the same by the enemy, had victory declared on their, or his side. Consequently, the man made a slave in this manner, might be said to be made so by his own consent, and by the indulgence of barbarous principles.

That Christian nations have not done all they might, or should have done, on a principle of Christian benevolence, for the civilization and conversion of the Africans; that much cruelty has been practised in the slave trade, as the benevolent Wilberforce, and others have shown; that much tyranny has been exercised by individuals, as masters over their slaves, and that the religious interests of the latter have been too much neglected by many cannot, will not be denied. But the fullest proof of these facts, will not also prove, that the holding men in subjection, as slaves, is a moral evil, and inconsistent with the Christianity. Magistrates, husbands, and fathers, have proved tyrants. This does not prove, that magistracy, the husband's right to govern, and parental authority, are unlawful and wicked. The individual who abuses his authority, and acts with cruelty, must answer for it at the Divine tribunal; and civil authority should interpose to prevent or punish it; but neither civil nor ecclesiastical authority can consistently interfere with the possession and legitimate exercise of a right given by the Divine Law.

If the above representation of the Scriptural doctrine, and the manner of obtaining slaves from Africa is just; and if also purchasing them has been the means of saving human life, which there is great reason to believe it has; then, however the slave trade, in present circumstances, is justly censurable, yet might motives of humanity and even piety have been originally brought into operation in the purchase of slaves, when sold in the circumstances we have described. If, also, by their own confession, which has been made in manifold instances, their condition, when they have come into the hands of humane masters here, has been greatly bettered by the change; if it is, ordinarily, really better, as many assert, than that of thousands of the poorer classes in countries reputed civilized and free; and, if, in addition to all other considerations, the translation from their native country to this has been the means of their mental and religious improvement, and so of obtaining salvation, as many of themselves have joyfully and thankfully confessed —then may the just and humane master, who rules his slaves and provides for them, according to Christian principles, rest satisfied, that he is not, in holding them, chargeable with moral evil, nor with acting, in this respect, contrary to the genius of Christianity.—It appears to be equally clear, that those, who by reasoning on abstract principles, are induced to favour the scheme of general emancipation, and who ascribe their sentiments to Christianity, should be particularly careful, however benevolent their intentions may be, that they do not by a perversion of the Scriptural doctrine, through their wrong views of it, not only invade the domestic and religious peace and rights of our Citizens, on this subject; but, also by an intemperate zeal, prevent indirectly, the religious improvement of the people they design, professedly, to benefit; and, perhaps, become, evidently, the means of producing in our country, scenes of anarchy and blood; and all this in a vain attempt to bring about a state of things, which, if arrived at, would not probably better the state of that people; which is thought, by men of observation, to be generally true of the Negroes in the Northern States, who have been liberated.

To pious minds it has given pain to hear men, respectable for intelligence and morals, sometimes say, that holding slaves is indeed indefensible, but that to us it is necessary, and must be supported. On this principle, mere politicians, unmindful of morals, may act. But surely, in a moral and religious view of the subject, this principle is inadmissible. It cannot be said, that theft, falsehood, adultery and murder, are become necessary and must be supported. Yet there is reason to believe, that some of honest and pious intentions have found their minds embarrassed if not perverted on this subject, by this plausible but unsound argument. From such embarrassment the view exhibited above affords relief.

The Convention, Sir, are far from thinking that Christianity fails to inspire the minds of its subjects with benevolent and generous sentiments; or that liberty rightly understood, or enjoyed, is a blessing of little moment. The contrary of these positions they maintain. But they also consider benevolence as consulting the truest and best interests of its objects; and view the happiness of liberty as well as of religion, as consisting not in the name or form, but in the reality. While men remain in the chains of ignorance and error, and under the dominion of tyrant lusts and passions, they cannot be free. And the more freedom of action they have in this state, they are but the more qualified by it to do injury, both to themselves and others. It is, therefore, firmly believed, that general emancipation to the Negroes in this country, would not, in present circumstances, be for their own happiness, as a body; while it would be extremely injurious to the community at large in various ways: And, if so, then it is not required even by benevolence. But acts of benevolence and generosity must be free and voluntary; no man has a right to compel another to the performance of them. This is a concern, which lies between a man and his God. If a man has obtained slaves by purchase, or inheritance, and the holding of them as such is justifiable by the law of God; why should he be required to liberate them, because it would be a generous action, rather than another on the same principle, to release his debtors, or sell his lands and houses, and distribute the proceeds among the poor? These also would be generous actions: Are they, therefore obligatory? Or, if obligatory, in certain circumstances, as personal, voluntary acts of piety and benevolence, has any man or body of men, civil or ecclesiastic, a right to require them? Surely those, who are advocates for compulsory, or strenuous measures to bring about emancipation, should duly weigh this consideration.

Should, however, a time arrive, when the Africans in our country might be found qualified to enjoy freedom; and, when they might obtain it in a manner consistent with the interest and peace of the community at large, the Convention would be happy in seeing them free: And so they would, in seeing the state of the poor, the ignorant and the oppressed of every description, and of every country meliorated; so that the reputed free might be free indeed, and happy. But there seems to be just reason to conclude that a considerable part of the human race, whether they bear openly the character of slaves or are reputed free men, will continue in such circumstances, with mere shades of variation, while the world continues. It is evident, that men are sinful creatures, subject to affliction and to death, as the consequences of their nature's pollution and guilt: That they are now in a state of probation; and that God as a Righteous, All-wise Sovereign, not only disposes of them as he pleases, and bestows upon them many unmerited blessings and comforts, but subjects them also to privations, afflictions and trials, with the merciful intention of making all their afflictions, as well as their blessings, work finally for their good; if they embrace his salvation, humble themselves before him, learn righteousness, and submit to his holy will. To have them brought to this happy state is the great object of Christian benevolence, and of Christian piety; for this state is not only connected with the truest happiness, which can be enjoyed in time, but is introductory to eternal life and blessedness in the future world: And the salvation of men is intimately connected with the glory of their God and Redeemer.

And here I am brought to a part of the general subject, which, I confess to your Excellency, the Convention, from a sense of their duty, as a body of men, to whom important concerns of Religion are confided, have particularly at heart, and wish it may be seriously considered by all our Citizens: This is the religious interests of the Negroes. For though they are slaves, they are also men; and are with ourselves accountable creatures; having immortal souls, and being destined to future eternal award. Their religious interests claim a regard from their masters of the most serious nature; and it is indispensable. Nor can the community at large, in a right estimate of their duty and happiness, be indifferent on this subject. To the truly benevolent it must be pleasing to know, that a number of masters, as well as ministers and pious individuals, of various Christian denominations among us, do conscientiously regard this duty; but there is great reason to believe, that it is neglected and disregarded by many.

The Convention are particularly unhappy in considering, that an idea of the Bible's teaching the doctrine of emancipation as necessary, and tending to make servants insubordinate to proper authority, has obtained access to any mind; both on account of its direct influence on those, who admit it; and the fear it excites in others, producing the effects before noticed. But it is hoped, it has been evinced, that the idea is an erroneous one; and, that it will be seen, that the influence of a right acquaintance with that Holy Book tends directly and powerfully, by promoting the fear and love of God, together with just and peaceful sentiments toward men, to produce one of the best securities to the public, for the internal and domestic peace of the state.

It is also a pleasing consideration, tending to confirm these sentiments, that in the late projected scheme for producing an insurrection among us, there were very few of those who were, as members attached to regular churches, (even within the sphere of its operations) who appear to have taken a part in the wicked plot, or indeed to whom it was made known; of some churches it does not appear, that there were any. It is true, that a considerable number of those who were found guilty and executed, laid claim to a religious character; yet several of these were grossly immoral, and, in general, they were members of an irregular body, which called itself the *African Church,* and had intimate connection and intercourse with a similar body of men in a Northern City, among whom the supposed right to emancipation is strenuously advocated.

The result of this inquiry and reasoning, on the subject of slavery, brings us, Sir, if I mistake not, very regularly to the following conclusions:—That the holding of slaves is justifiable by the doctrine and example contained in Holy writ; and is, therefore consistent with Christian uprightness, both in sentiment and conduct. That, all things considered, the Citizens of America have in general obtained the African slaves, which they possess, on principles, which can be justified; though much cruelty has indeed been exercised towards them by many, who have been concerned in the slave-trade, and by others who have held them here, as slaves in their service; for which the authors of this cruelty are accountable. That slavery, when tempered with humanity and justice, is a state of tolerable happiness; equal, if not superior, to that which many poor enjoy in countries reputed free. That a master has a scriptural right to govern his slaves so as to keep them in subjection; to demand and receive from them a reasonable service; and to correct them for the neglect of duty, for their vices and transgressions; but that to impose on them unreasonable, rigorous services, or to inflict on them cruel punishment, he has neither a scriptural nor a moral right. At the same time it must be remembered, that, while he is receiving from them their uniform and best services, he is required by the Divine Law, to afford them protection, and such necessaries and conveniencies of life as are proper to their condition as servants; so far as he is enabled by their services to afford them these comforts, on just and rational principles. That it is the positive duty of servants to reverence their master, to be obedient, industrious, faithful to him, and careful of his interests; and without being so, they can neither be the faithful servants of God, nor be held as regular members of the Christian Church. That as claims to freedom as a *right,* when that right is forfeited, or has been lost, in such a manner as has been represented, would be unjust; and as all attempts to obtain it by violence and fraud would be wicked; so all representations made to them by others, on such censurable principles, or in a manner tending to make them discontented, and, finally, to produce such unhappy effects and consequences, as have been before noticed, cannot be friendly to them (as they certainly are not to the community at large,) nor consistent with righteousness: Nor can the conduct be justified, however in some it may be palliated by pleading benevolence in intention, as the motive. That masters having the disposal of the persons, time and labour of their servants, and being the heads of families, are bound, on principles of moral and religious duty, to give these servants religious instruction; or at least, to afford them opportunities, under proper regulations to obtain it: And to grant religious privileges to those, who desire them, and furnish proper evidence of their sincerity and uprightness: Due care being at the same time taken, that they receive their instructions from right sources, and from their connexions, where they will not be in danger of having their minds corrupted by sentiments unfriendly to the domestic and civil peace of the community. That, where the life, comfort, safety and religious interest of so large a number of human beings, as this class of persons is among us, are concerned; and, where they must necessarily, as slaves, be so much at the disposal of their masters; it appears to be a just and necessary concern of the Government, not only to provide laws to prevent or punish insurrections, and other violent and villainous conduct among them (which are indeed necessary;) but, on the other hand, laws, also, to prevent their being oppressed and injured by unreasonable, cruel masters, and others; and to afford them, in respect of morality and religion, such privileges as may comport with the peace and safety of the state, and with those relative duties existing between masters and servants, which the word of God enjoins. It is, also, believed to be a just conclusion, that the interest and security of the state would be promoted, by allowing, under proper regulations, considerable religious privileges, to such of this class, as know how to estimate them aright, and have given suitable evidence of their own good principles, uprightness and fidelity; by attaching them, from principles of gratitude and love, to the interests of their masters and the state; and thus rendering their fidelity firm and constant. While on the other hand, to lay them under an interdict, as some have supposed necessary, in a case where reason, conscience, the genius of Christianity and salvation are concerned, on account of the bad conduct of others, would be felt as oppressive, tend to sour and alienate their minds from their masters and the public, and to make them vulnerable to temptation. All which is, with deference, submitted to the consideration of your Excellency.

With high respect, I remain, personally, and on behalf of the Convention, Sir, your very obedient and humble servant,

RICHARD FURMAN

*President of the Baptist State Convention*

His Excellency GOVERNOR WILSON

Notes

1. Historians have recently debated whether a widespread insurrection plot actually existed. See Michael P. Johnson, "Denmark Vesey and His Co-Conspirators," *William and Mary Quarterly*, 3rd ser., 58 (October 2001): 915–76; Douglas R. Egerton, *He Shall Go Out Free: The Lives of Denmark Vesey* (Madison, Wis.: Madison House, 1999); and the roundtable in the *William and Mary Quarterly*, 3rd ser., 59 (January 2002): 135–202.

2. Frederick Dalcho, *Practical Considerations Founded on the Scriptures Relative to the Slave Population of South-Carolina* (Charleston, 1823). For my portrait of Furman, I have relied

on James A. Rogers, *Richard Furman: Life and Legacy* (Macon, Ga.: Mercer University Press, 1985); Zaqueu Moreira de Oliveira, "Richard Furman, Father of the Southern Baptist Convention," in *The Lord's Free People in a Free Land,* ed. William R. Estep, 87–98 (Fort Worth: School of Theology, Southwestern Baptist Theological Seminary, 1976); Sylvia R. Frey, *Water from the Rock: Black Resistance in a Revolutionary Age* (Princeton, N.J.: Princeton University Press, 1991); Wood Furman, *A History of the Charleston Baptist Association* (Charleston, 1811); and the Richard Furman Papers, South Caroliniana Library, University of South Carolina. For the quotation from Furman's letter to Governor Bennett, see Jeffrey Robert Young, *Domesticating Slavery: The Master Class in Georgia and South Carolina, 1670–1837* (Chapel Hill: University of North Carolina Press, 1999), 169.

3. Benjamin Elliot (whose name was typically spelled in this fashion) was a Charleston jurist and author.

4. Leviticus 25:39–55.

5. Acts 22:28.

6. 1 Timothy 6:2.

# CHAPTER 13

# Charles Cotesworth Pinckney, 1829

THE PINCKNEY FAMILY COULD CLAIM one of the oldest, most accomplished and most respected lineages in South Carolina. During the colonial period, family members had coordinated the militia and served in prominent official capacities such as chief justice. During the Revolutionary and Early National periods, Charles Pinckney (1757–1824) and his second cousins Charles Cotesworth Pinckney (1746–1825) and Thomas Pinckney (1750–1828) entered the first ranks of the American leadership, gaining prominence for their military and diplomatic contributions (not to mention their roles at the Constitutional Convention of 1787 and their candidacies for and tenures in various political offices). Thomas Pinckney's son Charles Cotesworth Pinckney (1789–1865) was born soon after the ratification of the federal Constitution his uncle and namesake had helped to draft. Given his family's prominent role in the new nation, the younger Charles Cotesworth Pinckney maintained a relatively low profile. In 1811 he married Phoebe Caroline Elliott, the descendant of another elite Carolina family. Pinckney became a planter in Abbeville District, South Carolina, and he and his wife raised several children, including Charles Cotesworth Pinckney (1812–1898), a well-respected minister in the Episcopalian Church.[1]

By the end of the eighteenth century, the Pinckney family had already played an active role in the defense of slavery. In particular, Charles Cotesworth Pinckney (1746–1825) had helped to protect slavery from federal tampering during the federal constitutional convention. Alienated by the antislavery sentiment of many of the northern delegates, the elder Pinckney reminded them that "if slavery be wrong, it is justified by the example of all the world," including "the case of Greece[,] Rome & other an[c]ient States," not to mention "the sanction given [to slavery] by France, England, Holland & other modern States."[2] In private correspondence with his wife, Pinckney reflected organic assumptions about the master-slave relationship, lamenting evidence that some southern slaveholders failed to supply their bondservants with sufficient food and clothing. Charles Cotesworth Pinckney (1789–1865) clearly shared his uncle's vision of slavery as an institution that should recognize the slaves' humanity. Pinckney's wife, for example, reported in 1831 that Pinckney had invited a minister to the plantation to preach to the slaves, an act for which they "express much gratitude." When their son, Charles Cotesworth Pinckney (1812–1898), wrote a biography of his grandfather Thomas Pinckney, he took care to emphasize the mutual affections between slaves and masters in the Pinckney family.

Hence, when Charles Cotesworth Pinckney (1789–1865) addressed the South-Carolina Agricultural Society in 1829, he offered proslavery principles that were deeply ingrained in his family identity. During a period when state authorities grappled with the potential threat that Christianity posed against slavery, Pinckney emphasized the ways in which slave missions would buttress the institution by instilling a sense of obedience and duty among enslaved African Americans. His tract, which was immediately published and was sufficiently popular to merit a second edition, offered arguments that were perfectly consistent with those of colonial missionaries such as Thomas Bacon. No doubt these organic principles were ones that Pinckney had internalized as he grew to maturity in turn-of-the-century South Carolina. His decision to present them publicly signified the growing political momentum that such ideas generated during an era when slaveholders increasingly collided with antislavery voices.

<hr />

CHARLES COTESWORTH PINCKNEY, *An Address Delivered in Charleston, before the Agricultural Society of South-Carolina. At Its Anniversary Meeting, on Tuesday, the 18th August, 1829* (Charleston: A. E. Miller, 1829)

August 18th, 1829.

*On Motion*—*Resolved, "That the thanks of this Society be presented to* Mr. C. C. Pinckney, *for his very able and interesting Address delivered this day, and that a copy be requested for publication," which motion being seconded, was unanimously agreed to.*

*Extract from the Minutes.*

Charles E. Rowand, *Secretary.*

### Address.

Mr. President and Gentlemen:

I have endeavoured to select a topic of sufficient interest to attract attention, and to confine our observations within the stricter limits of agricultural speculation. This has proved no easy task to one, whose want of skill in those departments of the Science, precludes a possibility of advancing novel ideas, on the subject of Soils, Implements and Manures. These having already been fully and ably discussed, warrant a deviation from the usual course, to a theme, which has hitherto occupied a min[o]r share of public attention. Under this impression it is proposed to direct our thoughts to that class of beings, who, occupying a subordinate station in society, are of paramount importance in Southern Husbandry—whose actual condition is too little known to strengthen and fortify the support of our friends, or to repel the attacks of misguided and unwearied foes. That Slavery, as it exists here, is a greater or more unusual evil than befalls the poor in general, we are not prepared to admit; and apprehend that its extinction would be attended with calamity to the country, and the people connected with it, in every character and relation. Believing that no necessity exists for such extinction, it is proposed to demonstrate, that the situation of the slave of America, will not suffer by comparison with that of the labouring classes of Europe, or perhaps of our own more favoured land. In comparing the different degrees of misery attached to the operatives of free and slave-holding states, we may arrive at results not unfavourable to the latter, and in examining the long train of "ills that flesh is heir to," we may find, that if the absence of mental and bodily pain be the test of human happiness, the slave might sometimes be a loser, could he exchange places with half the freemen in the world. To form a correct estimate of the advantages attending their condition, we must review the evils of poverty, and examine in what degree they affect the welfare of the slave.

One of the greatest calamities which afflict the poor of the Old World is famine; we read of whole communities suffering from hunger and its consequent diseases, a shocking instance of which occurred a few years since in Ireland. It may be confidently asked, who ever saw a famished slave; every planter would gladly compound to furnish them with more than they can possibly consume, could he be protected from a system of plunder, carried on by the negroes, to provide, not the necessaries, but the luxuries of life—rum, sugar, tobacco and finery. The same dictates of policy and humanity which induce a man to feed his horse, or ox, compel him to feed his slave; and the latter has this advantage over his four-footed fellow-labourer, that he can tell his wants, and when his owner is barbarian enough to withhold the necessary food, he has always intellect, and generally opportunity, to supply the deficiency.

Sickness, another evil much aggravated by poverty, is rendered less grievous by their situation. From diseases of climate they are generally exempt; they thrive and increase, where the white man sickens and dies. Their agricultural occupation is more conducive to health than that of the Manufacturer, the Mechanic, the Merchant, or those who pursue the learned Professions; and when sickness, and even death approach, their bodily pains are not augmented by any surpassing agony of mind, for the future welfare of those, who are near and dear.

No situation can be imagined more thoroughly wretched than that of the free labourer, who feels the indications of disease, and is certain that abject penury and suffering must overtake and overwhelm his helpless family, deprived of his support. Slavery has no draught more bitter than this. Beyond mere animal suffering,

the slave has nothing to dread; his family are provided in food, shelter, and raiment, whether he live or die. The few proprietors who are devoid of humanity,
are instigated by interest, that never slumbering incentive, to provide for the
invalid, on whose health and labour their income depends. Careful females are
appointed to nurse the sick, and medical assistance generally procured: while the
poor, free man, suffering under the same disease, and unable to employ nurse or
physician, is frequently quacked into the bills of mortality, by the nostrums of his
charitable neighbours.

War is a third evil which falls with no unsparing hand on the labouring class of
older nations: and, to the poor inhabitant, is often accompanied by every variety
of wretchedness. To be wounded or killed without even knowing the cause for
which their lives are thrown away, is a special blessing, provided by their rulers,
for the poor and free; and is certainly a harder fate than that of the slave, who seldom receives a few stripes without knowing the reason; and whose punishments
are of a similar nature to those inflicted on sailors in America, on soldiers and
sailors in Great Britain, and on the great boys of her great seminaries, Eton, West-
minster, and Harrow. The knout of Russia, the bastinado of China, and the various
implements with which the few, who are rich and powerful, inflict summary justice on the many, who are weak and poor, either as penalties for crime or incen-
tives to labour; all tend to prove that human nature is the same in every period
and in every clime; and that coercion, or stimulus in some form, is an indispensable requisite to the performance of duty. In regulating the proportion between
transgression and its consequences, there is this exception in favour of the slave;
that, however heinous his offence, it is always in the interest of the owner, or overseer, that punishment be not excessive and stop short, not only of life or limb,
but loss of labour; and in numberless instances, they escape with less severity
than they deserve, from the apprehension, that in punishing them, the owner
may punish himself by the loss of their services. They have another advantage over
the ignorant poor of every description; the rule of law, "*ignorantia legis neminem
excusat,*" is evidently founded on the barbarous necessity of the case, and the free
poor are frequently its victims;[3] to punish a man for an action which he did not
know was illegal, is so replete with injustice and absurdity, that reason and religion both revolt at it; such, it has been shewn, are the privileges the slave enjoys,
that he often escapes merited castigation for wilful transgression; and many arrive
at what cannot be called a good old age, so laden with the sins of theft, bigamy,
and other enormities, that had they been born free, with the fabled lives of the
cat, they would have forfeited them all to the offended majesty of the laws. In
returning to our third head—the calamities of war—it may be necessary to dwell
on those evils which we only know by description, and for that reason are unable
to estimate in their full extent. The laurel, that solitary ornament of the forest, is

destined for the head that plans, but not the hand that executes, the most brilliant military achievements. The renown of the fairest fields of fame, seldom descends to any lower grade than general officers. In support of this position it may be stated, that with few exceptions, the name is unknown to history, of any private soldier who distinguished himself in battle, from the days of Hastings and Agincourt, to those of Waterloo. Now, take from war its only charms, the glory of conquest and the enjoyment of power, confined to a few; and what remains for the thousands who follow in its train, but every species of want, misery, and vice. Nor are these limited to the army of one power; a state of war implies different armies in different countries; and the poor inhabitants who are not enrolled, remain liable to all the privations and disasters incident of that region which becomes the seat of war, or that which is stripped of its most active population and valuable supplies, to invade an enemy's territory. It is not denied that war may be a necessary evil, wisely designed to reduce redundant population, preserve a balance of power, or accomplish other ends which human reason can neither develop or comprehend; it is only here intended to shew, that from all its miseries and horrors of every degree, from the sufferings of the French in the Russian campaign, down to the inconveniences of a militia fine; our slaves are happily and totally exempt. It has thus been our endeavour to prove, that those of the New World are not exposed to the three national imprecations of War, Pestilence and Famine.

Much has been said and written about the treatment and condition of these people, by Abolitionists and others, who are striving, against experience, to keep up that farce of Philanthropy. Not living among us, and having perchance seen some abolition pictures, where a white man is represented with a lash, and a black one with his hands tied, they charitably conclude, that such are the constant occupations of the Southern Planter. With these ideal views of Slavery, the advocates of its abandonment, disbelieving all statements from the South as interested or untrue, and preferring the suggestions of their own morbid sensibility, are invoking all the powers of Heaven and Earth to abolish Slavery; and, like Peter the Hermit, may yet preach a crusade, and send a band against us, as deluded, and we trust as unsuccessful, as that which attempted the rescue of the Holy Sepulchre.[4] The lucubrations of these visionaries are entitled to as much consideration from us, as a Treatise written in Florida, to enlighten our Eastern Brethren in the art of taking or preserving codfish, would command on the Banks of Newfoundland. Should courtesy dictate a more serious notice, we may safely declare, that we need no better rules of faith and practice, no other guides for human conduct, than the Scriptures afford. Numerous passages in the Mosaic dispensation sanction this system. The denunciations of Noah on the posterity of his second son, clearly indicate that state of servitude which has verified the prediction: nor have we yet discovered in holy writ, that the abolitionists of the nineteenth century, are destined to restore them to a level with the descendants of his brethren. If Slavery be inconsistent with the genius and spirit of Christianity, (as has been more frequently asserted than proved,) how shall we account for the total silence of its founders on this subject? At the period of the Christian era, it had long prevailed in various modifications over the known world. Yet in all the special instructions of our Saviour, in all his general references to the old Law, not one word condemns the practice. More recent scriptural authority is found in the writings of the great Apostle of the Gentiles. His instructions are even more minute than those of his master; is it possible that St. Paul, amid his multifarious directions, descending to the minutiae of domestic arrangement and female attire, would have omitted so important a topic, had he considered it a modern evil? In writing to Philemon, to intercede for his fugitive slave, Onesimus, (who had been converted by his preaching, whilst he was a prisoner at Rome,) he had an opportunity of reproving him for an evil practice, had the Apostle deemed it such, especially when we consider the eminent piety, "the love and faith towards the Lord Jesus, and towards all saints," which he ascribes to Philemon, the master of the runaway.*

* *Scriptural references, proving the antiquity and prevalence of Slavery.*
    Genesis, ch. ix. ver. 25; ch. xvii. ver. 13, 23; ch. xx. ver. 14; ch. xxxvii. ver. 27, 36.
    Exodus, ch. xxi. ver. 1–6, 20, 21, 26, 27.
    Leviticus, ch. xix. ver. 20; ch. xxv. ver. 39, 40, 44–46, 53.
    Deuteronomy, ch. xv. ver. 12, 17; ch. xx. ver. 14.
    II Kings, ch. iv. ver. 1.
  *References from the New Testament.*
    Matthew, ch. xviii. ver. 25.
    Epistle to Ephesians, ch. vi. ver. 5–8.
    Colossians, ch. iii. ver. 22–25; ch. iv. ver. 1.
    I. Timothy, ch. ii. ver. 9; ch. vi. ver. 1, 2.
    Titus, ch. ii. ver. 9, 10.
    Epistle to Philemon.

As the arguments drawn from the Sacred Writings, appear entirely in our favour, let us consider the objections of those who differ from us in opinion. The most plausible reason they urge, is, that the golden rule cannot apply to our case. If we understand this maxim, it signifies, that we should do unto others that, which, in an exchange of circumstances, we would wish them to do unto us. We do not interpret this rule to direct a rich man, who meets a beggar, to put him into immediate possession of his estate, and thus become a mendicant himself; but to bestow that charity which is adapted to the wants and condition of its object. These people are the poor whom we are bound to cherish and protect; the attachment existing between master and slave is a more active principle than that which unites the poor to the affluent under any other relation. In no free country, are the indigent so well treated by the wealthy, as our negroes are by their owners. Many Planters, not actuated by duty, or charity, use their people with all the kindness and equity

Another argument in favour of our system, which ought to satisfy unprejudiced minds, arises from the remarkable fact, that amidst all the plans and projects of abolition, no humane and rational means of carrying it into effect have ever been devised. Sad experience has already exposed the absurdity and cruelty of African colonization. Having sufficiently fertilized their first settlement with that richest of all manures, the human bodies of those who settled at the Isle of Sherbro; another charnel house has been selected under the appellation of Liberia. The avowed objects of the Society are, to furnish an asylum for the free blacks of the United States, and to afford a home to those who may hereafter be emancipated. We think both classes, bond and free, better in America. Accustomed to a comparatively healthy climate, they fall a prey to African diseases almost as readily as the whites. Their moral and intellectual condition here, is not such as to induce rational expectation of their evangelizing or civilizing that, or any quarter of the globe. There is greater probability that the few, who survive the ravages of disease, will return to the superstitions of their fathers, the prevailing creeds of the multitudes around them; than that the natives should be induced to embrace Christianity, by untaught and unconverted emigrants. We cannot but admire the skill with which this latter view, of a religious tendency, has been blended with the other, and real objects of the Society; whereby hundreds of pious enthusiasts are enlisted in what they deem a sacred cause, whose motives cannot but command our respect, while we deprecate their effects on the objects of their solicitude. Cordially approving the benevolent Missionary enterprises which distinguish the present age, and admitting that Africa presents a field "white for the harvest," we cannot perceive the necessity of sacrificing on her shores, hundreds of human victims, whose deaths are not conducive to the desired end. If the Colonists are designed to become instrumental in converting the natives, should they not be instructed in the doctrines they are to teach, before they are sent away? And, is it necessary, at great expense of life and treasure, to found and maintain Colonies merely to furnish Missionaries; when the sums expended in Colonization, would be amply sufficient to educate all, who are capable of becoming useful in disseminating the precepts of religion? An institution for this purpose, called the African Mission School, has been recently established at Hartford, (Connecticut,) which promises more benefit to benighted Africa, than all the colonial schemes, British and American, which have been pursued, with very limited success, for thirty-seven years. Whatever effect the

---

their situation permits, solely from the prudential motive, that it increases the value and production of this species of property: and though the rewards of a charity, so interested, may not be safely calculated on in a future state, its sable objects have the full benefit of it in the present. Our theory is strengthened by the fact, that not only good men are good masters, but others, who fail in the performance of many duties, are kind to their negroes.

exertions of these Societies may have produced in abolishing the Slave Trade, entitles them to the thanks of humanity, and the conscious gratification of having obtained *that* end. But considering their present design hostile to the Southern States, and the permanence of the Union; and particularly injurious to those whose welfare it pretends to promote, by rendering them discontented subjects, or suspected traitors: we are bound to watch their proceedings with an eye that never slumbers, and unite, in exerting additional influences, to counteract their injurious effects.

Nothing is better calculated to render man satisfied with his destiny in this world, than a conviction that its hardships and trials are as transitory as its honors and enjoyments; and that good conduct, founded on Christian principles, will ensure superior rewards in that which is future and eternal. A firm persuasion that it is both our interest and duty to afford religious instruction to the blacks, induces me to dwell on this subject. From obvious considerations, persons of colour must be our only domestics. Without education or instruction of any kind, they are placed in frequent, perhaps constant intercourse with the susceptible minds of white children; and the pernicious effects of their early lessons are often incalculable and irremediable. There needs no stronger illustration of the doctrine of human depravity, than the state of morals on plantations in general. Besides the mischievous tendency of bad example in parents and elders, the little negro is often taught by these, his natural instructors, that he may commit any vice he can conceal from his superiors; and thus falsehood and deception are among the earliest they imbibe. Their advance in years is but a progression to the higher grades of iniquity. The violation of the seventh commandment [forbidding adultery] is viewed in a more venial light than in fashionable European circles. Their depredations of rice have been estimated to amount to twenty-five per cent, on the gross average of crops, and this calculation was made after fifty years experience, by one, whose liberal provisions for their wants, left no excuse for their ingratitude.

While these defects in their character conduce to the injury of master and servant, another consideration presents itself of no trifling moment. If judicial punishment, or merited execration, pursue the owner who fails to provide for their temporal wants, will no obloquy attend the neglect of their more important interests? Is there no room for apprehension of future responsibility before a tribunal, whose Judge has expressly directed the dissemination of his doctrines? It may be questioned whether the consequences of guilt are as severe to an uninstructed sinner, to whom the path of duty has never been revealed, as when its arrows are barbed with consciousness of crime? Is it not prudent to inquire, whether part of the blame may not attach to the owner, who withholds, or neglects their instruction in the only way our policy can permit, viz: by unfolding, to their comprehension, the simple doctrines of religion? Let it only be admitted that the Scriptures are true, and our conclusions appear undeniable. The Saviour's injunction, that the Gospel should be "preached to every creature," and the conversion and baptism of an Æthiopian by Philip, both prove that Christianity was designed for all complexions. The poverty, which is inseparable from their condition, forms no bar to their obtaining the rich blessings of futurity. All the varieties of the human race, have some notions of religion: dark, irrational, and confused, when they spring from our own apprehension; but pure, and clear as light, when drawn from the infallible resources of Revelation. Between these widely differing systems, an election must be made by every human being; for man is a religious animal; if the doctrines of truth are withheld, he will imbibe those of error; the prevalence of Idolatry and Islamism in Africa and Asia, sanctions this position.

Were true religion propagated among this numerous and important class, a sense of duty would counteract their reluctance to labor, and, diminishing the cases of feigned sickness, so harassing to the Planter, would augment their numerical force, and consequent production. The social relations of life being better observed, a greater proportion of domestic happiness would prevail, and render them more contented with their situation, and more anxious to promote their owner's welfare. The absence, or diminution of theft, falsehood, and many other vices, would render the home of the Agriculturist far more agreeable than it can be, where guilt, which escapes human detection, knows not, and fears not, another tribunal. The necessity of punishment would decrease; for their want of Christianity prevents their owners from practising its dictates, in the forgiveness of injuries; so little good results from pardoning those, who are incapable of appreciating the motive, that it is frequently considered sufficient cause for repeating the offence.

That moral improvement would follow the introduction of religion among the blacks, may be argued from its influence on the white population of our own State. It has been remarked by our oldest Judges, that the progress of vice and crime, throughout the upper country, many years since, was more sensibly arrested after the Missionaries commenced their labours, than by the previous establis[h]ment of Courts of Justice. Public Schools were not organized until a much later period. There are some who object to the religious instruction of their people, on the ground that it has been the cloak assumed to cover the nefarious designs of insurrection. To this we reply, in the first place, that it was the only cloak it could assume. Secondly, that such instruction was the best antidote to this very disease. And, thirdly, that no arguments are entitled to so little weight, as those which condemn the use of any practice, because it has been abused. The most valuable medicines become active poisons, when improperly administered; and shall we forbid this medicine for the soul, because a few discontented wretches have perverted its sacred use?

To ensure security and comfort to the Planter, it is necessary to render those about him conscious of their advantages, and grateful to their Maker for his bounties. To produce this, a more efficient system of religious instruction should extend into the country, then prevails in the city. Every denomination of Christian teachers are willing and ready to send *white, Southern,* Missionaries to the plantations, (whose owners permit it,) to instruct the people *orally* in the duties and principles of Christianity. Such a state of moral culture would give us the advantage in argument over our Northern Brethren, whose numbers and principles are respectable; and whose objection to our system is partly founded on the deficiency of religious instruction. Were this more generally diffused, our national character would be relieved from its only real opprobrium. To their arguments we might reply, that these people have been removed from that quarter of the world, whose condition it seems as hopeless to improve, as to cultivate her deserts; to another, where they enjoy the greatest blessings of which our nature is susceptible. Their bodies are held in subjection, far more tolerable than they endured in Africa; and if their souls are released from the fetters of Paganism, and the truths of the Gospel brought home to their hearts and understanding, how great must be their gain? To exchange the barren, sultry, and idolatrous shores of their native country, for a genial climate and soil; and the gloomy, doubtful prospects of an unknown hereafter, for the glorious certainty of a blessed immortality.

Our State Polity imperiously denies to them, the advantages of education: but with all due deference to the Republic of Letters, it is affirmed, that human happiness does not so much depend on the cultivation of the intellect, as on the improvement of the disposition and heart; and it may be less than problematic to advance, that mankind would be happier, with religion, and without education, than with all the lights of Science, were they deprived of the comforts of Christianity. The cultivation of the powers of the mind, and the best affections of the heart, are by no means incompatible; we only contend, that where one must be avoided, the other need not be excluded. Religion is superior to liberty, or learning; for, give the latter all the praise their warmest advocates can imagine, they must terminate with our precarious existence; but the blessings of the former are only equalled by their eternal duration.*

---

*As usual, the Methodists were the pioneers of this enterprize. It was not without hesitation that they were employed by some planters, who had heard their black congregation accused of being deeply implicated in the affair of 1822. On investigation, it appears that all concerned in that transaction, except one, had seceded from the regular Methodist Church in 1817, and formed a separate establishment, in connexion with the African Methodist Society, in Philadelphia: whose Bishop, a coloured man, named Allen, had assumed that Office, being himself a seceder from the Methodist Church of Pennsylvania. At this period, Mr. S. Bryan, the local Minister of the regular Methodist Church in

Believing, therefore, that our peculiar Institutions are not repugnant to the spirit of the Bible, let us farther examine the condition of those people in their Agricultural capacity. The labouring classes, in all countries, constitute a large majority: the fruits of their toil are barely sufficient to afford them the necessaries of life. The profits, arising from the Mechanic Arts and Trades, from Manufactures and Navigation, are not returned, in any great proportion, to those whose industry produces them; but after paying in cash the slender stipend of the Workman, Manufacturer, or Sailor, the larger portion of the product remains in the hands of the capitalist. The difference between this mode of paying the workmen, and that practised on plantations, gives the superiority to the slave; a part of the product of his labour being always employed in providing for his personal wants; but when the other is paid his daily, weekly, or monthly wages, it rests with his own discretion, (wherein the poor do not abound,) whether the wages he has earned and received, shall be expended in necessaries for himself and family, or squandered at the gaming table and dram shop. The comparison is still more favorable when applied to the non-effective poor; dependant on the charity of their relatives, who with the best dispositions, are not always abled to assist them, and sometimes have not the will, when the ability exists; they may well envy the antiquated negro, who is supported for the work he has done, or the infant, who is nourished for the expected services of his maturity.*

---

Charleston, was so apprehensive of sinister designs, that he addressed a letter to the City Council, on file in the Council Chamber, dated 8th November, 1817, stating, at length, the reasons for his suspicion.

The General Methodist Conference in January last, appointed two Missionaries for the Northern and Southern plantations within the State. Their religious and political principles are guaranteed by the Conference, and the Rev. William Capers, the presiding Elder of this Circuit. They are not authorized to preach on any plantations without permission of the owners, and always request the attendance of the white residents. These Missions have been in operation several months: and their visits are continued throughout the year. The mode of instruction used is catechising and preaching to the elder negroes on Sundays, and in the evenings; and teaching the children the first rudiments of religion, while their parents are occupied in the field. The Missionary who attends North and South Santeé Rivers is so fully occupied, that he was compelled to decline the last application for his services.

*The annual expenses of a Rice Plantation where provisions are purchased, average about thirty dollars per head: the accounts of estates, passed and recorded in the Ordinary's Court, attest this fact. Let us suppose a family of six persons, whose joint labour amounts to that of three full workers. Their product, at eight or ten barrels to the hand, would be from twenty-four to thirty barrels: taking $250 as the average price of rice per cwt. the value would be from $360, to $450. According to the above rate of expense, this family will receive, for their services, $180, one half of the lowest estimate of the crop,

Without admitting the necessity of apology for continuing that course of life, wherein a bountiful Creator has apportioned our destiny, another justification arises, from considering the nature of our soil and climate. The Southern States are scarcely surpassed in fertility by any region in the world; but wherever the principal sources of national wealth—Cotton, Rice and Sugar—flourish, it is physically impossible for a white man to cultivate them; those who merely superintend the labors of the blacks, are poorly compensated for the risk of health and life, by any wages or emoluments they receive, and are usually paid the utmost that can be afforded.

In calculating the returns received by the slave for services performed, his profits are considerably augmented by the manner in which his work is executed; a day's labour being seldom more than half of that performed by free operatives at the North. Nor does it prove that the negro is less capable of equal exertions; for, in our mountain districts, where the climate permits a white man to work in the sun, the slave cheerfully keeps pace with his master, and fellow-labourer; and his performance is usually double that of the negro of the lower country, who has no white man working by his side to test the extent of his exertions.

A distinction favourable to these people, because it places the risk of the Aristocratic party, is, that the landholder incurs all hazard of loss of income, arising from storms, rain, drought, mismanagement, or low markets. His plantation expenses must be encountered, though indulgences may be curtailed. It is not thus under any other arrangement. When the Proprietor cultivates his own soil, and hires labourers, he avoids a large portion of expense by discharging his workmen, perhaps to starve, at any period of the year, when, from various causes, it becomes his interest to suspend his operations. If the landholder is not a cultivator, but farms out his land, then all the burden of risk falls on the poor tenant, who must pay his rent first, and afterwards provide for his family with the little surplus that remains.*

---

besides lodging and fuel, which are never included in plantation expenditures; and ought, perhaps, to increase their receipts to one half of the highest estimate, $225. It may be reasonably doubted whether the labouring poor, in any part of the world, are more aptly remunerated. On those plantations where provisions are raised, where the clothing is grown and made, and where the adjacent pine-barrens enable the owner to reside near his planting interest, and save Overseer's wages; the plantation expenses are materially diminished; whilst the advantages are increased to the slave: provisions and clothes, made at home, being superior to those which are purchased, and the superintendence of the owner, preferable to that of an Overseer. A rice crop has been selected for calculation, because when it is the only grain cultivated, every article of plantation supply is purchased, and the value more readily ascertained.

*The *Free Trade Advocate* of 11th July, 1829, contains an extract from the *Manchester Advertiser,* detailing the hardships of the Farmer-weavers of Over-Darwen. "Those domestic

Compounding of felony, a practice much reprobated by ancient law, is carried to a great extent in favour of the negro. Theft, of any article, worth more than twelve pence, is punishable with death by the Common Law of England, which is of force in this and several other states. The owner is generally the sufferer by depredations of far greater value than the limits of grand larceny; but never exacts a higher penalty than the law attaches to petty larceny; for, were he to proceed by judicial process to capital punishment, he would add the loss of the value of the

---

Manufacturers who till a small portion of land as well as ply the shuttle, of whom there are great numbers in this neighbourhood. The profits of their farming avocations are now utterly inadequate to clear the rates and other charges to which they are liable; and their scanty earnings, at weaving, are ill calculated to supply the deficiency. Their little property is therefore being sacrificed piecemeal in a hopeless struggle, until nothing, in some cases, is already left, but comfortless walls and a scanty bed of straw!" Then follow a statement of prices and regulations of the trade, which lead the Reporter to the following conclusions. "The above are, as we have stated, the list prices, which are seldom or never realized; but, taking them at their full extent, after the most careful inquiry, we find that the earnings of a good workman, would at that rate, amount to about *three shillings and ten pence per week,* to accomplish which, the devotion of from sixteen to eighteen hours per day to unremitting labour would be absolutely necessary. Out of this miserable pittance he has to pay rent, and support the ineffective members of his family." Speaking of the town of Blackburn, the Reporter says, "The little weaver-farmers, of whom we have before spoken, are, for ten miles round this neighbourhood, in a state of lamentable privation." The whole of this article, occupying less than four pages, has the appearance of impartiality, and deserves attentive perusal; not only as exhibiting a state of pauperism and hardship unknown in these Southern States, but shewing what our Northern Brethren may calculate on, when the American system shall have arrived at the maturity to which it seems rapidly approaching. It appears strange, that any numerous class in Great Britain can be reduced to the situation here described. The ample benefactions of her charitable, and patriotic Nobility and Gentry, shed a lustre on the land of our ancestors, more admirable than all her conquests. May we not hope that some portion of one rich stream of her bounty, which has hitherto flowed through an unproductive and pestilential soil, will be hereafter directed to furnishing the means of emigration to these Farmer-weavers, whose Agricultural knowledge, with industrious and economical habits, would render them eligible settlers in Canada, or New-Holland. The bounty referred to, is the ill-fated Colony of Sierra Leone; recent accounts state, that continued insalubrity has, at length, induced the Directors of this Institute to remove their settlement to the Island of Fernando Po, about five degrees nearer to the Equator. The mortality of the former place, amounting to one third, even of the negroes released from slave-ships, is certainly good cause for removal; but as the slave-trade is to cease by international compact in January, 1830, there can be no occasion for a receptacle for rescued captives on the Coast. The American and British Navies must be sufficient to interrupt and destroy all illicit attempts to continue the traffic.

negro, to that of the article stolen. But when the offense is more similar to the crimes of the free, and the slave plunders a neighbour whose interest does not immediately conflict with the highest punishment, the rigor of the law is seldom enforced: if the loser be a slave-holder, he knows not how soon one of his own may be in a similar predicament with the culprit; and interest, or courtesy have established the usage, that the offender is either chastised on the spot, as for petty larceny, or sent to his master, with a request that such punishment be inflicted as will prevent a repetition of the offence. When crimes of greater magnitude are committed, the commutation of capital punishment for transportation, (that humane feature of penal law,) saves many of its victims. It is applied, not only to those cases which policy permits, and humanity dictates, but whenever the welfare of society can be made to accord with the interest of the Proprietor. It is almost the only instance where they are sold singly, without consulting their inclination. Instead of being hurried to the gallows, "with all their imperfections on their head," they are removed to other States or Territories, where the absence of associate malefactors, and a total change of life, frequently under ameliorated circumstances; afford opportunity and inducement for improvement of character, with better prospect of success, than attends the condition of transported convicts, or galley slaves.

Whilst they are thus screened from that severity of the Common Law, which disgraces those governments that still retain the barbarous statutes and traditions of the darker ages, there are other offences, from which their situation, in a great measure, restrains them. Intemperance, that gigantic and prevailing vice of every age and clime, is much repressed among them, chiefly by the difficulty of procuring ardent spirits. From this vile and degrading servitude, they are more generally exempt, than the labouring class of any country where the means are attainable.

A sale of negroes, deemed an outrage on humanity by those who contemplate it from a distance, is often attended with beneficial effects. Bad masters are generally obliged to part with a species of property that does not improve in value when abused. Unproductive land, or depreciation of the staple, may occasion a sale, or removal of its cultivators: in either case an improvement of their condition is the probable consequence. The separation of near relatives, seldom takes place, except by their own desire; and when it does, their situation is not worse than that of the labouring class of all other countries, who are compelled to abandon their homes in search of subsistence, and often encounter more real perils and hardships, than are to be found in the romantic catalogue of the horrors of slavery.

In concluding this imperfect sketch of a subject not easily exhausted, it has been my object to prove, that the humble and useful beings, whose situation is here pourtrayed, do not require the succour, or the sympathy of distant friends. Their tender mercies have hitherto occasioned nothing but calamity; and their schemes, if persevered in, may produce consequences at which humanity shudders. In advocating a more benignant system of government than universally prevails, we are actuated by a conviction of practical beneficial results, where it has been already faithfully tried. Nor do we propose, in any measure, to relax the salutary restraints, *which our laws* and circumstances have rendered necessary; for while rewards of a more enduring nature, are held out for the performance of duty, the reproofs of an awakened conscience will be superadded to other punishments. In comparing their situation with that of the poor in other countries, we can perceive no reason for unusual commiseration; the wholesome restrictions to which they are subjected, and their immunity from all the anxieties, and many of the disasters that attend the poor man's pilgrimage below, appear to us equivalent to the privations and hardships of their peculiar lot; and sufficient to render them, and all who compassionate them, contented with their condition in that state of existence, where the All-Wise Disposer of Events has been pleased to locate them.*

*On a Plantation in Georgia, where, in addition to superior management, the religious instruction of the blacks is systematically pursued, the crops are invariable the best in the neighbourhood. The neatness and order which the whole establishment exhibits, prove that the prosperity of the Master, and the best interests of the negro, are not incompatible.

The same State furnishes another instance of this position. The people of an Absentee's plantation, were proverbially bad, from the abuse and mismanagement of an Overseer; (the Proprietor resided in England, and the Attornies in Carolina.) The latter dismissed the Overseer as soon as his misconduct was discovered, and employed another, who was a pious man: he not only instructed the negroes himself to the best of his abilities, but accompanied them every Sunday to a Methodist Church in the neighbourhood. At the end of five years their character was entirely changed, and has so continued ever since. After nearly fifteen years more, the surviving Attorney is now in treaty for the purchase of these very negroes, whom he formally considered a band of outlaws.

Other examples in favour of this plan have occurred in Carolina. In one instance, a gentleman invited a Missionary to attend his plantation. After some time, two black Preachers, who had previously acquired popularity, fell into disrepute, and were neglected by their former congregation. These statements are derived from unquestionable sources. The last case presents a view of the subject, which may have weight with those, who think other motives insufficient. We look upon the habit of black preaching as a widespreading evil; not because a black man cannot be a good one; but because, in the first place, they are not sufficiently instructed for the sacerdotal office: secondly, not being regularly appointed by any ecclesiastical authority, there is no security for their qualifications, or principles of any kind: thirdly, because they acquire an influence independent of the owner, and not subject to his control: and fourthly, because when they have possessed this power, they have been known to make an improper use of it.

Great efforts have been made to abolish this practice; but they have been attended with the usual effects of religious persecution, secrecy, and nocturnal meetings in old fields,

Notes

1. My introduction to Pinckney is drawn from the Charles Cotesworth Pinckney (1789–1865) Papers, Emory University; Mabel L. Webber, "The Thomas Pinckney Family of South Carolina," *South Carolina Historical and Genealogical Magazine* 39 (January 1938): 32–33; "Notes and Queries," *South Carolina Historical and Genealogical Magazine* 1 (January 1900): 103–5; N. Louise Bailey, ed., *Biographical Directory of the South Carolina House of Representatives*, vol. 4, *1791–1815* (Columbia: University of South Carolina Press, 1984), 186; Max Farrand, ed., *The Records of the Federal Convention of 1787* (New Haven, Conn.: Yale University Press, 1937), 2:371; and Charles Cotesworth Pinckney, *The Life of General Thomas Pinckney* (Boston: Houghton, Mifflin, 1895).

2. Jeffrey Robert Young, *Domesticating Slavery: The Master Class in Georgia and South Carolina, 1670–1837* (Chapel Hill: University of North Carolina Press, 1999), 95.

3. The Latin phrase expresses the principle that ignorance of the law excuses no one from the consequences of violating the law.

4. Peter the Hermit was a noted eleventh-century Catholic enthusiast popularly credited with spearheading the First Crusade against the Islamic presence in Europe.

and plantations where no white persons reside. We cannot but think it advisable, to afford them an opportunity of contrasting the sense and doctrine they hear in such places from men, whom they know to be only their equals, with the religious information to be derived from white teachers, whose superiority in knowledge of every kind, they cannot question.

The observations in this Address and Notes refer entirely to Plantation negroes.

# INDEX